NEW ADDRESS: APRIL

ERA
444 N MICHIGAN AVE #1960
CHICAGO IL 60611

(312) 527-3050
- 3783 FAX

THE SALES REPRESENTATIVES BUSINESS AND TAX HANDBOOK

Melvin H. Daskal C.P.A., M.B.A.

IRWIN
Professional Publishing

Chicago • Bogota • Boston • Buenos Aires • Caracas
London • Madrid • Mexico City • Sydney • Toronto

To Albert J. (Al) Bruning

Al was my first client and also my first sales rep. He is the one who got me started on this unusual and rewarding career path.

Al, you really changed my life.

This publication is designed to provide accurate and authoritative information in regard to the subject matter covered. It is sold with the understanding that neither the author or the publisher is engaged in rendering legal, accounting, or other professional service. If legal advice or other expert assistance is required, the services of a competent professional person should be sought.

From a Declaration of Principles jointly adopted by a Committee of the American Bar Association and a Committee of Publishers.

Editor-in-chief: Jeffrey A. Krames
Production manager: Laurie Kersch
Designer: Mercedes Santos
Compositor: Eastern Composition, Inc.
Typeface: 10.5/12 Palatino
Printer: Book Press, Inc.

Library of Congress Cataloging-in-Publication Data

Daskal, Melvin H.
The sales representatives business and tax handbook by Melvin H. Daskal.
p. cm.
Includes index.
ISBN 0-7863-0312-3
1. Manufacturers' agents—United States—Handbooks, manuals, etc. 2. Manufacturers' agents—Taxation—United States—Handbooks, manuals, etc. 3. Corporations—Valuation—United States. I. Title.
HF5421.D37 1995
658.8—dc20 94-2844

Printed in the United States of America
1 2 3 4 5 6 7 8 9 0 BP 1 0 9 8 7 6 5 4

Please Read This First

HOW TO USE THIS HANDBOOK

The average sales rep would probably rank reading this entire handbook at one sitting as preferable to losing a major line or an IRS audit, but not by much! This book is not intended to be read like a novel, or even like most nonfiction. It is a *reference manual* that should be sitting on or near your desk (even in these tough times, most reps still have desks), so that you can refer to the *particular topic* you need information about.

If you want to know how to value and sell *part or all* of your agency (most reps over the age of 35 would really like to do so!), refer to Chapters 31 though 38. They will provide you with current ideas, information, and pitfalls, major changes under the 1993 tax act, IRS problems, and my lifelong experiences in all these matters. Included are completely *different* ideas for selling only *part* of your sales agency.

If for some strange reason, you would like to avoid being audited by the IRS, see Chapter 25. If you want to decide the best form in which to operate your rep firm, check out Chapters 12 through 15. If you are ready for a retirement plan, peruse Chapter 10. If you want to legally avoid paying *corporate* income taxes, consult the information in Chapter 16. If you are nervous about estate planning, Chapter 23 will calm your nerves and help you to plan wisely.

If you are *not* interested in large and tax-free expense accounts, perhaps this book will not appeal to you, but if you are, it will. If you care to improve your expense account skills, you should certainly read Chapters 1 through 6.

A custom designed sales rep Chart of Accounts and bookkeeping system is provided (Chapter 17), revised to take into account the major changes of the Revenue Reconciliation Act of 1993. Also, chapters include such topics as independent contractor problems, stealing by your employees, insurance, and dealing with your banker. Check over the Contents and go for the knowledge that will help make you a more successful rep.

All the really thriving reps are good businesspeople and not just good salespeople. Here is your chance to get *all* the necessary business and tax information in one place to aid in the success of your sales agency. Your CPA and your lawyer are, of course, trying to help you professionally, but they usually lack any great or intimate knowledge of exactly what it is you *do* (a comment I hear over and over from sales reps). So buy each of them a copy of this book.

REPETITION IS DELIBERATE!

Each chapter has been designed to include "stand alone" information on that topic so you do not have to refer back and forth to different chapters. The result is that some information may appear in more than one chapter and in more than one form. For example, when you learn how to avoid an IRS audit the chapter includes information about the best way for a sole proprietor to prepare a Schedule C, but if you consult the chapter on proprietorships, you will find *similar* information about preparing the proprietorship Schedule C.

WHERE DID YOU GET ALL THE INFORMATION?

Ideas, knowledge, and lore came from more than 30 years of working with sales reps and more than 300 different rep firms at various times and in assorted ways; being involved in over 100 sales, mergers, or valuations of sales agencies; working for a half-dozen rep trade associations; speaking to various groups of sales reps all over the United States; and currently working with more than 100 sales rep clients in our own CPA firm.

CHANGING LAWS

The tax laws, regulations, and rules are changing almost continually. Changes in business mileage reimbursements, per diem travel allowances, auto leasing inclusions, and similar just represent new *numbers* and not new *ideas*. Don't be put off if a figure in this book has since been changed by the IRS or Congress. *The concepts and ideas will remain unchanged!* So be cool: You can use this handbook for years to come, and it may save you more money than some of your lines are worth.

Mel Daskal

Brief Table of Contents

Contents

Chapter One

Business Entertainment

Let's begin this book with a high priority. Entertainment expenses are an integral and major factor in the average sales agency by the very nature of the business. Therefore, you must meet the mandatory IRS recordkeeping requirements to avoid losing the tax deduction for any particular expenditure or possibly even your *total* tax deduction (of 50 percent) for a category like "entertainment." As sales reps, a lot of money is at stake.

WE SHALL OVERCOME

Unfortunately, reps have a special chromosome that carries two unusual genes that are usually paired. Gene 1 transmits great sales ability. Gene 2, which can be considered an "antigene," conveys the lack of desire and lack of ability to perform great feats of recordkeeping! So, there is a natural and hereditary conflict deep within your psyche, *which must be overcome,* and it's Gene 2 that needs the overcoming. Otherwise, financial disaster awaits you in the form of 70, 80, and 90 percent disallowances of your remaining tax deductions in the travel, entertainment, and auto expenses areas.

ENTERTAINMENT PHILOSOPHY 101

Business entertainment is, has been, and always will be subject to special IRS scrutiny, suspicions, mistrust, examination, inspection, and disallowance. The IRS simply cannot understand why food, alcoholic beverages, and partying should *ever* be tax deductible! So, there are many special rules that must be understood and followed, and they have consistently been made increasingly restrictive like the 50 percent entertainment disallowance.

In practice, the IRS barely concedes that there are major differences in the magnitudes of entertainment between various kinds of businesses (say a grocery store versus a sales agency). So, since the average IRS agent rarely comprehends the nature of your business, you generally start off on the wrong foot anyway.

Of course, those who understand the "rep business" know that someone in your calling can run up percentages of business entertainment that might be 50 to 500 times that of a neighborhood grocery store or similar. While individual agents *sometimes* understand these differences (but just infrequently, and only from time to time), my sad conclusion is that, in general, they and certainly their computer audit selection process essentially do not!

Therefore, those reps with large dollar (or as a percentage of gross commission income) amounts of business entertainment (almost all you readers) have two special warnings to consider:

1. You are much more likely to be audited.
2. When you are audited, your entertainment documentation (or lack thereof) will then be involved in defending major tax deductions!

> *TAXTIP*
>
> There is one overall idea to always keep in mind. The very fact that there *are* these special entertainment and recordkeeping rules (IRS Code Section 274) can really simplify your business life if you will recognize this one reality: because of these specific rules, your entertainment tax deductions are all or nothing! If you exactly follow the regulations, you will get *all* your claimed deductions (less the 50 percent disallowance that we will later discuss).

But, if you don't *exactly* conform, you will get *none* of your claimed deductions! Entertainment justification and recordkeeping are an all or nothing situation. Don't ever expect to get a percentage of your deductions, as a compromise, based on sloppy documentation. In such cases, you will get *nothing!*

The days of the estimates and the compromises are long over, and a careful study of and conformity to the rules should keep you from the dreaded 100 percent disallowance. Keep in mind that the IRS has the right to, and frequently does in fact do, statistical sampling of entertainment (and travel) records. If, for example, the auditor selects two sample months and the documentation *fails* in 83.9 percent of the test cases, you will end up with 83.9 percent of your *total* disallowed for the entire year!

> *TAXTIP*
>
> The courts have upheld the IRS on this audit technique.

"LET ME ENTERTAIN YOU" (AN OVERVIEW)

Entertainment expenses, including all meals (all of which are only 50 percent tax-deductible anyway), must meet all of the following requirements (note each *and* and the one *or*):

1. Must be "ordinary and necessary" expenses of your trade or business, *and*
2. such expenses cannot be "lavish or extravagant" (a threat not really defined and rarely enforced by the IRS), *and*
3. you must be able to prove the expenses by required recordkeeping, plus certain receipts, *and*
4. the expenditures must be:
   a. directly related to the active conduct of your trade or business, *or*
   b. the expenditures must be associated with the active conduct of your trade or business.

The rules are very rigid. You must meet 1. and 2. and 3. plus *either* of the two provisions of 4. It is generally the point 4. requirement that costs most reps their entertainment deductions, so let's begin with those critical regulations.

DIRECTLY RELATED ENTERTAINMENT

This category is the most typical of sales rep's expenditures and really provides the strongest reasons that uphold and defend your entertainment tax deductions. "Directly related" means, in the traditional sense, that *during* the entertainment, you "did business." To meet the directly related tests, you must meet *all three* of these conditions:

1. You had more than a general expectation of deriving income or some other specific business benefit at some future time.
2. You did actively engage in business (meeting, negotiation, discussion, or other bona fide business transaction) with the

person being entertained *during* the meal or entertainment period ("during" is the crucial requirement).

3. The main purpose of the combined business and meal or entertainment was the active conduct of business (i.e., a "business transaction").

Says the IRS,

> You are not required to show that business income or other business benefit *actually resulted* from each meal or entertainment expense. However, if the business discussion is only incidental to the meal or entertainment, it does not qualify.

That sums up the three mandatory conditions. However, the IRS, as always, has some further cautions for you. The entertainment is normally expected to take place in "a clear business setting." So when such entertainment does not take place in a clear business setting, there is a presumption that the main purpose was not business entertainment (also, see the later discussion of goodwill entertainment problems). In such cases, you will have to overcome that presumption by convincing proof. Here are IRS comments about some other suspect places:

> Expenses are generally not considered directly related when a meal or entertainment occurs where there is little or no possibility of engaging in the active conduct of business. Examples are meetings at nightclubs, theaters, sporting events, or essentially social gatherings, such as cocktail parties . . . at places such as cocktail lounges, country clubs, athletic clubs or vacation resorts. You *may prove otherwise* by showing you engaged in a substantial business discussion during the entertainment.

Under such circumstances, be prepared for a tough time proving your entertainment was "otherwise," since the presumption is against you. Note that the IRS uses that old word "cocktail lounges." In my hometown of Chicago, we cut to the heart of the matter and just call them "bars," while in Los Angeles they are sometimes called "attitude adjustment and psyche encounter fulfillment centers." (When I give a speech before some of the rep groups and scare the hell out of them about the IRS, my speech is usually followed by an "attitude adjustment" hour, since, by that time, the attitudes of many of the reps has slipped considerably.) Oh well.

There are still further entertainment locations where the IRS does not think that much business entertainment is really located, so to speak. So they continue with still more admonitions:

> Business is not considered to be the main purpose when business and entertainment are combined on hunting or fishing trips, or on yachts or other pleasure boats, unless you can show otherwise.

While the preceding locations are "not considered conducive" to "directly related" entertainment, you may still be able to (and more easily) sustain the same tax deduction under the "associated with" rules. Let's move on to that topic, regretfully leaving behind all those cocktail lounges, bars, and fond memories. And please try to keep your attitude adjusted about this whole topic.

ASSOCIATED ENTERTAINMENT

This alternate category means that either *before* or *after* (instead of "during") the entertainment you "did business." Now reread the first IRS series of quotes under the preceding section. The same three rules apply: expectation of income, actively engaging in business during, and the main purpose is business, except that in the second rule you change the word "during" to "before or after." In this case, the entertainment portion of the event itself can literally be entertainment only, without a business discussion, as long as the business discussion *preceded* or *followed* that entertainment.

Again, cogent quotes from IRS folks:

> You can deduct meal and entertainment expenses that do not meet the directly related test but are associated with your trade or business if the meal or entertainment directly precedes or follows a substantial business discussion . . . Meals and entertainment on the same day as the business discussions are considered directly before or after the business discussion . . . However, if . . . not on the same day, the facts of each case will be considered.

Not bad at all! You can have your big entertainment bash all by itself, as long as *sometime in the same day* you also had your substantial business discussion. Not bad at all! These properly documented "associated with" provisions frequently represent an easier-to-sustain kind of business entertainment.

GOODWILL ENTERTAINMENT

There is a common conception that goodwill entertainment is no longer deductible at all. For many of us, that is primarily correct but partially wrong. Creating or keeping business goodwill is still a legitimate objective of business entertainment, and goodwill entertainment *per se* is not automatically disallowed. However, it's wacha' do and how ya' do it that counts!

What has been changed is that goodwill entertainment is tax deductible only if it meets the same "directly related" or "associated with" rules and, even then, only if involving a "substantial business discussion." However, those simple-sounding changes really have eliminated the deductions for many of the goodwill situations that were formerly write-offs.

A typical situation involves the rep (or doctor or lawyer or CPA) who has 500 people, including many business associates, principals and customers (or for the other categories: other doctors and patients or clients), to a daughter's wedding and deducts most or all of those costs as goodwill entertainment. Similar types of entertainment include the 25th anniversary bash at the country club or hotel and parties of similar ilk. Those kinds of goodwill entertainment badly flunk on three counts under current rules:

1. They are *not* held in a "clear business setting."
2. The *main* purpose is not business.
3. You could *not possibly* engage in a substantial business discussion before, during, or after such kinds of entertainment with each and every guest!

So, while the goodwill rules may little influence or impinge on large or publicly owned corporations, many sales agents (and almost all doctors!) will be affected by these changes. The days of throwing a big party with some business-connected guests and claiming a big goodwill entertainment deduction is ended forever. But only that particular kind.

RECORDKEEPING AND RECEIPTS

The receipt requirements are easy! For every separate entertainment expense or business meal costing $25 or more, you *must* have a receipt or no tax deduction is allowed! However, this does not mean you should discard every receipt of $24.99 or less. *Au contraire*, save as many receipts as possible of such expenses, because they lend a tone of authenticity to your overall seriousness and competence as a recordkeeper! (As my dear mother used to say about her chicken soup: "It couldn't hurt!")

There are six required elements for entertainment recordkeeping and to remind you again, if you miss just *one* your *entire* deduction will be lost.

1. The amount of each separate entertainment expenditure.
2. The date of the entertainment.
3. The place and description of the entertainment (i.e., the location and whether dinner or theater or what).
4. The details of the business: purpose/benefit/discussion. This is the business purpose requirement usually missed by most reps and the one that will make or break your entire tax deduction!
5. The business names and business relationships of those entertained.
6. That you or one of your employees was present at any business meal involving a client or customer.

> ***TAXTIP***
>
> Keep in mind that these records must always show that the entertainment was either "directly related" or "associated with" as we have already discussed *ad nauseam*.

THE 50 PERCENT LIMITATION

The speech writer who thought up the phrase "the three-martini lunch" arguably did more damage to sales reps and their legitimate entertainment deductions than anyone in history! The result of that attitude, as the IRS carefully spread it through Congress, is that entertainment is now perceived as a major tax abuse. The IRS *always* thought so, and now they got Congress to agree! As a consequence, under the 1993 tax law you can only deduct *50 percent* of your business meals and entertainment, which includes your own travel meals.

This limitation applies to whomever is *deducting* these expenses on an income tax return—the employers, independent contractors, or employees who were not reimbursed for such expenditures (bad tax planning by the employer, that last one).

Employers can, of course, reimburse their employees at 100 percent (as is almost the universal custom). Such reimbursements, properly accounted for, are still 100 percent tax-free to the employee (not just 50 percent). It is when that employer *deducts that reimbursement* on the corporate (or other) income tax return, that the 50 percent limit comes into play.

As I have commented before, this provision unfairly penalizes those businesses that must incur high entertainment costs by their very nature (not only sales reps, but also entertainers, advertising agencies, public relations firms, and similar businesses).

You can only fight back by developing better awareness in Congress of the special problems of sales agencies *and also* by keeping the most comprehensive and impeccable entertainment records in history! There are only two possible areas in which you can improve your entertainment tax deductions:

1. Increased recording of each and every minor (under $25) business meal and entertainment expenditure that does *not require a receipt*.
2. Increased saving, safeguarding, and (then) recording of each and every business meal and entertainment expenditure backed up by a *cash* receipt, regardless of the amount. (Of course that's *in addition* to the usual entertainment *charge* expenses and receipts, which I assume you always record properly.)

So don't forget all those small (under $25) business breakfasts and lunches and other out-of-pocket cash expenditures, including cash tips, restaurant parking, and bar bills, that you never bothered to record before. Well, do so now and also *save every receipt you can get your hands on!* Those "extra" receipts you never saved before and extra-perfect recordkeeping for all those minor (under $25) expenditures will help offset the lost 50 percent.

A DRASTIC ALTERNATIVE

Some companies have thrown up their hands in disgust over both the 50 percent business meals and entertainment disallowance *and* all the preceding entertainment recordkeeping rules. Their new solution, particularly as far as officer/shareholders are concerned, is to *increase salaries* and then have such individuals pay their own entertainment expenses *without reimbursement*.

It works like this. Assume that the officer/shareholder averages $12,000 a year in business meals and entertainment expenses. The company increases that officer's salary by, say, $18,000 and he pays the $12,000 of business meals and entertainment *without reimbursement*. How does everybody come out?

1. The company now has an $18,000 salary deduction (plus related payroll tax costs) instead of a $6,000 (50 percent of $12,000) business meals and entertainment deduction.

2. The company is out $18,000 cash (plus related payroll tax costs) instead of $12,000.
3. The officer/shareholder is about even, since he has around a $12,000 *net* take-home pay from salary instead of a $12,000 tax-free business meals and entertainment expense reimbursement.
4. The officer/shareholder will possibly benefit from a *larger* retirement plan contribution as the result of the increased salary.
5. There are *no recordkeeping requirements* for the $12,000 of entertainment and business meals expenses, since neither the company nor the employer are claiming a tax deduction for that $12,000.
6. However, if the officer/shareholder *wants* to get involved in personal recordkeeping and individual income tax deductions, he *could* claim the business meals and entertainment as unreimbursed business expenses (a miscellaneous itemized deduction), by filling out Form 2106 ("Employee Business Expenses") and attaching it to Form 1040, Individual Income Tax Return. However, there are big *downsides* to this one:
   a. Only *50 percent* ($6,000) of the entertainment and business meals could be *initially* claimed by the individual.
   b. That 50 percent deduction is *further* reduced by 2 percent of adjusted gross income (AGI) of the individual taxpayer.
   c. Full entertainment *records* must once again be kept by that individual taxpayer.
   d. The chances of an IRS audit are *substantially* increased. (Yecch!)
   e. If the individual has a high enough income, there is a *phase-out* of itemized deductions, which would include the claimed entertainment deduction and *further* reduce the final net tax deduction, perhaps, in this example, to a final deduction of $3,000 or so.
   f. In calculating the alternative minimum tax (AMT) itemized tax deductions such as this are not allowed. For AMT purposes, they are *useless!*
7. Since the employer company now has either zero or far less entertainment costs claimed, the risk of an IRS audit is to some extent reduced (an indeterminate factor, but certainly one that should be considered, particularly by all you "entertainment cowards").

My personal opinion is that I am intrigued by the idea, *particularly for poor recordkeepers* of business meals and entertainment expenditures! However, I am considerably less attracted to the option described in point 6. But overall it's certainly worth considering, *particularly* if an IRS entertainment audit would devastate you financially.

> *TAXTIP*
>
> If you *do* adopt this overall idea, document this arrangement in your corporate minutes. It will help defend any individual income tax deductions claimed under point 6.

CLUB ENTERTAINMENT AND CLUB DUES

Special entertainment rules apply to deductible expenses at country, golf, social, athletic, and similar clubs, because special abuses of entertainment rules seem to hang around those places. Let's first consider the special rules for club *dues*. Under the Revenue Reconciliation Act of 1993, *all* tax deductions for *any* kind of club dues have been eliminated. *Period!*

Club entertainment is subject to all the general entertainment rules already discussed. That may not present a problem for business meals (properly documented) at the club! However, it sure can present a problem for all those golf games and club parties! About the best you can do for golf games is to try to conform to the "associated with" rules and do your business "before or after." Those club parties for members only also appear to be personal expenditures.

For all those (doctors and maybe some reps) with their weekly, Wednesday standing golf games and standing foursomes, who take turns paying and deducting for club "business" lunches and "business" greens fees, here is the IRS message:

> Reciprocal entertaining. Expenses are not deductible when a group of business acquaintances take turns picking up each other's entertainment checks without regard to whether any business purposes are served.

Don't misunderstand! The sales agent who takes a buyer to the club for lunch and a round of golf and then sells like crazy at the 19th hole bar has gotten the best ("associated with") entertainment tax deduction in the world (if properly documented). It's that other category of "standing date" golfers who are in real trouble if they are regularly claiming club entertainment, as is done in so many cases.

Entertainment at clubs must follow all the rules and recordkeeping already described, but it will always be more suspect and more subject to challenge by the IRS. Have a super day at the club, but with your principals and customers, I hope.

ENTERTAINMENT TICKETS

The rules are rather simple. You cannot deduct more than the face value of any ticket, except for a ticket to benefit a qualified charity. Excess payments over list price to scalpers or ticket brokers are *not* deductible at all.

Simple enough, but you must again meet all the other rules already discussed, and you still lose the entire deduction unless you meet either the "directly related" or "associated with" rules. Remember that entertainment, regardless of type or category, is never deductible unless it qualifies under one of those two provisions and satisfies every other applicable rule as well.

A common problem is buying season tickets and giving them away, from time to time, to good customers. In the olden days, that could have qualified as goodwill entertainment. Now, since you flunked both the "directly related" and "associated with" provisions, that ticket is no longer deductible! A similar incident is the World Series tickets given to a key purchasing agent and similar transactions. The actual purchase of the season tickets is never deductible *at that point in time,* since each ticket transaction must be documented and justified under the rules.

Of course you can accompany your customer, engage in a substantial business discussion, prepare the required documentation, and deduct away! It is the other (much more usual) ticket giveaway situation that has been killed.

CONVENTION EXPENSES

Attending a convention "to further your trade or business" is considered the equivalent of a "substantial business discussion." The flunker here, says the IRS, is that:

> The organization that sponsors the convention or meeting must schedule a program of business activities that is the *main activity* of the convention or meeting.

I recently saw the program for a so-called business convention in Palm Springs. There were three hours devoted to business out of an entire four-day (Thursday through Sunday) meeting! That one ain't gonna' fly! There are many such meetings and conventions that fall well inside the IRS gray zone, and all you meeting planners are well advised to "plan your plans" (design your programs) accordingly! No IRS agent is going to bend over backward to give you the tax deduction for a borderline business convention, particularly if the meeting is held in a resort area.

CONCLUSION

To sum up the major entertainment rules:

- You must actively engage in documented business discussions "directly related" (during) *or* "associated with" (before or after) the active conduct of your trade or business. *No other kind of entertainment is tax deductible!*
- There are six mandatory recordkeeping and meeting requirements, and you must meet *all* of them to sustain your tax deduction.
- Goodwill entertainment, club entertainment, and tickets are only deductible if they meet all the conditions of the above two bullets.
- Club dues, *no matter what kinds of clubs,* are *never* tax-deductible.
- Convention programs themselves can lose you your entire tax deduction if the business portion of the convention is too limited.

Finally, keep in mind all the following:

- Entertainment deductions are now an "all or nothing" situation. Meet all the rules and get your entire deduction. Miss even *one* requirement, and you lose the complete deduction!
- Save and record each and every receipt both *over* and *under* $25.
- Don't miss *any* of those minor "under $25" expenditures for which no receipt is required and enter *every one* in your expense accounts.

Chapter Two

Business Auto Leasing

As most reps know, there are severe restrictions when claiming depreciation of business autos that are considered "luxury cars." The definition of a luxury car is one costing more than $13,700 (that amount is indexed annually, somewhat, for inflation), which illustrates a typical difference between reality and the IRS perception of same. To prevent a full deduction for leasing autos costing more than the luxury car limits, the IRS has promulgated various rules and regulations covering business auto leasing. These numerous ordinances are supposed to effectively reduce the leasing tax deduction to the equivalent of the limited and allowable depreciation deduction.

There are different rules for different situations, all of them complex and each of them different. How well they really accomplish the IRS purpose is open to question, and some of them are so complicated that I suspect that certain regulations are honored more in the breach than in compliance. However, as always, these are the rules and the law is the law.

Not to keep you in suspense, the bottom line is, in my opinion, that even after scrupulously following the IRS rules that attempt to limit business auto leasing deductions, you are far better off *taxwise* if you lease your business autos, although leasing may *cost* more than owning. There are various leasing scenarios.

- A self-employed individual leases the auto.
- An employee leases the auto and pays the costs.
- An employee leases the auto and is reimbursed.
- The employer company provides the auto to the employee.

Of course there is no standard IRS method that applies in all these situations. In fact, there are different procedures, different income inclusion tables, and different calculation modes. Otherwise, how would you expect us poor, starving CPAs to make a living? Remember, the IRS made it this complicated without even being asked to do so by the accounting profession! They may have used the same guy who designed the original business auto log rules (the one where you had to pull off the road and make a 15-minute entry in your auto log after every 30-minute sales call). I think he designed the new business home office expense calculation and deduction procedures as well.

The following tables contain sample selections from the IRS inclusion tables. The table for cars first leased in 1993 and 1992 are just for reference, while the 1991 table will be used in our first example (for illustration purposes, the year really doesn't matter).

The IRS income inclusion charts reflect automobile price inflation adjustments from 1991, to 1992, to 1993. So, the final amounts you must include as income for personal use of business autos continue to *drop each year, for the same priced car*. Of course the *prices* of autos continue to rise, which is the IRS logic for the lower figures in each newer inclusion table.

TABLE 2–1

Income Inclusion Table for Autos First Leased in 1993[1]

	Year of the Lease				
Fair Market Value	*1st*	*2nd*	*3rd*	*4th*	*5th on*
$14,900–$15,200	$ 4	$ 9	$ 13	$ 15	$ 17
16,400– 16,700	13	27	41	49	55
18,000– 18,500	22	49	72	86	99
20,000– 20,500	34	74	109	130	150
22,000– 23,000	47	101	151	181	207
28,000– 29,000	81	176	262	313	362
32,000– 33,000	103	226	336	402	464
34,000– 35,000	115	251	373	446	515
36,000– 37,000	126	276	410	491	566
38,000– 39,000	137	301	447	535	617
40,000– 41,000	149	326	484	579	669
42,000– 43,000	160	351	521	623	720
48,000– 49,000	194	426	631	757	874
50,000– 51,000	206	450	669	801	925
55,000– 56,000	234	513	761	912	1,052
58,000– 59,000	251	550	817	978	1,130
60,000– 62,000	265	581	863	1,034	1,194
66,000– 68,000	299	656	974	1,167	1,347
70,000– 72,000	322	706	1,048	1,255	1,450
76,000– 78,000	356	781	1,158	1,389	1,603
85,000– 90,000	416	911	1,353	1,622	1,871
95,000–100,000	472	1,036	1,538	1,843	2,128

[1]Source: IRS Publication 917, "Business Use of a Car."

TABLE 2–2
***Income Inclusion Table for Autos First Leased in 1992*[1]**

	Year of the Lease				
Fair Market Value	*1st*	*2nd*	*3rd*	*4th*	*5th on*
$14,900–$15,200	$ 11	$ 23	$ 35	$ 43	$ 49
16,400– 16,700	23	52	76	92	106
18,000– 18,500	38	83	123	148	171
20,000– 20,500	55	120	178	214	247
22,000– 23,000	74	162	239	288	333
28,000– 29,000	124	273	405	486	561
32,000– 33,000	158	347	515	618	713
34,000– 35,000	175	384	570	684	789
36,000– 37,000	192	421	625	750	865
38,000– 39,000	209	458	680	816	942
40,000– 41,000	226	495	735	882	1,018
42,000– 43,000	243	532	790	948	1,094
48,000– 49,000	293	644	955	1,145	1,323
50,000– 51,000	310	681	1,010	1,211	1,399
55,000– 56,000	353	773	1,147	1,377	1,589
58,000– 59,000	378	829	1,230	1,475	1,703
60,000– 62,000	399	875	1,299	1,557	1,799
66,000– 68,000	450	987	1,463	1,755	2,027
70,000– 72,000	484	1,061	1,573	1,887	2,179
76,000– 78,000	535	1,172	1,738	2,085	2,407
85,000– 90,000	623	1,367	2,027	2,431	2,807
95,000–100,000	708	1,552	2,302	2,761	3,188

[1]Source: IRS Publication 917, "Business Use of a Car."

TABLE 2–3
***Income Inclusion Table for Autos First Leased in 1991*[1]**

	Year of the Lease				
Fair Market Value	*1st*	*2nd*	*3rd*	*4th*	*5th on*
$14,900–$15,200	$ 17	$ 36	$ 54	$ 64	$ 71
16,400– 16,700	32	68	102	121	138
18,000– 18,500	49	105	156	186	213
20,000– 20,500	68	148	220	263	301
22,000– 23,000	90	197	292	348	401
28,000– 29,000	149	326	484	578	666
32,000– 33,000	189	412	611	732	843

TABLE 2–3 (*concluded*)

	Year of the Lease				
Fair Market Value	*1st*	*2nd*	*3rd*	*4th*	*5th on*
34,000– 35,000	208	455	676	808	931
36,000– 37,000	228	498	739	885	1,020
38,000– 39,000	248	541	803	961	1,109
40,000– 41,000	267	584	867	1,038	1,197
42,000– 43,000	287	627	931	1,115	1,285
48,000– 49,000	346	756	1,123	1,344	1,551
50,000– 51,000	366	799	1,187	1,421	1,639
55,000– 56,000	415	907	1,346	1,613	1,860
58,000– 59,000	444	972	1,442	1,727	1,993
60,000– 62,000	469	1,026	1,521	1,824	2,103
66,000– 68,000	528	1,155	1,713	2,053	2,369
70,000– 72,000	567	1,241	1,841	2,206	2,546
76,000– 78,000	626	1,370	2,033	2,436	2,811
85,000– 90,000	730	1,596	2,368	2,838	3,276
95,000–100,000	828	1,812	2,687	3,221	3,718

[1]Source: IRS Publication 917, "Business Use of a Car."

A SELF-EMPLOYED INDIVIDUAL

This is a person who operates an unincorporated business and, accordingly, reports the business income and expenses on Schedule C "Profit or Loss From Business," of Form 1040. For a car first leased in 1991, that individual must use Table 2–3 (the IRS usually issues new charts *late* every year or so; your own CPA can supply them to you). This will be our first illustration (note that the applicable $32,000–$33,000 line on the 1991 table is italicized for you).

Of course, how to work that table is the trick! Here are the procedures:

1. Use the fair market value of the car on the first day of the lease.
2. Determine your business use percentage of the leased auto.
3. Prorate the dollar amount in the income inclusion table by the number of days in the first (and last) tax year.
4. In the last year of the lease, use the dollar amount shown in the preceding year of the lease.

The only possible way to follow this procedure is by example. Assume our individual business owner leased a car with a fair market value of $32,500 (the italicized line on Table 2–3), on July 15, 1991, for five years, with an annual lease cost of $8,900 and with 80 percent business use; our job is to figure the tax deduction for the full year of 1992. Based on Table 2–3, here are the various calculations:

Year	*Table Amount*	*Proration %*	*Business Use*	*Income Inclusion*
1991	$189	170/365	80%	$ 70
1992	*412*	*A year*	*80%*	*330*
1993	611	A year	80%	489
1994	732	A year	80%	586
1995	843	A year	80%	674
1996	843	196/366	80%	361

Note that the *$412* from the table is not the final amount used as the income inclusion; it's multiplied by the percentage of business use to arrive at the $330 income inclusion. However, that $330 is *not* the only adjustment required! The big hit lies in the fact that the lease payments are only deductible for the business use percentage anyway (80 percent in this example). So you have *two* calculations to make before this individual's Schedule C is properly completed. Let's continue our example, using the year 1992 to illustrate the final reporting number for this auto (first leased in 1991).

In the following calculation, note that the $330 shown above as the 1992 income inclusion is not reported as income but rather is used to reduce the lease payments when figuring the actual tax deduction.

Total lease payments	$8,900
Less: 1992 income inclusion (from previous calculation)	– *330*
Reduced lease cost	8,570
At business use percentage	× 80%
Net 1992 tax deduction	$6,856

COMMENT

Equate this $6,856 lease tax deduction with the comparable depreciation deduction for the same auto leased in 1991. Annual depreciation would be limited to:

First year	($2,600 × 80%)	$2,128
Second year	($4,300 × 80%)	$3,440
Third year	($2,550 × 80%)	$2,040
Each year thereafter	($1,575 × 80%)	$1,260

Consider those contrasting figures. The 1992 lease deduction is almost exactly *double* ($6,856 versus $3,440)! In most situations, I feel that business auto leasing still produces higher tax deductions, although the *economics* of leasing versus buying is another matter altogether. Leasing may or may not be cheaper than buying, but the net tax write-offs are usually higher.

> ***TAXTIP***
>
> If you study either leasing income inclusion table, you will note an anomaly. You are penalized (income inclusionwise) for longer leases! For example, a $50,000 auto first leased in 1991 for four years has total gross income inclusions of $3,671. If the same priced car is leased for two years and a similar car is leased for a second two years, the total income inclusions for the total four years would only be $2,268. So, the shorter the lease, the less the total income inclusions, and vice versa.

The presentation of these figures on Schedule C could possibly make the difference between an IRS audit and none! Please refer again to the earlier example. We showed a net tax deduction of $6,856 for auto leasing. If you simply list that amount on Schedule C, how does the IRS *know* that you have scrupulously followed the rules regarding leasing income inclusions and personal use of a business auto?

We always disclose those facts in one of two ways. In our example, we would list auto leasing expense at the gross amount of $8,900. Then we would either report $2,044 ($8,900 − $6,856) as "other income" on line 6 of Schedule C, or report $2,044 as a negative expense number on line 27 of Schedule C. In either event, we would describe that $2,044 as "Personal use of business auto, plus auto leasing income inclusion." Now the IRS knows that you have followed the rules and are probably the single most honest of all 130 million taxpayers, and they should never, never audit your tax return! *That's* IRS presentation!

EMPLOYEE LEASING AN AUTO AND PAYING THE COSTS

If the employee is a "statutory employee" (see Chapter 7), all the same rules of the preceding section would apply, since that particular class of employees can report and claim their expenses on Schedule C. But for the rest of you who fall in the *regular* employee category, Form 2106 ("Employee Business Expenses") comes into play. This IRS form is used for claiming employee business expenses on your personal tax return and it anticipates the leasing of luxury autos.

Naturally, the IRS changed the methodology from that of the preceding sections just enough to confuse anyone who has followed things so far. You do use the same income inclusion table and the theory is the same, but the application is different! Says the IRS:

> Compute the inclusion amount without taking into account your business use percentage . . . [then] report the inclusion amount . . . [finally] the net amount of vehicle rental expenses will be adjusted . . . to reflect the percentage of business use for the tax year.

Huh? Again, only an example can save the remaining shreds of your sanity. Go back to our original illustration and again compute for the year 1992. Now obtain a Form 2106, and we will fill out Part II. On line 24a, "Vehicle rentals," you would enter $8,900. On line 24b, "Inclusion amount," you would enter $412, the full amount of the inclusion figure from the table (this time without reduction to $330 for the business use percentage).

Line 24c of Form 2106 is then the net of $8,900 less the full $412 income inclusion, or $8,488. Finally, on line 27, the 80 percent business use would be applied to $8,488 for a net tax deduction of $6,790. Note that in our earlier illustration we obtained a Schedule C tax deduction of $6,856 versus this $6,790. Why? By changing the calculation *sequence* on Form 2106, the IRS has further reduced the net tax deduction! Probably eight people outside the IRS have ever noticed this fact, but now you have joined this select group of tax trivia, lost-deduction mavens.

EMPLOYEE LEASING AN AUTO AND REIMBURSEMENT BY THE EMPLOYER

This situation is almost funny! To reimburse an employee properly, accurately, and exactly for the business expenses of operating a leased auto for the employer, the most precise way would be to calculate the total amount of the auto expense reimbursement using Form 2106 and the procedures just described in the preceding section. The employers following this course, however, are about the same number as CPAs who can dance on the head of a pin! I personally am not acquainted with taxpayers doing so, or pin-dancing CPAs!

In the real world, employers reimburse employees in one of the following ways: at 29¢ a business mile; for a percentage of the lease, usually 80 to 90 percent; for 100 percent of the lease and then charging back a percentage (or flat dollar amount) as compensation to cover the personal use; or charging the employee with an income inclusion figure derived from an entirely different table that is only supposed to be used if the employer *provides* the vehicle to the employee (see Table 2–4).

So, that's the real world, and frankly IRS agents seem to be accepting any reasonable and fair method of reimbursement for an employee's leased auto, provided personal and luxury use of that auto is taken into account in some equitable form or another. That's no guarantee that I'm extending to you, readers, but it's our general experience to date. Wotta' mess.

EMPLOYER PROVIDING AN AUTO FOR THE EMPLOYEE

Everything changes! The inclusion table, the definitions, the calculation method, and even the definition of "lease." In this situation, forget everything you have learned to date, and we will start over. What we are after here is to figure the amount for "personal use of business auto," which will either be repaid to the company by the employee (preferable, since it *saves payroll taxes* for both employer and employee) or added to the employee's taxable compensation (subject to all payroll taxes).

The "Annual Lease Value Table" (sample selections following) supplies numbers that now include maintenance and insurance of the auto. This table can be used whether the company provides the employee a leased *or* company-owned vehicle. And, the calculation itself is opposite that of the previous table in that the inclusion amount is multiplied by the *personal* use percentage, rather than the *business* use percentage as in the previous cases.

NOTE

For autos with a fair market value of more than $59,999, the annual lease value equals: 0.25 × fair market value plus $500. For example, for a $100,000 leased car, the value would equal: 0.25 × $100,000 = $25,000 + $500 = $25,500. However, this does *not* mean you report that $25,500 as income.

Now, the IRS does not come right out and say that you only have to pick up the inclusion amount for the personal use percentage of the auto, but that's the real truth! However, they only explain it by indirection and obfuscation. And if someone is not very, very careful, they could end up charging their employees 100 percent of the

TABLE 2–4
Annual Lease Value Table[1]

Fair Market Value	*Annual Lease Value*
$ 1,000–$ 1,999	$ 850
2,000– 2,999	1,100
3,000– 3,999	1,350
4,000– 4,999	1,600
5,000– 5,999	1,850
7,000– 7,999	2,350
10,000– 10,999	3,100
12,000– 12,999	3,600
15,000– 15,999	4,350
20,000– 20,999	5,600
25,000– 25,999	6,850
32,000– 33,999	8,750
40,000– 41,999	10,750
46,000– 47,999	12,250
50,000– 51,999	13,250
52,000– 53,999	13,750
56,000– 57,999	14,750
58,000– 59,999	15,250

[1]Source: IRS Publication 535, "Business Expenses."

inclusion amount on the basis of this IRS language, which *implies* a 100 percent income inclusion:

> If you provide an employee with an automobile for an entire calendar year, you can use the automobile's annual lease value to value the benefit . . . Determine the fair market value on the first date the auto is made available . . . for personal use . . . Use the Annual Lease Value Table . . . to find the annual lease value.

In another IRS publication, place, and context (like my favorite quote from *Star Wars:* "In another universe, on another planet, far, far away . . .") the IRS states that:

> A working condition fringe is any property or service provided to you by your employer that you can deduct as an employee business expense if you had paid for the property or service.

You must combine those two scattered fragments of IRS *Star Wars* Information to recognize that if the auto provided by the employer is used, say 80 percent for business, *that* element of the annual lease value is a "working condition fringe" and is not taxable to the employee! Only then would you arrive at the correct conclusion that after you obtain the annual lease value from the table you should multiply that value by the *personal* use percentage to get the true income inclusion. It ain't easy!

Let's go back to our original example of a $32,500 car. Referring to the "Annual Lease Value Table" (Table 2–4), we find that the annual lease value is $8,750 (see italics). Using our example of 20 percent personal use, the employee is only liable for $1,750 (20% × $8,750 = $1,750) that must be repaid the employer or it will be treated as additional taxable compensation. The income tax on $1,750 is not such a terrible annual penalty to pay to drive an employer-provided luxury car worth $32,500. Even a $50,000 auto at 20 percent personal use only results in an annual $2,650 ($13,250 × 20% = $2,650) in personal use income. Not bad!

Remember, the value of maintenance and insurance is included. Remember, this lease value table applies to both company leased *or* company-owned vehicles. Further, this table applies for up to four years, without change, for any particular vehicle, and if you go past that point, you begin anew with the (lower) fair market value as determined at the beginning of the fifth year.

The annual lease value table does not include the cost of fuel provided by the employer. For that event, the IRS allows a ("safe harbor") short-cut rate of a flat 5.5¢ a mile for fuel costs. So, if the employee is driving 3,000 personal miles a year, the sum of $165 (3,000 × 5.5¢ = $165) would be added to the personal use figure. Alternatively, you can use actual fuel costs in this calculation, but who wants to bother?

TAXTIP

Since the lease value remains the same for four years (and then drops in line with the fair market value), there is no built-in penalty, as with the first three income inclusion tables. In the case of leasing, the longer the lease, the higher the income inclusion. Be aware that is not true in this case of an employer-provided auto.

TAXTIP

Any employee is better off when the employer supplies the auto to the employee and then pays or exactly reimburses expenses. The employee

(continued)

thus avoids filling out that terrible Form 2106, substantially reduces the chances of an IRS audit, is not subject to an expense disallowance of 2 percent of adjusted gross income, and can even claim a standard tax deduction if beneficial.

SUPER TAXTIP

If the auto is leased by the employer company, by properly charging (or getting reimbursed for) the appropriate annual lease value to the employee, the employer company gets a *100 percent* tax deduction for the lease payments regardless of the amount! This puts owning and depreciating a company-owned luxury car to shame! Taxwise, that is.

For example, under IRS rules, it would take about 60 years to depreciate a company-owned car costing $100,000 (e.g., the S class Mercedes, which has nothing to do with S corporations). That car might be leased by the company for, say, $18,000 a year with those lease payments deducted in full (as described above). In such a case, with 20 percent personal use, the annual personal lease value to the employee would be $5,100 (20% × $25,500), and the annual tax cost to the employee (assuming a 35 percent federal/state tax rate) would be $1,785 (35% × $5,100 = $1,785). *So*, for $1,785 a year, our employee drives a $100,000 car and the company deducts 100 percent of the lease payments!

FINAL TAXTIP

If after reading all this you are still buying business autos, the right way to get the maximum tax deduction is to always *sell* them and never *trade* them on your next car. If you trade the auto, the undepreciated balance is just added to the tax basis of the next vehicle, and you begin that very limited depreciation cycle all over again. However, if you *sell* the car, the difference between the selling price and the (usually large) undepreciated tax basis becomes an immediate tax deduction ("depreciable property used in a trade or business and sold at a loss, results in an ordinary income tax deduction"). So, as a rule, never trade your business auto. Taxwise, that is.

CONCLUSION

Self-employed individuals should follow the rules and example described in our suggested Schedule C presentation for personal auto inclusions and personal use amounts. An employee leasing an auto and paying the costs should exactly follow our instructions in filling out Form 2106.

An employee leasing an auto and being reimbursed falls into an area of alternate scenarios. Certainly a 29¢ per business mile reimbursement is perfectly safe. Beyond that, we get into various options where employers charge personal income inclusions or reimburse expenses for only a business use percentage or who knows what else. It's the least precise area once you leave the 29¢ arrangement.

Finally, when the corporation leases an auto for an employee we come to probably the most favorable *tax* (not necessarily economic) arrangement of all. Reread the preceding example and consider that option carefully. Remember, you can lease any price category of auto.

Chapter Three

Business Travel

There are three general kinds of business expenses that the IRS dislikes the most, because, in each case, the IRS believes that there is a strong possibility for "abuse." In IRS jargon this means attempted tax deductions of what really are personal expenses. They consider the three most "abusive" expense areas to be: (1) entertainment, (2) auto, and (3) travel.

Over recent years, the IRS convinced Congress that special and unusually restrictive rules were needed to govern and control the deduction of such expenses. They passed the exceptionally strict recordkeeping requirements for documenting entertainment (see Chapter 1) and all estimated and approximated entertainment deductions under the old "Cohan rule" (based on a case won by George M., no less!) were eliminated. In 1986, 20 percent (in 1994, 50 percent) of all entertainment and business meals were made nondeductible.

Auto expenses have been subjected to the onerous "auto log" and intricate auto recordkeeping rules, while probing questions about auto mileage and auto usage were added to all types of tax returns (using Form 4562, "Depreciation and Amortization"—Part III), as well as new rules for taxing income from "personal use of business autos." Then came the special restrictions on so-called luxury autos. Allowable auto depreciation was also reduced to the current level of absurdity, where it will take over 30 years to fully depreciate a mid-priced Mercedes. Finally, auto leasing deductions (see Chapter 2) are also limited by various and complex personal income inclusion tables and leasing tables that are barely understood by anyone.

IRS rules and special IRS requirements regarding business travel are compounded by the *kind* of business travel being claimed. There are different rules for travel in the United States, travel outside the United States, luxury water travel, travel with your spouse, travel without your spouse, travel with your secretary, travel to conventions, travel as a form of education, investment-related travel, and for any personal (i.e., vacation) element in any business travel.

Then we have the special disallowance of 50 percent of all travel meals with which to cope. In addition, there are overall recordkeeping and receipt rules for any and all business travel.

TRAVEL RECORDKEEPING

There are four different recordkeeping requirements and you must satisfy *all four*, for each trip, or you will invariably lose your *entire* travel tax deduction:

1. The dates of your departure and return and the number of business days spent on the trip.
2. The destination (described by city or town or similar designation).
3. The itemized costs of the trip such as lodging, transportation, and meals. You can total the cost of meals into one daily amount and also total the cost of each category of incidentals (e.g., taxi fares, tips, telephone calls, parking) into one daily amount for each category.
4. The business purpose of the trip or the business benefit gained or expected to be gained from your travel. Here is where many of you flunk the entire recordkeeping and tax-deduction process!

Remember, three out of four does not get you to third base in this IRS ballgame. It's a strike-out *and* you lose 100 percent of all your claimed travel deductions! Most of you miss item four, or you forget the additional matter of keeping receipts.

RECEIPTS

Besides the preceding documentation, you must also provide the receipt for *all* lodging expenses, regardless of the amount and receipts for all other expenses of $25 or more. As mentioned earlier (Chapter 1), keep records and receipts for expenses *under* $25 as well!

THE 50 PERCENT LIMITATION

I trust you know by this time that you can only deduct 50 percent of your travel meals. It does not matter if you have that travel meal alone or as part of business entertainment. The 50 percent limitation applies in both instances, which is why travel *meals* must always be shown as a separate item on your travel expense account.

As with business entertainment, the common question is who "loses" that 50 percent. Is it the employer, the employee, the reimburser, the reimbursee, or the self-employed? The easiest way to remember is that the limit applies to whomever is *deducting* the travel meals on that income tax return. Almost all employers who reimburse their employees for business expenses in general reimburse travel meals and all entertainment at 100 percent, which is really appropriate. In such cases, it is the *employer* who forfeits 50 percent of the business meals and entertainment expense deductions (Schedule M-1 of Form 1120 "U.S. Corporation Income Tax Return" even has a preprinted line for the 50 percent disallowance).

However, if an employee is *not* reimbursed and is claiming the travel meal deduction on her personal income tax return (on Form 2106, "Employee Business Expenses"), then it is that employee who loses the 50 percent. Similarly, the self-employed individual is always going to forfeit 50 percent of the deduction (on Schedule C).

NONDEDUCTIBLE TRAVEL

Let's get the easy stuff out of the way first. If you travel as a form of *education,* and the travel itself serves an educational purpose, you cannot deduct any expenses of the trip (this one is primarily aimed at teachers and travel agents).

If you engage in investment-related travel (for example, to an investment-type convention, investment-type seminar, or stockholders' meeting), rather than travel directly related to your trade or business, you cannot deduct any expenses of the trip (this one is primarily aimed at doctors).

You cannot deduct any expenses for attending a convention, seminar, management conference, or similar outside the "North American area" unless:

- It is as "reasonable" to hold the meeting outside that specified area as in it (good luck with proving this one!).
- The meeting is "directly related to your trade or business" and not for any other reason.

The "North American area" (the definition keeps expanding) includes the United States, its possessions (Puerto Rico, Guam, Virgin Islands, and Samoa), Canada, Mexico, the Trust Territory of the Pacific Islands, Barbados, and Jamaica. This provision is directed at "seminars" held in Paris, London, Rome, and similar destinations by doctors, lawyers, accountants, insurance agents, sales reps, contractors, importers, manufacturers, wholesalers, retailers, and all other categories of taxpayers responsible for the past abuses of foreign meetings and their related travel deductions!

If a trip is primarily a vacation, the *entire* cost of the trip is nondeductible except for any directly provable business expenses. The IRS has a rather interesting commentary on this:

> A trip can be a vacation even though a promoter advertises that a trip to a resort or on a cruise ship is primarily for business. The scheduling of incidental business activities during a trip, such as viewing videotapes or attending lectures dealing with general subjects, will not make what is intended to be a vacation into a business trip.

TRAVEL IN THE UNITED STATES

If you can meet the recordkeeping and receipt requirements and if your trip was in fact entirely for business (as shown by your documentation), your trip is 100 percent deductible (except for your travel meals and entertainment, both of which are only 50 percent deductible).

The problems arise where there is a *mixture* of business and personal travel. What the IRS is after are business trips that are nothing more than disguised vacations! Such trips usually involve travel to a seminar, management conference, continuing education meeting, convention, or sales meeting, rather than just a trip to sell customers or visit principals in another city and then back home.

If your trip was primarily business, however, and you added a side trip to see your parents, you must disallow the additional costs of that side trip, but all the transportation expenses to and from your business destination are fully deductible.

Of course, there are many legitimate business seminars and meetings being held, but even in the United States many of those suspect business meetings are held at luxury resorts, with ample golf, tennis, swimming, spas, and other vacation facilities, and some with rather limited business schedules. This does not mean that you cannot hold a legitimate business meeting in a resort area (in fact, I try to limit my speaking engagements to exactly such meeting locations). It just means that the IRS is particularly suspicious of those kinds of vacation-oriented gatherings.

The following quote from the *Audit Technique Handbook* for IRS agents applies equally to domestic and foreign meetings:

> Conventions and meeting agendas—these should be scrutinized carefully in determining the business relationship. Items to consider are as follows:
>
> 1. The exact nature of the business conducted.
> 2. The amount of time truly spent on business.

3. The social events included in the agenda.
4. Is the site and time of the meeting vacation-oriented, such as a resort area in season?

Based on those considerations, you might find to your horror that your entire meeting expenses, including transportation, are disallowed under the following IRS rule:

> If the trip was primarily for vacation, the entire cost of the trip is a nondeductible personal expense, except for any expenses you incurred that are directly for and properly allocable to your business.

"Meetings" that involve two hours of business discussions and eight hours of golf and tennis on both Thursday and Friday, followed by Saturday and Sunday sight-seeing and shopping tours (and lavish cocktail parties and banquets each evening) just will not pass the IRS test. I find it particularly laughable when the meeting programs themselves indicate that about 80 percent of all the activities are social events! In some cases, the meeting programs can really hang you.

The final killers are the side trips that follow the meeting. For example, the meeting itself lasts two days, in a motel in Carbondale, Illinois, followed by a three-week side trip to China, Hong Kong, and Katmandu to get "potential new lines" or something similar!

Such abuses are even more common where foreign meetings are involved; some meeting organizers let you jump to the conclusion that (somehow!) the side trip from the London meeting, to Madrid, Barcelona, and Majorca is just as deductible as the meeting itself! In about 98 percent of the cases, that's simply not true; but while they don't *say* it, they let you *think* it. So check out the deductibility of side trips before you go tripping off.

TRAVEL OUTSIDE THE UNITED STATES

Since the IRS feels that the majority of disguised and expensive vacations will be outside the United States, there are totally different and special rules that govern foreign travel. If your foreign trip was primarily for business and if you meet any *one* of the following four conditions, you can deduct 100 percent of your *transportation* costs (not *total* costs) of the trip:

1. If your foreign business travel does not exceed one week (not counting the day you depart but counting the day you return).
2. If your foreign business travel was over one week (counting both the day you depart and the day you return) *and* you spent less than 25 percent of the total time on nonbusiness activities.

3. You lacked substantial control over arranging the details of the trip (e.g., attending a foreign trade show or being instructed to go by your employer).
4. You can establish that a personal vacation was not a "major consideration," even if you own the business or have substantial control over the arrangements for the trip (a great loophole, if you can *prove* your position—not just say it!).

Remember, if any one of the preceding conditions are met, this will only allow you to deduct 100 percent of your *transportation*. In all events, you must keep detailed records of business and personal days and expenditures and you can only deduct *other* travel expenses (hotel, meals, etc.) for the business days of your trip.

If you do not meet any one of the preceding four conditions, your transportation costs must be divided (prorated) between business and nonbusiness days, and only the business percentage of the transportation can be deducted. For example, if your trip was 20 days and you had 12 days of business travel, you can only deduct 60 percent (12 business days divided by 20 total days) of your transportation costs plus the other documented expenses of those 12 days only.

At what point does your foreign trip cease to be *primarily* for business and become *primarily* a vacation? What if your 20-day trip had only 5 days of business travel? If your foreign trip is primarily a vacation, you cannot deduct any expenses except for the minor ones (e.g., registration fees at the business seminar) directly related to your business! The following example from the IRS illustrates that point and is kind of funny (unless you are a doctor):

> Example 1. You are a doctor practicing medicine and a member of a professional association. The association sponsored a two-week trip to two foreign countries with three professional seminars in each country. Each seminar was two hours long and was held in a different city. You also made an optional side trip to a well-known tourist attraction in each of the countries visited. At the end of the trip, you received a Certificate of Continuing Education in Medicine . . .
>
> Your participation in the professional seminars did not change what was essentially a vacation into a business trip. Your travel expenses were not related primarily to your business. You had no other expenses that were directly for your business. Therefore, you may not deduct your trip as an ordinary and necessary business expense.

To complete this section on foreign travel deductions, another quote from the *Audit Technique Handbook* will illustrate what you may be faced with in any case involving "disguised" foreign vacations:

In reviewing travel outside the United States, the taxpayer's itinerary should be reviewed to determine the number of days spent on business and personal activities. An examination of . . . passport, auto rental receipts and dates of credit card purchases, may reveal personal side trips . . . Inspection of the taxpayer's passport and airline tickets may reveal personal side trips before, during and after the period of the convention.

LUXURY WATER TRAVEL

Even if your travel is 100 percent business, there is a limit on the cost of your transportation by ship. The total cost deductions for such business travel are limited to twice the highest per diem travel allowance of US government employees. If that amount, which changes annually, is, for example, $185 a day, your limit is twice that, or $370. The deduction includes each and every expense of the water travel. Even for a 10 day round-trip on the QE2 (to and from a bona fide business meeting in London), you could only deduct a transportation total of $3,700 (10 × $370) for the 10 days (while the actual cost might be $10,000 to $15,000 for such a round-trip, depending on shipboard accommodations).

BUSINESS MEETINGS ON CRUISE SHIPS

There are special limitations on the expenses that can be claimed for attending even the most legitimate business meeting, convention, or seminar aboard a cruise ship. You must meet *all* the following conditions, or you cannot deduct anything:

- The cruise ship must be registered in the United States (a "US flag ship").
- All the ports of call are located in the United States or its possessions.
- You must attach to your income tax return a written statement that you sign, giving the following information: *(a)* total days of the trip, *(b)* total number of hours each day devoted to scheduled business activities, *(c)* a program of the scheduled business activities.
- You must also attach to your income tax return a written statement signed by an officer of the organization, giving the total number of hours each day you attended the scheduled business activities, and a schedule of the business activities of each day of the meeting.

- If you meet all the preceding conditions, your maximum total deduction is then *limited* to $2,000, or any lesser amount actually spent!

> ***TAXTIP***
>
> With that $2,000 maximum business cruise deduction limit, you are better off with a shorter (or cheaper) cruise meeting, since a longer (or more expensive) cruise will just result in more and more expenses becoming nondeductible once you exceed the $2,000 maximum deduction limit.

Remember, you still must prove that this cruise is a directly related expense of your business and does not fall into that terrible disguised vacation category! Finally, it is possible that if *both* spouses can qualify (e.g., two "working spouses") for a deduction under the preceding rules, then the $2,000 limit would be doubled to $4,000! However, this is not an easy deduction to obtain and sustain.

CONVENTIONS

Conventions are another special hang-up of the IRS, because it is more usual for the spouse to be along than in most other business travel situations. Such disguised vacations also include meetings labeled "management conferences" or "educational seminars."

Another cogent quote from the IRS:

> Convention expenses. You may deduct travel expenses for yourself, not your family, to attend a convention if you can show that your attendance benefits your own trade or business . . . If the convention is for investment . . . or other purposes unrelated to your trade or business, you may not deduct the expenses. Nonbusiness expenses such as social or sight-seeing expenses, are personal expenses and are not deductible.

In other words, as with all other kinds of business travel, the travel must be related to your trade or business (and not a disguised vacation), and you still must eliminate those expenses that apply to the personal portion of the convention. This last idea is frequently ignored or misunderstood by many convention attendees, as is the following problem.

YOUR SPOUSE AT A CONVENTION

It is unfortunately still true that it is easier to deduct your secretary's expenses at a convention than those of your spouse! In fact, *I* can take your spouse to a convention and deduct him or her easier than you can! There is a virtual automatic assumption by the IRS that when your spouse is along with you, it's for vacation purposes only, while if he or she travels with me, the purpose is more likely work-related. Even a true working spouse will forfeit the travel deductions by not attending business sessions and spending the entire time on shopping, golf, tennis, and sight-seeing! (However, as meeting planners become more knowledgeable about these rules, I am being asked more and more to address the spouses on topics such as estate planning.)

In the Revenue Reconciliation Act of 1993, the IRS finally got Congress to settle the perceived problem about abuse in these situations to the detriment of all you convention-bound reps. The new law states that *no deduction will be allowed* for expenses paid or incurred with respect to a *spouse, dependent, or other individual* accompanying a person on a business trip *unless* the accompanying person is a (bona fide) *employee* of the person or company paying for the trip, there is a (bona fide) *business purpose* for that person's *presence* and travel on the trip, *and* the expenses are otherwise deductible (i.e., "legitimate").

The new law really makes it extremely difficult to continue the deduction for a spouse or "friend" at the average business meeting. Either meet *all three* of those conditions or just consider eating part of the costs. That's not the end of the world, if you will consider that the only expenses lost are the *differentials* between single and double occupancy, bargain airfares, meals, registration, and so forth, and not necessarily a full 50 percent of each of those costs.

CONCLUSION

You should now be aware of the tough rules, restrictions, and recordkeeping requirements for business travel, as well as the *new* law regarding those who *accompany* you to business meetings. Have a nice trip, anyway.

Chapter Four

Business Use of Your Home

U.S. v. SOLIMAN

In January 1993, the US Supreme Court ruled against Dr. Nader Soliman and struck down his claimed $2,500 home office deduction. The Court said the fact that the work he performed in his home was essential to his business was not enough, since he failed to meet either of the two standard conditions. To be deductible, a home office must either be the taxpayer's (1) "most important" (i.e., "principal") place of business, or (2) a place used regularly to meet patients, clients, or customers (those were the exact rules in effect *before* this trial). The Court said his home office (1) was not his principal place of business and, (2) was not used to meet with his patients. So he lost.

In that same case, however, the Supreme Court suddenly defined "principal place of business" as the most important place where you generally spend the bulk of your workday. Dr. Soliman did not spend the "bulk of his workday" at his home office, and, thus, it was not his "most important" (i.e., "principal") place of business. Let's consider that new definition for a sales rep whose only office is in his home, because a lot of new trouble and lost tax deductions will come from this reassessment of the entire idea of a tax-deductible home office.

The IRS is now certainly going to rule that the sales rep's bulk of the workday is spent out in the field calling on customers, and therefore the most important place of business is in the field. There will be no deduction allowed for any claimed home office! This is not just idle speculation on my part, but instead is a new fact of life already confirmed by many tax authorities!

Accordingly, everyone (not just sales reps), who has an office in the home should be prepared to prove one of the following to the IRS:

- That you truly spend the most important–bulk of the workday in your home office and not in the field (in which case, for many of you, how are you earning a living?), *or*

- That you regularly meet customers/principals/sales managers in your home office. Note that *occasional* meetings are not sufficient. It's "regular" or you lose!

If either of those conditions are absent upon audit, you will almost certainly be denied any home office deductions! It may really pay (tax-wise) to rent an office outside your home; this new attack is only on *home* offices.

MANY OTHERS WILL ALSO LOSE!

Just for the record, reps are not alone! Here are some of the other grim possibilities being bandied about by some of the warped minds of various tax experts.

- A CPA's only office is in his home. Each day he goes out in the field and works at the offices of various clients. He loses his entire home office deduction, since the bulk of his workday is spent in the field! (According to the Court's logic, the "field" is the principal and "most important" place of business, as it may be for you reps.)
- The same situation would exist for many other independent contractors: plumbers, electricians, carpenters, painters, social workers, insurance salespeople, and any others who fit the pattern. They are out in the (most important) field doing their jobs the bulk of the workday. Ergo, no home office deduction.
- A real estate agent spends most of each day showing houses to prospective customers. That's the most important–bulk of the workday and no home office deduction will be allowed.
- A chestnut vendor in New York City roasts the chestnuts in his home kitchen and then spends all day selling them on various city street corners. The most important–bulk of the workday is spent on street corners with the same terrible result!

To summarize, anyone with a home office who spends most of the time at (most important) other places and locations can no longer deduct a home office, even if it's the only one the poor soul has.

THE IRS

The IRS is so happy about this unexpected turn of events that they can hardly speak. Their fondest hope was to win the *Soliman* case and prevent a potential liberalization of the standard home office rules. They not only won the case, but with the almost casual reference by the Supreme Court to the "most important" and "bulk of the workday" they have a super opportunity to disallow the entire home office deductions of tens of thousands of taxpayers.

IRS celebrations doubtless made most Super Bowl celebrations look tame. Now IRS agents can spend the bulk of *their* workday gleefully disallowing thousands of home office deductions!

WHAT TO DO

If you are going to take the position that the most important–bulk of your workday is in fact spent in your home office, by all means keep a daily diary in an appointment book or calendar to prove this fact. You can certainly expect to be happily challenged on this point by almost any IRS agent you encounter during any future audit you ever undergo.

SOLIMAN CONCLUSION

This certainly was not a Solomon-like decision. Thanks a lot, Oh Honorable Supreme Court justices of highest esteem, supreme intelligence, great renown, and unlimited empathy for the small businessperson!

GENERAL INTRODUCTION

Despite the *Soliman* case, there is still the potential for some reps to sustain a home office deduction under various conditions and circumstances. A portion of your home may be used for trade or business purposes for the following reasons:

- As a self-employed (unincorporated) sales rep.
- For an incorporated sales agency.
- As an employee, receiving reimbursement for home office expenses from your employer.
- As an employee, claiming a personal tax deduction for unreimbursed home office expenses.
- As a statutory employee, claiming a tax deduction for unreimbursed home office expenses.
- As an employee, leasing the home office to your employer.
- As an independent contractor, leasing the home office to a client/customer.

THE BASIC RULES

Naturally, different rules apply to the different cases and situations and here they are.

You must use a portion of the home *exclusively* and *regularly* for your trade or business. "Exclusively" means a specific part of your home used only for business purposes with no personal use ever allowed. "Regularly" means on a continuing basis and not just occasional or incidental use.

Besides exclusive and regular use, the home office must also be (1) your principal place of business (now defined as the most important place where you usually spend the "bulk of your workday"), or (2) a place to meet and deal with customers (clients or patients), or (3) a separate structure that is not attached to your home. (You can have different home offices for each different business.) If you are an employee, there is a further condition that the home office use must also be "for the convenience of your employer" and not merely be "appropriate" or "helpful" in the conduct of your employment.

If you store inventory in your home, you do not have to meet the exclusive use test, but you do have to meet *all five* of these new tests:

1. The inventory is for use in your trade or business.
2. You must be selling at retail or wholesale.
3. Your home is the only fixed location of the trade or business.
4. The storage space is used on a regular basis.
5. The space must be a separately identifiable space suitable for storage.

SELF-EMPLOYED (UNINCORPORATED) INDIVIDUALS

Individual sales reps in this category file Schedule C. A Schedule C filing automatically makes them bad people in the eyes of the IRS. Not only does the IRS audit them (4–6 times) more often, but a Schedule C audit itself is perhaps more extensive and detailed than regular individual IRS audits.

FORM 8829

As if that were not enough, the IRS created Form 8829, "Expenses for Business Use of Your Home," that must be used in conjunction with every Schedule C (to claim expenses for business use of a home).

This form consists of 42 lines of information for the IRS to paw over, examine, question, and audit.

For example, in Part I the IRS asks you to calculate the percentage of business use of your home. The IRS urges you to use the "area basis" method, which is based on square feet of exclusive business use (including inventory storage) to total square feet of your residence, although you can use "any other reasonable method."

HOW TO INCREASE YOUR HOME OFFICE DEDUCTIONS

For those of you who can still qualify for a home office deduction after the *Soliman* decision, the key to enlarging home office deductions lies in the *method* you use to calculate the percentage of business use of the home.

The IRS is quite vague, however, as to exactly how you do the calculation. There are generally *three* recognized methods, and they frequently produce different results. Try all three and use the one with the most beneficial result.

1. *Number of rooms method.* Using this method, if the rooms are of similar size and there are 10 rooms in the home, one room used as an office will result in *10 percent* business use.
2. *Square footage method.* If the office is 200 square feet and the house is 1,800 square feet, you could claim *11 percent* business use (200 divided by 1,800).
3. *Net square footage method. Reduce* the total square feet in the house by the amount of square feet in the common areas used for both business and personal purposes. If those common areas are, say, 300 square feet for the house in the example above, we would divide the 200-square-foot office by 1,500 square feet (1,800 minus 300). The business use percentage would be *13 percent.*

TAXTIP

Whatever percentage you calculate will affect all your home office deductions, so the higher (more generously) you figure the square feet, the higher all your deductions will be!

Direct expenses are the first category to list on Part II of Form 8829. These are expenses that only benefit the business and are not subject to any percentage allocation, since they are 100 percent deductible. Examples are painting the home office or repairs to the home office space.

> *TAXTIP*
>
> In our experience we found few or no items in this category, but if some exist in your own situation you are probably better off simply claiming them on the Schedule C itself under the expense categories (Part II).

Indirect expenses are those expenditures necessary to maintain the entire house; they benefit both the business and personal areas of the dwelling. These expenses will later be subject to the business use percentage you arrived at earlier. Examples are mortgage interest (or rent), real estate taxes, utilities, insurance, repairs, maintenance, and depreciation of the actual home office itself.

CORPORATIONS

Interestingly, the IRS requires no special forms and makes no special rules for corporations operating out of a private home. They probably figure, correctly, that there are few of them indeed. Of course, if there is an IRS audit, the corporation would have to prove any claimed home office deductions. Undoubtedly, the IRS agent would use something like a square foot business percentage in examining those expenses, and we recommend exactly such a procedure in determining a corporation's deductible home office expenses. However, no Form 8829 is required and no special IRS attention is called to the corporation tax return.

> *TAXTIP*
>
> Many corporations occupying home offices pay many expenses (maintenance, insurance, utilities, repairs, etc.) *directly* and simply deduct them in the various expense categories.

EMPLOYEE RECEIVING HOME OFFICE REIMBURSEMENTS

If you account to your employer for any business expenses (by the usual documentary evidence) and are exactly reimbursed, you do not have to report the reimbursement on your personal tax return, nor does the employer report it to the IRS or include it in your Form W-2 income. This arrangement is the best method for business expenses in general, and such reimbursements can include the employee's expenses for a home office!

To qualify in this particular case, the home office must be:

- A place to meet or deal with customers.
- For the "convenience of your employer."
- Used exclusively for business.
- Used regularly for business.

You do not qualify if the office is only used to make or receive business phone calls, and you must meet all four of the preceding conditions.

NOTE

You do not have to meet the new most important–bulk of the workday interpretation.

> ***TAXTIP***
>
> **If the employee qualifies, a substantial benefit (big bucks!) can be obtained by way of tax-free reimbursement for home office use! (Further, remember that owners of corporations are also employees. Think about that!)**

EMPLOYEE CLAIMING UNREIMBURSED HOME OFFICE EXPENSES

The home office deduction qualifications are the same as described in the preceding section. But in this situation, the employee must first elect to claim itemized tax deductions on her individual income tax return, giving up the chance to claim the standard deduction, and then fill out Form 2106, "Employee Business Expenses," which in turn generates a "miscellaneous itemized deduction." Such deductions are further disallowed to the extent of 2 percent of the employee's adjusted gross income. Also, the odds of an IRS audit are sharply increased. The end result is, therefore, nowhere near as attractive as in the foregoing case.

> ***TAXTIP***
>
> The tax-free reimbursement arrangement described above is far preferable to this one, even if the individual's compensation has to be *reduced* by a similar amount.

STATUTORY EMPLOYEE CLAIMING UNREIMBURSED HOME OFFICE EXPENSES

The same home office deduction qualifications apply as for all other employees, but this special category of employee is allowed to avoid the expense reporting (and 2 percent disallowance) of the regular employee class and claim his expenses on Schedule C (see Chapter 7), as does the self-employed (unincorporated) individual. (The statutory employee must also fill out and attach Form 8829, detailing all home office expenses.)

EMPLOYEE LEASING A HOME OFFICE TO THE EMPLOYER

When leasing is involved, the law prevents the employee receiving the rent from deducting *any* expenses of a home office. Period! But there are other considerations.

> ***TAXTIP***
>
> There is nothing to bar the employer from paying *rent* to an employee and the employer getting a full tax deduction. But if that employee has unused passive losses from other property investments (tax shelter partnerships, rental property, etc.), the gross amount of the rental income from the employer is fully offset by other such passive losses, and those rental payments are then received tax-free! This arrangement might be worthwhile even if the employee's salary is cut by an amount similar or identical to the rental payments. (In that event, you are replacing taxable income with tax-free income and reducing the Social Security/Medicare tax bite as well!)

Comment

Note the dramatic difference in the tax rules governing an employee who is exactly reimbursed for home office expenses and an employee who is simply paid home office "rent." The former receives the most favorable tax treatment possible, while the latter is under stringent limitations and is, in effect, punished. Consider these facts when discussing home office payments to employees. There is a big difference, tax-wise!

INDEPENDENT CONTRACTOR LEASING A HOME OFFICE TO A CLIENT/CUSTOMER

The same restrictions as in the preceding section apply to any independent contractor who "leases to the party for whom she performs services." In such a situation, the law again *prevents* the deduction of any home office expenses and the gross amount of the rent received must be reported as rental income.

> ***TAXTIP***
>
> When hiring a sales sub-agent or any other independent contractor in which a home office rental might be involved, simply negotiate an increased fee or commission rate (if necessary) and don't even *mention* any implied rental concession. The independent contractor will receive the same dollar amount expected *and* can still deduct all his home office expenses.

THE LIMIT AND SEQUENCE OF HOME OFFICE DEDUCTIONS

The IRS has two reasons for forcing the use of Form 8829, which is mandatory in every case where a Schedule C is being filed, *and* there is a deduction for business use of a residence. The first and more obvious reason is to make taxpayers supply detailed information about the exact expenses and calculations underlying the deductions for their home office.

The second motive is to implement the home office limitations that were part of the Tax Reform Act of 1986. Simply stated: The deductions for the business use of a home are limited to the gross income of the business in such a way that they can never be used to create a tax-deductible *loss* in any year.

The limit on the home office deduction is calculated in the following sequence:

1. The gross income from the business (Schedule C, line 7);
2. Less total expense deductions (wages, supplies, auto, travel, promotion, taxes, etc.) as required by Schedule C, line 28;
3. Less the business percentage of mortgage interest and real estate taxes (Form 8829, line 14). Whatever *that* net amount may be is the final limitation (Form 8829, line 15) on your deduction for *other* home office expenses and the depreciation of the home office.

Remember, these calculations can never produce a *currently deductible tax loss;* instead, any such loss only becomes a carryover to future years. (A home office carryover loss keeps the exact character of the type of expenses involved, when claiming them in future years.) The best you can ever show, because of home office expense deductions, is a breakeven for any particular year, but never a loss.

Here is an example using the mandatory IRS expense deduction sequence of Form 8829 and assuming 20 percent business use of the home:

Gross income from the business	$36,000
Less Expense Deductions	
1. Business expenses not relating to home office use (payroll, taxes, auto, materials, travel, etc.)	*28,000*
Overall limit on home office deductions	8,000
2. Mortgage interest and real estate taxes (20% of $25,000)	*5,000*
Limit on further home office deductions	3,000
3. Home office expenses (20% of home: insurance, utilities, maintenance, etc.)	*4,000*
Preliminary loss carryover to next year	(1,000)
4. Depreciation of home office (20% of total home depreciation)	*1,500*
Final loss carryover to next year	$(2,500)

Study what really happens in this example. The mortgage interest and real estate taxes are deductible *anyway,* whether you have a business or not! But by using this mandatory deduction sequence, you have lost a current deduction for home office expenses and depreciation. In the olden days, we would have claimed the $5,000 in mortgage interest and real estate taxes as part of a $25,000 itemized deduction without relating them to the business at all. Then all the home office expenses would have deductible in full. We now have a sly and devious (albeit legal) way of further limiting home office deductions!

It is also mandatory that the carryover be calculated and classified as follows. You must move in reverse sequence for this computation. So first, the $1,500 depreciation deduction carries over in full, which leaves $1,000 of the preceding category of home office expenses to carry over to next year, for a total carryover of $2,500. Remember, the carryover expenses keep their same expense category classification in future years.

Thus, in our illustration, the taxpayer reports a loss for the current year, and moreover faces a reduced itemized tax deduction for mortgage interest and real estate taxes of only $20,000 ($25,000 less $5,000 "used up" in this home office deduction). The final insult is that the carryover items are of the lowest priority the last to be deducted in tax deductions again in the next year and may very well be further disallowed and carried over to still another year, *ad infinitum!*

TAXTIP

If you have a borderline profitable (or losing) business operating out of your home, consider *not* claiming home office expenses, *not* filing Form 8829, and simply claiming your mortgage interest and real estate tax deductions in the conventional manner. You will certainly be reducing the probability of an IRS audit, and all you are giving up are some home office expense carryovers that may or may not *ever* result in future tax deductions. This advice only applies, of course, to businesses that are dubiously profitable (or not at all) and will usually apply to minor, secondary, minimal businesses.

AN INTERESTING RESULT

For those of you operating relatively successful unincorporated rep firms out of your home, the mandatory business deduction for mortgage interest and real estate taxes has produced some unexpected consequences. We have seen this in a number of cases where the IRS limitation on losses was not the issue, since the business was producing substantial profits.

In some such cases we found that using Form 8829 and including some substantial mortgage interest amounts produced a larger than expected home office deduction. This result then served to reduce the taxpayer's Social Security/Medicare taxes, which are figured on the net profit (after the home office deduction). Some of those combined mortgage interest and real estate tax deductions were in the $10,000 range (e.g., 20 percent of $50,000), which, in cases where net profits were below the maximum Social Security limit, generated a gross Social Security/Medicare tax savings of $1,530 (15.3 percent × $10,000)! An unexpected outcome indeed, and one that can increase as the mortgage interest deduction (and the business use percentage) becomes larger.

SALE OF YOUR HOME

If you are planning to sell and replace your home in a tax-free rollover, be very, very careful about claiming home office expenses. There are costly tax pitfalls lurking!

TAXTRAP

If you claim part of your home for business in the year of sale, you can only postpone recognizing gain on the nonbusiness portion. So if you claimed 20 percent business use in the year of the sale, 20 percent of any gain would become taxable income and could not be deferred!

SOLUTION

Never claim home office business expenses in the year of sale.

TAXTRAP

If you claimed (or could claim) any depreciation on your home for business use, you must lower the basis of the home by those amounts when figuring the deferred gain on the tax-free rollover. Further, such depreciation is figured on the amount taken or that could have been taken. Finally, if you used an accelerated depreciation method, some of that gain may be treated as taxable ordinary income ("depreciation recapture") in the year of sale and not deferred at all.

SOLUTION

You may be better off claiming 40-year straight-line depreciation on the business portion of your home. Using the straight-line method avoids any taxable (recapture) income that can result from using an accelerated depreciation method. The 40-year life serves to reduce the annual depreciation, which might not be deductible anyway under the various limitations discussed, and thus *increases* the rollover basis of the home. See your tax adviser for more on this complicated subject.

BUSINESS TELEPHONE IN YOUR HOME OFFICE

> *TAXTIP*
>
> By all means get a *second* telephone line in your home, if you are claiming home office expenses under any circumstances.

Tax deductions cannot be claimed for the base cost (including taxes) of the first telephone line in any residence. A business telephone adds about $15 a month to a telephone bill in Los Angeles and up to about $30 a month in other parts of the country. Strangely, the IRS considered this change a major victory when they got Congress to pass this provision as part of the 1988 tax law.

Further, by having a second telephone line you automatically segregate business and personal telephone use by the selection of the two different lines. This avoids any IRS proration of the cost of a single line above the disallowed base costs of any single line.

Finally, and ideally, you might arrange for your employer to directly pay the cost of the phone bill for that second line (or at least get exactly reimbursed, but direct payment is even better).

TRADE OR BUSINESS

The home office must be used for your "trade or business." This phrase is significant whenever taxpayers try to justify home office tax deductions for investment activities. Says the IRS:

> You cannot deduct any expense if you use part of your home, even though exclusively and on a regular basis, to read financial periodicals and reports, clip bond coupons, and perform similar activities for your own investments, because these activities are not a trade or business.

A MEETING PLACE

Here is the IRS explanation of what really is a major exception (i.e., loophole) to the principal place of business home office rule:

> If, in the normal course of your business, you meet or deal with patients, clients, or customers in your home, even though you may carry on business at another location, your expenses for the part of your home used exclusively and regularly for this business are deductible.

For those who do have a home office used as a meeting place, keep in mind that it can be a second (and nonprincipal, non–bulk-of-the-workday) office and still afford some interesting tax opportunities. Remember, however, that an employee must also meet that added test of "for the convenience of the employer" before a home office is deductible at all.

CONCLUSION

For the self-employed (unincorporated) sales agent operating out of her home, Form 8829 is now a fact of life. Follow the rules, as explained and consider all the other comments, information, and ideas provided. Pay particular attention to the new "most important–bulk of the workday" attack on your entire home office deduction. Some sales reps may, in fact, lose *all* such deductions under the new *Soliman* interpretation, which I don't consider a very Solomon-like decision. Keep in mind the three alternate ways of figuring the business use percentage of your home.

For employees, including the officers/shareholders of incorporated rep firms, the potential for home office expense *exact reimbursements* has not been exploited to the full limits of the law. My advice is to reread and restudy this information. In some form or other, it can hopefully benefit most of our readers.

Chapter Five

Business Auto Recordkeeping

As I travel around the United States, giving seminars on taxes and matters financial, I always get the same reaction from some sales rep in the audience the moment I get to business auto recordkeeping: "They changed the law back to what it used to be, and we don't have to keep any auto log!" My answer is always the same: "Well, yes—and no."

The background, as most of you may remember, is that Congress first passed a law that mandated a "written contemporaneous business auto log." That law required an individually written entry for each and every individual business auto stop or trip. So, after each and every sales or business call, salespeople had to whip out business auto logs and make the required bookkeeping entries, frequently causing auto accidents (deductible?) in the process. This was a typical example of "IRS overkill." The idea was good and somewhat appropriate, but the execution was awful!

So, after an absolutely enormous and horrendous outcry from the entire American business community, Congress held further hearings and again changed the law over the bitter objections of the IRS, who thought the then existing requirements were perfectly reasonable and easy to implement! The sequence of events has caused considerable misunderstanding, particularly for many reps; the law was changed *somewhat*, but it is still stricter and more demanding than in days of old, when knights were bold and auto logs weren't invented.

AUTO LOGS

Here are some current quotes from the IRS (emphasis mine):

> A contemporaneous log is not required *but* you should prepare and maintain the account book or similar record at or near the time of the expense or use while you can still remember it accurately.

You should keep an account book, diary, *log*, statement of expense, trip sheets, or similar records and documentary evidence that, in combination, may prove your business expenses."

Generally, an adequate record must be *written*.

While there was no longer the absolute requirement for a written auto log, with an entry for each and every stop, Congress, at the same time, issued a warning and explanation of preference and priority. It went approximately like this and is still the law of the land:

1. Every taxpayer must substantiate business auto expenses by "adequate records or by sufficient written or oral evidence." However,
2. Written evidence carries greater weight than oral evidence.
3. The value of written evidence is still greater, the closer it is made to the time of the expenditure, which means that contemporaneous written records are still the best evidence!

Thus, while a contemporaneous record is not required (the major change when Congress amended the law), a written and contemporaneous record is still the *best evidence* of a business auto expense. It is the most easily acccepted by the IRS, it carries the most weight, it is the most persuasive, and it is the number one passer of the "IRS smell test" for veracity, probity, honesty, virtue, rectitude, verity, and *DA trooth!*

TAXTIP

The best advice is to continue to maintain a *written* record of business auto use with all entries being made close to the time of the trip. However, you don't have to make an entry for each and every call! Therefore, how often should you record your trips, mileage, and business purpose in a business auto log? Ideally, once a day, at the end of that day. A poor second choice: once a week. I don't feel that a once a month entry even comes close to the "contemporaneous" idea. How long does it take to write in the names of the places you drove to, a brief description of business purpose (not always required; see following), and the mileage for the day? Ten minutes? Five minutes? Two minutes?

Further, if you have repetitive calls on customers for deliveries, sales calls, or similar, you do *not* have to enter the business purpose! Here is that good news, direct from the IRS:

> If the business purpose . . . is clear from the surrounding circumstances, a written explanation is not required.

As an example of the preceding rule, the IRS specifically refers to manufacturers' sales agents (which should gladden the hearts of our readers) with the following example:

> A sales representative who calls on customers on an established sales route does not have to submit a written explanation of the business purpose for traveling that route.

Note that you are getting a "pass" on the *business purpose* of such auto expenses, but you still should maintain a written, contemporaneous record! And, you still must list "business purpose" for all entertainment and other business expenditures.

Here's an IRS quote confirming my earlier advice about making one entry a day for all your business auto use (emphasis mine):

> Uses which may be considered part of a single use, such as a round trip or *uninterrupted business use*, may be accounted for by a single record.

So, at least for most salespeople, a written and contemporaneous auto log is a simple thing indeed. The IRS will let you skip the recording of business purpose, with an "established sales route," and they confirm that one entry a day is acceptable. Why not settle for exactly that?

To sum up business auto logging, by all means keep a *written* log. Once you accept that discipline, a contemporaneous, or once a day, entry is the best way to go! The time required is minimal and the (IRS) rewards in upheld auto deductions are great!

SUBSTANTIATION OF EXPENSES

An auto log is just one part of business auto substantiation. There are *four* elements involved in completely satisfying the IRS. You must prove:

1. The amount of each separate expense for a car, such as the cost of buying the car, capital improvements to the car, lease payments, maintenance and repairs, gas and oil, and all other auto expenses.
2. The mileage for business use and the total miles for the year, so business use percentage can be accurately determined. This requirement really makes an auto log essential!

3. The date of the expense or use (auto log!).
4. The business reason for the expense or use (subject to the special waiver described earlier).

As you can see, while an auto log is not required, it is virtually impossible to fully satisfy the IRS without such a log or something equivalent. Receipts are generally the best proof of most auto expenditures, so listen to the IRS again.

> A receipt is ordinarily the best evidence to prove the amount of an expense. A canceled check together with a bill from the payee will establish the cost. However, a canceled check alone does not prove a business expense without other evidence to show that it was for a business purpose.

That's clear enough, but that last sentence bears some extra study. There is a frequent misunderstanding among taxpayers in general that a canceled check is all the IRS proof needed for any business expenditure. Not true! A canceled check alone is proof of nothing but that a payment was made! It does not, in and of itself, prove that such a payment was deductible. For example, a canceled check for $423 to the Jones Motor Company may prove that you made a payment to that company. But, was it for the repairs of your business auto? Or your spouse's car? Or for your brother-in-law's car? Was it for maintenance? Was it to repay a loan to Mr. Jones? Was it for a capital expenditure (new stereo for your car)? Was it for a pool motor for your swimming pool? Or a new motor for your furnace? Get the point? The check alone will *not* satisfy the IRS.

EMPLOYEE AUTO RECORDS

A frequent question is whether the employee must keep duplicates of expense records submitted for reimbursement. Generally not, unless the employee is claiming expenses in *excess* of those reimbursements. Says the IRS:

> Employees who give their records and documentation to their employers and are reimbursed for their expenses do not have to keep duplicate copies of this information. However, employees who claim deductions for expenses that are more than reimbursements . . . may be required to prove their expenses.

By all means keep duplicate records if you are claiming expenses in *excess* of reimbursements. Further, if you receive a flat (e.g., $400 a month) auto or other expense allowance, you, the employee, must maintain and preserve all your own expense documentation in case of an audit. As always, any employee is better off with exact expense reimbursements and nothing claimed on the individual income tax return. The exact reimbursement arrangement materially reduces the chances of an individual IRS audit.

PARKING

Parking presents every employer with an opportunity to save the employees some taxes, while the employer also benefits. That's because every employer can pay or reimburse for employee parking *tax-free*. But, if the employee pays her own parking without reimbursement, no deduction can be claimed. (As of January 1, 1993, the maximum tax-free payment/reimbursement was $155 a month, indexed annually for inflation in $5 per month increments.) So here we have a rare IRS win-win situation (emphasis mine):

> The value of parking provided by your employer on or near the employer's business is a working condition fringe and is therefore excluded from income. The exclusion applies whether the employer owns or rents the parking space.
>
> A reimbursement or allowance to you for renting a parking space on or near the business premises of the employer is also a working condition fringe which is excluded from income.
>
> The parking space working condition fringe does not apply to any parking facility or space . . . for *residential* purposes by the employee.

TAXTIP

Any employer with employees paying their own parking should change such arrangements. The employer will save payroll taxes on that parking allowance/payment, and the employee will receive that portion of compensation tax-free (except, as noted, for any portion exceeding the maximum allowable by law).

EXCLUDED VEHICLES

I get many questions about whether special vehicles, trucks, and vans can be excluded from the onerous auto logging requirements. The answer is again: "Well, yes—and no." You can exclude many such vehicles under IRS rules—but not all.

The basic rule is that any vehicle designed to carry cargo, with loaded gross vehicle weight of over 14,000 pounds, is exempt from the auto logging requirements and is *never* considered a "personal vehicle." That one doesn't help most of our readers. However, trucks and vans under 14,000 pounds *may* qualify as "nonpersonal use" (i.e., 100 percent business use) vehicles under certain circumstances:

1. A van if it is clearly marked with special advertising, paint or decals; has seats for only the driver and one other person; and has permanent shelving that fills most of the cargo area. Or if the cargo area is open but the van is always carrying merchandise, material or equipment during business hours.
2. A pickup truck if it is clearly marked with special advertising, paint, or decals and it is specially equipped with a hydraulic gate, power winch, tanks and drums or other heavy equipment. Or if it is primarily used for transporting a particular type of load in connection with construction, manufacturing, or similar and has been specially designed or modified accordingly.
3. Delivery trucks with seating only for the driver plus a folding jump seat.
4. Police, fire, bus, special farm, ambulance, and similar vehicles.

Since most reps are interested in qualifying vans or pickup trucks as nonpersonal vehicles, here is the overall IRS rule:

> A pickup truck or van is not considered a qualified nonpersonal use vehicle, unless it has been specially modified with the result that it is not likely to be used more than minimally for personal purposes.

In view of the preceding, perhaps a specially modified Mercedes SL600 two-seater convertible pickup truck or van would be the way for us to go! With permanently affixed decals bearing the name of my accounting firm.

COMMUTING EXPENSES

It is impossible to fully discuss business auto recordkeeping if you don't understand that auto mileage *always* includes "personal commuting," which is a term clearly defined by the IRS:

> You may not deduct the costs of driving your car between your home and your main or regular place of work. Those costs are nondeductible personal expenses. You may not deduct commuting expenses no matter what the distance between your home and your regular place of work or if you are employed in different locations on different days.

> *TAXTIP*
>
> For those of you who go to and from the same office location every day, you're stuck. For those of you who are going to different locations each day (e.g., most salespeople), you should arrange your schedule so the first and last trips each day are close to your home.

The IRS has anticipated and barred most attempts to convert personal commuting to business. They particularly mention that *none* of the following will save your trip from becoming personal commuting:

- Using a car phone while commuting.
- Having business associates ride with you and discussing business with them.
- Hauling tools or instruments in your car.
- Displaying advertising material on your car.

The one exception to these personal commuting rules seems to be when your only office is in your home. The IRS has generally allowed all the mileage of business auto trips that begin or end at your (only) home office. The theory seems to be that when you leave your (only) home office, you have already *made* that first personal commute and are now driving from your office to your next business stop. The IRS lost a significant Tax Court case in 1992, when they strangely took a contrary position on business driving from the (only) home office, so this practice has been upheld.

CONCLUSION

I have failed miserably if any sales rep still thinks that a business auto log is a poor idea or rarely required. And remember, even the recommended auto log is just *one* element of perfect business auto recordkeeping and substantiation. By following this advice, you should be rewarded with some handsome increases in after-tax dollars.

Many days a salesperson can make more money by saving taxes through expense recordkeeping than through earning sales commissions! Business recordkeeping (auto/travel/entertainment) can pay a high hourly rate in tax savings. So think of it as another way to earn "commissions" and put real dollars in your pocket.

Chapter Six

Employee Expense Reimbursements

Many rep business owners are still not aware that legislation enacted way back in 1988 requires that any employee expense reimbursements or expense allowances that fail to meet specific IRS accountability conditions ("criteria") *must* be reported on wage statement Form W-2, "Wages and Tax Statement," box 1, as taxable "additional compensation." Those payments then become subject to mandatory income tax withholding and payment of all payroll taxes, just like any other wages. This law became fully effective for all such expense payments/allowances made on or after July 1, 1990, but we find that some sales agency owners are still wasting money and reimbursing employee expenses in the wrong manner.

Whether business expense reimbursements are wages subject to withholding and payroll taxes or not depends on whether such expense arrangements are paid under an "accountable" or a "nonaccountable" plan, which will be discussed in full later in this chapter.

AVOID ISSUING A FORM W-2 AND A FORM 1099 TO ANY EMPLOYEE

Let's deal with one common error first. The IRS does not want, under any circumstances, an employer reporting any employee's compensation or expense payments on both a Form W-2 (wage statement) and a Form 1099 "information return." They want forms of compensation of every kind and type reported on a Form W-2 (the only exceptions are interest, rents, dividends, and so on—payments in an entirely different category).

We have seen a few cases where the IRS has returned a Form 1099 (made out to an employee) to the employer with instructions to reissue a corrected Form W-2 that was to include the amounts previously reported on the Form 1099 information return. The IRS has three excellent motives for their stubborn actions:

1. The obvious reason is to concentrate all reported income and other transactions between an individual and the employer in one document (Form W-2). This improves both the speed and efficiency of the IRS in tracking and computer auditing each employee's total dealings with his employer.

2. While 100 percent of Forms W-2 are matched to the related individual income tax returns, a lesser (and secret) percentage of Forms 1099 are so matched—rumored to be around 90–92 percent (but in actuality, probably in the 70–80 percent range). Obviously, whenever possible, the IRS prefers Form W-2 reporting only.

3. Perhaps the main reason the IRS wants compensation and such expense payments reported on the Form W-2 is that many collateral payments to employees, such as "nonaccountable" expense allowances, are now subject to social security and other payroll taxes! When these payments are reported on a Form 1099 information return, they just might slide by IRS scrutiny without such taxes being collected, or the tax payments might be reduced (expenses would be deducted from the expense allowance by the employee and Social Security/Medicare taxes only paid on the net income, if any).

This mandatory Form W-2 reporting also results in substantially increased tax revenues for the government—a state of affairs most passionately desired, wanted, dreamed about, coveted, and craved by the Internal Revenue Service!

ACCOUNTABLE EXPENSE REIMBURSEMENT PLANS

An accountable plan is any expense reimbursement or expense allowance plan in which the employee accounts (of course) to her employer, within a reasonable time, and, in so doing, meets the substantiation requirements of IRS Code Section 274. It also must be a plan in which any excess amounts *not* accounted for are returned to the employer: "No W-2 reporting is required for reimbursements that are equal to or less than the employee's substantiated expenses."

TAXTIP

The general IRS definition of "substantiation" (i.e., "accounting for") includes any IRS-approved dollar amounts of "flat" (i.e., fixed amount) payments such as per diem travel allowances and business mile reimbursements. This represents a big and legal loophole through which you can drive many expense reimbursements so they're not subject to the payroll tax/taxable compensation rules.

Please reread the information in this section, since this is the "guts" of what every employer and employee should ideally strive to achieve. If you meet all the conditions, all the expense payments to the employees are tax-free to them, are not reportable to the IRS, and are not subject to employment taxes and income tax withholding. If you don't, they ain't!

> ***IRS Quiz***
>
> Question:
>
> When you get a dreaded IRS "CP 2000" letter, which states that you have failed to report some of your income, do you know what the letters stand for?
>
> Answer:
>
> The rumor is that "CP" stands for "Crooked Person."

NONACCOUNTABLE EXPENSE REIMBURSEMENT PLANS

If even one of the requirements of accountable plans are not met, all such expense reimbursements or allowances (or excess reimbursements *not* accounted for and *not* returned to the employer) are:

- Treated as part of taxable wages.
- Includible in the employee's gross income.
- Considered "additional compensation."
- Reported as such on Form W-2 (in box 1).
- Subject to all payroll taxes and income tax withholding.

As the IRS so succinctly puts it, "A nonaccountable plan is any plan that fails to satisfy all the requirements of an accountable plan."

The current employee expense rules have been pronounced final by the IRS, and there is little chance that they will be changed in the foreseeable future. So, learn 'em—and live by 'em! You have no choice.

A MISHMASH OF ACCOUNTABLE AND NONACCOUNTABLE EXPENSE PAYMENTS

Of course many of our employer readers will manage to mix up the two kinds of plans, the two kinds of payments and, thus, the two kinds of rules! This certainly increases their business complexities, to say nothing of their accounting fees!

In such multifarious cases, the IRS says that insofar as any kinds of expense payments *are* accounted for, that *portion* is considered to be a nontaxable reimbursement. To the extent they are *not* accounted for, they are treated as additional taxable wages and, of course, now subject to payroll taxes and income tax withholding. This hodgepodge usually occurs when the employee is being paid a flat expense allowance, such as $300–$1,000 per month from which the employee pays auto, entertainment, and travel expenses. If the employee never turns in any expense accounting, the payments are fully reported as wages under the nonaccountable expense rules already discussed. However, the IRS had really bent over backward to offer an attractive compromise. In the case of a fixed reimbursement allowance, only that portion not accounted for by "substantiation or government specified rates" is to be reported as additional taxable wages.

EXAMPLE 1—SUBSTANTIATION

You pay an employee $800 a month as a fixed expense allowance. The employee turns in properly substantiated and properly receipted travel expenses of $637 for the month. The employee does not return the $163 difference to the employer, nor is he required to do so.

SOLUTION 1

$163 ($800 − $637) is added to the employee's taxable wages (usually in the month following), subject to full income tax withholding and payroll tax deductions. The $637 is a tax-free reimbursement to the employee and is *not* reported to the IRS.

EXAMPLE 2—GOVERNMENT SPECIFIED RATES

You pay an employee $800 a month as a fixed expense allowance. The employee turns in documentation that indicates she drove 2,000 business miles for the month, using her own car for this business driving. If the current government specified rate for business mileage reimbursement is 29¢, the employee mileage report accounts for $580 (2,000 miles × 29¢). The employee does not return the $220 difference (and was not required to do so).

SOLUTION 2

The sum of $220 ($800 − $580) is added to the employee's taxable wages (usually in the month following), subject to full income tax withholding and payroll tax deductions. The $580 is a tax-free reimbursement to the employee and is *not* reported to the IRS.

EXAMPLE 3—GOVERNMENT SPECIFIED RATES

You pay an employee $800 a month as a fixed expense allowance. The employee turns in the time, place, and business purpose (no lodging receipt is required in this case) of a five-day business trip that month to a "high cost" city (as so defined by the IRS). If the current government specified rate for travel reimbursements covering lodging, meals, and incidental expenses to high cost cities is $150 (it usually changes every year), that employee travel report accounts for $750 (five days × $150). The employee does not return the $50 difference and was not required to do so.

SOLUTION 3

The sum of $50 ($800 − $750) is added to the employee's taxable wages (usually in the month following), subject to full income tax withholding and payroll tax deductions. The $750 is a tax-free reimbursement to the employee and is *not* reported to the IRS.

TAXTIP

This special per diem travel arrangement technically cannot be used by those owning over 10 percent of the employer company. However, this doesn't really prevent company owners from using the same arrangement. It just means that *if there is* an IRS audit, you must be prepared to prove that your actual expenses equaled or exceeded the flat allowance.

EXAMPLE 4—EVERYTHING COMBINED

You pay an employee $800 a month as a fixed expense allowance. In one month, the employee turns in the following expense accountings, with proper documentation, receipts, and records—as required for the different expense categories under rules covering both "substantiation" and "government specified rates":

Itemized travel expenses for one business trip	$ 84
One-day trip to a high cost city—flat rate	150
One-day trip to a low cost city—flat rate	94
Log documenting 1,000 business miles at 29¢	290
Itemized "in town" entertainment expenses	240
	$858

SOLUTION 4

Nothing is added to the employee's taxable wages since the documented expenses (by both "substantiation" and "government specified rates" *exceeded* the $800 expense allowance. Further, the employee has a potential tax deduction of $58 ($848 – $800) on his individual income tax return.

In summary, an employee can use any combination of methods to account to the employer for any fixed expense allowance. To the extent such an allowance is not accounted for, it is reported as additional taxable wages, and the employer will incur additional payroll-tax costs on the increment. A lose-lose situation. Let's discuss the damages after this next TAXTIP.

> ***TAXTIP***
>
> Employees who drive inexpensive and economical cars and put on very high annual business mileage can be paid *unlimited* business mileage reimbursements at 29¢ (1994 rate), all tax-free, and make a substantial tax-free *profit!*

THE DAMAGE TO EMPLOYERS AND THE SLAUGHTER OF EMPLOYEES

The worst thing the employer can do is to pay a *fixed* amount expense allowance to an employee, with *no* further expense accounting required! By so doing, the employer increases the company payroll tax and incurs additional Social Security/Medicare taxes, federal and state unemployment compensation tax, workers' compensation insurance, and additional retirement plan contributions as well. The extra cost to the employer (easily avoided by proper expense accounting) is about *15 percent or more* of any fixed (and unaccounted for) expense allowance! A total waste of company funds.

The employee is in even worse shape! In order to deduct those business expenses on an individual income tax return, the employee is forced into an extremely adverse tax situation. This is what happens:

- Contrary to past years, an employee can only claim unreimbursed business expenses as an itemized tax deduction. The option of claiming a flat standard deduction (no questions asked) is then lost by such forced itemization.

• The employee must complete and attach Form 2106, "Employee Business Expense" to the individual income tax return Form 1040: a nice and complicated additional disclosure document, designed by the IRS to pin down your claimed business expenses—and to also pin you down—to the IRS audit mat!

• The employee loses part of the business expense deductions equal to 2 percent of that individual's adjusted gross income (AGI). For example, if AGI is $50,000, then $1,000 (2 percent × $50,000) of the business expenses are not deductible.

• The employee can only deduct 50 percent of entertainment costs and travel meals. On the other hand, when employers pay reimbursements for such costs, they are usually paid at *100 percent*.

• The employee had to pay one-half the cost of Social Security/Medicare taxes, levied on the entire "nonaccounted for" fixed expense allowance. This cost, currently 7.65 percent for the employee, is not recovered by any subsequent business expense deductions on that individual's income tax return. That tax is just paid and "gone" into the bottomless coffers of the Internal Revenue Service.

• The employee has absolutely boosted the chances of being audited by the IRS, since unreimbursed business expenses are one of the highest IRS audit triggers presently known to humankind.

If you factor in all the preceding points, the total tax loss to the employee is approximately 30 percent; the same loss to the employer is around 15 percent. Adding the two together, the overall loss to the "tax community" of employer and employee is perhaps 45 percent of that "nonaccounted for" fixed expense allowance! Which ain't too smart an arrangement.

BETTER ALTERNATIVES

Many employers who do not require an accounting from their salespeople, do so because they want to control and limit their total cost of employee compensation. So they usually pay a higher salary with the understanding that the employee pay her own business expenses, without reimbursement and account only to the IRS.

Such an arrangement, as just explained, might result in combined additional tax costs of about 45 percent. One solution is a "compensation pool," a fixed dollar amount that is the agreed on maximum cost to the employer. However, all properly documented expenses of the employee are exactly reimbursed (tax-free) *first,* and the balance of the pool limit is paid as the *variable* monthly salary. Under this plan, all the additionally described costs to employer and employee completely disappear! About a 45 percent saving.

A second alternative is to reclassify qualifying outside sales employees as statutory sales employees (see Chapter 7). In brief, this allows the employee to claim all business expenses *as if* the employee were an independent contractor (on Schedule C of Form 1040). The employer is not required to withhold income taxes from statutory sales employees, and the employees, as a result, receive considerably higher take-home pay and much more flexibility in tax reporting and payment of taxes. The employer still has the option of lowering payroll tax costs by exactly reimbursing the statutory employee's expenses and can use a compensation pool arrangement as well.

CONCLUSION

Some employers just don't want to be bothered with employee expense accountings. However, to incur added payroll costs of about 15 percent represents a terrible business and management decision. So reread the two preceding alternatives and *do something!* How many 15 percent lines do you represent?

Chapter Seven

Statutory Sales Employees

If you will refer to a Form W-2, "Wage and Tax Statement," near the bottom, in section 15, are some boxes to be checked. The very first box is identified as "statutory employee." Almost nobody knows exactly what defines such an employee, although one of our rep clients wanted to identify *all* his employees as such "because they all stand around like a bunch of statues, instead of working." That's not exactly the right definition, although that comment may have some merit.

ADVANTAGES OF BEING CLASSIFIED AS A STATUTORY EMPLOYEE

Think of a statutory employee as being a "quasi-independent contractor," or as being part employee and part independent. An IRS ruling in effect since the end of 1990 (Revenue Ruling 90-93) can be of great benefit to some employees (primarily salespeople) and can also afford some interesting benefits to the employer as well. The advantages in being classified as a statutory employee rather than just a plain old "regular" (common-law) employee are:

1. A statutory employee can report income and expenses on Schedule C of Form 1040, "Profit or Loss from Business (Sole Proprietorship), *as if* she were a self-employed independent contractor. This allows that individual to deduct all expenses in *full*, without the disallowance (2 percent of adjusted gross income) of such expenses when otherwise claimed as an itemized deduction.
2. The statutory employee is not subject to *income tax* withholding, although the employer must deduct the employee's Social Security/Medicare taxes at normal rates, and the employer must pay the other one-half of that tax as usual. However, this tremendously increases such an employee's take-home pay, and, although the employee must then pay income taxes by quarterly estimate, such estimates are only based on the *net* income reported on Schedule C.
3. Despite filing on Schedule C, the statutory employee is not

liable for self-employment tax since Social Security tax has already been paid (one-half by withholding and the other half by the employer).

The two indications to the IRS that someone is a statutory employee are the appropriate box has been checked by the *employer* in Section 15 of Form W-2 and the *employee* indicates this status in the box on Schedule C, line 1 (the line that reports gross income). On that same line, the IRS has also added this instruction: "*Caution:* If this income was reported to you on Form W-2 and the 'statutory employee' box on that form was checked . . . check here."

STATUTORY EMPLOYEE DEFINED

The IRS has four categories of individuals who can be statutory employees. Three categories, of less concern for purposes of this chapter, are full-time life insurance salespeople, agent-driver or commission-driver, and home worker performing work according to specifications. Our interest is in category 4, the statutory salesperson:

> A traveling or city salesperson . . . who works full-time (except for sideline sales activities) for one firm or person getting orders from customers. The order must be for items for resale or use as supplies in the customer's business. The customers must be retailers, wholesalers, contractors or operators of hotels, restaurants, or other businesses dealing with food or lodging.

Except for sales to *manufacturers,* who are not covered by the preceding definition, the IRS conditions are rather easy to meet. The customers are either buying for resale or consume the product in their own business (the only other category that would not fit the definition is the salesperson selling a *service,* rather than a product). Further, consider those salespeople who *do* sell to manufacturers as well as wholesalers and retailers. Would the IRS bother to audit and question that situation? I think generally not.

Based on our experience to date, if the employer checks the "statutory employee" box on Form W-2 and the employee checks the same box on Schedule C, the IRS is little inclined to question that classification. It would hardly pay them to do so. Now we come to the crux of the matter. We have determined that it is generally advantageous for an individual to be classified as a statutory employee. We have further determined that salespeople are one of the four possible statutory employee categories. The only remaining hurdle is to pass three rather easy tests.

THE THREE TESTS

The IRS says if the salesperson, as qualified previously, meets three simple conditions, then he is a statutory employee!

> You are a statutory employee if your employment is described in the following list [i.e., the list of four categories that included "traveling or city salesperson" as category 4] and you meet all three tests below:
>
> 1. It is understood from the service contract that you will perform the services [i.e., in our case, "selling"].
> 2. You do not have a substantial investment in facilities (other than transportation) used to perform services.
> 3. Your services involve a continuing relationship with the person for whom they are performed.
>
> If you are a statutory employee, you are self-employed for reporting purposes. If you deduct your business expenses as a statutory employee, report your income from box 1 of your Form W-2 on line 1 of Schedule C.

If an individual who works for you meets the above three tests and the salesperson definition, you do not have to withhold federal income tax from his pay. However, even if a salesperson is a statutory employee his pay will still be subject to Social Security/Medicare (FICA) and federal unemployment (FUTA) taxes.

If you employer reps will review the salesperson definition and the three requirements, you will quickly see that many or most of your salespeople are statutory employees; you remain liable for FICA withholding and FUTA taxes, but are not responsible for federal income tax withholding. As already stated, take-home pay will frequently jump and any unreimbursed expenses can be deducted in full on Schedule C.

BENEFITS TO EMPLOYERS

The rep employer can offer the sales employee much higher take-home pay and an opportunity to file a tax return (and claim expenses) on a more favorable basis! That arrangement, in turn, may allow an employer to attract salespeople!

If a rep employer is presently treating certain salespeople as independent contractors, but is nervous about whether that arrangement is really legal, a wonderful compromise would be to convert them to statutory employees; they can still do their tax reporting as independent contractors, but will no longer have to pay Social Security/Medicare tax with their Schedule C! Most salespeople will not object to the change and will welcome the chance to save the employee share of FICA. They really have nothing to lose.

The independent contractor compromise will cost rep employers one-half the Social Security/Medicare, plus the federal unemployment compensation tax. However, such employers might be able to negotiate commission arrangements, since they are now paying half of the Social Security/Medicare costs that the independent contractor used to pay. If you think this idea may be applicable, discuss the idea with your tax advisers and review this chapter with them before approaching your "independent contractors."

WHAT'S IN IT FOR THE IRS?

I think the IRS is more interested in seeing questionable independent contractors (ICs) converted to statutory employees than the change-over of regular employees to statutory employees. The ruling eliminates their present hassle of auditing and deciding just who is or is not an IC. Also, remember that *more* Social Security/Medicare taxes will be paid if the statutory employee is paying all her expenses, because Social Security tax is figured on *gross* (Form W-2) earnings, while ICs only pay Social Security on *net* income. Total IRS tax collections may go up, while their IC audit problems may go down!

> ***TAXTIP***
>
> Whether you convert independent contractors or regular employees to the statutory employee category, you (and they) will pay far less in Social Security/Medicare taxes if you first exactly reimburse them for all expenses. This is the pool concept of compensation described in Chapter 35 and elsewhere.

OUR CLIENTS' REACTIONS

The category of statutory sales employees created quite a stir. We found a high degree of interest among most of our reps who employ outside salespeople. However, one of our clients objected to this on the basis that "once you give a salesperson the money he'll never put a dime aside to pay [quarterly estimated] income taxes." I certainly agreed with that comment and since this rep is quite protective of his employees, together we devised an informal alternative to keep his statutory sales employees out of tax trouble.

While there is no *requirement* for income tax withholding, a voluntary agreement between the statutory employee and the employer is not barred (nor would the IRS object to collecting taxes faster). So we took each employee's salary, reduced it by estimated deductible business expenses, and continued to withhold income taxes from each check based on estimated net compensation (after deductible expenses).

As an example, a statutory employee was paid $3,500 a month and paying all her own expenses. Assume those expenses were estimated at $1,200 a month. We continued to withhold income taxes as if that employee was paid $2,300 a month ($3,500 − $1,200 = $2,300), with the proper number of exemptions claimed against that $2,300. The statutory employee does not have to pay quarterly estimated taxes (and fuss with those complicated rules), and take-home pay has still increased considerably, but even more important, the employee should be about even with the IRS when income tax filing time rolls around!

We found some clients confused about paying or reimbursing expenses for statutory sales employees, but there are no special expense restrictions on this particular employee category. Any of the expense arrangements discussed in this book can be used. Or you can allow them to pay all their own expenses without reimbursement, and at least they'll get a special tax break when filing their individual income tax returns.

YOUR OWN REP FIRM

From time to time, we hear stories about reps who are afraid they'll be considered employees of a principal that they represent. The fact is that sales agency owners usually have a substantial investment in facilities, do not work full time for *one* firm, and invariably exhibit most or all the independent contractor characteristics. I really think you reps are safe (a recent ruling from the IRS held that the sales agency representing the factory was indeed an independent contractor), but certainly use the information in this chapter if the question is raised by either the IRS or a principal regarding your own sales agency.

STATE REGULATIONS AND STATUTORY EMPLOYEES

Check if your own state follows the federal rules on statutory employees. In California, only state unemployment and disability insurance must be paid and withheld for statutory employees, but state income tax withholding is not required.

CONCLUSION

For those of you who kneel at the side of your bed every night and send this prayer—"Bless my Mommy and Daddy, and I pray they don't audit me about those I have classified as independent contractors!"—the newly revised statutory employee category for your salespeople may be the real answer to your prayers!

Also, keep in mind that classifying an employee as a statutory employee *costs the employer nothing*, but when classifying an independent contractor as a statutory employee the employer can *reduce* the new payroll tax burden by exactly reimbursing all expenses using the compensation pool idea and a variable net salary. The payroll tax burden will be eased considerably and *still* limit the employer's overall compensation costs.

Since some of you are so nervous about the problems of classifying individuals as independent contractors, as you should be, the next chapter is about that topic.

Chapter Eight

Independent Contractor or Employee?

According to the IRS there are four categories of employees:

1. Common-law employees.
2. Statutory employees.
3. Statutory nonemployees.
4. Independent contractors.

We have already discussed statutory employees in Chapter 7. Statutory nonemployees are, by law, a special two-class category only for direct sellers or licensed real estate agents.

Common-law employees are "regular" employees, or, defined another way, if an individual working for another does not fit one of the *other* three categories, then he is a common-law employee. If you study the IRS definition of what a common-law employee is, you will find out what an independent contractor is *not*.

> Common-law employees. Under common law rules, every individual who performs services subject to the will and control of an employer, as to both what must be done and how it must be done, is an employee. It does not matter that the employer allows the employee discretion and freedom of action, so long as the employer has the *legal right* to control both the method and the result of the services.
>
> Two usual characteristics of an employer-employee relationship are that the employer has the right to discharge the employee and the employer supplies the employee with tools and a place to work.
>
> If you have an employer-employee relationship, it makes no difference how it is described. It does not matter if the employee is called an employee, partner, co-adventurer, agent, or independent contractor. It does not matter how the payments are measured, how they are made, or what they are called. Nor does it matter whether the individual is employed full-time or part-time.

> No distinction is made between classes of employees. Superintendents, managers, and all other supervisory personnel are all employees.

If you search through all the literature and court cases, you will not find a better or more accurate statement of the IRS position than the preceding quote. As you can see, many more individuals *are* common-law (i.e., "regular") employees and are *not* independent contractors than some rep employers would like to think.

MY DEFINITION OF INDEPENDENT CONTRACTOR

An independent contractor is someone like your lawyer, CPA, or doctor. They are not under your "direction and control." Generally, they render services for many individuals and companies. Usually they have their own offices, their own employees, their own business licenses, their own equipment, and their own capital at risk.

> The general rule is that an individual is an independent contractor if you, the employer, have the right to control or direct only the *result* of the work and *not* the means and methods of accomplishing the result [emphasis mine].

In other words, you hire your CPA to prepare your income tax return or you hire your lawyer to create a contract, but you don't instruct them exactly *how* (the "means and methods") they will accomplish that task. They both use their own independent and professional judgment and expertise in performing those services, and you barely know what they are really doing (or sometimes why it costs so much). See the difference between the common-law employee and the independent contractor?

RECENT DEVELOPMENTS

A warning from the IRS for arrant and brazen misclassifiers (emphasis mine):

> If you classify an employee as an independent contractor and you have no reasonable basis for doing so, you will have to pay employment taxes for that worker . . . Further, if you do not withhold income and social security taxes from his or her wages, you may be held *personally* liable for a penalty of 100 percent of the tax if you are the person responsible for the collection and payment of withholding taxes.

Almost everybody knows about the tremendous IRS crackdown on employers misclassifying employees as independent contractors. The IRS (and most states) have found that as the cost of payroll taxes have climbed, more and more employers are stretching matters, going the independent contractor route with some who really are employees. The IRS crackdown is because this area contains the combined two things that the IRS loves the most: a perceived abuse of the law and the potential to collect very large sums of money (in payroll taxes, interest, and penalties). In 1991 the IRS examined about 20,000 small business returns, reclassified over 80,000 independent contractors as employees, and assessed well over $100 million in additional payroll taxes, interest, and penalties!

The IRS publishes a list of 20 factors that supposedly test whether an individual is an employee or an independent contractor (see Chapter 9). However, the IRS does not give any *weight* to any of these 20 elements and, in fact is not much help in arriving at a decision:

> The degree of importance of each factor varies depending on the occupation and the context in which the services are performed.

This fighting between the IRS (and also many states, particularly California) and employers has reached such proportions that Congress is slowly getting involved. In 1991, a pronouncement from a House of Representatives Subcommittee Report to Congress was to the effect that absolute guidelines be established so every employer would have a perfect way of determining independent contractor categorizations, without living in fear of a reversal from an IRS auditor. Further recommendations were for an amnesty from back taxes and penalties for employers that "honestly misclassified workers." However, Congress has so far refused to act. Someday we may reach that perfect state of independent contractor affairs, but right now, even with 20 "guidelines," many independent contractor characterizations are simply a judgment call by the employer and his tax advisers playing independent contractor audit roulette"!

Eventually something will be done to help the borderline calls, but in the meantime the number of IRS and state independent contractor audits doubles and triples every year. So, for you blatant misclassifiers with your necks stuck way out, I urge you to review and reconsider your independent contractor classifications. Or sooner or later they will getcha'.

IRS INSTRUCTIONS TO THEIR AGENTS

From various government publications and sources, here are IRS guidelines and instructions to their employees about judging *your* employees:

- A title, designation, or written agreement defining a person as an independent contractor is to be considered meaningless.
- Required compulsory compliance with instructions as to when, where, and how a person is to work usually means that the individual is an employee.
- The right to control a person implies that person is an employee. It does not matter if that right is seldom used.
- If a worker must devote full time to the business of the employer, he is under the employer's control.
- A continuing relationship between the parties, set hours of work, payment of expenses, requirement of written reports, participation in fringe benefits, and so forth usually mean that the individual is an employee.

The items mentioned in the last point are a good tip-off as to the particular kinds of things that will cause you IC trouble, while the others are an overview of basic rules and the broad strokes. So, for example, if you are requiring an IC to submit daily sales reports, you are helping defeat your own IC position. Similarly, if you are reimbursing the IC for expenses, you are jeopardizing the situation even more so (in that case, adjust the commission rate or compensation level upward and have the IC pay her own expenses). Also, group insurance or other fringes for the IC count as *major* evidence of an employee relationship. Please study that last point again!

According to the IRS, the following are independent contractor and not employee characteristics:

- Has a business license.
- Has a separate (and own) place of business.
- Has a separate listing in the phone book(s).
- Is usually paid on an hourly or "job" basis.
- Hires, pays and directs any assistants.

OK, reps, now how many of you can really qualify your, er, ah, "independent contractors" as really being independent contractors? Be honest with yourself and your (IRS) chances!

A FEW EXAMPLES

Taxpayers continue to lose most of the court cases involving the independent contractor issue. Here are a few random samples:

- Perhaps the most famous case of all. The women at the notorious Mustang Ranch brothel (in a county in Nevada where such activities *are* legal) were held to be employees and not independent contractors. The taxes, interest, and penalties assessed effectively and financially broke the entire operation. The total assessments were in the millions and the IRS auctioned off the ranch.

• In a similar vein, go-go girls working at a bar who were required to dance, socialize with customers, and hustle drinks were held as employees.

• Baby-sitters provided through a state licensed agency were held as employees.

• Boat salespeople were paid on a commission basis, separately licensed by the state, and had no restrictions as to where or when they performed their services. They were held to be independent contractors.

• Pollsters for a public survey organization were held to be employees.

• Negotiators were hired by an education association to represent teachers in salary negotiations. They were held to be employees.

• Examination graders for the American Institute of Certified Public Accountants, who grade the semi-annual CPA exams were held to be employees.

SUB-AGENTS AND THE DASKAL DISTANCE DOCTRINE

Like everyone else, the typical sales agent would prefer to hire all salespeople as independent contractors, and some of them foolishly do so regardless of the (ultimate, potentially terrible) consequences. I have even come across more than one instance where the boss's secretary and company receptionist were both categorized as independent contractors, which is nonsense that would not hold up for five minutes of IRS scrutiny! Absurd!

However, there are circumstances that offer a winning possibility for many sales agents, but please be warned that this advice is based on my logic and my experience in similar cases, neither of which are necessarily prized or even highly regarded by the IRS. Regardless of what the IRS thinks of me, "I don't take it personal," as we usta' say on the South Side ah Chiccago—from whence I groo upp.

TAXTIP

Ideally, you can avoid all payroll tax and related costs if you can hire sales agents (independent contractor type) as sub-agents to represent you in a

(*continued*)

particular part of your sales territory. Hiring a sub-agent isn't as easy as simply characterizing your attorney or CPA as an independent contractor, but it's far from impossible, given one important characteristic: The *further away* your sub-agent resides (and territorially sells), the stronger your argument that she is an independent contractor. Why? Because of that key definition of an employee: "direction and control." In my opinion, both direction and control *fade with distance!*

Let's consider my favorite example. You are a Los Angeles sales agent and you hire two additional salespeople who live and sell in Phoenix, Arizona, and San Francisco, California (those sales territories are generally described as "Arizona and Northern California"). Both are over 400 miles away from Los Angeles. Given those circumstances it is likely you can sustain an independent contractor arrangement, because in my opinion, distance insulates from employee status. In *my* opinion. Also, you really don't know what they are doing on a day-to-day basis. They never come to your (Los Angeles) office. You don't assign them any particular customers to call on. You don't tell them what particular lines to sell. In summary, you don't exercise "direction and control," nor could you at that distance.

That sample situation seems to be fairly clear-cut. The problem arises when we start reducing the mileage spread from 400 miles to 200, to 50, to 10, to 2!! Obviously, the same conditions, assertions, and protections rapidly erode, and the IRS moves in closer and closer, as your sub-agent moves closer and closer to you. The claimed independent contractor status will usually *fade* as distance to the home office *decreases*. Accordingly, the IRS will usually move in and audit your employee (mis)classifications in an inverse ratio to the aforementioned decreases in the mileage separation between the home office and the office of the sub-agent.

There is no real answer to this mileage problem except good judgment and getting advice from your trusty advisers. The most common mistake I encounter is that the employer made the decision for independent contractor status all alone and (motivated by desire) just to cut costs. That's a dangerous way to decide!

At least apply some common sense. I think that at 400 miles away you can arrange and then defend independent contractor status. Obviously, anything over that distance is also, in my opinion, "safe" (given proper contracts, conditions, etc.). As that distance decreases, however, two things happen:

1. In general, it becomes more likely that a line of "direction and control" will be established.
2. Far more important is the fact that as distance decreases we

may have that person operating out of the *main office* of the agency, which puts him right under the thumb of the boss! That o'l debbil' "direction and control" is just oozing all over the office, and onto everything and everybody.

You see, in our example, the key point was not just that there was a 400 mile distance from the main office. That was maybe 25 percent of the argument. The other 75 percent really lies in the fact that the person did not operate from or come into the home office. He was based elsewhere, in either a branch office or operating from that person's home. But not from the main office! Thus, that person was literally removed from the possible exercise of "direction and control"! And that's the Daskal Distance Doctrine.

THE COSTS, OH, THE TERRIBLE COSTS!

The first thing to understand is that if you get "caught," the dollar costs will not be calculated or limited to a single payroll tax quarter or a single year! The minimum assessment will usually be for the normal three years under the general IRS statute of limitations. That can represent a startling amount of money! However, to further ruin your day, if you have not been filing payroll tax returns at all the IRS *may* take the position that there is no statute of limitations protecting you in such a case, since the statute only begins to run with the actual filing of an applicable tax return.

Generally, the IRS will report their findings to your state. If the state initiates the examination, they will generally report their findings to the IRS (both are true in California). In either case you are talking about a double whammy of IRS plus state payroll tax assessments.

Along with payroll taxes, interest, and penalties, they can also insist that you pay the income taxes that should have been withheld if they cannot satisfy themselves that the individuals involved reported their IC income and paid their income taxes. If you want to estimate your dollar exposure, figure 30 percent to 50 percent of the total dollars you paid in questionable IC compensation in the last three years. That's an approximation of the taxes, interest, and penalties you could be charged (see Chapter 9 for methods of legally and materially reducing penalties and interest if you are audited).

Another threat is absolutely mind-boggling, horrendous, and scary! That's a potential disallowance of all your retirement plan contributions! How is that possible? Follow this simple logic. Your retirement plan cannot be "discriminatory" by law, which means that it must include all employees who qualify for coverage. However, if you have been classifying three common-law employees as ICs (and you got caught), you have been discriminating against those employees by not covering them under your retirement plan! If your retirement plan *is* discriminatory, the contributions to the plan are not deductible, which results in a three year (or more) disallowance of all the contributions!

In our experience, we have had agents threaten such disallowances as a *negotiating* ploy to get us to agree to reclassification of some ICs as employees. We have never really had them act on this threat, but one of you reps may be the unlucky one that gets this hit. It's certainly not impossible.

EVEN FURTHER (COSTLY) COMPLICATIONS/CONSIDERATIONS

Consider this scenario. The person you have been classifying as an IC gets out of line or doesn't perform. Naturally, you fire her. So she promptly applies for unemployment compensation! The state, however, has no record of her being covered or reported as an employee, but she says, "I worked for that bum for three years and then he fired me! I want my unemployment compensation!" Well, sez the State, we will launch a little investigation. Give us the bum's name, address, and identification number. Just get it off the Form 1099, "Information Return," that he gave you, since you weren't treated as an employee and did not get a Form W-2. Then sit tight, and you will probably get all your unemployment compensation." What follows could be a very *hostile* audit of your payroll and other records, followed by all the horrendous assessments previously described! And, consider the next scenario.

One of your ICs gets badly injured while on the job and files a claim for workers' compensation. He may not be covered under your workers' compensation insurance policy, depending on how honest you were with your insurance agent or whether or not your state requires that ICs be covered by this type of insurance (California insurers now require this coverage). So if your IC was *not* covered and should have been, or your IC is really an employee and naturally should have been insured all along, guess who gets sued?

Another horror scenario. Because of your nonemployee classification, a person is not covered by your group medical insurance. As luck would have it, the same person is involved in a terrible auto accident while on company business. The medical bills are about $400,000 and that individual has no medical insurance coverage. Guess who gets sued?

Now you know what the various exposures can be if you carelessly make an employee into an IC. So think it over very, very carefully and please consult your tax advisers before you make this serious decision. Do it cautiously or not at all!

HOW TO SWITCH

The sales rep who has misclassified the ICs now wants to begin reporting them as common-law employees. But the question I get asked repeatedly is, If I just start reporting them on the next payroll tax return, won't the IRS wonder why I just suddenly began to report them?"

If you are anywhere near the beginning of the calendar year, begin the employee classifying and reporting as of January 1. If you are not, my best advice is to just bite the bullet and begin with the first day of the next calendar quarter. Or, if you are now completely paranoid and costs be damned, file corrected payroll tax returns retroactively to last January 1 (you could then play catch-up with income tax withholding over the balance of the calendar year). Discuss this with your CPA before you decide.

A NEAT BUT COMPLICATED ALTERNATIVE

There is one way to preserve independent contractor status for each and every employee. That is simply for the employee to incorporate. You then hire that *corporation* (by a written contract) to provide sales services and suitable personnel for your company. So far we have not heard of any IRS attempts to overthrow this arrangement (of course, nothing can ever be guaranteed where the IRS is concerned). It would help immensely if the new corporation renders services or represents a few minor lines for one or more other companies as added window dressing.

However, the average (unsophisticated) "employee-IC" reacts with horror to the suggestion that she incorporate, as she considers corporate tax returns, formal books, payroll tax returns, corporate minutes, board meetings, recordkeeping, legal fees, accounting fees, and extra bookkeeping. Still, that person might be much better off incorporating, and the company would solve a major problem (and exposure) once and for all. Again, consult your tax adviser. The employee-IC should also get some good tax advice. You both may be surprised at the answers!

That new IC corporation can adopt a retirement plan and fiscal year, pay generous expenses for the officer/shareholder, provide a company car, and so forth. The employer/company could pay the cost of incorporation, or even of continuing bookkeeping, accounting, and tax services. If I were a salesperson-IC and this was offered to me I would grab it for the many tax and fiscal advantages that could be obtained (see Chapter 12). The complexities are well worth the game.

CONCLUSION

If you do continue to have ICs, be sure you have a written contract. Your lawyer should draw that up and it should include details that the IC is responsible for all Social Security/Medicare and income taxes, as well as obtaining all necessary business licenses. Beyond that, your lawyer should follow the guidelines we have cited.

Now let's return to some ways to survive an IC audit and to minimize the dollar damage.

Chapter Nine

Independent Contractor Audits and the IRS Tests

The 1993 Social Security/Medicare Tax deductions from earnings were 6.20 percent Social Security tax up to $57,600 (a maximum of $3,571.20) and 1.45 percent Medicare tax up to $135,000 (an additional maximum of $1,957.50). The employer must match those withholdings for each employee. Thus, at $135,000 or higher, the employer's 1993 cost per employee was $5,528.70 (and the maximum cost to the employee was another $5,528.70). When we add federal and state unemployment compensation, workers' compensation insurance, and retirement plan contributions the total costs to the employer can easily reach 25–30 percent of payroll.

Further, for 1994 and after, there is *no limit on the 1.45 percent Medicare tax deduction* (and the matching 1.45 percent as the employer's share), no matter how high the salary may be. These tremendous costs are a *powerful* motive to classify workers as independent contractors and avoid those expenses! Powerful, and frequently illegal.

The IRS estimates that one out of every seven workers is misclassified as an independent contractor (IC) instead of an employee. As a result, they estimate that they are losing $1.6 billion annually in tax revenues due to these mischaracterizations. Increased examinations of payroll tax issues will continue to accelerate in the foreseeable future. The IRS is out to collect taxes and not to listen to your arguments with "sweet reasonableness"! This is a revenue raising issue with the IRS!

One of our tax publications summed up these audits very well. To paraphrase: There is an incessant attack by the IRS on the status of workers doing business as ICs and the audits have continued unabated over the last few years. They are *adversarial* audits from the moment they begin. No matter what information you give the IRS auditor, whatever facts and whatever explanations, they will all be used with but one goal, to convert your independent contractors to employees!

Accordingly, you must change your thinking and adjust to the fact that these audits are not like "normal" (ha!) IRS income tax audits.

Your evidence and proof will frequently be ignored, downplayed, rejected, or twisted to the auditor's own ends. These audits are not fair! They are not evenhanded. They are really intended to raise tax revenues at virtually all costs, something like the current IRS audits of retirement plans.

So if you normally regard an IRS auditor as an adversary, you ain't seen nuttin' yet! Persuasive arguments and even hard facts are frequently of little avail. Accordingly, you should prepare for the audit with extra care, but perhaps what is more important, you should take steps now that may protect you from eventual audit disallowance. Remember, there was about a 40 percent increase in IC audits *each* year since 1991!

INDEPENDENT CONTRACTOR OVERVIEW

Says the IRS (emphasis mine):

> Anyone who performs services is an employee if the employer can control what will be done and how it will be done ["direction and control"]. This is so even when you give the employee freedom of action. What matters is that you have the *legal right* to control the method and the result of the services . . . If an employer-employee relationship exists, it does not matter what it is called . . . it does not matter how payments are measured, what they are called, or whether the employee works full- or part-time.

These horrendous audits are also based on this IRS quote:

> Treating employees as nonemployees. You will be liable for income tax and employee Social Security and Medicare taxes [and possible interest and penalties!] if you don't deduct and withhold these taxes because you consider an employee as a nonemployee.

THINGS TO DO BEFORE YOU ARE AUDITED

Review the status of your workers with your CPA, attorney, or both, in effect conducting an internal IC audit. Cure the blatant and obvious misclassifications voluntarily and immediately. In certain cases, the form and substance of the relationship can be altered to increase the likelihood of the worker being classified as an IC.

Sometimes we find such absurdities as a secretary, receptionist, or file clerk classified as an IC. As delicately as I can put it, "Gimme a break, will ya'?" Also, officers of the corporation who are truly working in the business are *by definition* employees, as is the salesperson who works out of your office (not a home office) and comes in every morning for a daily dose of "direction and control." Study the borderline cases that you were nervous about before reading this (and the preceding chapter) and make some new and even more careful reappraisals.

As noted in Chapter 8 (but it bears repeating), perhaps the best single move you can make is to *incorporate* any IC who just might be an employee (I will give this move a better than 90 percent success rate). That new corporation will have its own federal identification number and you are *not* required to file a Form 1099, "information return," for your payments to a corporation although this may change, but so what. If it is a C ("regular") corporation, it can generally report on a fiscal year. Every corporation can have its own retirement plan, provide group insurance and other fringe benefits, reimburse expenses, pay expenses directly, provide an auto for the owner, and so forth, all of which help to reduce the taxable salary of the new corporate owner and former IC. Again, it is most helpful if that new corporation renders services, even minor ones, for one or more other companies besides the main sales agency.

There should absolutely be a written contract between your company and the new corporation (as there should always be between your company and *every* IC). Again, we have seen a number of cases where the costs of incorporation were partly or fully paid by the "employer" company. The tax advantages to the IC should be explained in great detail, since they do exist and are substantial.

Other than incorporation, some of the other techniques that we have seen work in IC cases are for the individual salesperson to: have a business license, operate under a DBA ("doing business as") like "John Smith Sales Associates," render *monthly billings* to your company, have a federal identification number, have a separate office even if in the home, have a written contract (of course), and work for more than one company. The more of these attributes the better!

If the individual does operate under a DBA and has a federal identification number, by all means file the Form 1099 using both the DBA and that identification number, not the individual's Social Security number and not the individual's name. This may be of some help and it couldn't hurt. If you don't file a Form 1099 *at all*, for whatever reasons, you are absolutely *dead* if there is an audit, and that very act of omission may trigger an audit! You *must* file a Form 1099 for every unincorporated IC who was paid $600 or more in the calendar year. That is the law!

WHAT TO DO AT THE BEGINNING OF THE AUDIT

Carefully marshal and review all your documentation and evidence with your CPA. Go over each and every IC who might be reclassified by the auditor. Get all the facts straight, give your CPA all possible information, and go over the likely exposures. Remember the words "direction and control" during this overview and in erecting your IRS defenses.

For example, we had a case where an individual set up store displays for one of our clients and was paid about $5,000. The Form 1099 showed only her name and Social Security number. The IRS agent proposed a change to employee status. A check with the client revealed that this woman performed similar services for over 30 different companies and had a real IC business going (there was even a contract they forgot to give us). In this case, the additional facts saved our client, but this is the kind of information to give your CPA before the audit begins.

HOW YOU GET SELECTED FOR AN IC AUDIT

The IRS (and some states, like California) do a kind of "reverse auditing," where they go from the IC's tax return to your sales agency. The Form 1099 is the heart of this program and it works like this. First they pull all 1099s that report over $10,000 in compensation (and cases where those payments represent the ICs *only* source of income). Then, they pull the payer company for audit (*not* the IC, as is thought by some who have really missed the point of reverse auditing).

For example, your rep firm paid John Smith $31,297 in sales commissions, which were reported on a Form 1099. On John Smith's personal tax return, he filed a Schedule C (as an unincorporated business) and his total gross income is shown as $31,297! Tilt! His return is not audited (why should it be if he reported the correct amount of income)? Instead, the IRS audits you, the *payer* of the $31,297. I call this "reverse auditing," and the reason for using this technique to trigger audits is that the IRS (and many of the states) feel that any time an individual receives 100 percent of their business income from *one* company, that is *prima facie* ("at first glance") evidence he is an employee (some state auditors take the position that 80 percent of income from one company is also proof of the employee status of an IC).

The IRS recently stated that thousands of supposed ICs have claimed to be employees *after* losing their jobs in order to claim unemployment compensation. That can also trigger an IC audit! During IRS income tax audits the auditors always review payroll tax returns (Form 941, "Employer's Quarterly Federal Tax Return"), information returns (Form 1099), and other records looking for possible IC misclassifications. They rarely did so in the past.

THE IRS SECTION 530 SAFE HARBOR

If the IRS has its way, Code Section 530 will someday be eliminated or restricted. If Congress ever gets around to clarifying or changing the IC definitions and law, the IRS will ask that Section 530 be eliminated since they hate it because of the protection you can claim. However, that may not happen and even if it does, this law can afford you protection for all prior years, and some or all of it may remain untouched. As with everything in this book, here is the law, at this writing.

If the requirements of Section 530 are met, the worker is treated as an IC and cannot be reclassified as an employee by the IRS for employment tax purposes (unfortunately the various states are not bound by these rules and California auditors tend to ignore them, as may other state auditors). You have to pass *all four* of these tests to sail your ICs into this IRS safe harbor:

- *Past Treatment.* The employer must not have treated the worker as an employee for any period ending before 1980.
- *Consistency over Time.* The worker must have been treated as an IC on every tax return filed for all periods beginning after 1978.
- *Consistency.* No other worker in a substantially similar position can have been treated as an employee for any period after 1977.
- *Reasonable Basis.* The employer must have had a "reasonable basis" (not just to save payroll taxes!) for treating the worker as an IC. Any *one of the following will create a reasonable basis:*
  a. *Precedent.* Judicial precedent, published rulings, or technical advice.
  b. *Past audit.* In any past IRS audit, no worker in a substantially similar position was reclassified by the IRS (even though the past IRS audit was not an employment tax audit, but just an income tax audit). This is the item the IRS *hates* and will weaken or eliminate in any new law!
  c. *Long-standing industry custom.* A large segment of the industry traditionally treated substantially similar workers as ICs.
  d. *Any other reasonable basis.* Any other reasonable basis will suffice such as lack of direction and control over the workers.

Please, please remember: You must pass *all four* of the tests and under that last test ("reasonable basis") you must meet at least *one* of those conditions.

Remember, the IRS is *increasing* their independent contractor audits despite the many complaints from small businesses. They are now instructing their field agents to specifically search for "employees who are misclassified as independent contractors" in *every audit* they perform! Why? The 1978 "safe harbor" law (Code Section 530), *bars* the IRS from reclassifying independent contractors as employees if, among other things, there was a *previous* IRS audit and "no worker in substantially the same position was reclassified from independent contractor to employee." This protection can apply *even if the previous audit did not even address or examine that issue!*

Since the IRS hates that provision, they are determined *never* to conduct another field audit without considering the independent contractor issue, which is particularly bad news for the many reps who are *still* treating all, or most, of their salespeople as independent contractors! In recent experiences with IRS field audits, we find that many of the auditors *begin* the audit with an examination of payroll tax returns and a review of every independent contractor reported on information return Form 1099. That not only gets this mandatory part of the examination out of the way, but it also provides an early indication to the IRS auditor if she is going to easily pick up $10,000 to $150,000 in this area.

WHAT TO DO AFTER THE AUDIT

Of course if you just plain win hands down, give your CPA a bonus and plan a nice (tax-deductible) company celebration party! For the other 90 percent (you IC losers), believe it or not there are legal ways to *reduce* the amount of the IRS bill! Since, in quite a few cases, we have found that the IRS auditors do not point out all these potential reductions (gee, probably just an honest oversight), we shall now helpfully save them the trouble! There are four different ways to save taxes, interest, and penalties. These IRS code sections are provided for the convenience of your own tax advisers:

1. *Section 3402(d) Income Tax Relief*. This section generally allows a reduction in the employer's income tax withholding liability, insofar as it can be shown that the employee paid the income tax. File Form 4670, "Request for Relief from Payment of Income Tax Withholding," and Form 4669, "Employee Wage Statement" (signed by the employee). This relief only applies to the withholding liability itself and not to any penalties or interest for the failure to deduct and withhold.

2. *Section 6521 FICA Relief.* This section generally allows the employer to obtain a credit for its (one-half) liability for Social Security Medicare taxes to the extent the employer's share was paid by the employee's self-employment tax but only if the employee is barred by the statute of limitations from seeking a refund of those taxes.

3. *Section 3509 Relief.* This section generally provides for a reduced retroactive employment tax liability as long as the employer did not intentionally disregard that liability. If the employer filed the appropriate Form 1099 for the IC who was now reclassified as an employee, the following reduced liability for the employer may be obtained:

a. Withholding taxes of 1.5 percent of the employee's wages.
b. FICA taxes of 20 percent of the amount that would otherwise be the employer's liability.

If the Forms 1099 were *not* filed, the following reduced liability for employers may be obtained:

- Withholding taxes of 3.0 percent of the employee's wages.
- FICA taxes of 40 percent of the amount that would otherwise be the employer's liability.

If you claim relief under this section, federal unemployment taxes must be paid in full and no additional relief can be claimed under the two code sections (3402[d] or 6521). Finally, if this code section applies, the employee's tax liability is not subject to adjustment, and the employee may not obtain a refund of self-employment taxes. *This may afford big tax savings for some of you!*

4. *Section 6205 Interest Relief.* This section generally provides that the income tax withholding and the FICA liabilities (but not federal unemployment tax) may be paid by the employer (after the reclassification of ICs) without the payment of interest *if* the employer reports the underpayment of taxes before the last day of the report period in which the underpayment was ascertained. (The IRS has held that the reporting of the underpayment in the period during which all levels of administrative appeal have been exhausted will qualify for Section 6205 interest relief.) Another potential money saver!

APPEALING THE IRS FINDINGS

If the audit is not resolved at the examination level, you have the usual right to meet with the agent's group manager. You then have the further right to protest this matter to the Appeals Division of the IRS. Finally, you can go to court.

However, to the great surprise of many readers, you *cannot* go to the Tax Court, since the Tax Court does not have jurisdiction to hear employment tax disputes! Therefore, you can only file a suit for refund in the US District Court or the US Claims Court, but only after payment of the tax, and filing a claim for refund.

> ***TAXTIP***
>
> To prevent large initial employment tax payments, you can use the following technique to pay only a small amount of tax before you sue. Since employment taxes are "divisible" taxes (e.g., applicable separately to each employee and each reporting period), only a *partial* payment is required to bring a valid suit for refund. The employer could pay only the tax for *one* employee (representative of the group) and for *one* tax period, and then bring suit. (The IRS will normally counterclaim for the additional taxes, but will sometimes forgo collection efforts for the taxes of other periods and other workers.) If you try this technique, you had better be doing it under the careful guidance of your lawyer and with the prudent advice of your CPA!*

THE 20 IRS COMMON LAW TESTS

The IRS supplies 20 "factors or elements" (i.e., tests) to help determine if an individual is an employee or an IC, but the IRS refuses to give any *weight* to any one of these tests over another; in fact, the IRS goes out of its way to say that everything depends on the particular "facts and circumstances" of each case.

So, with typical IRS obfuscation, the tests are just an introduction to future misinterpretation and fighting with the IRS, but should be used as important guides in determining the IC question. (*Note:* Following this list, we will also present an internal IRS training document that *interprets* the 20 tests in a different and more helpful manner.) Here are the "fabulous 20" with my comments interspersed:

1. *Instructions.* A worker who is required to comply with other peoples' instructions about when, where, and how to work is ordinarily an employee. This control factor is present if the person for whom the services are performed has the right to require compliance

---

*My thanks to attorney Richard A Corleto of Encino, California, for supplying all the legal research and legal information included in this and the preceding sections of this chapter.

with the instructions whether or not that right is exercised in any particular situation. (This is the big one about "control.")

2. *Training.* Training a worker to perform services in a particular method or manner indicates that person is an employee. Independent contractors generally receive no such training and use their own methods and techniques. (This is the big one about "direction.")

3. *Integration.* Integration of a worker's services into the business operations indicates that worker is subject to "direction and control" (see 1 and 2) and is generally an employee.

4. *Services Rendered Personally.* An employee must render the services personally (indicating the employer is interested in the "methods and results" of the work). (Conversely, an IC, such as your lawyer or CPA, may well supply a *different* individual to perform some or all of the services you require.)

5. *Hiring, Supervising, and Paying Assistants.* An IC hires, supervises, and pays assistants, and is only responsible for the results of the services (e.g., your CPA when preparing your tax return). An employee works for some other person who does that hiring, supervising, and paying.

6. *Continuing Relationship.* A continuing relationship between the worker and the person for whom the services are being performed is an indication of employee status. This can be true even if the work is performed at frequently recurring but irregular intervals.

7. *Set Hours of Work.* An employee has set hours of work (an indication of "control.") An IC sets her own hours.

8. *Full Time Required.* An employee generally works full-time for the employer, and the employer has control over the amount of time spent working. (This by implication restricts the employee from seeking other work; the IC, however, can work whenever and for whomever she chooses, and may work for more than one company or individual.)

9. *Doing Work on Employer's Premises.* Work performed on the premises or at a location or route designated is an indication of "control" and of employee status, especially if the work could be done elsewhere but was not. Conversely, work done off the premises, such as at the office of the worker, indicates some freedom from control. (However, this factor alone is not sufficient to establish that the worker is an IC.)

10. *Order or Sequence Set.* An employee is one who must perform services in the order or sequence set by the employer (even if the order or sequence is not set, or infrequently set, but the employer retains the *right* to exercise the order of services).

11. *Reports.* A requirement that the worker submit reports indicates a degree of control and implies employee status in that the worker must account to the employer for her time and actions. (This

can certainly affect "sub-reps" being treated as ICs by any sales rep company.)

12. *Payments.* Payment by the hour, week, or month generally points to an employee-employer relationship (provided this is not simply a convenient way of paying an agreed upon lump sum for a job). Payment by the job or on a straight commission basis is an indication that the individual is an IC.

13. *Expenses.* Payments or reimbursements for business and travel expenses are a strong indication that the individual is an employee. Only an employer is able to control an employee's expenses, which generally means the employer also retains the right to regulate and control that person's business activities ("direction and control" again). (You don't pay or reimburse the expenses of your lawyer, doctor, or CPA, who are all ICs.) This can be a telling point in the sub-rep situation; the solution is to pay a higher commission rate and have the sub-agent pay all expenses.*

14. *Furnishing of Tools, Materials.* The furnishing of significant tools, materials, and equipment tends to indicate an employer-employee relationship. (You don't furnish your CPA with a car or computer; however, if you do, please let me know if the job is open!) Again, furnishing an auto to an ostensible sub-rep would be a major point against IC status, but paying a higher commission rate and having the sub-rep supply her own car would not!)

15. *Significant Investment.* A significant investment in facilities (office, equipment, furnishings, computers, autos, etc.) used in performing services for someone else is one good indication of an IC. On the other hand, the lack of significant investment suggests an employee.

16. *Profit or Loss.* An IC is "at risk" in that business and can suffer a loss or make a profit. An employee is generally not.

17. *Working for More than One Firm.* The more the better (a strong indication that person is an IC). Working for "multiple unrelated firms or persons" is typical of ICs—not employees.

18. *Services Available to the General Public.* Offering services to the general public on a regular and consistent basis indicates an IC relationship.

19. *Right to Discharge.* The right to discharge a worker indicates an employer-employee relationship. An employer exercises "direction and control" through the threat of dismissal, which causes the worker to obey the employer's instructions. On the other hand, an IC cannot be fired as long as the IC produces the result that meets

---

*Note: All you reps who are hiring ICs should pay special attention to 11, 12, and 13, keeping in mind that these are just 3 of the 20 factors to consider. However, if you ignore these three you probably killed any chance of IC status for your sub reps!

the specifications of their contract (absent unusual circumstances). (You do not "fire" ICs, you "terminate the contractual agreement" with them.)

20. *Right to Terminate.* An employee can quit the job at any time without incurring liability. An IC is generally responsible for satisfactory completion of a particular job (absent fraud, nonpayment, etc.) and otherwise could be held liable.

AN IRS INTERNAL TRAINING DOCUMENT

We have obtained internal IRS material "designed specifically for training purposes only." The unusual thing about this unofficial IRS guide is that this version of the famous 20 question test *compares* common-law employees and independent contractors! In the past, all we have ever seen is the basic and highly confusing list of these 20 factors (Revenue Ruling 87-41), along with a typical IRS cop-out: "Employee status is determined by applying 20 factors to a particular case to determine whether an employer-employee relationship exists. The degree of importance of each factor varies depending on the occupation and the context in which the services are performed." (Not a lotta' help in arriving at a decision!)

In this unusual training material, the IRS has *restated* and broken up the 20 factors into a two-column approach that is potentially very beneficial. Here, then, is an exact reprint of their *comparative* listing. You may very well want to save this list for years to come. Note particularly the second section of number 10 about a "salesperson," as well as many others that apply to any individual working for sales reps in some capacity or other.

20 Common Law Factors

Employee	*versus*	*Independent Contractor*
1. Instructions		
Complies with instructions about when, where, and how work is to be performed.		Works his or her own schedule. Does the job his or her own way.
2. Training		
Trained by an experienced employee working with him or her. Required to take correspondence courses. Required attendance at meetings and by other methods indicates that the employer wants the services performed in a particular manner.		Uses his or her own methods and receives no training from the purchaser.

3. Integration

Services of the individual are merged into the business. Success and continuation of the business depends upon these services. Employer coordinates work with that of other workers.	Success and continuation of business aren't dependent on his or her services.

4. Services Rendered Personally

Services must be rendered personally. Not able to engage other people to do the work.	Contractor able to assign one of his or her people to do the job.

5. Hiring, Supervising, and Paying Assistants

Hires, supervises, and pays workers at the direction of the employer (acts as foreman or representative of the employer).	Hires, supervises, and pays the other workers as a result of a contract under which he or she agreed to provide materials and labor and is responsible for the results.

6. Continuing Relationship

The individual continues to work for the same person year after year.	Hired to do one job. No continuous relationship.

7. Set Hours of Work

The hours and days are set by the employer.	Is master of his or her own time.

8. Full Time Required

Must devote full time to the business of the employer. Restricts him or her from doing other gainful work.	Free to work when and for whom he or she chooses.

9. Doing Work on Employer's Premises

Implies that the employer has control; is physically within the employer's direction and supervision.	Works off employer's premises, uses own office, desk, telephone.

10. Order or Sequence Set

Performs services in the order or sequence set by the employer. Salesperson reports at the office at specified times, follows up on leads, and performs certain tasks at certain times.	Services performed at his or her own pace. Salesperson works own schedule and usually has own office.

11. Reports

Required to submit regular oral or written reports to the employer.	Submits no reports.

12. Payments

Paid by the employer of regular amounts at stated intervals.

Paid by the job on a straight commission.

13. Expenses

The employer pays the person's business and traveling expenses.

Takes care of own expenses and is accountable only to himself or herself for expenses.

14. Furnishing of Tools, Materials

Employer furnishes tools, materials, etc.

Furnishes his or her own tools.

15. Significant Investment

Has a lack of investment and depends on the employer for such facilities.

Has a real, essential, and adequate investment.

16. Profit or Loss

Cannot realize a profit or loss by making good or bad decisions.

Can realize a profit or suffer a loss as a result of his or her services.

17. Working for More than One Firm

Usually works for one employer.

Works for a number of persons or firms at the same time.

18. Services Available to the General Public

Does not make his or her services available except through some company or business he or she does not have an interest in.

Has own office and assistants. Holds business license, listed in business directories, or maintains business telephone. Advertises in newspaper, etc.

19. Right to Fire

Can be discharged at any time.

Cannot be fired so long as he or she meets contract specifications.

20. Right to Terminate

Can end his or her relationship with employer at any time.

Agrees to complete a specific job. Is responsible for its satisfactory completion or is legally obligated to make good.

COMMENT

Obviously, this list will be carried and used by IRS agents making audit determinations between independent contractor and employee status. Obviously, you are better off having this list *before* any potential audits! Obviously, you're welcome!

Now, I know almost every rep would rather sell than read, but I urge you to carefully restudy this IRS comparative list as well as all the preceding information. Check off the ones that can cause you trouble and go over them with your CPA or other tax adviser. I would rather you anticipate trouble than wait until it's facing you in the form of a bill for payroll taxes, interest, and penalties, plus accounting and legal fees.

CONCLUSION

Be sure to check for any further Congressional developments before you count on each and every point in this chapter. Although the *concept* of who is an employee or who is an independent contractor will *never* really change, we may get easier rules to determine those classifications.

The very attractive option of sales agents in turn hiring sub-reps should only be taken after study of this and the preceding chapter, and then only after expert advice. The rep with poor judgment does it first and tells his advisers after the fact (or not at all). That rep is probably out there slowly twisting in the (IRS) wind. Is it *you* who can you feel that knot tightening around your neck?

Chapter Ten

Retirement Plans and IRS Plan Audits

There are only two ways that the average sales rep can assure financial security for retirement. One way is to "cash out" by selling the sales agency (usually to the employees). As we will discuss in the last eight chapters of this book, serious financial risks and other problems can accompany that sale, such as lost lines and incompetent buyers. It is just not always possible.

The better way to guarantee financial security is through systematic (and tax-deductible) contributions to retirement plans. In many cases, we have seen small rep owners accumulate as much as $1 million over a 20-year period. (Annual contributions in the $25,000 range, plus the compound effect of tax-deferred earnings on those contributions, can easily reach $1 million in 20 years or less.) It's not impossible to become a millionaire from a rather small sales agency, given enough time and the *discipline* to make those annual contributions.

Books have been written just on the rules and details of various retirement plans, so by necessity, we will give you only an overview to help you understand, discuss, and select a retirement plan with the help of your own tax adviser or even a retirement plan administrator or plan designer.

WHY HAVE AN ERISA-QUALIFIED RETIREMENT PLAN?

The tax advantages available for an Employee Retirement Income Security Act (ERISA)-qualified retirement plan are overwhelming! These plans offer reps and their employees the single greatest opportunity to accumulate large amounts of money for retirement. An ERISA-qualified plan is virtually anything you have heard about *except* an Individual Retirement Account (IRA) or Simplified Employee Pension (SEP).

The incredible benefits of ERISA-qualified plans are:

• The contributions to the plan are deductible by the company making the payment.

• All plan participants defer taxes on those contributions until they receive their retirement plan distributions.

• The earnings of the plan assets compound tax-deferred until payout.

• Favorable (special) tax treatment may be available on lump-sum distributions from the plan, unlike an IRA or SEP.

• These plans allow more investment flexibility than in an IRA or SEP.

• Qualified plans can be self-trusteed, saving the trustee's fees that may be paid for an IRA, SEP, or Keogh plan.

• Unlike an IRA, SEP, or Keogh, participants may be able to borrow from the plan.

• These plans attract and motivate quality employees.

• The plans can be arranged to allow employees to contribute additional funds, and such payments will also enjoy tax-deferred growth (not possible for an IRA or SEP).

• The vesting schedule of the plans rewards employee longevity.

• The plans can, to a great extent, be custom designed to meet specific needs (not true of an IRA, SEP, or Keogh).

• Plan contributions can be used to purchase whole life insurance, essentially allowing for deductible life insurance premiums (not allowed in an IRA, SEP, or Keogh).

• Now for a big one! ERISA-qualified plans provide protection against lawsuits, as well as against creditors in a bankruptcy proceeding. In June 1992, the US Supreme Court unanimously ruled in the case of *Patterson* v. *Shumate* that assets in these plans are *exempt* from bankruptcy proceedings and that creditors cannot reach or attach such assets! This means that individuals in financial difficulty can rely on the assets of their ERISA-qualified plan *after* they are discharged from bankruptcy.

WARNING

While the Court did not consider Keogh plans, we have been cautioned that these plans are not protected from creditors unless there are other participants *besides* the owner (or owner and spouse). Otherwise, they are not immune to creditors.)

TAXTIP

If you are in financial difficulty, never transfer retirement plan assets from an ERISA-qualified plan to an IRA rollover account! By so doing, you lose

(continued)

that protection against creditors. Similarly, never establish a SEP instead of an ERISA-qualified plan if you have monetary problems! Again, you would lose all shielding of your retirement plan assets. So IRA accounts, IRA rollover accounts, most Keogh plans, and SEPs have serious drawbacks for those in serious fiscal trouble.

With all caveats firmly in mind (and I won't repeat them each time), let's move on to the description of the many kinds of plans.

SIMPLIFIED EMPLOYEE PENSION PLAN

The Simplified Employee Pension (SEP) plan can be used by both incorporated and unincorporated businesses, is simple to adopt and use, and is cheap to set up and administer. Given the increasing complexities and administration costs of most other plans, we often recommend the SEP alternative to our rep-clients.

In a corporation, the employer makes (tax-deductible) SEP contributions into a separate IRA for each eligible employee; these funds are immediately and fully vested and under the complete control of each employee (just like any IRA). The contribution is not income to the employee, and the amount paid in by the employer can vary each year from 0 to 15 percent of compensation, up to a maximum of $30,000 for each employee. The SEP must cover all eligible employees, that is, those who are age 21 or over, worked for the employer three of the preceding five calendar years, and were paid at least $350 a year (indexed annually for inflation).

In a noncorporate form of business, the SEP contributions for the employees are subject to the same rules. However, SEP contributions are limited to 13.0435 percent of net profits (i.e., the net self-employment income of the business) for the self-employed *owners* of proprietorships and partnerships. The unincorporated owner can make a variable (tax-deductible) contribution of 0 to 13.0435 percent of net self-employment income each year, up to an annual maximum of $30,000. Eligible employees must also be covered by the same gross percentage contribution of their compensation (i.e., 13.0435 percent of net profit is really 15 percent of the net profit remaining after the SEP contribution is deducted), which means a 15 percent (of compensation) payment for employees while the owner's contribution is 13.0435 percent of net profits.

For SEPs, annual reports do not have to be filed with the IRS, the annual administration fees are low (like any IRA), and you can establish the plan right up to the due date of your corporate or individual or partnership income tax return (including any extensions of time to file). The SEP contribution is always deductible in the applicable tax year even though the actual payment is not made until the due date (or extended due date) of the tax return in the following year.

For many reps with modest corporate profit-sharing plans or Keogh plans or just plain IRAs, the SEP is a more attractive alternative!

CORPORATE PROFIT-SHARING PLAN (DEFINED CONTRIBUTION)

This fixed percentage ("money purchase") plan really has nothing to do with the *profits* of the company. A variable 0 to 15 percent of employee *compensation* can be contributed (tax-deductible) each year up to an annual maximum of $30,000 for each employee. The same percentage must be contributed for all employees each year, whatever percentage is selected for that year. The contribution is not income to the employee.

There are various eligibility, nondiscrimination, and vesting rules. Annual reports (Form series 5500, "Annual Returns/Reports of Employee Benefit Plan) must be filed, and there are administration fees to pay for set up, amendments, recordkeeping, and filing. The same rules apply for establishing the plan and the time for making and deducting the payments as detailed for the SEP.

SELF-EMPLOYED PROFIT-SHARING KEOGH PLAN (DEFINED CONTRIBUTION)

All Keogh plans *must* be established by December 31 of the first year involved, and a minimum payment must be made at that time (otherwise you cannot make a Keogh contribution for that year). *Then* you have until April 15 of the following year to pay the balance of the contribution into the plan, and that date can be extended by any extensions of time to file your tax return. (For those who miss that December 31 opening date, you can elect to have a SEP instead, because there is no similar December 31 requirement.)

The unincorporated owner can make a variable (tax-deductible) contribution of 0 to 13.0435 percent of net self-employment income each year up to an annual maximum of $30,000. Eligible employees must also be covered by the same gross percentage contribution of their compensation (i.e., 13.0435 percent of net profit is really 15 percent of the net, net profit remaining after the SEP contribution is deducted), which means a 15 percent (of compensation) payment for employees while the owner's contribution is 13.0435 percent of net profits. The contribution is not income to the employee.

There are various eligibility, nondiscrimination, and vesting rules. Annual reports (Form series 5500) must be filed, and there are administration fees to pay for set up, amendments, recordkeeping, and filing.

CORPORATE PENSION PLAN (DEFINED CONTRIBUTION)

The same fixed percentage of employee compensation is contributed, tax-deductible, each year. The maximum percentage that can be adopted under this plan is generally *10 percent*, which added to the maximum corporate profit-sharing plan of *15 percent*, provides the traditional overall maximum contribution of *25 percent* of employee compensation for these two retirement plans combined. The annual maximum employee contribution for *both* plans is still $30,000. The contribution is not income to the employee.

There are various eligibility, nondiscrimination, and vesting requirements. Annual reports (Form series 5500) must be filed, and there are administration fees to pay for set up, amendments, recordkeeping, and filing. The same rules apply for establishing the plan and the time for making and deducting the payments as are detailed for the SEP.

SELF-EMPLOYED MONEY PURCHASE KEOGH PLAN (DEFINED CONTRIBUTION)

This plan usually incorporates the profit-sharing Keogh plan; the owner can make a variable (tax-deductible) contribution of up to 20 percent of net self-employment income each year, up to an annual maximum of $30,000. You can *vary* the profit-sharing portion of the contribution each year, while the balance of the plan represents a fixed percentage contribution.

Eligible employees must also be covered by the same gross percentage contribution of their compensation (i.e., 20 percent of net profit, which is really 25 percent of the net, net profit remaining *after* the Keogh contribution is deducted), which means (trust me!) a 25 percent contribution (of compensation) payment for employees while the owner's contribution is 20 percent of net profits. The contribution is not income to the employee.

There are various eligibility, nondiscrimination, and vesting requirements. Annual reports (Form series 5500) must be filed, and there are administration fees to pay for set up, amendments, record-keeping, and filing. The same rules apply for establishing the plan and making the payments as are detailed for the profit-sharing Keogh plan. Again, the SEP is an alternative if you miss the December 31 date for establishing the Keogh plan the first year.

CORPORATE DEFINED-BENEFIT PENSION PLAN OR SELF-EMPLOYED DEFINED-BENEFIT KEOGH PLAN

The annual contribution to a defined-benefit plan is not a fixed percentage of compensation or profits, but varies based on age and compensation of participants, interest rates and net earnings of the plan, "defined" benefits promised at retirement, planned date of retirement, life expectancy, and so forth. The actual contribution is calculated and certified annually by an actuary. There is no theoretical limit to the annual contribution (e.g., 100 percent of salary is possible), but individual retirement benefits are limited (but adjusted upward annually for inflation). The most recent retirement cap was about $103,000. The contribution is not income to the employee.

There are various eligibility, nondiscrimination, and vesting requirements. Annual reports (Form series 5500) must be filed, and there are administration fees to pay for set up, amendments, record-keeping, and filing. The administration fees are higher than for any other kind of retirement plan because of the actuarial requirements and the overall complexities of the plan.

For the corporate plan, the same rules apply for establishing the plan and making and deducting the payments as are detailed for the SEP. For the Keogh plan, the same rules apply for establishing the plan and making the payments as for other Keogh plans. The defined-benefit plan frequently results in a higher contribution than any other plan and is generally beneficial for owners who are at least age 50 (the older the better!).

401(K) AND 403(B) PLANS (DEFINED CONTRIBUTION)

The 401(k) and 403(b) are similar plans, but the 403(b) is for nonprofit organizations only. These plans permit each employee to earmark part of her salary as a contribution to the plan; that amount is not reported as gross income (on Form W-2, "Wage and Tax Statement") for income tax purposes, although it is reported for Social Security/Medicare tax purposes. As with all other IRS "qualified" retirement plans, the earnings accumulate and compound tax-deferred until funds are withdrawn at retirement.

The amount each employee can defer is currently limited to $9,240 ($9,500 for 403[b] plans) annually, adjusted upward for inflation each year. Special nondiscrimination rules limit the deferral percentage for higher-paid employees to the percentage lower-paid employees choose to defer.

The employer company can match all or part of each employee's contribution. Nearly two-thirds of large corporations make matching payments, sometimes 50 percent (25 percent the most typical) of the employee's contribution. The employee may literally earn these percentages each year by electing to join the 401(k) plan, yet a pathetic number of employees don't sign up! Of 24 percent of eligible employees nationwide, only 14 percent have signed up, and most of them are at the higher income levels. Where else can you earn an annual 25 percent tax-deferred income for your retirement? Don't turn this plan down!

INDIVIDUAL RETIREMENT ACCOUNT

If you have earned income from wages, self-employment, or alimony you can have an Individual Retirement Account (IRA). The maximum tax-deductible contribution is the lesser of $2,000 or your total earned income (the contribution *must* be paid by April 15 of the following year). You and your spouse can each contribute up to the $2,000 limit, if you qualify, or either spouse can contribute up to $2,250 on behalf of both.

However, those contributions are not always deductible. If neither you nor your spouse is covered by another retirement plan the full IRA contribution is always deductible. If either of you are covered by another plan, the IRA contribution is only deductible if your income is below certain limits (currently $25,000 for single filers and $40,000 for joint filers), and the IRA tax-deduction is phased out as your income climbs above those stated income limits.

Always, always, always make IRA contributions if they are fully deductible! If you began when you were young and made these contributions for 30–40 years, an IRA could be worth $1 million at retirement! Even a child who baby-sits and mows the lawn can qualify for the early start!

> ***TAXTIP***
>
> Pay your children for chores around the house, have them report the earnings, and pay 100 percent (up to $2,000) into an IRA.

If an IRA contribution is not deductible, however, I recommend that you do not make a contribution; if you do, you'll be forced into special tax reporting procedures each year until retirement, and you can't freely and easily withdraw those funds. Instead, invest the same amounts annually in a tax-exempt bond or money market fund, and you will be better off and have ready access to your funds, if needed.

EMPLOYEE STOCK OWNERSHIP PLAN

Through an Employee Stock Ownership Plan (ESOP), the employees are given stock (i.e., ownership) in their employer company. Employers are encouraged to do this by the substantial tax breaks that are offered for ESOPs.

The ESOP is funded with either the stock of the employer company or with cash that is used to *buy the stock of the owners* (see Chapter 33). If the corporation funds the ESOP with a cash contribution, the company gets a tax deduction. The ESOP then uses the cash to buy part of the stock from the corporation owner(s), or from the corporation. That stock is independently appraised at *market* value. Therefore, the owner ends up with cash (capital gain), which has already produced a tax deduction for the company! A wonderfulness indeed!

> ***TAXTIP***
>
> If the owners of the company stock roll over the proceeds into other listed stocks, they can *defer all tax* on the gain until the *new* stocks are sold!

Another arrangement is for the ESOP to borrow the money to buy the stock (independently appraised at market value) from the owner.

The bank making the ESOP loan can exclude from taxable income 50 percent of the interest on such loans, and thus the ESOP can borrow at lower than normal rates. The corporation subsequently makes annual cash contributions to the ESOP or pays cash dividends to the ESOP on the stock the ESOP has acquired, which supplies the funds for the ESOP to repay the bank loan. Under these special rules, *either* the dividends *or* the contributions to the ESOP are deductible by the company!

The employees end up owning part of the company, the corporation gets substantial tax deductions, and the company owner gets cash at market value for corporate stock! The ESOP is almost always a great deal for the owner, but only sometimes for the sales agency employees, depending on how well the company is doing financially and other factors.

PRIVATE PENSION PLANS

This is a major retirement plan idea involving life insurance. Recently there was a minor scandal when it was revealed that certain Metropolitan Life Florida insurance agents were selling insurance policies to nurses, described as a "Nurse's Retirement Plan," without clearly disclosing that they were actually life insurance policies (failure to describe any insurance product as "insurance" is against the law). Subsequently, *The Wall Street Journal* wrote that agents for New York Life, Allstate, and Prudential were doing exactly the same thing. These insurance policies are a version of the latest product called "private pension plans."

These plans do have a lot to offer, but also have potential drawbacks that are rarely mentioned. Since the whole idea has become a major life insurance marketing tool, it deserves your careful and informed consideration.

THE MONEY AND TAX ANGLES

The private pension plan is a life insurance product that offers both an investment benefit and a death benefit. It takes full advantage of these favorable tax rules, which govern life insurance policies in general:

1. As premiums are paid, the cash values of life insurance increase *tax-free* each year (the so-called inside buildup).
2. Payments from a qualified retirement plan are fully taxable as received, but withdrawals from life insurance policies are *tax-free* to the extent of all premiums paid.

3. Borrowings from life insurance policies are *also tax-free* up to the cash surrender value of the policy. (The "policy loans" in points 2 and 3 do *not* have to be repaid, and the entire outstanding loan balance, plus interest, will eventually be deducted from the death benefit paid.)

4. Contrary to a qualified retirement plan, no tax rule *forces* you to begin these withdrawals at age 70½, and there is no surcharge levied if the annual withdrawals exceed $150,000.

5. If you wish, by selecting a *variable life* insurance policy you can choose any investment mix of domestic and foreign stock funds, balanced income funds, or common stocks to try for a higher (tax-free) cash value buildup. You can change the investment mix as often as you want, without any tax consequences, and you may hire an investment manager to make your investments. Alternatively, you can opt for a more traditional policy and let the life insurance company invest the money conservatively (by law) for you.

6. If the individual dies before retirement, the policy proceeds, as is normally the case with all life insurance, are income tax free. Additionally, they would qualify for the unlimited marital (spousal) deduction and escape estate taxes as well. In most cases the proceeds would be received by a surviving spouse free of both income and estate taxes.

THE CONCEPT

In effect, private pension plans are set up as *nonqualified* retirement benefit plans and do *not* require IRS (or other regulatory) approval; they are in the category of *other* benefit plans that need no IRS consent such as split-dollar insurance, deferred compensation, executive bonus plans, salary continuation plans, and so forth. Private pension plans are not subject to Department of Labor or IRS administrative reporting rules and only negligible plan administration is involved. A private pension plan can be used to benefit just owners or just other employees, or both.

A major benefit of this arrangement is that it can be offered on *a discriminatory* (i.e., "selective") basis. A private pension plan can be established by any size corporation (C or S) as well as *non-profit* organizations. The premium ("funding") costs are tax-deductible to the corporation and are income to the employee (see next section), but the *after-tax* costs to the employee are insignificant. The employee owns the policy and can name the beneficiary.

This plan is often used in situations where the company owner:

- Is personally *fully* funded in the company qualified retirement plan and now wants to obtain additional retirement benefits.

- Wants to reward *certain* employees with additional retirement benefits.
- Desires that additional retirement benefits start accumulating for herself, even though her qualified plan is *not* fully funded. (Under current law, only $150,000 in annual compensation is counted toward *qualified* retirement plan contributions, and remember, those retirement benefits are *taxable* when paid!)
- For whatever reasons, does not want a company retirement plan at *all* and simply wants to provide this private pension plan for himself, which is not that uncommon an arrangement.

THE MECHANICS

Let's assume a company owner wants to reward a key manager with a private pension plan and the annual premium selected is $10,000 a year. There are two options: The manager can be paid an annual bonus of, say, $14,000 and, after taxes, there will be about $10,000 available to pay the premium, or the manager can be paid a $10,000 bonus and take a *tax-free* dividend withdrawal from the insurance policy of $3,000–$4,000, which will about pay her taxes on the bonus.

The company will have either a $14,000 or a $10,000 tax deduction, depending on the option chosen. As long as the manager's *overall* compensation package is not deemed "unreasonable," these payroll costs are deductible under IRS Code Section 162(a). The manager, after taxes, will have no net out-of-pocket costs. This procedure can also be used to reward company owners as well as other selected employees.

In the case of self-employed, unincorporated individuals, the same kind of insurance policy can be purchased. The key difference is that the policy premiums are not tax-deductible, since no tax-deductible bonus is paid to cover the premium. It's a pure life insurance and investment vehicle, but with the same money and tax angles detailed earlier.

THE DANGER: PROJECTIONS

Variable life and *all other kinds* of ordinary life insurance policies are sold with illustrations of future values. However, they are nothing more than projected *estimates* of what *may* happen in the future! In the case of the variable life policy, if the stock market drops so will the return on the policy. In the case of the conventional investment-type life insurance policy, if interest rates drop so will the return on the policy. Of course, the more optimistic the illustrations the easier it is to sell these policies to you, since *the apparent cost is lower*. Understand that:

- Future projected *interest rates and investment earnings* are only *estimates*, therefore
- The predicted *rate of return* is only an estimate, therefore
- Future *cash values* are only an *estimate*, and
- Future *dividends* are only an *estimate*.

The same considerations apply to *every life insurance policy that you buy!* In a conventional policy, if the projections are too optimistic, your future premiums will increase or the total number of required annual premium payments will increase. In this case, if the projections are too optimistic *it's your planned retirement benefits that will drop!*

Said another way: A conventional policy is purchased *primarily* for the *death benefit* of a stated amount while these policies are purchased *primarily* to achieve a certain future level of *retirement* plan funds. Big difference!

KEY POINT

The projections must be pragmatic, sober, practical, and realistic! Not pie-in-the-sky rosy projections, intended to sell you on the cheap. What's a hardheaded and pragmatic number for projecting current policy earnings? At today's interest rates, for a conventional policy with the insurance company doing the conservative (by law) investing in high grade corporate bonds and US government obligations, I would figure about 5–6 percent. For a variable life policy, with a mix of common stock funds and balanced income funds, I would figure 10–11 percent. If you get a quote on a conventional policy using a 9.5 percent interest rate (see the following story) or on a variable life policy projecting 15 percent, you are not dealing with an honest insurance agent in the real world of 1994!

We recently had a case where a wealthy widow was buying a *conventional* multimillion dollar life insurance policy to cover future estate taxes. Two insurance agents bid for the policy. The first presented figures based on *realistic* current interest earnings (since the insurance company was doing the investing) of 6 percent. The second agent's figures for the *same kind of policy* were based on 9.5 percent current interest projections (casually mentioned once and never referred to again) and naturally he quoted a much *lower* annual premium. Despite the advice from both her attorney and myself, she bought the cheaper policy. It *won't* be, in a few years.

THE DANGER: POLICY LAPSE

You *cannot* let the private annuity policy lapse once you begin major borrowing! If the policy lapses or you surrender the policy, all loans in *excess* of the premiums paid, plus any remaining cash value in the policy, will become *ordinary taxable income to you!*

For example, if you paid a $10,000 a year premium for 20 years ($200,000 total) and then, after retirement, withdrew $30,000 a year for 15 years ($450,000 total), if the policy lapsed you would owe ordinary income taxes on at least $250,000 ($450,000 – $200,000)!

As a worst case, if interest rates or the stock market fell, your borrowings could so erode the cash values of the policy that you would have to pay *additional* premiums just to keep the policy in force! And, as explained, you *cannot* let it lapse if you borrow more than the premiums paid.

To avoid these situations, the stated premiums and planned retirement withdrawals must be mapped out so as to leave a cushion in the policy. If you don't want to reduce the retirement withdrawals, *the premiums must be realistically high enough* to produce the projected retirement benefits *and* eliminate the need for future premium payments at, or before, retirement. I'd suggest you have your CPA or other independent tax adviser review all life insurance proposals.

YES OR NO?

You are wrong if you think the preceding was intended as an indictment of private pension plans. I happen to like them very much, *in the right circumstances*. For example, we have a new client about 10 years from retirement, with a seven-figure annual income that appears to be stable. We simultaneously set up a defined-benefit pension plan for his corporation and a private pension plan. At the end of 10 years, his annual retirement income from both sources will be well into six figures, and the private pension plan portion will be *tax-free*, under current law. We are playing catch-up for all the years he was without *any* retirement plans (or good advice).

> ***TAXTIP***
>
> Both owners and other employees should *first* max out all possible contributions to their 401(k) plans, IRAs, and Keoghs, however, and *then* consider a private pension plan as a retirement supplement.

I like the private pension plan as a method of *selectively* rewarding key employees as well as owners. Another benefit is that all life insurance (except term) is a method of *forced savings* for the individual involved, and about 90 percent of all of us need that kind of financial discipline (starting with me!).

I particularly like the idea of variable life insurance and the wide investment *choices* available. Another advantage to variable life is that the assets are *not* part of the insurance company's general account and are legally walled off from all other insurance company assets. In the event the insurance company gets into financial trouble (e.g., Mutual Benefit Life), the assets in these segregated accounts are safe, inviolate, and untouched. Not a trivial consideration. However, I strongly suggest the use of an experienced investment manager if big money is to be invested in a variable life policy.

OTHER PLANS

There are also other (qualified and nonqualified) plans such as subsidized thrift, target benefit, stock bonus, deferred compensation, and phantom stock, which are of less interest to the average rep. A "nonqualified" plan (frequently recommended by insurance agents as a way to sell large amounts of life insurance) means it has *not* qualified with the IRS for the qualified plans' triple benefits of tax-deductible contributions by the company or individual, payment not considered as being income to the employee, and compounded, tax-deferred earnings. There are many, many nonqualified plans and variations on that theme, some good, some bad, and some just designed to sell a lot of life insurance.

RETIREMENT PLAN ADMINISTRATION

It is impossible for the average businessperson to comprehend the incredible complexities that the IRS has inflicted on retirement plans! Many of these rules and regulations were designed by the IRS to stop perceived abuses, of which there were many indeed in the early days: unlimited borrowing from plans, minimal repayments of such loans, blatant discrimination between the highly paid and the lowly slaves, and so forth.

However, as is almost invariably the case when the IRS attempts to stop abuses, their overkill is simply monumental! For example, the Tax Reform Act of 1986 contains about 250 pages of changes in retirement plan regulations. In the last 10 years or so, the design and administration of retirement plans has become a new profession. We refer 100 percent of such business to two or three such experts in whom we have confidence, and we no longer attempt to perform these functions (or charge fees for same) in our own CPA firm. Indeed, this is a new, specialized, and highly sophisticated calling.

Those labyrinthine rules and regulations have naturally been accompanied by comparable and tremendous increases in the fees for plan administration. Therefore, if you have simple and minimal retirement plans in place, but the administration fees are getting out of hand in dollars or percentage, consider changing to a SEP and reread that section of this chapter. For some reps, SEPs are looking better and better (unless you plan to go bankrupt, as discussed earlier).

RETIREMENT PLAN INVESTMENTS IN LIMITED PARTNERSHIPS

Here is a generalization that will infuriate many of those "investment adviser" sharks who can smell your retirement plan money from the same great distance that other sharks smell blood: Don't invest *any* retirement plan funds in limited partnerships! Why? Because they are illiquid investments, and you can't get your money out whenever you want; up to 25 percent of your funds can go off the top in commissions to those sharks; they are usually mediocre investments at best; and the IRS now insists that all plan assets be valued at market and not initial cost or book/capital account value, which is immensely difficult and costly in the case of limited partnerships. To sum up, we have had nothing but *bad* experiences with them!

Here are direct quotes from a 1992 IRS letter that was sent to a company (not our client) at the conclusion of the IRS retirement plan audit. The company had invested retirement plan funds in a number of limited partnerships and one had already gone belly-up.

> After carefully reviewing the explanations for the foreclosed partnership, it appears the taxpayer did not exercise prudence in managing the assets of the plan, and did not ensure that the portfolio was adequately diversified. As a plan fiduciary he must diversify plan assets to minimize the risk of large . . . losses. The taxpayer's lack of familiarity with an investment is no excuse for making an imprudent investment. Under an objective standard of prudence, trustees are judged according to the standards of others acting in a like capacity and familiar with such matters. Where trustees are themselves ill-equipped to evaluate the soundness of a proposed investment, their duty is to seek outside assistance. It appears this was not done, resulting in a violation of the exclusive benefit rule which could disqualify the plan.

The IRS is referring to the "prudent person" rule, as well as diversification as a standard technique. Keep in mind that not only can the IRS disqualify a plan, but your *employees* can take action against you for improperly managing plan assets! Investment stupidity is no excuse and, if necessary, you should seek outside help in making investment decisions.

The IRS letter then discusses annual valuations of these wonderful limited partnerships. Note the significant concluding sentence.

> All . . . plans must provide for an annual valuation of investments held by the trust on a specified valuation date, in accordance with a method consistently followed and uniformly applied. You must use fair market value for this purpose, and you should adjust the respective accounts of participants based on the valuation (Revenue Ruling 80-155). You are not doing this with the limited partnerships held by the trust. The capital account shown on the Schedule K-1 [Partner's Share of Income, Credits, Deductions, Etc.] is *not* fair market value. Your failure to perform this annual valuation could result in incorrect allocations and discriminatory distributions. Both prohibited discrimination (in favor of the highly compensated) and failure to follow the plan document could result in plan disqualification . . . Limited partnerships can also create unrelated business income which is taxable. You should carefully consider the prudence of such investments for a retirement plan trust.

You must have annual valuations at fair market value, and the capital account of a limited partnership is *not* that value. Finally, the last sentence is as close as the IRS can come to a flat statement that you should not invest in limited partnerships at all! That's my advice also, and if I'm being too diffident in expressing my opinion, what part of "no" don't you understand?

The best advice is to invest conservatively. This is your *retirement* you are gambling with and not just a weekend in Vegas! You will have plenty of time to double and quadruple your money in conservative investments through the guaranteed magic of tax-deferred compounding (just start early and contribute regularly). And remember, you could get sued by your employees for not investing their funds as a "prudent person" would. Investing retirement funds is not like selling, because you *can* take it easy (be conservative) and still get rich! To sum up retirement plan investing: Don't shoot craps!

RETIREMENT PLAN DISTRIBUTIONS

Again, the rules are complicated, intricate, knotty, and involved! You will need advice about such options as: lump-sum distributions,

IRA and other rollovers, 10-year forward averaging, 5-year forward averaging, capital gains treatments, partial distributions, partial rollovers, early retirement, plan loans, life insurance, required distributions, estate planning, annuities, and so on.

To illustrate, here are just the *penalty* rules on distributions:

Why	*How It Applies*	*Penalty*
Too soon	Distribution before age 59½	10%
Too late	Distribution delayed beyond age 70½	50%
Too little	Distribution below minimum required	50%
Too much	Distribution above certain limits	15%

Now let's discuss those various penalties in more detail.

EARLY WITHDRAWAL PENALTY

A 10 percent penalty applies to early withdrawals (before age 59½) from all qualified retirement plans (pension, profit sharing, Keogh, 401(k), SEP, IRA, etc.) unless you can meet one of the exceptions. The penalty will not be applied if the early distribution is:

- Due to disability or death.
- Due to early retirement after age 55 (but this exception does not apply to IRAs).
- Due to a qualified domestic relations order (QDRO) (i.e., divorce) and the payment is to another payee (i.e., spouse). This exception does not apply to IRAs.
- Due to termination of employment and the distribution is made in substantially equal payments over your life or life expectancy.
- To pay medical expenses that are deductible (i.e., currently over 7.5 percent of adjusted gross income). This exception does not apply to IRAs.
- Your own after-tax employee contribution (but not any earnings thereon generated while in the plan).

The 10 percent penalty tax will apply to early withdrawals (distributions) before age 59½ from any and all of your retirement plans if you don't meet any of the above situations. Also, a virtual "catch-22" is built into the current retirement plan rules. Here's a damned if you do, damned if you don't situation:

- You must make certain minimum distributions from your retirement plan, or there is a penalty tax.

- If those required minimum distributions are too high, there is another penalty tax.
- If you die leaving too much still remaining in your retirement account, there is still another penalty tax.
- If you take out all the money in a lump-sum distribution, the favorable averaging options have been weakened considerably and there is a further penalty if the lump-sum distribution is too much.

MINIMUM DISTRIBUTIONS

Many well-paid executives and successful owners would prefer to leave their retirement plans intact to avoid paying taxes on any distributions and to compound the tax-deferred earnings as long as possible. However, the law requires that you *must* begin drawing their retirement benefits (from any and all plans) by April 1 of the year you turn 70.

You cannot simply draw some minimal amount. You must draw out benefits at a rate actuarially estimated to consume the entire plan assets (including all additional earnings while distributions are being paid) over your life expectancy and that of any beneficiary (e.g., spouse). Further, these required minimum distributions cannot be rolled over into an IRA or other retirement account. *A 50 percent tax is imposed on any such required distributions that are not actually made!*

EXCESS DISTRIBUTIONS

The "catch-22" continues! We just learned the rules for minimum distributions that must be made. But if those required minimum distributions are too large, you are subject to another penalty tax because of that very fact!

Here are those rules:

- There is a penalty tax of 15 percent on all excess distributions, including those paid from IRAs.
- The tax is imposed on combined annual retirement distributions that exceed $150,000 from all plans (or exceed a somewhat lesser amount if a special election was made some years ago).
- The tax is applied to any excess distributions paid over those stated annual limits and all distributions from all retirement plans are included in the penalty tax calculation.

- The 15 percent penalty tax (technically an excise tax) does not apply to distributions that are rolled over into an IRA or other plan, made to a beneficiary after the person's death, made under a qualified domestic relations order, or a return of your own after-tax employee contributions.

So, you pay a 10 percent penalty tax if you take distributions before age 59½ that are not subject to the exclusions. Then, you pay a 50 percent penalty tax if you don't take the required minimum retirement payments from April 1 of the year you turn 70. But, if those payments exceed $150,000 annually from all plans, the excess is subject to a 15 percent penalty tax!

AFTER-DEATH DISTRIBUTIONS

Finally, a new penalty tax ("additional estate tax") of 15 percent is applied to any excess retirement accumulation that is left in your estate. The "excess retirement accumulation," is

> The excess (if any) of the value of the decedent's interests in all qualified employer plans and IRAs over the present value of annual payments equal to the annual ceiling (generally $150,000) over a period equal to the life expectancy of the decedent immediately before death.

In other words, if you leave so much money at your death that, if it was invested in a life annuity that would generate annual payments of (generally) over $150,000, that excess accumulation will be taxed in your estate.

I was given the following quote, which summarizes things beautifully:

> Pity the senior citizen who depends on the private pension system. The poor soul is taxed if he or she: (1) receives too much of a retirement distribution, (2) takes too little of a retirement distribution, (3) takes the retirement money too early, or (4) takes the retirement money too late.

IRS AUDITS OF RETIREMENT PLANS

For the next few years, at least, the IRS intends to aggressively examine qualified retirement plans. This is a major audit initiative, and don't be surprised if your itsy-bitsy insignificant plan wins the audit lottery. The IRS has shifted from auditing just the actuarial assumptions of pension plans (a humiliating disaster for the IRS, as it has turned out!) to a search for all the technical defects of retirement plans. Given the legal complexities of almost any retirement plan (except those like the good old SEP), this gladiatorial examination arena could find such "defects" everywhere!

IRS ANNOUNCEMENT 92-182 TO IRS AUDITORS OF RETIREMENT PLANS

As stated in IRS Announcement 92-182 (December 28, 1992), the IRS will audit the following areas with extra special emphasis on points 1 and 2:

1. Were there prohibited transactions, self-dealing, dealing in company real estate or securities, improper loans to anyone or excessive loans to participants? Were loans properly collateralized as required? And so on.
2. Were there improper plan asset valuations? (This is a special IRS priority within the special retirement plan audit program!)
3. Were all required amendments to the plan actually and timely made? Did they meet all the various pension law changes of the last 10–15 years?
4. Was the plan properly and timely funded each year?
5. Were plan distributions always reported as income by all employees? What about the reporting of any annual PS–58 (these are the insurance premium costs paid in excess of the cost of term insurance for each applicable policy) insurance costs?

> ***TAXTIP***
>
> It is foolish not to report any and all PS–58 costs each year, since by doing so you reduce the eventual amount of life insurance proceeds from the plan that will be considered a *taxable* distribution at the time of death. You are much better off picking up some of that income each year and *reducing* any eventual tax hit.

6. Were there excessive deductions claimed involving insurance contracts and insurance plans?

To that last point, I have already indicated that limited partnership interests must be valued at market value (please reread "Retirement Plan Investments in Limited Partnerships" on page 107). The IRS further insists that this rule be applied to all such plan assets (e.g., real estate, collectibles, closely held corporate stock, and limited partnership interests). Annual independent appraisals will be required, and the IRS will monitor the dates of the last appraisals and insist on updates in a timely manner (IRS Form series 5500 has been changed to ask for the date of the last independent appraisal of such property). It ain't gonna' be a great few years for retirement plan audits.

IRS Announcement 92-182 concentrates on two audit areas: valuation of plan assets, and loans to plan participants (a prohibited transaction). Violation of the rules in either of the two areas can cause complete disqualification of your plan, including disallowance of all retirement plan contributions! The summary heading for this announcement makes interesting reading: "Plan qualification: Plan examination guidelines: Prohibited transaction rules and plan asset valuation." Get the picture?

Here is a cogent quote:

> VI. Effects of Improper Valuation. A. Qualification. 1. Rev. Rul. 80-155 requires that a defined contribution plan's assets be revalued at least annually. If the requirements of Rev. Rul. 80-155 are not met, the plan is not qualified.

Not "maybe," not "perhaps," not "give 'em a break," just "not qualified."

And another:

> V. Specific Type of Plan Assets. A. Partnerships. 2. Examination Steps. a. Ask for information regarding how and when the fair market value of the partnership was determined. Determine the basis for the valuation of the partnership, i.e., if the value of the partnership was based on the original cost of the investment, or the capital account . . . Such valuations may not reflect the fair market value of the partnership. b. The fact that a partnership has no earnings may indicate that the partnership is worthless.

Further:

> II. Valuation Information on Form 5500. B. Examination Steps. A valuation problem may exist if you find any of the following items on Form 5500. 1. Determine whether the plan reports assets with level values in successive years. a. If the same value for an asset has been reported on Form 5500 for the prior year, this is an indi-

cation that a yearly valuation may not have been performed, requiring further examination.

And:

I. General. A. Importance of Accurate Assessment of Value. An accurate assessment of fair market value is essential to a plan's ability to comply with the requirements set forth in the (IRS) Code and in Title I of ERISA. For instance, a prohibited transaction exemption may not apply unless the fair market value of assets is accurately determined. Similarly, a failure to properly establish fair market value may cause an exclusive benefit violation.

Finally:

II. A. Loans to Parties in Interest. B. Exemptions for Loans to Participants . . . permits loans to participants and beneficiaries that: 1. are adequately secured; 2. are available on a reasonably equivalent basis to all participants in the plan; 3. are not made available to highly compensated employees in greater amounts than other employees; and 5. are made in accordance with specific plan provisions governing such transactions.

To summarize, the greatly expanded IRS audits over the next years will be conducted by IRS agents looking for trouble and carrying a complete copy of IRS Announcement 92-182 in their grubby little hands. Additionally, these audits will not result in slap-on-the-wrist-type action, but in many cases they will propose a complete disallowance of your retirement plan, followed by a deficiency bill of such magnitude that it will exceed the annual budget of most small European countries!.

The IRS will: Disallow three years of retirement plan deductions; tax all supposedly tax-deferred earnings of the plan; tax all loans to participants; assess penalties and charge interest (compounded for three years); plus other horrible things even I cannot imagine! Have I made my point?

CAFETERIA PLANS

A cafeteria plan is an employer-sponsored written benefit package that offers all eligible employees a choice between taking cash compensation (taxable), certain qualified fringe benefits (not taxable), or a combination of the two up to a stated dollar maximum amount. Thus the employee can "shop" the various benefits offered, as if going down the line in a cafeteria, select certain ones to put on her "tray," and reject other offered benefits that are not attractive in that employee's particular situation.

These flexible benefit plans were created by Internal Revenue Code Section 125. They encourage the employees to share the responsibility of choosing the appropriate benefits best suited to their lifestyles. Under a cafeteria plan, all eligible employees can voluntarily elect to reduce their taxable compensation (up to the stipulated maximum of the plan) insofar as they choose tax-free cafeteria benefits in lieu of some of their (taxable) cash compensation. Many of these benefits would not be deductible if paid directly by the *employee*.

The amount by which salary is reduced is put into a fund to pay or reimburse certain selected expenses of the employee tax-free. At the beginning of each plan year, the employees must decide how much to set aside for each benefit, and this decision cannot be changed later in the plan year. The cafeteria plan allows employee flexibility, choice, and tax savings, a seductive package for most of us.

CAFETERIA BENEFITS AVAILABLE

The following are the *only* benefits that can be included in a cafeteria plan entirely tax-free (the first four items may be changed if a national health plan is adopted):

- Medical insurance premiums.
- Medical costs not covered by the insurance.
- Dental insurance premiums.
- Dental costs not covered by the insurance.
- Group term life insurance premiums.
- Disability income insurance premiums.
- Accidental death insurance premiums.
- Qualified dependent care costs.
- Group legal services costs.
- Contributions to a qualified 401(k) pension plan.

A cafeteria plan need not offer all the preceding choices and, in fact, some large companies only offer a choice between various medical insurance plans. Limiting and controlling the total medical insurance costs of each employee is a motive in such cases. For example, one California employer offers each employee a cafeteria plan maximum of $5,000 a year to be spent on any one of a number of medical plans. If the employee spends over $5,000, the excess is deducted from his salary; if the employee spends less than $5,000, the difference is added to salary. Thus, it never costs the employer over $5,000 annually for the medical insurance premiums of any single employee.

A cafeteria plan cannot pay fringe benefits other than those already listed, although the employer might be able to under various other IRS rules and circumstances, such as:

- Educational benefits (scholarships or fellowship grants). Limited to $5,250 a year for each employee, spouse, and dependents. Further limited for company owners to *5 percent* of the total amount paid out each year.
- Employer-provided transportation between home and work.
- Deferred compensation.
- Working condition benefits, such as parking, business dues, subscriptions, business use of employer's auto, or similar fringes.

NONDISCRIMINATION RULES

Naturally, cafeteria plans cannot discriminate. The key to a successful plan is that it must provide benefits that are so attractive to the lower-paid employees that they all elect to go with the plan. Otherwise, you are up against the loss of the tax-free status of the benefits for higher-level employees. In that case, the entire plan loses all the advantages discussed and should probably be aborted (similar in concept to the requirements for adoption of a 401[k] plan).

The nondiscrimination rules are quite technical and will be limited to a general overview, sufficient only to enable you to intelligently discuss the matter with your own experts. Here is an IRS summary:

> Nondiscrimination rules. If, in any plan year, your cafeteria plan discriminates in favor of highly compensated individuals [$99,000 for 1994] as to eligibility to participate in the plan or in favor of highly compensated participants as to contributions or benefits, highly compensated participants are taxed on the amount of the taxable benefits that could have been elected.
>
> If qualified benefits provided to key employees are more than 25 percent of the total of these benefits provided for all employees under the plan, key employees must include in income the value of the benefits that could have been elected.

Thus the plan becomes discriminatory and benefits to the top people become *taxable* under any of three scenarios:

1. The benefits paid for "key" employees exceed 25 percent of the total benefits.
2. The benefits paid for "highly compensated" employees as a percentage of compensation are "significantly" higher.
3. The eligibility (participation) requirements discriminate in favor of highly compensated employees.

For example, your company has a cafeteria plan and the key employees received nontaxable benefits of $25,000. The total benefits for all employees were $110,000. Since the key employees' benefits were less than 25 percent of the total benefits, your company passes the first test. However, say that $25,000 represents 15 percent of highly compensated employee compensation, while the remaining $85,000 ($110,000 – $25,000) represents 5 percent of nonkey employee compensation. Since the key employee percentage benefit (15 percent) is significantly higher than the nonkey employee percentage benefit (5 percent), your company flunks the second test!

In that event, all those benefits for highly compensated employees ($25,000 in this example) becomes taxable to the individual, but the benefits for the nonkey employees remain nontaxable. Not a great result for the top company people!

Note that while the term "significantly higher" has not yet been defined by the IRS for cafeteria plans, for other plans it has been defined as any excess over 1.25 times the nonhighly compensated employees amounts, while in our example it was three times as much, that is, 15 percent versus 5 percent.

"HIGHLY COMPENSATED" AND "KEY" EMPLOYEES DEFINED

A "highly compensated" employee is defined by the IRS as a person who fits any one of these four categories:

1. Any company officer.
2. Any owner of over 5 percent of the company stock.
3. Anyone considered highly compensated under the "facts and circumstances on a case by case" basis.
4. A spouse or dependent of anyone described in points 1, 2, or 3.

A "key" employee is currently defined as a person who fits any one of these four categories:

1. Any company officer earning over $45,000 a year.
2. Any of the 10 highest-percentage owners of the company who earn over $30,000 a year.

3. Any owner of over 5 percent of the company stock.
4. Any owner of over 1 percent of the company stock who earns over $150,000 a year.

As you can see, those definitions fit virtually everyone but the rank and file, which is exactly the intention of the IRS.

ELIGIBILITY

Finally, the plan cannot discriminate as to eligibility of employees for participation in the plan. This condition is somewhat easier to meet: no more than three years of employment can be required as a condition of participation, and, after the three years, employees must participate in the plan on the first day of the next plan year. Of course, employees cannot be unreasonably left out of the plan because of their employment classification (e.g., clerical or warehouse, etc.).

LIMITS ON CAFETERIA AMOUNTS

The revenue code does not state any dollar limit on cafeteria plan benefits *per se;* however, *other* sections of the law place other restrictions and limits on certain of those cafeteria snacks, meals, and desserts.

Group term life insurance can be purchased through the plan but is limited to $50,000 coverage per employee (Code Section 79), just as if it were purchased outside the plan. If more than $50,000 is purchased on any single employee, the cost of the excess coverage is determined by a special IRS insurance cost table and that amount is taxable to the employee.

> ***TAXTIP***
>
> The IRS tables are not favorable for over $50,000 coverage.

Similarly, only a maximum of $5,000 a year can be paid for qualified dependent care (Code Section 129) and special rules cover eligibility, reporting on the employee's tax return, and so forth. A further requirement is that at least *55 percent* of the benefits paid must be for *nonhighly* compensated employees.

Medical insurance premiums and reimbursements for uninsured medical expenses are not limited in amount, but these plans must also meet special nondiscrimination rules.

Contributions to a 401(k) plan are limited to $9,240 for 1994 (adjusted upward annually for inflation), and these plans are subject to the same nondiscrimination rules as the cafeteria plans.

Disability insurance premiums are not limited in amount, but you should be aware of a potential taxtrap.

> *TAXTRAP*
>
> If the employer pays and *deducts* the premiums, any disability benefits then received by the employee are *taxable.* If the employee pays the premiums directly, indirectly, or by payroll deduction, any disability benefits then received are *non*taxable. Think that one over.

You *could* adopt a cafeteria plan with a rather high limit (e.g., $25,000 or more for each employee), but you have to conform to the additional restrictions noted above.

RECORDKEEPING AND REPORTING

The necessary recordkeeping and reporting is about equal to any retirement plan, and the same IRS Form series 5500 must be filed each year for every cafeteria plan. A quote from the IRS:

> Reporting requirements. Every employer that maintains a cafeteria plan is required to keep complete records showing: 1) The number of employees of the employer. 2) The number of employees eligible to participate in the plan. 3) The number of employees participating in the plan. 4) The total cost of the plan for the tax year. 5) The name, address, and TIN [tax identification number] of the employer. 6) The type of business in which the employer is engaged. 7) The number of highly compensated employees who are employed, the number who are eligible to participate in the plan, and the number who do participate in the plan.

Additionally, the plan must be written and describe the benefits, coverage, eligibility, and so forth, and records must be kept of each employee's compensation, contributions to the plan, and benefits paid. Remember, to avoid taxation, a participant must elect the cafeteria benefits *before* the cash benefits (i.e., wages) have been earned, meaning "due and payable."

The employer company pays into the plan the stated amount for each employee. Then, the plan pays the cafeteria benefits and, at the end of each plan year, any excess or unused funds are returned to the employer. The employer gets a tax deduction for the net payments to the plan, just as if they were contributions to a qualified retirement plan.

A fair amount of new recordkeeping and complexities. Is it worth it? Let's consider some pros and cons.

PLAN CONSIDERATIONS

The employer may hold on to employees better if a cafeteria plan is offered, as the plan can meet individual needs. Another big plus is that the Social Security/Medicare tax costs of the employer and employee will be reduced since the salary reduction amount of the cafeteria plan is not subject to those taxes (however, 401(k) contributions *are* subject to Social Security/Medicare taxes). Besides Social Security/ Medicare taxes, employees also save on income taxes because of the salary reductions in the cafeteria plan.

Once again, the big drawbacks for employers are the onerous IRS recordkeeping and reporting requirements. Make no mistake about it, this is just like adopting another retirement plan as far as IRS requirements are concerned. It's a big pain but well worth it to some employers! See your advisers and consider going down the cafeteria counter.

MY CAFETERIA OPINION

I particularly like the cafeteria plan if you have a 401(k) plan and you can just fold it into an overall cafeteria plan. This makes the cafeteria plan much more attractive, since you have already set up a plan with recordkeeping and conformed to the nondiscrimination rules. So, in my opinion, the first people to consider a cafeteria plan are those who already *have* a 401(k) plan. The next group are those about to install a 401(k) plan. The rest of you can at least consider the cafeteria plan in light of your overall tax planning. Remember, a cafeteria plan offers a way to control the medical insurance costs of employees, which may be a major objective for some employers.

WITHHOLDING ON RETIREMENT PLAN DISTRIBUTIONS

As of January 1, 1993, a mandatory 20 percent withholding is in effect on almost all retirement plan distributions paid to the individual rather than directly to a financial institution (i.e., to a rollover IRA or even to another plan). This law applies even if the employee intends to and does roll over the distribution within 60 days. In other words, it is now virtually impossible to get your hands on a retirement plan check made out to *you* without that distribution being reduced by the mandatory 20 percent withholding!

For example, in January 1994, you receive a check for your lump-sum distribution of $10,000 from a profit-sharing plan. However, the check is for $8,000 because of the compulsory 20 percent withholding tax. To avoid being taxed on that distribution, you must place it in a rollover IRA within 60 days of the postmark date on the envelope containing the check. You intend to do so. However, you have only $8,000. How can you roll over the $10,000 distribution? Your choices are to:

• Roll over only the $8,000, in which case when tax time comes around on April 15, 1995, you will owe the taxes on the $2,000 portion of the distribution that you "kept" (you will also have credit for $2,000 in income tax withheld). You may also be liable for a 10 percent IRS penalty on that $2,000, as a premature distribution, if you were under age 59 in January 1994. You may also be liable for a state income tax penalty (2.5 percent in California) on that premature distribution. Finally, realize that your rollover account, earning interest tax-deferred to retirement, has *shrunk* by 20 percent ($8,000 went into it and not $10,000).

• Put up an additional $2,000 out of your own funds and roll over the total $10,000. This will cause an immediate personal cash drain on you, and you will only get credit for that $2,000, in the form of additional tax withheld when you file your tax return 15 months later on April 15, 1995.

THE WITHHOLDING SOLUTION

The IRS pushed for this new law to prevent you from having 60 days to play with a distribution before it had to be rolled over. In my opinion, neither of the preceding solutions make any sense. So choose one of the following alternatives so as *not* to be subject to the 20 percent withholding tax:

• Have the funds transferred *directly* by your employer to a rollover IRA or another qualified plan. That's what the IRS wants to force you to do, and this action indeed eliminates the 20 percent withholding.

• If directly transferred to a rollover IRA, *then* you can withdraw funds from *that IRA* without the mandatory 20 percent withholding, since this withholding rule does *not* apply to *IRA* distributions). Of course, you may still be liable for the penalty if you are under age 59½.

• Leave the money in your former employer's plan for now (if possible) where it will continue to grow tax deferred. At some future date have the direct transfer made.

• Begin periodic withdrawals of the funds now. If the distributions continue to age 59 or for five years, whichever is later, there is no 10 percent premature distribution penalty, and you will only pay regular income tax on the portion received each year.

About the only good news is that this law now permits you to roll over *partial* distributions into an IRA; the previous law allowed this if the rollover distribution was at least 50 percent of the balance of the plan. My advice is to always use a *separate* rollover IRA when you transfer such funds, or you lose the right to later transfer to a new employer's retirement plan or to elect averaging when the money is finally withdrawn.

The new law simply makes it uneconomical for anyone who intends to roll over the full distribution to receive and hold it for 60 days. Use one of the four preceding options only. If you intend to keep and pay tax on part of a distribution you can receive the funds directly, keeping in mind that there will be 20 percent withholding, and you then must plan accordingly.

There is some talk about getting this onerous new withholding law canceled. If that does happen by the time you read this, save this information for that future day when they again reinstate such withholding!

RETIREMENT PLANS AND PERSONAL BANKRUPTCY

Please reread the last point on page 94. To reiterate, you will lose all bankruptcy and creditor protection of your plan assets if you either roll them over from an ERISA-qualified plan to a rollover IRA or adopt and keep your retirement assets in a SEP or a Keogh, which has no other participants except the owner (or owner and spouse).

Accordingly, any ERISA-qualified plan participant with serious financial problems who is nearing or contemplating bankruptcy should seek legal advice before *ever* rolling retirement plan funds from an employer's plan into an IRA. And understand that your assets in a SEP are without any protection from creditors. This is your second and final warning!

CONCLUSION

As stated at the beginning of this chapter, retirement plans offer the primary or only security for most sales reps. I cannot urge you strongly enough to consider setting up one or more plans immediately. If you already have these plans in place, you now have a brief look at possible penalty taxes lurking about, and if you indeed have large amounts already accumulated by all means do some estate planning (see Chapter 23). Remember, this entire, long chapter is just the briefest overview of the most complicated topic we will discuss in this book. The advice in this chapter may be your best opportunity to end up rich!

Chapter Eleven

The New Threat to Retirement Plan Bank Accounts and Other News

A law took effect on December 19, 1993, that changed the Federal Deposit Insurance Corporation (FDIC) insurance coverage for bank accounts of IRAs, Keoghs, 401(k) plans, and 457 (nonprofit organization) plans. Before you think this may not apply to you, remember that many corporate retirement plan accounts end up *rolled over* into IRA accounts by the individual participants.

Effective December 19, 1993, for all those accounts, the FDIC only insures \$100,000 total *per individual, at any one bank,* instead of \$100,000 *for each account*. For example, if one individual depositor has \$150,000 spread over three IRA, Keogh, and 401(k) retirement plan accounts *at the same bank,* and the bank fails, she would lose \$50,000 (\$150,000 total accounts − \$100,000 maximum FDIC insurance = \$50,000 not insured). Under the old rules you were perfectly safe, since the insurance coverage was \$100,000 *per account*.

Keep in mind that this new rule *only* affects IRAs, Keoghs, 401(k), and 457 accounts (all being the so-called self-directed accounts) and not the traditional *corporate* pension and profit-sharing accounts (see below).

TAXTIP

If you do have that much money in bank accounts, currently drawing the pitiful interest they pay, consider putting some of the money into conservative mutual funds such as stocks, bonds, and US Treasuries. Our firm generally recommends the Vanguard funds, since they traditionally have the lowest operating expenses of all funds and are also "no load" (no commission when buying *or* selling their funds). Sometime in 1993, the assets

(continued)

---

of all mutual funds exceeded *$2 trillion!* I'm not sure exactly how much this is, or how many zeros go after the "2," but I do know it's even more than I owe on all my credit cards! In any event, a lot of smart money seems to be leaving banks for mutual funds of all kinds. (The banks are fighting back by starting their *own* mutual funds.)

Finally, there is even a threat to *corporate* retirement plans, traditionally considered insured by the FDIC up to $100,000 per *participant*. This is a tough one to interpret, since the FDIC says (effective December 1992) they will only continue this full "pass-thru" insurance for certain "well capitalized" banks or "adequately capitalized banks that meet additional requirements." For banks that do not meet the criteria there will only be $100,000 FDIC insurance *per pension plan* and not per individual participant. How is the poor rep supposed to know which bank is which?

Well, the latest "clarification" goes like this (my emphasis):

> The FDIC insurance will continue to be available to each participant in a plan, *only if* the financial institution is eligible to accept broker deposits *or* if it is adequately capitalized.

The warning is that if you, the employer, are the plan fiduciary, *YOU are responsible* for determining the capital status of the FDIC insured institution. You are advised to check into this matter immediately!

TAXTIP

You are virtually *forced* to concentrate your pension plan assets into very strong banks if banks are where you want to keep these assets at all. Otherwise, if "superconservative" is your name consider direct investments in US Treasury obligations, zero-coupon US Treasury bonds, or US Treasury money market funds (like Vanguard), all direct obligations of the federal government. Many clients ask us where I keep my own retirement plan assets and the answer is: 100 percent in various US Treasuries. I am admittedly very, very conservative, but if I were 10 years younger I would probably invest most of it in assorted mutual funds stock.

INDEPENDENT CONTRACTOR AUDITS

The bad news is that the IRS is *increasing* its independent contractor audits, despite the many complaints from small businesses. It is now instructing its field agents to specifically search for "employees who are misclassified as independent contractors" in *every audit* they perform!

The IRS is being so headstrong because they have been repeatedly stung by certain taxpayer protections granted in a 1978 law. This law frequently *bars* the IRS from reclassifying independent contractors as employees if, among other things, there was a *previous* IRS audit and "no worker in substantially the same position was reclassified from independent contractor to employee" (Code Section 530). This protection can apply *even if the previous audit did not even address or examine that issue!*

As mentioned in an earlier chapter, the IRS hates that provision, and to fight back they are determined to *never* conduct another field audit without considering the independent contractor issue. Bad news for sales reps who are *still* treating all (or most) of their salespersons as independent contractors! In our recent experiences with IRS field audits, we find that many of the auditors *begin* the audit with an examination of payroll tax returns and a review of every independent contractor reported on information return Form 1099. That not only gets this mandatory part of the examination out of the way but it also provides an early indication to the IRS auditor if she is going to easily pick up some "big money" in this area. Which the IRS loves.

> ***TAXTIP***
>
> If you *do* catch an IRS field audit and you *do* suffer a major reclassification of independent contractors to employees, refer your CPA to the following IRS Code sections for possible substantial tax savings under various "mitigation" provisions: Section 530, the "safe harbor"; Section 3402(d), for income tax relief; Section 6521, for FICA relief; Section 3509, for reduced liability relief; and Section 6250, for interest relief.

The various *states* are *not* bound by these rules. From our own experience, California state auditors ignore these federal statutes as do many other state auditors. This problem ain't gonna' go away.

DEDUCTING 100 PERCENT OF HEALTH INSURANCE PREMIUMS WHEN YOU ARE NOT INCORPORATED

Self-employed individuals are only allowed to deduct 25 percent of their health insurance premiums. If they are employees of their own corporations, the corporation can deduct 100 percent of the premiums. Not a very fair arrangement.

Here is an alternative method that can achieve the same 100 percent tax deduction for unincorporated individuals (who file Schedule C):

1. *Hire your spouse* as a bona fide employee.
2. Obtain a health insurance policy that covers "employees and *spouses* of employees."
3. Have your *spouse* cover *you* under the policy.

Now 100 percent of the health insurance premiums would be tax-deductible since you can fully deduct health insurance premiums paid for *employees* as long as the regular rules for employees' tax-free fringe benefits are met.

> ***TAXTIP***
>
> This arrangement will *not* work for partners in partnerships or S corporation owners, but it *was* approved in IRS Revenue Ruling 71-588 for proprietorships.

THE DREADED TAXPAYER COMPLIANCE MEASUREMENT PROGRAM AUDITS WILL CONTINUE

The IRS had planned to phase out Taxpayer Compliance Measurement Program (TCMP) audits in which they audit every single line of your tax return. There are about 50,000 of such audits every three years. Unfortunately, the General Accounting Office says they are "very useful in measuring taxpayer behavior," so the IRS will continue them.

UNREIMBURSED PARTNERSHIP EXPENSES

The IRS has now ruled that a partner can deduct partnership expenses on his *personal* tax return *if* there is an *agreement* that these expenses are *not* to be reimbursed by the partnership. Further, because these are business expenses of the partner, they can be deducted from the individual's *gross* income and the 2 percent of income disallowance for miscellaneous itemized deductions can be avoided.

TAXTIP

Remember, the partner must be *required* to pay certain partnership expenses out of his own funds, *without* a right to reimbursement, to achieve this beneficial tax effect.

However, for the average sales rep in a partnership, the best arrangement is still to have *all* business expenses reimbursed or paid directly by the partnership, and the same is true no matter what the form of your rep business.

TAXTIP

Always take your expense reimbursements *first* and taxable compensation *last*. And if you can't take 100 percent of both, reduce only your *taxable* compensation. That's always the best procedure taxwise.

BUSINESS TRAVEL

A reminder that, effective January 1, 1993, the law was changed to eliminate business travel expense deductions for business travel to one place for *longer than one year*. For example, if a sales employee of a rep firm were sent from Los Angeles to *reside* in the Phoenix area for 18 months and then to return to Los Angeles, this would be considered a *permanent* move (over 12 months) and housing, meals, and so forth would not be tax-deductible. Before the new ruling, if you took the position that the move was temporary (and the employee did in fact return), you could usually claim all those wonderful travel expense deductions even if the period of time was more than 12 months. Now it's only possible for a "temporary assignment" of one year or less.

For 1994, the IRS "no questions asked" flat daily travel allowance to cover lodging, meals, and incidentals was raised to $95 a day generally and to $152 for "high cost" areas. "High costers," as you might guess, include New York City, Los Angeles, Chicago, Boston, Philadelphia, Washington, DC, and San Francisco. All the employee needs to do is establish the time, place, and business purpose of the trip. Receipts are not required (not even for lodging).

The per diem IRS travel allowance rules are akin to the 1994 rate of 29¢ per business mile auto allowance in that they are "deemed substantiated and accounted for." Per diem travel allowances can be paid, instead of actual expenses, to all employees except *owners of over 10 percent* of your rep firm. This avoids the usual documentation hassle for business travel expenses and should be a welcome alternative for rep firms trying to control business travel expenses. To emphasize: This flat reimbursement is deductible by the employer *and* tax-free to the employee.

HOME OFFICE DEDUCTIONS

The 1993 Supreme Court *Soliman* decision drastically cut the possibility of home office deductions for most sales reps. The Tax Court has continued this trend with a recent decision (Crawford, TC Memo. 1993-192).

In the *Soliman* case, Soliman saw *no* patients at his home office, which otherwise could have been the loophole that permits a home office deduction. In this new case, a doctor *occasionally* saw patients in an office in his home, but the Tax Court said the home office was not his *principal* place of business since he spent 75 percent of his time ("bulk of the workday") at hospitals. Ergo, no home office tax deduction. This trend will continue, and the reps who spend the bulk of their workday in the field, selling their brains out, will be major losers.

IRS AUDITS

Five "special audit targets" were announced by the IRS because they have low levels of compliance and handle lots of cash. They are: auto dealers, commercial fishers, lawyers, morticians, and taxi drivers.

More important to sales reps, the IRS will be issuing special audit guides on other business lines including: *entertainment,* travel agencies, garment manufacturers/contractors, trucking, gas stations, and laundromats.

As you can see, the audit thrust continues against businesses that handle a lot of cash as well as businesses where there have been other abuses. The entertainment issue has always been a rep area that stood out because of both abuses and poor recordkeeping. This new crackdown, coupled with entertainment expense deductions lowered to 50 percent, should give every rep *more* incentive to improve recordkeeping and receipt habits. There is a lot of money at stake!

Chapter Twelve

The Form of Your Business: The "Regular" (C) Corporation

Probably 75 percent of our reader-owners are already operating as corporations (the Electronics Representatives Association states that 94 percent of its members are incorporated). This chapter should be used by all those who *are* incorporated as both a checklist to see if you have fully utilized your corporation and taken advantage of every fringe benefit and option available to you, and to verify that you are operating in accordance with all the corporate requirements. In other words, to see what you are doing right, to add some new ideas, and to avoid the pitfalls of corporate existence. For those presently *not* incorporated, this chapter may well change your mind, or, perhaps, the new limited liability company may catch your interest.

A NEW TYPE OF BUSINESS ENTITY: THE LIMITED LIABILITY COMPANY

Before we go into a discussion of the traditional C corporation, let me point out a new type of business entity that you may want to consider or check out with your lawyer and CPA. This is the limited liability company (LLC). It is a hybrid kind of entity that is an alternative to C corporations, S corporations, or partnerships (it is not a substitute for proprietorships, since it must have two or more owners). It offers some of the best of two worlds.

LLCs are taxed like partnerships, but provide the limited liability of corporations! Thus, they deliver the limited liability that is missing in general partnerships (see Chapter 14 for the potential double liability of partners). The LLC also avoids the tricky tax rules of S corporations (see Chapter 13) as well as the potential double taxation of C corporation earnings (discussed below).

If you reside in one of about 30 states that have adopted or will shortly adopt LLC laws, it's something new to consider. Compare the LLC to the tax advantages and disadvantages (and even fringe benefit options) discussed in these chapters. First read about the various traditional forms of business entities so you have a basis for comparison. This will help you understand why I don't feel the double taxation of C corporation profits is really much of a threat for the average rep firm (if you are worried, also see Chapter 16 on how to "zero out"). I suspect that the IRS may limit the fringe benefits of the LLC owners just as they do in S corporations and in partnerships. Again, check with your own tax advisers and consider all the business alternatives before you decide.

Now let's go into a discussion of the C corporation, which is my general favorite for reasons you will discover.

WHAT IS IT AND WHAT DOES IT DO?

A corporation is a legal entity established by compliance with state laws. It can be thought of as an artificial person, created for the purpose of conducting business. The corporation can hire employees, enter into contracts, acquire assets, incur debt, pay taxes, and be sued. It issues shares of its stock as evidence of ownership to those persons who contribute the money (or assets), which the corporation will use to conduct its business. It can have any number of shareholders or just one.

WHY INCORPORATE?

The main reason for incorporation is usually to limit the *personal liability* of the owners for the debts, taxes, and other liabilities of the business to the amount they have invested. It also can provide the owners with a personal shield against product and other liability claims. Generally, shareholders in a corporation are not personally liable for claims against the corporation and are at risk only to the extent of their investment in the corporation.

Similarly, the officers and directors of the corporation are not liable for the corporation's debts, although in some cases they may be held liable for failure to withhold and pay the income taxes from employees' wages (many states have similar laws regarding employees' withheld income taxes, and California also has a comparable rule regarding sales taxes).

Another reason for incorporation may be to obtain the many fringe benefits that are tax-deductible by the corporation and tax-free to the individual employee (including the owner). In many cases these fringe benefits *cannot* be treated in the same tax beneficial manner for the unincorporated (these benefits are discussed in detail later).

Finally, many business owners incorporate because they are attracted to some or all of the following corporate features.

- *Perpetual Life.* The continuity of the operation is not interrupted by the death of a shareholder or transfers of interest (i.e., changes in shareholders). Creditors, suppliers, principals, and customers often prefer to deal with a corporation because of the assured continuity that is implied by the corporate form.
- *Limited Liability.* In general and under normal circumstances, liability is limited to the corporate assets only, and the legal exposure/liability of the individual shareholders is limited to their investment in the corporation.
- *Management Is Centralized.* The elected officers and the board of directors run the company.
- *Ease of Transferability of Ownership.* Stock transfers for any amount can happen at any time and do not affect the operations or continuity of the corporation. This can even include the sale or merger of the entire business (essentially, you just hand over the stock certificates).
- *Title to Property.* Title is held by the corporation.
- *Your Investment.* Your investment in the capital stock of the corporation cannot be easily withdrawn, although it can be sold (see above).

TAX CONSIDERATIONS

The net income of a corporation may be subject to double taxation in that the corporation first pays federal taxes on that net income at graduated rates of 15 percent on the first $50,000, 25 percent on the next $25,000, 34 percent on the next $25,000, 39 percent on the next $235,000, 34 percent from $335,000 to $10 million, and 35 percent over $10 million (if any reps are interested in that last figure). If the corporation then declares and pays dividends from those earnings, those profits are taxed *again* as ordinary income to the shareholder.

However, in most sales rep and other service corporations, there is usually minimal or no taxable income remaining after paying the compensation of the officers (who are usually the shareholders) and the tax-deductible retirement plan contributions.

In similar fashion, even for many small nonservice corporations engaged in manufacturing, distribution, or retailing, dividends are rarely declared as these companies must retain every dollar to build working capital, expand facilities, carry inventories, and so forth. In such cases there is only a single corporate tax paid and again the threat of double taxation is really moot. As one tax book states, "Most incorporated small businesses, with good tax planning, can avoid double taxation and can often use the corporation to actually *save* taxes."

Taxes can really be minimized since income is "split" between the shareholders and the corporation, and both sides stay out of higher tax brackets. Say the corporation has net profits of $150,000, before the only owner/officer's salary. If a $75,000 salary is paid, the owner is taxed on $75,000 and the corporation is taxed on the other $75,000. Neither is in a very high tax bracket and the working capital of the corporation is being increased by the net income retained.

In the corporate form, all payroll tax costs can be saved to the extent legitimate payments are made to the shareholders for rent or interest instead of salary. Additionally, the shareholders can further benefit if they can offset that rental income with other rental losses, or if they can offset that interest (i.e., "investment") income with other investment expenses. You could personally end up with essentially tax-free income *and* your corporation could get a tax deduction! See your tax adviser for a full explanation (and see the later discussion in this chapter on real estate ownership).

Even the corporate fringe benefits (see pages 135–138) may be a tax motive for incorporation. Some of these fringes can be so material in amount that they are received instead of taxable salary (particularly by owners).

Dividends received by the corporation on stocks it owns of other companies generally receive a 70 percent federal tax exemption in the form of a deduction from taxable income. This allows accumulation of such income at very low tax rates. For example, if the corporation receives $1,000 in dividends from IBM and AT&T, only $300 ($1,000 less the 70 percent deduction) will be included in the taxable income of the corporation. If the corporation is in a 15 percent tax bracket, the tax on the dividends is only $45 (15% × $300), a 4.5 percent tax rate! As the birdie said, "Cheep, cheep!" Think about this method of investing surplus corporate funds rather than in fully taxable interest obligations.

TAXTIP

This 70 percent deduction will be reduced if your corporation borrows money (and pays interest) to purchase dividend-paying stocks.

Finally, the continual and horrendous IRS audits of unincorporated (Schedule C) businesses is driving some business proprietors to consider incorporation for that reason *alone*. IRS audits of Schedule C are 4 to 6 times as frequent as IRS audits of small business corporations! Additionally, the scope and intensity of the Schedule C audit is much greater and more difficult and costly to handle than that of a small corporation.

SELECT A FISCAL (NOT CALENDAR) YEAR

All C corporations (except a special category of "qualified personal service corporations") can select a fiscal year for tax reporting purposes. There are generally tax advantages in doing so, and we virtually always recommend a *fiscal* rather than a calendar year-end for all sales agencies.

For example, assume your corporation reports on a July 31 fiscal year and also assume that there are bonuses payable for that year to the officers/shareholders. If the corporation reports on a cash basis or if the officers/shareholders own over 50 percent of the stock, the bonuses, if paid in July, are deductible in the fiscal year ending July 31; but if you pay them in August, they are deductible in the following fiscal year that began August 1. The timing of corporate tax deductions can lead to some clever tax planning. However, *payout timing does not matter to the individuals receiving the bonuses,* since in either event they will report those bonuses in their *calendar* year of January through December.

Only eight special qualified personal service corporations, which do not include reps, cannot select a fiscal year, and they also pay a *flat* 35 percent tax on all net corporate income. These eight are those performing 95 percent or more of their services in the fields of: law, health (medicine), accounting, engineering, architecture, actuarial science, performing arts, or consulting. Note that you sales reps are not in one of those eight categories and *can* select a fiscal year. Do it!

It can be highly advantageous to select a fiscal year that ends with the close of your "cycle of business activity." In theory, this is when commissions receivable and business activity in general are at a low point and just before a new business cycle begins. For many sales agencies, spring or summer is the low point and September is considered the beginning of the business year.

Consult with your accountant before you make the fiscal year selection and don't think this is a minor decision. Once you do pick the fiscal year, you cannot change it without permission of the Commissioner of Internal Revenue (permission is frequently denied). Do you really want to go through that IRS begging process and call all that attention to your company? Since my religious persuasion is "devout cowardice," I don't!

USE THE CASH METHOD OF TAX REPORTING

Whenever possible, the *cash* method of tax reporting should be elected! In general, sales reps and any other service business can opt for the cash method as long as their gross receipts (commissions, not sales) average less than $5 million. The eight special personal service categories listed earlier (and farming corporations) can generally report on a cash basis no matter how high their gross receipts may be. (This special break was put in the law for the particular benefit of the large national CPA firms. As you can see, *they* know the tax benefits of cash basis reporting, so learn from them!)

If inventories (i.e., purchases) are a "material income-producing factor," the company *must* use the accrual method of tax reporting. This includes manufacturers/assemblers and wholesaler and retailer since their businesses are always inventory intensive (but see your CPA for the possible use of the combination hybrid method).

Selecting the cash method of reporting offers even more potential tax-saving advantages than selecting a fiscal year! Since you reps can qualify for cash basis reporting, grab it! Again, if you are already using the accrual method, you must state your reasons and request permission of the Commissioner of Internal Revenue to change to the cash method. Be sure and tell them the reason is "to pay less taxes," since that will make a big hit with the IRS (just kidding)!

FRINGE BENEFITS

As a generalization, the best and the most fringe benefits obtainable from any form of business can be procured for the owners (officers/shareholders) of a regular (C, not S) corporation. (C corporations are governed by Subchapter C of the Internal Revenue Code, while those S corporations are controlled by Subchapter S.) However, because many such benefits are only available to employees and not sole proprietors, partners, *or even S corporations*, the owner must incorporate in order to be legally classified as an employee.

Consider the following C fringe benefits as fully tax-deductible by the C corporation and fully tax-free to the individual employee receiving or profiting from the benefit:

• Group medical and dental insurance, which must be nondiscriminatory in coverage. You cannot provide greater benefits to officers or "highly compensated individuals" than you offer the rank and file. However, higher premiums paid for older employees are not considered discriminatory. The employee is not required to include either the cost of the premiums or the benefits paid by the insurer in taxable income (and dependent coverage is optional). Note that, in contrast, the unincorporated, self-employed individual can only deduct 25 percent of health insurance premiums, and even that limited privilege is subject to almost constant review by Congress.

• Disability insurance, which can be purchased for certain individuals only and in virtually any amount.

> ***TAXTIP***
>
> **If the corporation pays the premiums, disability benefits to the employee will be taxable; if the employee pays the premiums, any disability benefits received will be tax-free.**

• A $5,000 tax-free death benefit for the beneficiary of any or every deceased employee. That tax-free payment can be made from the retirement plan account of the demised employee, thus reducing the (eventually taxable) distributions from the plan.

• Up to $50,000 of group term life insurance coverage for every employee.

• Accidental death insurance, which can be purchased for certain individuals only and in virtually any amount.

• A nondiscriminatory self-insured medical reimbursement plan that can pay those expenses not covered by the group medical insurance for employees and even their dependents. It includes, for example, the insurance deductible, the co-insurance percentage portion ("co-pay" in medical insurance jargon), psychiatric services, dental work (which could include orthodontic work and dental implants), medical transportation, prescription glasses and contact lenses, or anything else *not* covered by the group insurance. This arrangement is attractive because medical expenses cannot be deducted on an individual income tax return except for any amounts that may exceed 7.5 percent of adjusted gross income. Although this plan option is frequently overlooked, many employees would prefer, say, $3,000 or $5,000 a year of this medical benefit to $3,000 or $5,000 of taxable salary (an example of how the corporate cafeteria plans work).

• The various corporate retirement plans represent the biggest benefit of all! It is often said that retirement plans are the last great tax shelter. The amounts contributed to each plan, up to certain limits, are not only deductible by the corporation and tax-deferred for the employee, but their earnings compound tax-deferred within the plan. When the funds are finally paid out, at your retirement, you will probably be in a lower tax bracket. Thus, you not only defer the payment of any tax, but the tax you finally pay may be at lower rates. A major difference between C corporation retirement plans and Keogh, SEP, IRA, or S corporation plans lies in the fact that *only* the C corporation employee is able to *borrow* (up to $50,000) from the plan. That's major!

• Qualified dependent care assistance programs, up to $5,000 a year for each employee (however, at least 55 percent of the average benefits provided must be for *nonhighly* compensated employees).

• Company loans of up to $10,000 to any single employee (interest need not be charged or imputed).

• Group legal services.

• Employee discounts.

• Educational benefits, such as scholarships or fellowship grants for employees or their children, up to $5,250 a year per employee (however, not more than 5 percent of the total amount paid out during the year can be for the *owners* of the company).

• Flexible benefit cafeteria plans that offer the employees a choice between taking cash compensation, certain fringe benefits, or a combination of the two (see Chapter 10).

• Company paid parking or parking allowances (up to a maximum of $155 a month for 1993 and then indexed for inflation in monthly increments of $5).

• Business dues (not club dues), subscriptions, and publications.

• Employee gifts up to $25 annually, employee prizes and awards, company parties, holiday gifts, employee eating facilities, employee athletic facilities, supper money when working late, occasional tickets to entertainment events, coffee and breakfast snacks, transit passes, moving expense payments, sick pay, and so forth.

Now consider these additional benefits and working condition fringes that may be fully tax-free or only partially taxable to the employee. They are all highly beneficial to the employee and any taxable income reported by the individual is usually far outweighed by the benefits provided:

- Country club memberships (even though the club dues are no longer deductible).
- Company provided autos.
- Key employee or split-dollar insurance.

- Salary continuation plans.
- Home computer and home telephone.
- Employer-provided transportation to and from work.
- Company trips involving combined business travel and personal vacations.
- See your tax adviser for more of the same!

SECTION 1244 SMALL BUSINESS STOCK

Here is a win-win situation that you should elect at the time of incorporation (it can be difficult later on). A corporation generally qualifies as a small business corporation if, at incorporation, it is capitalized for $1 million or less. In that event, the stock of the company should always be issued pursuant to Section 1244 of the Internal Revenue Code. What does that accomplish?

If the corporation fails (or is failing), any individual owning Section 1244 stock (but not for any other stock) can claim an *ordinary* loss on her individual income tax return, and then offset that loss against all other forms of income being reported. The maximum amount of this ordinary loss that can be claimed in any one year is $100,000 on a joint income tax return or $50,000 on a single filer's income tax return. It is possible to establish and claim worthlessness of *part* of the stock in successive years and thus claim total cumulative ordinary losses of more than the single year limit of $100,000.

You have absolutely nothing to lose by attempting to qualify and set up your original stock issue under Section 1244, and you have everything to gain if the corporation does not succeed. Always do it in every possible case! Further, if you are sitting with apparently worthless small business corporation stock, check into the feasibility of claiming one or more Section 1244 (ordinary loss) write-offs.

PIERCING THE CORPORATE VEIL

This legal term of art describes a dangerous situation when the courts ignore the fact that the corporation is a separate legal entity, and hold the shareholders of the corporation personally liable for actions that were conducted by the corporation (thus "piercing the corporate veil" of liability protection). Since limited liability is one of the most attractive features of doing business in corporate form, you should do everything possible not to get pierced! Piercing generally occurs when the corporation was not adequately capitalized, corporate formalities were not observed, or the corporation was not properly operated, three factors that would have protected the interests of the creditors in a manner to be expected by the standards of normal corporate conduct. While this is primarily a legal matter, in general those three kinds of actions can potentially expose you to the danger.

Corporation Not Adequately Capitalized

In the first action, also called "thin incorporation," or starting a corporation on a shoestring, the courts may hold that you did not start the corporation with enough money to make it a viable legal entity, particularly if very little money was invested in capital stock and large sums of money were borrowed as beginning working capital.

We have dealt with one careful tax attorney who refuses to incorporate even the smallest service business if the initial investment in capital stock is less than $10,000. The IRS takes a very dim view of corporations that begin with shareholder loans exceeding four times (or more) the investment in stock, and under such circumstances the IRS may reclassify some of the loans to capital and then reclassify the related interest payments to nondeductible corporate dividends. Also, the courts may frown on a beginning capitalization with an excess of loans in ratio to the stock (no matter what the source of borrowed funds).

So, incorporating for $100 or $1,000, as I have unfortunately seen some attorneys suggest, is not really a good idea. Neither are beginning ratios showing excess loans.

Corporate Formalities Not Observed

Failure to observe corporate formalities is probably the most common failing in many small business corporations. Too many such reps and other businesspeople treat their corporation as if it were their own pocketbook and virtually ignore the fact it is a separate legal entity. You do so at considerable risk!

Some of the key formalities that should be observed are complete corporate and financial records, written minutes of shareholders' meetings, including approval of the actions of the officers and directors, and written minutes of periodic directors' meetings, including approval of the actions of the officers. Ya gotta' do it!

Corporation Not Properly Operated

As to the final item, acts of fraud or even bad faith can expose you to personal liability. Indeed, the careless withdrawal or corporate funds as shareholder loans (see Chapter 21), without proper documentation or interest payments and while creditors remain unpaid, can be construed as an act of bad faith if not fraud. Repeated payments of the personal expenses of the officers/shareholders fall in the same class, and also can bring down the terrible wrath of the IRS. And, until you've been wrathed by the IRS, you ain't been wrathed at all!

For all the advantages of the corporation, you must understand and remember: it is a separate legal entity that must be dealt with scrupulously and at arm's length. The courts, the creditors, and the IRS are all looking over your shoulder. Consult your lawyer and your CPA before you ever make a questionable corporate move or omit an essential corporate procedure. As simply as I can put it: Don't mess up! I think incorporation is usually well worth it, but you must accept the responsibilities that accompany the many advantages. As I also put it: There ain't no free lunch! So stop snacking and get cracking.

COSTS OF INCORPORATION

There are both initial and recurring costs of incorporation. Initially the corporation will incur legal fees, costs for stock books, minute books, and the corporate seal, state franchise or incorporation fees (in California, the initial $800 franchise tax is refundable only if the corporation ends), and so forth. We estimate that whole package at $1,500 to $3,000 in California, but of course buy-sell agreements, employment agreements, stock options, and so forth can add thousands of dollars to the beginning costs. But you only spend it once!

Remember, these are all legal matters that fall within the province of your attorney. However, do consult with your CPA regarding the possibility of cash basis tax reporting, fiscal year elections, and similar matters that should *not* be decided by your lawyer. Many lawyers seem to love or know only calendar years and S corporations, and they wouldn't know about adopting cash basis tax reporting if you hit them over the head with the cash! Be sure to coordinate your two professional experts when incorporating, and read the next chapter before you even *consider* becoming an S corporation.

The good news is that all these costs of incorporation (and any start-up expenses) can be written off and claimed as a tax deduction within the first 60 months. We do this IRS Section 248 election automatically for all our newly incorporated clients. If there is no such election, these costs can never be deducted until the corporation is dissolved (accountants who fail to make the election should also be hit with whatever you have handy, including their bills for services rendered!).

Additionally, the corporation will also incur annual costs. Many corporate actions must be formalized and minutes must be kept, for example, of shareholders' and directors' meetings. There are annual fees to the state (in California there is a minimum annual franchise tax of $800) and more formal and complete accounting records must be maintained, which is why the IRS audits fewer small corporations than unincorporated proprietorships filing on Schedule C. Of course, I feel that incorporation is well worth it for the many reasons already stated, but this is where some of you start to balk: "Waddya' mean I gotta keep books and spend $3,000 to incorporate! Waddya' nuts?" Please don't just get stubborn and give this more thought.

YOUR FAMILY ON THE BOARD OF DIRECTORS

It is perfectly proper to elect your spouse or adult children to the board of directors of the corporation. As long as they attend board meetings and function in a responsible manner, they can be paid directors' fees. These amounts can be anything from "reasonable" to "reasonably generous" for the services truly performed. (Some board members of public companies receive compensation in the $60,000–$100,000 per year range, whether they attend board meetings or not. Then they put their executive friends on *their* boards, and their friends reciprocate and put them on *their* boards. Next, they vote huge pay raises for the other, and always approve them! And guess who pays that bill?)

Anyway, such directors' fees are considered self-employment income to the recipient and are subject to Social Security/Medicare taxes. However, each board member can then set up a Keogh plan and pay up to a tax-deductible 20 percent of those fees into that retirement plan (or even adopt a defined-benefit Keogh plan with much higher possible contributions). In the case of a spouse, it does not matter if that spouse is covered by a corporate retirement plan because such Keogh contributions are still fully tax-deductible. If there is no corporate retirement plan, the spouse could choose between a Keogh plan and an IRA.

The children have the option of adopting a Keogh plan or an IRA. If directors' fees are minimal, say $2,000 a year, each child could annually pay and then deduct a $2,000 IRA contribution. The only tax cost would be the Social Security/Medicare taxes on the $2,000 (but each is accumulating and compounding $2,000 a year, tax-deferred!). These tax-free fees can be further increased to $5,700 by also using the $3,700 standard deduction against earned income (more in Chapter 29 on this whole topic of family members in your business).

YOUR SPOUSE AS A CORPORATE EMPLOYEE

This is a tough call. If your spouse works full time in the business and if you have a corporate retirement plan, it may be worth it to pay salary to your spouse to obtain the retirement plan benefits. But absent those conditions, the incredibly high costs of payroll taxes, workers' compensation insurance, and possibly higher group medical insurance costs make this generally uneconomic.

It is usually unlikely that the spouse will ever draw Social Security benefits from his own Social Security account, since in most cases the benefit from the other (fully and permanently employed) spouse's Social Security account will be higher. In that common case, all the payroll taxes of the one spouse will be wasted!

Under the conditions of full employment and a good retirement plan only, it may be well worth while to pay your spouse as high a salary as possible and shoot for a high retirement plan contribution (then some "income shifting" could also be considered, but talk it over with your tax adviser before you add your spouse to the payroll). (See Chapter 29 for further discussion.)

YOUR CHILDREN AS CORPORATE EMPLOYEES

Again, high payroll taxes and other costs are sometimes a discouragement, but minimal salaries for minimal services can result in the same benefits as if your children are on your board of directors. About a $2,000 a year salary for part-time work can allow them a $2,000 a year IRA (tax-deductible) contribution. The only tax costs are the payroll taxes but they're minimal, based on the small amount of compensation. As mentioned earlier, each child can be paid an annual $5,700 tax-free, since they can claim their own $3,700 standard deduction against earned income and then deduct a $2,000 IRA contribution as well.

Also consider that if they are old enough and work enough for the corporation, they can earn up to $22,100 and still stay in the 15 percent tax bracket. Again, you must discuss this idea with your tax adviser to consider who claims their exemption, if they are full-time students, their age, their investment income, and so forth. But it is sure worth considering. (See Chapter 29 for further discussion.)

CORPORATE LIFE INSURANCE

Some real magic can be worked with your individual corporation when it comes to life insurance, estate planning, buy-sell agreements, and retirement planning. Some extremely clever but sometimes complicated ideas must be worked out in conjunction with your life insurance agent, your accountant, and a good estate planning attorney. To discuss and explain every possible idea and option would take about 100 pages, so I'll just plant some seeds, sow some ideas, and you take the harvest from there. Here are some of my ideas:

- Key employee insurance is used by the corporation to insure that employee against death. The premiums are not tax-deductible by the corporation, but generally all life insurance proceeds are received free of regular corporation income taxes.
- In a similar manner, many multiple owners of corporations are insured and the proceeds at death are tied into a buy-sell agreement to redeem the corporate stock from the widow or widower.
- Split-dollar insurance (see Chapter 24) represents a very clever way to provide cheap life insurance to employees, since the premium costs are split in a very favorable manner between the corporation (the cash values) and the employee (pure insurance only).
- Deferred compensation plans can be funded by corporate life insurance cash values or by the purchase of annuity policies. (However, check current laws about their present tax treatment, since numerous proposals under consideration will make annuities and tax-free life insurance buildups much less attractive. In general, I don't go for most annuity policies.)

A major complication is the corporate alternative minimum tax (AMT), which is a flat 20 percent tax levied on certain kinds of corporate income and certain deductions. A very simplified explanation (of a very complicated calculation) is that this 20 percent tax will generally be levied on 75 percent of any life insurance proceeds collected by the corporation after a $40,000 exclusion, which slowly phases out and disappears at $310,000 of income. If the corporation collects $100,000 in life insurance proceeds, there is no regular corporation income tax on this sum, but there *could be* an AMT of $15,000 to pay (75% × $100,000 × 20% AMT = $15,000). At best the entire $40,000 exclusion would apply.

There are two solutions to this problem. The first is to increase all your life insurance coverage by enough to cover the AMT. The second (perhaps more common in the case of buy-sell insurance), is to have the individuals cross-insure each other and then bonus them with enough funds to pay the premiums. The individuals will receive the life insurance proceeds completely tax-free, and they then buy out the widow or widower's stock (and get a higher tax basis for that stock in case it is later resold).

In complicated buy-sell arrangements with multiple owners, special partnerships are sometimes formed just to hold the life insurance and collect the proceeds. By now you can see that you really will need some expert advice to do your corporate life insurance planning, but it's well worth it!

RESTRICTED STOCK

Many closely held corporations place restrictions on their stock to prevent the stock from falling into unfriendly hands, to force an ex-employee to sell stock back to the company, or to provide for mandatory redemption of a deceased employee's (including an owner's) stock.

The corporation and its shareholders must be given a chance to equal the best bona fide offer from outside parties ("right of first refusal"). The corporation also has the option to buy the shares at a specified price before they can be sold to an outsider. These situations require the services of your lawyer.

Major restrictions are usually required in a buy-sell agreement between the owners. Such terms will help avoid future litigation, prevent outsiders from gaining ownership of your company, and prevent having the widow as your partner. If you have more than one owner and you ain't got a buy-sell, get one!

My lawyer friends tell me that any restrictions on the shares must be conspicuously noted on the stock certificates themselves. If this is not done, the restrictions against transfers of the shares will usually be unenforceable against an "innocent holder in due course."

ACCUMULATED EARNINGS

Every corporation can accumulate $250,000 in retained earnings without having to pay dividends and without any threat of the accumulated earnings tax. However, in the case of those eight special categories of service businesses described earlier, this exemption drops to $150,000 from the standard $250,000, but not for sales agents.

If additional accumulations above the $250,000 cannot be justified as necessary for future "reasonable needs of the business" (e.g., expansion, working capital, inventories, equipment) a flat penalty tax of 28 percent is imposed on "improperly accumulated earnings."

This tax is in addition to the regular corporate income tax. If you have those kind of funds accumulated, you also have enough money to hire and pay some expert tax advisers!

UNREASONABLE COMPENSATION

Drawing salary (deductible by your corporation) is always preferable to receiving dividends on your corporate stock (not deductible by your corporation). However, if your salary (including bonuses, retirement plan contributions, and fringe benefits) is "unreasonable," the IRS can reclassify part of it to dividends. The tax consequences are very painful!

Generally, until you get to the very large sales agencies, compensation is always "reasonable," since the owner is a major source of the commission income. Only in a rep firm so big that the owner is primarily in administration do we sometimes encounter this problem (see Chapter 22).

LOANS TO SHAREHOLDERS

The IRS does not like it when you borrow money (tax free) from your corporation and don't repay it in an orderly manner, don't pay periodic interest on the borrowing, don't execute notes with a fixed repayment schedule, the loans are in proportion to the stockholdings, or the corporate books do not record the withdrawals as loans. In any and all such cases, there is a clear and present danger that they'll call the loans a "dividend." You'll personally be taxed on those funds and the corporation won't even get a tax deduction! (See Chapter 21.)

Still another danger is if you have an accumulated earnings problem. The very existence of loans to stockholders makes it very difficult to argue that the corporation is accumulating those earnings only for the reasonable needs of the business. A big fat TAXTRAP! A separate line on the corporate tax return (Schedule L balance sheets) gives the IRS the clue. (See Chapter 21.)

OWNERSHIP OF REAL ESTATE

We usually recommend that the real estate occupied by the corporation be individually owned by the shareholders and then leased to the corporation. If the building appreciates, the individuals will profit. Deductions for depreciation, mortgage interest, and other expenses will benefit in some cases by saving actual taxes and in other cases by allowing substantial rental income that can be sheltered from taxes. In all cases, the rent paid should be "reasonable," get some documentation and some rental comparables together for the eventuality of an IRS audit and challenge.

If the individual owner has other real estate investments generating tax losses, a generous, but reasonable, rental from the corporation will result in little or no additional tax liability, since the net income from the one property is offset by the net losses from others. So another tax arranging area unfolds, like flowers welcoming the first rays of the sun! How poetic the planning of taxes can be.

CONCLUSION

These pages offered a checklist for those already incorporated and a discussion for those considering incorporation. Hopefully, everyone has benefited from a careful reading. Remember, this is just an overview of some of the tax planning opportunities that can apply to you and your corporation. There are tremendous openings for estate planning, income splitting, classes of stock, gifting of stock, buy-sell agreements, reducing estate taxes, providing for ownership succession, and dozens more! Use this as your first survey and take it from there.

To sum up, I am a great fan of regular corporations (and full employment for all CPAs!). Now, on to S corporations, which everybody loves but me!

Chapter Thirteen

The Form of Your Business: The S Corporation

The S corporation is no different from the C corporation in terms of limited liability of shareholders, corporate law requirements, unlimited life, or any other aspect except tax treatment. Since all other legal characteristics of C corporations (Chapter 12) are identical for the S corporation, we will limit our discussion in this chapter primarily to the advantages and disadvantages in the *tax treatment* of S corporations. There are many to consider.

While there are clearly benefits in some corporations electing S corporation status, I personally feel that they have been oversold in the case of many small businesses and particularly for the average sales agency. The glib and casual comment to most reps at the time they are incorporating is that "Of course you should go S corporation, you avoid double taxation that way." This refers to the fact that S corporations generally pay no taxes and "flow thru" the profits and losses to shareholders, like a partnership.

However, most rep C corporations pay little or no corporate taxes anyway. Bonuses to owners and other employees, plus retirement plan contributions, usually "zero out" all but the largest sales agencies (see Chapter 16 if you need help). In that event, absent a few special circumstances, the C corporation continues to offer considerable advantages over the S corporation. I know this position is contrary to that of most tax advisers, but rep firms are special animals, and you may be convinced by the time you finish this chapter. (In our accounting firm, we have only three S corporations out of over 100 sales rep clients.)

ADVANTAGES OF THE S CORPORATION

There are unquestionable advantages if you fit these *particular* categories or circumstances:

• Losses incurred by the S corporation, particularly likely in the first few years, can be passed directly thru to the shareholders, deducted (generally) on their personal tax returns, and thus offset their other income. (In such cases, we usually do go S corporation for a few years, but then switch to a C corporation.)

• You avoid the unreasonable compensation (see Chapter 22) of officers problem that sometimes occurs when officers' salaries are so high that there is a risk that the IRS will reclassify part as nondeductible dividends. (This threat is rarely raised in the average rep organization, since in all but the largest firms there is a direct relationship between commission income and the personal sales efforts of each owner/officer.)

• They avoid the accumulated earnings tax (IRS Code Section 531) that may be levied on accumulations of more than $250,000 (but since most rep firms have accumulated earnings in the $100 to $300 range, this is not a threat for the majority of you).

• For the larger rep agency, an S corporation can continue to use the cash method of accounting after gross receipts exceed $5 million, while the C corporation *cannot*. So when the sales agency tops $100 million in sales at an average 5 percent commission rate this can indeed be a big deal. (However, we usually wait and switch to S corporation status at the last legal minute, which is only after the *three-year average* exceeds the $5 million.)

• It avoids the flat 20 percent alternative minimum tax (AMT) for corporations, which can be levied (after a $40,000 exemption) on such items as corporate life insurance proceeds, and/or 75 percent of the excess of "book" income over taxable income, plus municipal bond interest, all dividends, and a number of other "preferences."

> ***TAXTIP***
>
> In a C corporation, if you do have corporate life insurance on an officer or shareholder who is quite ill, you should quickly consider a possible S corporation election or, with good tax advice, transfer the policies out of the corporation.

• The "book" income problem is a constant pain. Whenever any sales agency corporation is seeking a bank loan, the bank frequently asks for an accrual basis financial statement although we keep the books on the cash basis (see Chapter 26). Usually that statement shows a higher profit, since we zeroed out on the cash basis for tax purposes. That accrual basis financial statement can then be used by the IRS as proof of "book" income and the AMT levied on 75 percent of the difference between "book" and "tax" income (after the $40,000 exemption).

TAXTIP

Most bankers don't seem to understand the AMT danger at *all*, so we tactfully try to explain and then ask that they accept an accrual basis financial statement that is not prepared at the fiscal year-end, but rather for an interim period. That very act could avoid the AMT trap! (See Chapter 26 for an entire "banker" discussion.)

• By gifting S corporation shares to other family members, the profits of the S corporation will be divided among a number of individuals based on their percentage of ownership. This can limit the profits the original owner will be taxed on but still keeps the money in the family, and those profits are frequently taxed in lower brackets as they are spread around the family.

TAXTIP

This income will be passive income to the other family members who are not active in the business, so only gift it to those dependents age 14 or older (or it will still be taxed at your highest tax bracket). Those cash distributions to children could even be used to pay their college education! (However, the operator of the business must draw a "reasonable" salary and not just split all the corporation income with the other shareholders; more on that later.)

TAXTIP

The fact that passive income can be passed thru to certain shareholders provides a tax planning opportunity. If those same shareholders have passive *losses* from other investments (i.e., old "tax shelter" partnerships), they can then offset one against the other. In such circumstances, the result can be that all the income from the S corporation is tax-free to that individual.

TAXTIP

With an overall top corporate rate of 35 percent, a top personal income tax rate of 39.6 percent, plus the itemized deduction and exemption

(continued)

phaseouts, some individual taxpayers can reach an effective tax rate of around 41 percent. Therefore, if you want to keep the profits *in* the business and at generally *lower* tax rates, the C corporation is the way to go. (Before the Revenue Reconciliation Act of 1993 raised individual tax rates *above* the corporate rates, this was generally not true.)

• If you are bonusing or selling stock in your corporation to key employees, the S corporation election may provide a substantial monetary benefit to those employees, since they will also receive their pro rata share of any S corporate profits as well. (See Chapter 33.) Keep in mind that this idea will really benefit the other employees and not the owners.

DISADVANTAGES OF THE S CORPORATION

Let me count the ways:

1. There is no possibility of income-splitting between the owner and the S corporation, as can be accomplished with the C corporation, since *all* the income is taxed to the individual shareholder (whether distributed in cash or not).

2. Health insurance premiums paid by the S corporation receive extremely unfavorable tax treatment for "2 percent or more" shareholders. While such premiums are deductible by the S corporation, that same amount becomes taxable income to those shareholders and must be reported as such on Form W-2. However, the IRS finally decided the premiums are not subject to Social Security/Medicare taxes, after much flip-flopping back and forth. The shareholder is limited to a *possible* maximum tax deduction of only 25 percent of that premium. However, even that 25 percent deduction is lost if the amount to be deducted is more than the wages received from the S corporation (e.g., a family member who receives no salary, but owns 5 percent of the stock). The 25 percent deduction is also lost if the shareholder or spouse is eligible to participate in another health plan of another employer. In either of those cases, the entire premium paid is taxable income to the shareholder, but there is no individual tax deduction at all (in the best of circumstances only 25 percent is deductible). This is a big, big negative. (However, there is some talk in Congress about repealing this provision, as well as the following points, but you never know.)

3. Owners of 5 percent or more of the S corporation's stock cannot borrow directly or indirectly from the corporate retirement plan. In a

C corporation there is no such restriction, and borrowings of up to $50,000 are permitted.

> ***TAXTIP***
>
> If you are presently operating as a C corporation and plan to elect S corporation status, you must *repay* any such loans before the election is operative. Otherwise, you are in violation of this rule and subject to penalties and even possible disqualification of your entire retirement plan!

4. There is no 70 percent deduction for dividends received on other corporations' stock as there is for C corporations.
5. Most S corporations *must* use a calendar year. There are complicated and involved rules plus special required tax payments for any S corporations that elect to report on a fiscal year.
6. The S corporation cannot have an employee stock ownership plan (ESOP).
7. Certain states do not recognize S corporation status and continue to tax them as regular corporations. Thus, federally tax-free S distributions may be subject to state taxes. Some states that recognize S corporations still levy a special or minimum franchise tax (e.g., California, $800) or a flat percentage tax on profits (e.g., California, 2.5 percent); and some states are considering going back to nonrecognition of S corporations as a revenue measure.
8. The overall law regarding S corporations is unusually complex. You will require continuing tax advice and monitoring of the business operations to avoid many special tax pitfalls and to maximize tax benefits. You should expect to pay fairly substantial additional legal and accounting fees, or you may otherwise fall into tax traps you did not even know existed! For example, consider the next point.
9. That attractive S corporation feature of passing through and deducting losses on the shareholder's tax return has severe limits. Such losses can only be deducted to the *extent* of the shareholder's investment in the stock of the corporation plus any loans made from the shareholder to the corporation. Once that basis is used up, no further losses can be deducted by the individual, unless further loans are first made to the S corporation once again to increase the basis. Constant monitoring of each shareholder's stock and loan account, accompanied by the related professional fees and other costs to do so, is involved. Also, there are limitations on losses and credits from passive activities. (Complexity, thy name is S corporation!)

TAXTIP

If you do want to loan additional funds to the corporation to increase your basis, don't just personally *guarantee* a bank loan to the corporation, since the IRS won't allow that stratagem (and the Tax Court has upheld the IRS). Instead, borrow the money personally and *then* loan it to the S corporation. Your basis *cannot* be increased by a bank loan that you just guarantee.

10. In addition to the special medical insurance premium problems already discussed, the following other fringe benefits, when paid by the S corporation, are *not* deductible by the corporation but are passed through as taxable income to shareholders of 2 percent or more of the stock: (*a*) accident and disability insurance premiums, (*b*) self-insured medical reimbursement plans, (*c*) group term life insurance of up to $50,000 (Code Section 79), and (*d*) death benefits paid of up to $5,000 (Code Section 101[b]). In effect, the S corporation is treated as if it were a partnership for these and most other purposes.

11. In certain circumstances, an S corporation may still be subject to corporate taxes under quite intricate rules involving (*a*) excess net investment income, (*b*) certain capital gains, (*c*) built-in gains, (*d*) recomputing a prior year's investment credit, and (*e*) last-in first-out (LIFO) inventory valuation method recapture.

12. As mentioned earlier, the Revenue Reconciliation Act of 1993 pushed individual income tax rates *higher* than corporate tax rates, so the previous idea of using an S corporation to take advantage of *lower* individual rates is no longer effective. In the past, this was a major reason for many of the recommendations to elect S corporation status.

TRYING TO AVOID PAYROLL TAXES

A dangerous piece of advice from some tax advisers has been for the actively participating officer/shareholder of the S corporation to refuse any salary. The idea is to avoid all payroll taxes by taking the same funds as S corporation dividend distributions. The apparent loophole is that such payments, even to active shareholders of S corporations, are not subject to self-employment tax (although the same payments, if made to active partners of a partnership, are indeed subject to self-employment tax).

Speaking of "active," the IRS has caught on to this ploy and is "actively" auditing S corporations that do not list any officers' salaries. They are then enforcing a 15-year-old IRS ruling that lets the IRS reclassify shareholder distributions as wages when "appropriate." Then the IRS collects all the applicable payroll taxes, plus penalties and interest!

> ***TAXTIP***
>
> In this same situation, if you take a modest salary, you may avoid being picked for an IRS audit. Further, if you are audited, the IRS agent is faced with the judgment call problem of trying to claim the salary is too small. On the other hand, if you took no salary at all, the IRS agent can set up any salary that appears "reasonable" and *you* are faced with the problem of trying to overcome that IRS assumption. See the difference?

TAX PREDICTION

There is talk in Congress about changing the rules for taxing the S corporation income of active shareholders. The proposal is to tax 100 percent of their income as self-employment income, no matter how much is classified as salary and *regardless* of whether or not the income is actually withdrawn from the corporation. This would put the tax treatment at parity with similar partnership income. My prediction is that this change will come to pass.

QUALIFYING AS AN S CORPORATION

Most sales agencies can qualify and meet the requirements for an S corporation, which essentially are:

• No more than 35 shareholders. (Generally, joint owners are counted separately, except for shares held by husband and wife.)

• It cannot be a member of an affiliated group of corporations or have a subsidiary.

• Only a single class of stock can be issued that confers identical rights to corporate profits and liquidation proceeds to all shareholders. However, within that single class there can be both voting and nonvoting stock, and different terms for transfers, repurchase, and redemption rights of the stock. (This is a big and welcome change over the previous IRS position, which defined a "single class of stock" in much more restrictive terms.)

TAXTIP

You can sometimes do some "tax magic" when you issue *non*voting stock to your children and keep the voting stock for yourself. For example, you could keep 10 shares that represent 100 percent of the voting rights and give 90 shares to your children. Accordingly, they would receive 90 percent of the profits, but you would have 100 percent control. In some cases this diversion of taxable income could be highly beneficial to the owners. This also can be a great way to pass your sales agency on to the next generation and still keep control with as little as one share of voting stock. Of course, you can have the same stock arrangement in a C corporation, but it won't divert the *profits* in the same slick manner. Ask your tax advisers to comment.

- It must be a "domestic" corporation.
- The shareholders can only be individuals, estates, testamentary trusts, grantor trusts, voting trusts, and qualified subchapter S trusts. Partnerships, corporations, and foreign trusts cannot be shareholders.
- Individual shareholders cannot be nonresident aliens.
- Passive investment income (royalties, rents, dividends, and interest) cannot exceed 25 percent of gross receipts, although the IRS now allows certain exceptions for rental income from self-developed real property or where significant services are provided or substantial costs incurred in the rental business.

TAXTIP

These two quite new exceptions provide a fresh opportunity to operate certain kinds of real estate ventures in S corporation form for the first time.

Your tax adviser can steer you thru the rather easy qualifications if you decide to elect an S corporation.

ELECTING AS AN S CORPORATION

Every shareholder must consent in writing to the election. If the election is for the year in which it is made, any person who was a shareholder at any time during the year must consent even if he no longer owns the stock. Because of co-ownership rules and community property laws in some states (like California), most tax advisers (and we) insist that the consent of every spouse be included in all cases (mandatory in community property states).

The election is made on IRS Form 2553 ("election by a small business corporation"), and the form is filed with your applicable IRS Service Center. The shareholder consents should accompany this form. The election is effective for your current tax year provided this form is filed by the 15th day of the third month of the tax year for which the election is to apply. It can also be filed at any time during the previous tax year, effective for the following tax year. If the election and consents are not timely sent by certified mail, return receipt requested, you may live to regret it, and regret it, and regret it!

If you fail to get even *one* shareholder's consent, or necessary spousal consents, your entire election can be ruled invalid. I know of one California case where $600,000 in losses were disallowed because one spouse's name was typed on the consent but they failed to get the actual *signature* on the line next to it. They lived to regret it, and regret it, and regret it!

REVOKING S CORPORATION STATUS

The election can only be revoked by people holding over 50 percent of the stock. The revocation operates under the same timing rules as the election. If made by the 15th day of the third month of the tax year (or earlier) it is effective for that entire year.

> ***TAXTIP***
>
> After that 75 day period, a revocation can be effective on any day specified beginning with the date of the revocation, which affords the opportunity for some special tax planning by diverting personal S corporation income back to the "shelter" of a C corporation.

The revocation is in the form of a statement to the IRS and includes the following information:

- The corporation is revoking its election to be treated as an S corporation under Section 1362(a) of the Internal Revenue Code.
- The number of shares of stock outstanding at this time.
- The specified date of the revocation.

The consents of the shareholders and their number of shares (shares of over 50 percent required) must be attached to the revocation statement. And don't forget spousal consent!

INVOLUNTARY TERMINATION OF S CORPORATION STATUS

Termination occurs when any of the eligibility requirements for S corporation status are violated (e.g., more than 35 shareholders, a subsidiary is acquired, two different classes of stock are issued, another corporation or a partnership acquires some of the stock of the S corporation, and so forth.

When a terminating event occurs, the S corporation loses its status as of *that day* and not retroactively to the beginning of the tax year, which will certainly help provide full employment to CPAs and lawyers! The corporation is required to report the terminating event to the IRS, including the cause and the date. There are certain circumstances under which the IRS can waive inadvertent termination of an election, but you must request and receive permission from the IRS under Code Section 1362(f) to be able to treat the terminating event as if it had never occurred.

Once there is an involuntary termination, the tax year is divided into two segments (before and after) and, in effect, two sets of books must be maintained and two corporate tax returns must be filed: A Form 1120S (S corporation) for the first period and a Form 1120 (C corporation) for the second period. (Lotta' fun and lotta' bucks for your CPA!)

REELECTING S CORPORATION STATUS

In general, after termination of an S election (whether voluntary or involuntary), a corporation must wait five years before making another S election.

CONCLUSION

About as many long books have been written about S corporations as about corporate retirement plans. My best advice is to carefully reread the sections dealing with advantages and disadvantages and then have a discussion with your tax advisers. If they're still uncertain, sell them a copy of this book (including your commission, of course)! Also, keep in mind that the 1993 tax act increased individual income tax rates above corporate tax rates and changed the thinking about S corporations in many circumstances. As I warned in the beginning, the S corporation is not my favorite choice for most sales reps, unless they fit those special circumstances. Now you know why.

Chapter Fourteen

The Form of Your Business: Partnerships

A "partnership" is an ongoing consensual relationship formed by two or more individuals or entities to conduct a business and to produce profits (or losses) that will be divided among the partners. A partnership is much like a sole proprietorship, except that it has two or more owners.

Partnerships are a bit like marriages: they usually start out with a great deal of trust and have a high break-up rate. And like marriages, partnerships are easy to get into, require a lot of patience and understanding to live with, and are often costly and painful to end.

While partnerships can be superb business vehicles for the ownership and operation of real estate and certain other investment ventures, they are my *least* favorite form for operating a sales agency.

GENERAL CHARACTERISTICS OF A GENERAL PARTNERSHIP

A partnership consists of two or more partners who are co-proprietors and co-owners of the business in every sense of the word. They share (in an agreed-upon ratio) profits, losses, management decisions, and all the activities of the business. They share all the risks of ownership and have unlimited *personal* liability for all phases of the business. Each partner is a business agent of the partnership and can enter into written or verbal contracts on behalf of the partnership. Each partner can legally obligate the partnership and the other partners.

Liability extends to all the *personal* assets of each partner and not just to the partnership assets. An individual partner may be held personally liable for the acts or omissions of another partner acting for the partnership. This is an open-ended exposure that every partner assumes on behalf of every other partner, and this vulnerability is the biggest problem in operating any general partnership.

Limited partnerships are not within the boundaries of this discussion. They are rarely used by sales reps, but are common in fields such as real estate syndication, gas and oil, and other investment-type ventures. For the record, in these special partnerships you *can* limit the liability of such partners to the partnership investment, but this format is generally more typical of passive partnership real estate.

The typical sales rep general partnership does not have perpetual existence like the corporation, but rather a life limited by the partnership agreement. A danger of involuntary termination of the partnership under circumstances such as death, withdrawal, and changes in partnership interests requires a carefully drawn partnership agreement that averts termination, provides for continuation of the partnership, and covers all eventualities. The partnership agreement should absolutely include a buy-sell agreement for the partners. Otherwise, you may be standing out in the cold without a partnership when you thought you had one! Or, you may suddenly have a surviving spouse as your new partner! Or, you may end up in a chilly courtroom, litigating with a cold ex-partner, his icy lawyer, and a glacial judge.

A partnership is a separate legal entity with its own identity for legal and tax purposes. It can sue and be sued. It can also be thought of as an aggregation of sole proprietorships, linked together in a common enterprise.

TAX CONSIDERATIONS

For income tax purposes, partnerships are conduits that pass through separately, each and every element of income, losses, and certain deductions directly and proportionately to each partner. Each partnership must fill out IRS Schedule K-1 (with Form 1065; see below), "Partners Share of Income, Credits, and Deductions," reporting each share of the partnership's operating income, self-employment income (subject to Social Security/Medicare taxes), operating losses, investment income, investment losses, charitable contributions, tax credits, capital gains, capital losses, tax preferences, and dozens of other such items. This tax reporting is virtually identical to that for S corporation shareholders, who also receive a similar IRS Schedule K-1.

Although the partnership does not pay any taxes, it is still a separate legal entity for tax reporting, IRS audits, and similar purposes. It files Form 1065, "U.S. Partnership Return of Income," which includes a copy of each partner's Schedule K-1. A partnership generally must report on a calendar year, because it must choose the same year-end as its principal partners, and since virtually all individuals are on a calendar tax year, virtually all partnerships must use the calendar year (not of any tax advantage and not true of C corporations).

A rep agency partnership can elect to report on the cash method in all cases, even if the commission income exceeds $5 million annually. It is only the C corporation that is forced to switch to accrual reporting above the $5 million. However, if a C corporation is a partner in the partnership, then the partnership must switch to accrual reporting if the $5 million income is exceeded, a danger to watch for in cases when reps form a partnership and one of them uses his C corporation as a partner. We have had a few complicated cases like that among our accounting firm's clients.

ADVANTAGES OF THE PARTNERSHIP

There are some advantages of a partnership:

- A partnership is easy to start, as it entails minimal filing procedures.
- The accounting and tax reporting is somewhat less complex than that of a corporation.
- A partnership is not subject to double taxation because of the pass through nature of the partnership.
- Income and deductions can be allocated disproportionately by guaranteed payments to partners, which come off the top before profits are distributed by ownership percentage; by specially allocated depreciation; or similar arrangements because of the partnership agreement itself (the Internal Revenue Code, however, contains certain restrictions on special partnership allocations to prevent tax abuse).

TAXTIP

You are better off using only guaranteed payments instead of special allocations, since the latter generate great interest and suspicion by the IRS. Guaranteed payments can usually accomplish the same allocation purpose and with a much lower IRS audit profile.

- Income and losses "retain their character" as they are reported for tax purposes by the individual partners and can sometimes provide offsets against other similar income of the partners (e.g., real estate losses can be deducted from other real estate income).

DISADVANTAGES OF THE PARTNERSHIP

A partnership form has many disadvantages, some very serious:

- The prime and most weighty disadvantage of a partnership is the matter of personal liability. Not only are all personal and business assets at risk to begin with, but you are generally liable for all the actions of *other* partners taken on behalf of the business. There is no other form of business quite like this! In both C and S corporations your exposure is limited to your investment. Operating as a proprietorship, you do have unlimited liability, but only for your *own* actions. In the partnership form you have unlimited liability per se and further unlimited liability for the business actions of your partners!
- Fringe benefits are severely limited, exactly as in an S corporation (see Chapter 13).
- The partnership does not have unlimited life.
- Partnership interests are hard to sell and any transfer may be further restricted by the partnership agreement. You may have difficulty withdrawing from a partnership and when you finally do, there are sometimes totally unexpected and adverse income tax consequences.
- Your share of the income in the partnership is taxed to you whether or not you actually receive any of it in cash.
- If you are active in the partnership, you are subject to self-employment tax (Social Security and Medicare) on your proportionate share of the partnership income, again, whether it was distributed to you in cash or not. The same earnings in an S corporation are subject to Social Security/Medicare taxes only on actual salaries paid.

TRANSFERS TO THE PARTNERSHIP

If you contribute cash to the partnership, there are no special tax implications. If you contribute property to the partnership, generally no gain or loss is recognized to either the partner or the partnership, and the property is recorded on the books of the partnership at the contributing partner's tax basis.

If you contribute services to the partnership, gain may be recognized to the extent of the fair market value of any partnership interest received. If you receive an "equity interest" (a capital account balance with the partnership) for those services, that's income. If you receive only a future profit-sharing interest, the IRS has pretty much conceded that you do *not* have income at that time.

SALE OF A PARTNERSHIP INTEREST

A partnership interest is generally a capital asset and thus subject to capital gain and loss tax treatment; however, payments to a retiring partner are not always tax-deductible by the partnership.

ADJUSTING THE BASIS OF PARTNERSHIP PROPERTY

When there is a transfer in partnership interest because of the death of a partner or the sale of a partnership interest, the partnership (*not* the partner) may optionally elect to increase (or even decrease) the basis of partnership property accordingly. This is called an IRS Section 754 election.

To clarify: Assume a partner dies and the surviving spouse inherits a partnership interest that is "recorded on the books" for $10,000, but has a fair market value of $50,000 because the partnership owns a building that has increased in value. If the partnership *chooses* to make the IRS Section 754 election, the $40,000 difference between the $10,000 capital account and the $50,000 fair market value becomes an item subject to additional depreciation each year on the surviving spouse's tax return. The surviving spouse might have reported partnership profits of $1,000 a year, for example, but then might also be entitled to, say, a $600 annual Section 754 tax deduction. The result would be that she or he was only taxed on $400 ($1,000 – $600). The same election rules can apply when a partnership interest is sold for more or less than book value (IRS Section 743[b]), or even when property is distributed by the partnership. But the *partnership* must make the election, or choose not to.

Once the election is made under Section 754, it applies both to all transfers and all distributions made during the tax year and to all subsequent tax years unless the election is revoked (in accordance with IRS Reg. 1.754-1[c]). The election must be made in a statement that is filed with the partnership's timely filed tax return, but an automatic 12-month extension to make the Section 754 election can be obtained (per Rev. Proc. 92-85). Very complicated, but your tax adviser can steer you through this tax labyrinth.

CONCLUSION

If you want all the advantages of a partnership while avoiding the terrible personal liability exposure just explained, simply go for an S corporation, which is nothing but an incorporated partnership with essentially the same tax treatment. But the S corporation provides you with corporate *limited liability* as well as other advantages of the corporate form. While I really love C corporations by far the most, I'd go for an S corporation any day in preference to a dangerous sales agency general partnership!

Chapter Fifteen

The Form of Your Business: Sole Proprietorships

Now we come to the simplest and most common form of business, usually the initial format when reps first begin their careers. Virtually every sales agent started as a sole proprietorship. While it's not necessarily the best form, it certainly is the most universal, as when there was just Adam and Eve and a rep selling apples. . . .

GENERAL CHARACTERISTICS

A proprietorship is a business enterprise with one owner and operator. It is the easiest and least expensive business to form; you simply open your business and start operating. Of course, depending on individual state and local laws, various permits, licenses, and registrations will usually be required as with all other forms of business. It is the easiest and simplest, however, it is not always the smartest, as you will quickly learn.

The duration of a sole proprietorship is until the proprietor decides to end the business, since it can be terminated at will. A sole proprietorship also stops upon death or incapacity of the sole owner, which makes any rep agency exceptionally difficult to sell (even if the surviving spouse continues the very same business, it is legally a new proprietorship). The sole proprietorship can, however, easily be converted to a corporation at any time during the lifetime of the owner.

Estate planning and succession planning are *very* difficult, because the proprietorship terminates at death. Thus, there is a total lack of continuity in this form of business, unlike the perpetual existence of a corporation. Since continuity is what every principal wants, many lines and many sales agencies simply disappear soon after the death of the proprietor. Thus, the estate receives little or nothing for the proprietorship rep firm.

The business purpose may be anything not contrary to law. The size of the business is technically unlimited, although other considerations eventually limit the size of proprietorships.

As with partnerships, perhaps the single biggest drawback to this form of business operation is unlimited personal liability. The individual business owner can be held personally liable for all acts, omissions, and decisions. This personal liability cannot be delegated away or contracted away. All personal assets of the proprietor are always at risk in the proprietorship business!

In contrast, a corporate (whether S or C) shareholder's personal liability is generally limited to the investment in capital stock. In the case of a limited partner, the personal liability is generally limited to the partnership investment. In a typical general partnership, each partner has the same unlimited liability as a proprietor, plus the additional unlimited liability for the business actions of all the other partners (the worst-case scenario!).

The chief advantage of the sole proprietorship is simplicity of operations. One individual owns all the assets and liabilities, and accounting and tax reporting are therefore less complex. A separate income tax return is not required; the profit or loss is reported on Schedule C ("Profit or Loss From Business—Sole Proprietorship") of the owner's individual income tax return (Form 1040). A balance sheet is not required for tax reporting purposes as with all corporations and most partnerships.

The proprietorship is under the sole control of the owner and all decisions are made without shared authority. Centralized management is a given.

There is no double taxation of proprietorship income as may be the case for a C corporation. Funds can be contributed or withdrawn from the business at will, and neither action has *any* tax effect whatsoever. The raising of capital, however, is usually limited to the proprietor's personal assets and personal credit, although corporations can sell additional stock and partnerships can sell additional partnership interests (and both will usually bring in far more in new funds). There is no sharing of profits.

CASH BASIS TAX REPORTING AND OTHER TAX CONSIDERATIONS

As mentioned before, there is no double taxation of proprietorship profits and the tax reporting (on Schedule C) is as easy as possible (given the extremely complicated tax laws and IRS rules and regulations that apply to all taxpayers anyway).

Even though the rest of the individual income tax return is reported by the cash receipts and disbursements method, business income and expenses on Schedule C may be reported using either the cash or the accrual method. As with all other possible forms of a sales agency business, the cash basis method of accounting is always to your tax advantage and far simpler to use than the accrual basis method. Income is reported (and taxed) only when actually received, and expenses are deducted only when actually paid, providing considerable leeway in the *timing* of payments.

Proof positive that the cash method of reporting is to your advantage lies in the fact that the IRS has expended great efforts to *limit* the use of such tax reporting. For example, the cash method of reporting is not allowed for larger C corporations and tax-shelter syndications. Think about it: If the IRS hates cash basis reporting, then you had better love it!

Whatever method of reporting you adopt, you must use the same method year after year for that form of business. When you file your first Schedule C (or first tax return for any other business configuration), you can *choose* the appropriate method of accounting without permission of the IRS. However, if you change your mind at a *later* date, you must obtain the consent of the IRS (Form 3115, "Application for Change of Accounting Method") to switch reporting methods.

If you do apply for a change from the accrual to the cash method (since you just found out how much that will save you in taxes), be warned that the IRS has an entire group of individuals whose sole job is to roll on the floor with hysterical laughter before they deny almost all such requests! Why should they grant you an obvious tax benefit when it is completely at their discretion to approve or deny such requests? (Your CPA and lawyer should have advised you about this election the day you went into business. If you were advised to use the accrual method for a conventional rep firm, you had really bad advice!)

TAXTIP

If you are already operating as a proprietorship and reporting on the accrual basis, you might consider incorporating as a way to change back to cash basis reporting. The corporation is a new taxpayer in the eyes of the law and the IRS, and as such, a carefully formed new corporation can make new elections and adopt new accounting methods!

The tax reporting year of a sole proprietorship must be the same as the tax year of the owner, which is almost invariably the calendar year. There is nothing you can do about this, although it is somewhat of a tax drawback compared to a fiscal year-end for the C corporation.

Interest expense of the sole ownership is fully deductible as business interest *provided* the borrowed funds are used for (and can be traced to) a business purpose. Funds borrowed by the business but then withdrawn by the owner for nonbusiness uses can result in the loss of tax deductibility of the interest paid. The IRS now requires that a tracing method be used to properly associate interest expense and the uses of the related debt, so don't assume you can always deduct all the interest paid by a proprietorship!

At this writing, the self-employed business owner can deduct 25 percent of the amount paid for medical insurance (of both the owner and family), but not more than the taxable income shown on Schedule C. This deduction can be made whether or not tax deductions are itemized, but it cannot be claimed if either the owner or spouse is covered by another employer health plan.

Most of the traditional and deductible C corporation fringe benefits (tax-free to all employees, including the owner) are simply not available to a proprietor, for example, group insurance (medical, life, disability, accident) as well as many other tax-free perks. These fringe benefits are sometimes a major consideration in the pros and cons of incorporation. Also, stock options or other forms of shared ownership cannot be offered by the sole proprietor to others.

As the taxable earnings bases continue to rise, more and more income is subject to Social Security/Medicare taxes (the Medicare portion is subject to *unlimited* amounts of earnings or compensation). The tax basis includes the net profits of the proprietorship without regard to how much of those earnings were *withdrawn* by the owner. Thus, if the business earned $50,000, but $25,000 was reinvested in new equipment, the sole owner would pay Social Security tax on the entire $50,000, even though the actual draw might have been only the $25,000 of net cash available.

In a small corporation, however, the owner probably would have taken only the remaining $25,000 as salary and thus would have paid one-fourth as much self-employment tax (the corporation paid the other one-fourth) on the monies actually received. With both earnings tax rates and the earnings bases rising, Social Security/Medicare taxes have become an increasingly major burden on the sole proprietor, because the same payroll tax rate now applies to all business entities. Remember, the sole owner pays both halves of Social Security and Medicare taxes as compared to an employee because the other half of those taxes are paid by (and deducted by) the employer company. Self-employed individuals can deduct one-half of their self-employment tax from their income, but that's only a partial solution.

If the proprietor has bona fide full-time employees, including family (see the following and Chapter 29), the business can establish the same traditional employee fringe benefit plans as corporations (subject to nondiscrimination rules). However, such costs are fully tax-deductible and tax-free only for the *employees*. Such plans cannot provide any tax benefits to the owner other than the limited medical insurance deduction previously mentioned.

HOW TO DEDUCT 100 PERCENT OF HEALTH INSURANCE PREMIUMS EVEN IF YOU ARE NOT INCORPORATED

As sole proprietors, self-employed individuals are only allowed to deduct 25 percent of their health insurance premiums, but if they are employees of their own corporations, the corporation can deduct 100 percent of the premiums. Not a very fair arrangement.

Here is an alternative method that can achieve the same 100 percent tax deduction for unincorporated reps (who file Schedule C):

1. *Hire your spouse* as a bona fide employee.
2. Obtain a health insurance policy that covers employees and *spouses* of employees.
3. Have your *spouse* cover *you* under the policy.

Now 100 percent of the health insurance premiums are tax-deductible, since you can fully deduct health insurance premiums paid for *employees* as long as rules for employee tax-free fringe benefits are met.

TAXTIP

This arrangement will *not* work for partners in partnerships or S corporation owners, but it *was* approved for proprietorships in IRS Revenue Ruling 71-588.

IRS AUDITS OF SCHEDULE C

With the audits of tax shelters slowly dwindling, Schedule C is now probably the single highest IRS audit priority on individual income tax returns (two close ones are deductions for unreimbursed business expenses and home offices). The IRS has made no secret of this fact.

The IRS's own audit statistics show that Schedule C audits have the single highest individual audit frequency, and their various publicity releases and pronouncements keep emphasizing the same fact. A recent release stated that of the $100 billion of income that escapes taxes (how do they really know how much, if it escapes them?), $20 billion was unreported income on Schedule C!

Another IRS release threatened an audit for every Schedule C with either gross income of over $100,000 or net income of over $50,000. Still another release stated that while the original IRS audit thrust was aimed at finding personal expenses that are deducted as business expenses on Schedule C, they later found that a high percentage of returns contained an understatement of income as well!

Therefore, if you do get an IRS audit of a Schedule C, it will be unlike any other audit you have ever encountered unless you were unlucky enough to undergo their dreaded Taxpayers Compliance Measurement Program (TCMP) statistical audit. During a Schedule C examination, the IRS audits *every* kind of money account you have, both personal and business, to determine if taxable income has been diverted from the business account to any other account. In the process, they ask you to explain the source of *every* deposit to *every* account! That's savings, checking, money market, stock broker, and whatever else applies in your case.

Each IRS district sends a two-page, single-spaced "information request" to the taxpayer when a Schedule C audit is involved. Here are selected excerpts from one such IRS letter.

> Dear ______:
>
> To help us complete the examination of your 19__ return, please include the following information with your records (which will then be audited):
>
> 1) All bank statements, canceled checks and deposit slips, both business and personal, savings and checking for the 14 month period from December 19__ through January __.
>
> 2) Records of all savings and invested funds for the year (i.e., money market accounts, certificates of deposit, etc.).

3) Records of all other business and personal receipts such as loans, insurance proceeds, inheritances, salaries, gifts, social security benefits, transfers between bank accounts, etc.
4) Purchase invoices or closing statements for acquisitions and dispositions of capital items, business and personal. This includes real estate, automobiles, machinery and equipment, etc.

Those questions just relate to the *income* side of Schedule C. They are, of course, designed to discover undisclosed income. Except in the case of fraud or a TCMP, I know of no other kind of IRS audit that asks for this incredible amount of recordkeeping detail. Be prepared to pay the price in time, taxes, aggravation, and professional fees if you operate a sole proprietorship and are audited!

Of course, your solution and protection is to identify the source of every deposit to every single account you have. Ideally, you should deposit everything into only *one* account and identify each deposit. Then, everything placed in any other account is a *transfer* from that first account. This solution can save you time, taxes, accounting fees, and your sanity!

The IRS information request then inquires into business expenses. Here are some of the worst of their many requests:

1) Log books and other records to support the business mileage claimed. Repair receipts . . . and any other records showing total mileage for the year. [See Chapter 5.]
2) Appointment book or calendar of your business activities during the year. [This one frequently triggers urgent requests from clients like, "By any chance, do you happen to have a blank appointment book for 1990?"]
3) A log or a diary for travel costs incurred while away from home on business. Verification of the number of days away from home overnight for business purposes [see Travel Recordkeeping in Chapter 3].
4) Records and receipts for entertainment expenses you claimed. These records should show the name and business relationship of the person entertained, purpose of the entertainment, place, date of the entertainment, and the amount of the expenditure. (See Recordkeeping and Receipts in Chapter 1.) Keep in mind that someone really tried selling filled-out receipts to other individuals, but the IRS stopped them!

Those are just some selected questions; however, the preceding four points are audit questions that *any* rep could be asked by the IRS in most business circumstances. Reread them, and use them as a partial guideline for all business travel, entertainment, and auto recordkeeping (see Chapters 1, 3, and 5).

This IRS audit crackdown on Schedule C now enters into our discussions with clients as to when to incorporate and what form to choose for their business. It is no longer a trivial consideration.

RETIREMENT PLANS FOR THE SOLE PROPRIETOR

A sole proprietor has quite a few retirement plan options to consider and should get early and expert advice before grabbing whatever is offered. Three different Keogh plans, Simplified Employee Pension (SEP) plans, and Individual Retirement Accounts (IRA) are available. All the plans permit a tax deduction equal to whatever the mentioned contribution may be. Here is just enough information to let you consider the choices intelligently (see Chapter 10 also).

An IRA contribution is limited to $2,000 annually and is further limited (or possibly lost) if a spouse is covered by another retirement plan. Usually the IRA permits the smallest contribution (and therefore has the lowest tax deduction). Administration fees are usually very low and IRS reports do not have to be filed. You have until April 15 of the following year to establish and pay into the plan for the preceding year, but no extensions of time to pay are allowed.

The SEP permits a contribution of up to 13.0435 percent of net self-employment income (i.e., your net profit), up to a maximum of $30,000. You can vary the contribution percentage each year (from zero to 13.0435 percent). You have until April 15 of the following year to establish and pay into the SEP for the preceding year, and that date is extended by any extensions of time obtained to file your income tax return.

The profit-sharing Keogh plan, like the SEP, also permits a contribution of up to 13.0435 percent of net self-employment income, up to a maximum of $30,000, and again, you can vary the contribution percentage each year (from zero to 13.0435 percent). Administration fees are usually higher than with an IRA or SEP and Forms series 5500, "Annual Returns/Report of Employee Benefit Plan," must be filed with the IRS. The plan must be established by December 31 of the first year involved and a minimum payment made at that time (otherwise, you cannot make a Keogh contribution for that year). You then have until April 15 of the following year to pay the balance of the contribution into the plan, and that date is extended by any extensions of time obtained to file your income tax return.

The money-purchase Keogh plan, which usually incorporates the profit-sharing Keogh plan, permits a contribution of up to 20 percent of net self-employment income, up to a maximum of $30,000. The profit-sharing contribution portion of the plan can vary each year, while the balance of the plan represents a fixed-percentage contribution. Administration fees are usually somewhat higher than for a profit-sharing Keogh and annual reports (Forms series 5500) must be filed with the IRS. The timing rules for establishing the plan and for payments are identical to the rules of the profit-sharing Keogh plan in the preceding paragraph.

The annual contribution to a defined-benefit Keogh plan has no fixed percentage *at all* but varies from year to year, based on age, interest rates, projected retirement date, net earnings, (defined) benefits at retirement, life expectancy, and similar criteria. A defined-benefit Keogh plan requires the services and certification of an actuary. There is no theoretical limit to an annual contribution, but there's a limit on retirement benefits of $90,000 a year (annually adjusted upward for inflation). The actuarially determined contribution must be paid each year. Administration fees are substantially higher than any other plans, because of all the complexities and the additional costs of the actuary, and annual reports (Forms series 5500) must be filed with the IRS. The timing rules for establishing the plan and for payments are identical to the rules of the other Keogh plans. This plan has the potential to produce the highest contribution/deduction of all!

Use these descriptions as your guide to retirement plans, but definitely consult an expert in the field before making your decision. Don't just drift into any financial institution or broker and grab the first thing they are offering that particular day. For many reps, these retirement plan accumulations represent their biggest (and frequently *only*) source of financial security and salvation! Plan for your retirement!

WARNING

Please reread the bankruptcy information in Chapter 10. Your IRA, rollover IRA, or SEP assets are *not* protected in the event of bankruptcy, while the assets in ERISA-qualified plans *are* fully sheltered from creditors. This is a major point if you are in any kind of financial difficulty!

HIRING YOUR SPOUSE AS AN EMPLOYEE

This is a tough decision, since there are both advantages and disadvantages. If you do hire your spouse as an employee, a careful record of hours worked and services performed should be kept to justify and substantiate that the spouse is a bona fide employee. Salary payments should be reported on quarterly payroll tax returns, appropriate withholding of all taxes should be made, and a Form W-2, "Wage and Tax Statements," (not information return Form 1099) wage statement should be issued at year-end. In other words, treat your spouse like every other employee.

The decision whether or not to hire your spouse is difficult because of the high cost of Social Security/Medicare taxes. The Revenue Act of 1987 changed the rules and imposed payroll taxes (currently more than 15 percent) on the spouse working for the proprietorship. If the proprietor-owner's income exceeds the maximum Social Security limit, then the spouse's Social Security tax cost is an extra tax that could have been avoided. The additional tax cost on $20,000, for example, is over $3,000.

The main consideration is whether the spouse will ever draw Social Security benefits from his *own* account. The spouse can only draw benefits from that account, if the benefits exceed the 50 percent of the benefits that can be drawn from the proprietor/owner's account. In other words, in most cases the Social Security/Medicare contributions of the spouse are wasted because benefits are drawn from the other spouse's Social Security account.

However, in return for being a true (documented!) employee, the spouse is entitled to tax benefits, most of which are not even available to the proprietor-owner.

- As a *full-time* employee (subject to discrimination rules), the spouse is entitled to the standard employee benefits of medical insurance, uninsured medical reimbursement plan, group life insurance (up to $50,000), disability insurance, and other employee fringe benefits. Such employee benefit costs reduce both the income taxes and the Social Security/Medicare taxes of the proprietor-owner, but are tax-free to the spouse-employee.
- As a full-time employee, the spouse can participate in the retirement plan of the proprietorship (Keogh, SEP, or IRA) and thus increase the total tax-deductible retirement plan contributions and tax-deferred accumulations of the family unit.
- As a full-time employee, the spouse may be eligible for a child care income tax credit on the joint income tax return.

You will have to consider whether the extra payroll costs of a spouse working *full time* or *part time* are outweighed by the potential tax benefits just discussed. Usually it does not pay.

HIRING YOUR CHILDREN AS EMPLOYEES

As with the spouse, if you do hire your children as employees, keep careful records of time worked and duties performed. These family hirings are always more suspect than others in the eyes of the IRS.

Wages paid your children under age 18 are still exempt from Social Security taxes; however, the same Revenue Act of 1987 that applied payroll taxes to the earnings of the spouse-employee, did the same for children-employees 18 years or older.

In many cases, you have nothing to lose if you employ your children (including stepchildren or foster children) under age 18. The proprietor-owner gets a tax deduction, there is no payroll tax cost, and each child can pay up to $2,000 into an IRA. (It is generally projected that if you pay into an IRA for 30 or more consecutive years beginning as a young adult, you will have over $1 million at retirement!)

The wages paid to minor children frequently shift income from the proprietor's higher tax bracket to the minor child's lower tax bracket. However, with sufficient income, a child under 14 may be forced to file a tax return and have any unearned income taxed at the parent's tax rate! Also, such wages could cause the loss of the dependency exemption on the parent's tax return if the salary contributed to over half the child's total support.

With a child 18 years or older, Social Security/Medicare tax costs must be considered. As with a spouse, those tax payments may be wasted this time because such payments will probably not result in higher Social Security retirement benefits some 45 or 50 years later. However, the income tax savings between the child's lower tax bracket and the proprietor's higher tax bracket still make this very attractive. As explained in Chapter 29, we generally recommend *against* the spouse as an employee, but *for* the children as employees, regardless of their age.

If the child is a full-time employee (generally unlikely, because of schooling requirements), all the employee fringe benefits and retirement plan benefits can be obtained. Use these various considerations to decide whether or not to employ your children, keeping in mind the different rules for those under 18 years of age and for older children.

HOW TO FILL OUT A SCHEDULE C AND (POSSIBLY) AVOID AN IRS AUDIT

Here is some advice if you fill out your own Schedule C or when reviewing one prepared by your CPA. I am using a 1993 Schedule C as reference. (Also see Chapter 25.)

The "principal business code" number (question B, near the top right of Schedule C) is more critical than you may think. This business code number (selected from the list accompanying the Schedule C) categorizes your business return in the eyes of the IRS audit selection computer! If your business is improperly categorized your gross profit may seem too low, your travel and entertainment may seem too high, or a dozen other expenses may seem out of line with the secret averages in the IRS computer. The obvious result would be an unnecessary and costly IRS audit!

The IRS uses a different set of business codes for proprietorships than those used for corporations or partnerships. The only two appropriate codes for the average rep firm are *2634* or *2675*, both of which are "agent or broker for other firms—more than 50 percent of gross sales on commission." The code numbers are for "durable goods" and "nondurable goods," respectively.

Many times I see the wrong code used by a tax preparer who doesn't know a rep from a reptile. For example, "3533–Automotive tires, accessories and parts" promptly takes an automotive rep out of the commission/sales category and classifies her in *retail trade*. That mistake can easily cause an IRS audit, since the IRS computer compares the rep's "travel and entertainment" to that of the average retail store, and the IRS audit computer goes "Tilt!" A similar error is to classify hardware reps as "4457–Hardware" (retail).

Question F asks about your accounting method. If your method is "cash," you should *not* be showing any great amount of inventory and preferably none on page 2, Part III, "cost of goods sold." Inventories and purchases are the major test of mandatory *accrual* reporting!

Question H asks about any changes in determining beginning and ending inventories. Obviously, if you do report inventories, a "yes" answer is not good.

Question I, "Did you 'materially participate' in the operation of this business during 1993?" is also aimed at limiting the deduction of any losses.

Part II—Expenses, line 9, asks for "bad debts from sales or services." If you earlier stated you report on the cash basis, it would be very unusual to claim *anything* on this line. For accrual taxpayers, only direct write-offs are now allowed, and not any additions to a reserve for bad debts (one of many concealed audit triggers).

Line 10, "car and truck expenses," is another IRS area of suspicion. They are always looking for personal use of business autos. If you claim expenses on this line, then in almost all cases Form 4562, "Depreciation and Amortization," should be attached with answers to all questions about auto mileage, auto use, and auto recordkeeping filled out in Part V, Section B. Don't irritate the IRS with noncompliance!

Line 14, "employee benefit programs," has two catches. First, you should not be deducting anything on this line if you don't have any employees! Second, the IRS is always looking for abuses in this area and will compare this total claimed to (at least) your total payroll. Obviously, if employee benefits are double the payroll, you are a very generous person and probably a tax cheater!

Line 16b, "other" interest, is of increasing *interest* (joke!) to the IRS. We discussed earlier how Schedule C interest deductions are limited and are subject to the IRS tracing the use of loan proceeds. The IRS also claims that "personal" interest is sometimes deducted on Schedule C because it is no longer allowed as an itemized tax deduction, so excessive amounts on this line can be another audit trigger.

Line 20, "rent or lease," segregates "vehicles, machinery and equipment" leasing (line 20a) from leasing of "other business property" (line 20b). Line 20a is of particular concern to the IRS, since they are looking for lease deductions that actually are lease-*purchase* payments, that is, situations where equipment can be purchased after the lease expires. In such cases, you *cannot* deduct the lease payments you made; you must capitalize the equipment as a purchase and may then claim depreciation, which is usually much less of a tax advantage than lease payments.

Line 21, "repairs and maintenance," is a dangerous line to use. The IRS is looking for expenditures that should be capitalized and depreciated, rather than just deducted as paid. A relatively big number here can spell trouble.

Line 24a, "travel," is a danger whenever it is relatively high (as in the case of most sales agents), because of IRS perceived abuses.

Line 24b, "meals and entertainment," ranks equally high with "travel," but there is the additional requirement of a 50 percent (1994 on) disallowance (line 24c). If you enter anything on line 24b, there had better be an *exact* 50 percent deduction on line 24c! Further, if you enter anything under "travel" (line 24a), there had better be something reasonably related under "meals" (line 24b), unless you know a way to travel out of town without eating! If so, you can explain it to the IRS auditor, who will probably be fascinated by your diet, and your pitiful tax records as well!

On your Schedule C, all these interrelationships and stand-alone danger signals can be digested by the IRS computer in less than a second. There are undoubtedly other IRS computer tests being applied that I have yet to learn. While the advice in this section cannot necessarily "audit-proof" your Schedule C (your gross or net income amounts alone may trigger the audit), this discussion of proper presentation of a tax return may help you avoid needless additional cause for audit.

Chapter 17 includes a special rep Chart of Expense Accounts and a full discussion of how to break down travel and entertainment into a number of smaller accounts. There is nothing to prevent you from entering all such accounts (and amounts) on the open lines (page 2, Part V), of Schedule C. Just remember to indicate that they all have been "reduced by the applicable 50% of meals and entertainment." Chapter 17 also includes information about reporting "personal use of business autos" as a separate income amount on Part I, line 6 of Schedule C. All this is what we call "tax presentation."

CONCLUSION

By all means, open a *separate* business checking account for a proprietorship! This simple move will save you more time and money in bookkeeping, accounting, tax preparation, and IRS audits than you can imagine. Conversely, if you mix personal and business transactions into one single bank account, the unscrambling can be costly and the IRS will have no choice but to concentrate on this one scrambled account! This is major and serious advice! Ignore it and suffer!

Be aware that as a proprietorship you may need to obtain a federal employer identification number (FEIN) which is mandatory if you have employees; a certificate of assumed name; business license; business property registration; sales tax permit; workers' compensation coverage; payroll tax registration and forms; and so forth.

Finally, because of the unlimited liability of the proprietor-owner, it is absolutely essential that you obtain as much *liability insurance* (product, business, etc.) as you can possibly need and possibly afford (see Chapter 24)! Nowadays your liability exposure is virtually unlimited, so do the absolute best you can. And good luck in your proprietorship, unless I could interest you in a nice little C corp instead.

Chapter Sixteen

"Zeroing Out" at Fiscal Year-end

Over the years, our CPA firm has devised and perfected a special set of instructions that are sent to each of our reps (and other cash-basis clients) at the end of the eleventh month of their fiscal year. They thus have one month to follow our instructions, warnings, explanations, and even begging, to do the smart thing, which is, of course, to "zero out" their corporation and avoid payment of corporate taxes (and other reasons; see Chapter 25).

Up to now, we have carefully restricted this information to our clients only and asked them to keep these instructions confidential. Now, for the first time, we share this information and instructions with our readers in the same form it is sent to our clients. The following is a copy of our mailing to those clients.

SPECIAL INSTRUCTIONS FOR YOUR CASH-BASIS BUSINESS: HOW TO "ZERO OUT"

By Melvin H Daskal, CPA and Morris Spector, CPA

Everybody wants to legally minimize taxes, and the cash method of tax reporting that is available to most service businesses affords a special and particular advantage. You can legally time your tax deductions by paying, or not paying, tax-deductible expenses in one tax year or in another. Since our firm has so many service-business clients and sales reps, we have created a special set of instructions that are sent to each cash-basis client at the close of the eleventh month of business. Thus you have 30 days to implement these instructions. By using these legal cash-basis techniques, you can zero out your company or at least reduce your taxable income.

This information is restricted to our clients only. It is confidential and proprietary and should not be shared with outsiders. It is you, our client, who has paid for this; you should not casually give this valuable information away to others. Keep this competitive edge for your own business!

CASH BASIS

These instructions apply only to businesses using the cash basis of tax reporting. Such firms pay their taxes based only on income actually *collected* and expenses actually *paid*. Examples of such businesses are sales agents, doctors, lawyers, insurance agents, entertainers, consultants, accountants, and most other service businesses. It does not matter what the form of your business is—a corporation, a partnership, or a sole proprietorship—you can still usually report your service business on the cash basis.

If you have received these instructions from us, your business *is* reporting on the cash basis (for income tax purposes). These instructions should be followed carefully, unless you don't care about saving income taxes!

ZEROING OUT

The idea behind zeroing out is simply to make all possible legitimate payments that are currently tax-deductible *before* the end of your fiscal year. By so doing, you can legally reduce or eliminate all taxable profits (and thus corporate income taxes). Not every payment is immediately tax-deductible, but the point is to pay currently deductible expenses (e.g., salaries, bonuses, and other operating expenses) before fiscal year-end.

BANK ACCOUNTS

The *first* measure to use to zero out your taxable income is your bank account. In essence, if your bank balance is near zero at the end of your fiscal year, many times your taxable income is as well. However, there are some variations to consider, as we will discuss. But to begin with just watch your bank account(s), and we will monitor your profit and loss figures at the same time.

If you have brought your bank balance(s) very close to zero at fiscal year-end, you have done *most* of what you can do to reduce your taxable income. However, three warnings are in order:

1. Your payments should only be for currently *deductible* expenses and not for anything else (e.g., loan payments or purchasing a new car).
2. When disbursing those funds, remember to pay out the total balances of *all* your bank accounts. Leaving $50,000 in a money market account or a Certificate of Deposit is not zeroing out, and it will not accomplish these goals. Zero *all* cash accounts.
3. Do not *overdraw* all your bank accounts. Get close to zero in *all* your cash accounts and then stop. The IRS can disallow the deductions for expenses paid with checks that overdraw your bank account (except if you had previously arranged with the bank to honor all such overdraft checks).

RETIREMENT PLAN CONTRIBUTIONS

Do *not* pay these contributions before your fiscal year-end. Why? These contributions represent the *only* tax deduction that can be claimed on a cash basis without actually being *paid* before the fiscal year-end! Any current payment of these contributions is wasting cash that could be used to pay *another* tax-deductible expense.

While you can deduct these retirement plan contributions as if paid in your current fiscal year, the actual due date for payment is 2½ months after the end of your fiscal year. Further, by automatically filing six-month extensions for tax returns, the due date for the retirement plan contribution is *also* extended another six months to a final due date of 8½ months after your fiscal year-end (but still deductible in your *present* fiscal year). (In similar manner, we can extend the due date of an *individual's* Keogh or SEP contribution by filing an automatic four-month extension to August 15 of each year.)

A six-month extension not only allows extra time to pay your contribution, but, in many cases, an automatic six-month extension for corporate income tax returns is made at the request of retirement plan administrators. There are two good reasons:

1. The tax return extension also automatically extends the time for filing of the retirement plan reporting forms (the various Forms 5500), which is time the administrator frequently needs.
2. In many cases, the extension is needed to calculate the exact amounts of the retirement plan contributions, especially true

for defined-benefit plans which require special actuarial calculations (and actuarial certifications to the IRS).

THINGS NOT TO PAY FOR OR BUY

In addition to retirement plan contributions, there are other payments that will not generate an immediate income tax deduction, so avoid them if possible and if they will not damage your credit:

- The *principal* amounts (not interest actually due) of any bank loans until after fiscal year-end.
- Capital purchases, such as equipment, furniture, computers, copiers, phone systems, machines, usually cannot be deducted currently, but can only be depreciated (mostly over seven years).

NOTE

Up to $17,500 a year of such expenditures can be *immediately* charged off as an expense (IRC Sec. 179) in each fiscal year, but we may have already *done so* during the previous 11 months, so check with us first!

- Advances, loans, or loan repayments to employees do not generate any tax deductions at all.
- Purchases of automobiles produce virtually no current tax deduction when bought this late in the year and are further limited by the luxury auto depreciation rules.

OFFICER/SHAREHOLDER LOANS FROM YOUR CORPORATION

These loans represent a special problem. If during the year, you have borrowed money from your corporation, your company may be short of funds with which to pay the necessary tax-deductible expenses at fiscal year-end. The best solution is obvious. If possible, *repay* such loans before the fiscal year-end.

Said another way, if you have borrowed funds from your company, your company has used that money to make a nondeductible expenditure (i.e., a personal loan to you), and accordingly, the company is left with less tax-deductible expenses paid. By all means repay the loan (with interest, as required) and have your company immediately expend those monies on properly deductible expenses before the fiscal year-end.

By repaying the loan before the fiscal year-end, you also avoid another problem. The IRS is taking an increasingly aggressive stance by reclassifying such loans as dividends (or sometimes as additional compensation) to the officer/shareholder. These reclassifications result in the officer/shareholder being taxed on the amount of the loan in all such cases. Further, if the loan is classified as a dividend the corporation does not get a tax deduction for this adjustment (if "classified as additional compensation," it does). It is an issue we find being raised in almost every IRS audit of a company where such loans exist.

In any case, the individual officer/shareholder will end up with additional income, additional taxes, plus interest, plus penalties. All because a few dollars were needed for some personal purpose, and you just never got around to repaying the money until it was too late.

If you absolutely cannot repay such loans, you should understand that you have damaged the zeroing out process of the business. However, in that unhappy event, you should try and avoid these loans being reclassified to you as additional income (as explained in Chapter 21). Remember, the IRS has such a hang-up about these loans that you are required to disclose any such loan details on the balance sheets of the corporate tax return (Form 1120, Schedule L, page 4, lines 7 and 19). What does that tell you? Don't take them, or at least follow these recommendations:

- All officer/shareholder loans to and from your company should be authorized in the corporate minutes, preferably with a good reason for the loan being granted.
- All loans must be evidenced by a note, which specifies fixed repayment dates of principal and calls for a current (market) rate of interest.
- Interest must be paid *at least* quarterly or, ideally, monthly.
- The repayment of principal must be at reasonable intervals and not after an absurd length of time. If it looks like a sham, the IRS will call it a sham!

OFFICER/SHAREHOLDER LOANS TO YOUR CORPORATION

Loans that you make to your corporation are almost as dangerous as the loans taken from your corporation. In this case, you have not shorted your corporation for payment of fiscal year-end bills, but you have created the beginning of a taxtrap for the officers and shareholders personally!

In this event, the IRS will play another reclassification game when they audit you. If you casually put money into your corporation, and leave it there for quite some time, the IRS is prone to reclassify those loans as "additional permanent capital." Then, when you *do* make loan repayments to yourself, they reclassify them as taxable *dividends* to you, since your loans no longer (in effect) exist! Although these "dividends" are *not* deductible by the corporation, they are income to *you* personally!

The obvious solution is not to loan the corporation any money (and be warned that those lines 7 and 9 on the corporate tax return cover loans *to* as well as loans *from* your corporation).

However, if such loans do exist, it is important that you follow the four procedures described in the preceding section. You simply cannot casually treat your corporation as a personal pocketbook, or you will live to regret it.

Having said all that, there is one case where short-term loans to your corporation can be helpful. While zeroing out is frequently accomplished by just running the bank account to near zero, this is *not* true when substantial amounts of the annual cash-basis profits have already been used to repay old loans, acquire luxury autos, pay for leasehold improvements, pay the prior year's retirement plan contributions, and similar expenditures, all of which are *not* tax-deductible in the current fiscal year.

For example, if $50,000 of your profits were already spent to repay a $50,000 bank loan (or pay cash for a $50,000 auto), running your bank account down to zero will still leave your company with a $50,000 profit (give or take). In that event, a $50,000 loan from you or someone else will provide the necessary cash to zero out by paying a final $50,000 in expenses.

PAYROLL TAX DEPOSITS

A very common error occurs when you pay extra bonuses at your fiscal year-end. Those bonuses result in a much *higher* payroll tax liability, and you may have three days or less to deposit your total federal payroll taxes.

WARNING

Under the rules for semiweekly payouts, your payroll tax deposits are due after each payday, according to the following schedule:

Paydays	*Deposit By*
Wednesday, Thurday, or Friday	Following Wednesday
Saturday, Sunday, Monday, or Tuesday	Following Friday

If you are under the alternative monthly deposit rules for smaller companies, all payroll taxes for salaries and bonuses paid during the month must be deposited by the 15th of the month following that payroll.

Every business is directly notified by the IRS; you should be aware of whether you are subject to the semiweekly or the monthly deposit rules. If you don't know, please contact us immediately!

Please be sure to budget for payment of extra payroll tax deposits when deciding on fiscal year-end bonuses (and also any payment of any back salaries). Frequently, we find that in the process of following these procedures and zeroing out at the end of the fiscal year the owner completely forgets the cash requirements for payroll taxes.

SUMMARY

You can legally zero out your cash basis business at fiscal year-end by paying (currently tax-deductible) expenses, salaries, and bonuses. When the balances in all your bank accounts and other cash equivalent accounts approach zero, you have done *most* of your job, but see the earlier discussions for other details.

Do not materially overdraw the combined bank accounts. Do not pay retirement plan contributions, or items not currently tax-deductible, such as bank loan repayments, or payments for a new car. If loans are due from officers/shareholders, try to get them repaid before fiscal year-end and immediately use those funds to pay expenses and salaries. Study the circumstances described where a short-term loan to the company near year-end can materially aid the zeroing out process. Watch your cumulative payroll tax liability resulting from any additional salaries and bonuses, and be aware of the semiweekly and monthly payroll tax deposit rules. Finally, consider whether the special Section 179 deduction for new purchases of up to $17,500 can help solve your tax problem.

Above all, please contact our office *before* your fiscal year-end with any questions or clarifications you may require. Since we cannot appear at each and every company with a fiscal year-end on the same day (some months we have over 50 such simultaneous closings), we ask for your help in this most important procedure. We are always available by phone and fax to help you on your fateful tax day! After you have done your part, we will take over for the fiscal year-end adjustments and the actual closing of the books, and the rest of the financial and tax work is up to us.

Good Luck, and Go for the Zero!

Best regards,

Mel Daskal & Morry Spector

CONCLUSION

And that's our "zeroing out" letter to all our sales rep clients. Hopefully, many of you readers (and perhaps even some of your CPAs) will now have a better understanding of "what to do and how to do it."

Chapter Seventeen

A Bookkeeping System for the Manufacturers' Sales Agency

There are two wonderful reasons why you should adopt a more or less standard chart of accounts for your rep firm. First, properly used, it may actually help avoid an IRS audit, and secondly, it can produce meaningful information for your use in managing and operating your rep firm. Additionally, such standardization permits future surveys to be conducted of the income and expenses of sales agencies. Finally, this system also provides automatic segregation throughout the year of those expenses for business entertainment and business meals, which are only 50 percent tax-deductible (the 6000 series).

You don't have to be a CPA to understand the way the bookkeeping system works, or to understand the financial statement that is the final result. First, let's understand the 50 percent entertainment rule.

THE 50 PERCENT ENTERTAINMENT RULE

Virtually *all* entertainment categories are limited to a 50 percent tax deduction:

• The most typical form of entertainment is *any business meal* where you entertain anyone, be it a customer, purchasing agent, principal, factory sales manager (how come they never pick up a check?), prospective customer, your CPA, or similar. This entertainment category is the same whether or not such entertainment is *in* town or *out* of town. It's *all* such entertainment involving a *meal* (and includes liquor, tax, and tip as well).

• Your own meals and those of your employees dining *alone* while out-of-town on business travel. The "solitary" business travel meal is tax-deductible, but the solitary meal in town is not.

• Virtually anything else that is classified as entertainment, whether in town or out-of-town, such as conventions, seminars, trade shows, factory meetings, board meetings, sporting events, dinner meetings, parties, and "nights on the town." If it qualifies as entertainment under any of these categories, it's only 50 percent tax-deductible.

Minor exceptions are still 100 percent tax-deductible, for example, traditional recreational events for employees (company parties, holiday outings, summer outings) and a subsidized eating facility for employees.

Ticket costs that are more than face value (i.e., scalper prices) are not deductible unless the premium paid is for a charity affair. Further, there is no tax deduction for a table at a business dinner if the host or his representative does not attend.

For all the described entertainment categories the net results are simple but devastating. You spend $100 on business entertainment, and your income tax deduction is $50. It's that simple, but it sure isn't enjoyable! Unfortunately, this law falls with far greater force on the owners of rep firms than on the rest of the general business population. Obviously, nobody in Congress or at the IRS thought or cared about that distinction.

As stated earlier, the 50 percent reduction also applies to taxes, tip, and liquor at entertainment meals.

NOTE

The *employer* still can (and usually will) reimburse all employees at *100 percent* of their expenses. The 50 percent tax reduction will occur when the employer files the business tax return. Thus, the *employee* is not penalized under this arrangement (unless she is not reimbursed for such expenses), but the employer will be, as will all unincorporated reps.

THE 6000 SERIES

As already mentioned, the 6000 expense series is designed to segregate those expenses that are 50 percent tax-deductible, while the 5000 expense series is for all other (100 percent tax-deductible) business expenses. If you do not continually make this segregation and distinction throughout the year, the cost of segregating each and every individual entertainment expense for an entire year, when it's time to prepare your tax return, will be enormous!

Understand the bookkeeping rules clearly. You do *not* reduce those expenses in the 6000 series as they are entered into your bookkeeping system, but at the end of your fiscal year the 50 percent tax reduction can be made to the *totals* in the 6000 series accounts. In other words, a five minute job.

The computer bookkeeping system we use for our rep-clients, *combines* the 5000 series and the 6000 series expenses for each category on the monthly financial statement. For example, the expense category "travel" may include 100 percent tax-deductible transportation (in the 5000 series) and 50 percent tax-deductible travel meals (in the 6000 series), but the *financial statement* will show one figure for travel expenses at the full 100 percent cost for both accounts. It's only on the *tax return* that the 50 percent entertainment reduction is made. Thus, the financial statement makes sense, reflects your *full* costs, and is easy to read despite the 50 percent entertainment tax-deduction complication.

INSTRUCTIONS FOR YOUR BOOKKEEPER

For the convenience of all bookkeepers, we have listed each applicable 6000 account in the following Chart of Expense Accounts next to the basic 5000 account. In that way, you will not have to refer to a different part of the Chart of Expense Accounts to find those other numbers; they are right there, and you can decide which one to use without shifting your eyes. Note that the numbers are *identical* for each account except for the first digit.

REMEMBER

The 6000 series is only for the 50 percent tax-deductible expenses as defined earlier, but you still charge the 6000 accounts with such expenses at the full (*100 percent*) amount.

HOW TO USE THE CHART OF EXPENSE ACCOUNTS

The first thing to understand is that you should use *only* those accounts that are reasonably applicable to your size sales agency. Don't try to use most or all the expense accounts unless you are running a really big rep operation (as a generalization, say $3 million or more in annual commissions). Also, don't be intimidated by the size of the chart; as they say in computer jargon, this is just a menu to choose from. Stay with us while we walk through a simple computer bookkeeping scenario.

Chart of Expense Accounts

Numbers **5000 (6000)**	*Description* **Expenses (master account)**
5010	Advertising
5020	Amortization
5030	Automobile expenses
5040	Auto expense reimbursements
5050	Automobile leasing
5060	Business gifts
5070 (6070)	Business promotion
5080	Catalogs, literature, and samples
5090	Commissions paid
5100	Computer service bureau fees
5110	Computer supplies and expenses
5120	Computer leasing
5130 (6130)	Continuing education
5140	Contributions
5150 (6150)	Conventions
5160 (6160)	Customers' costs and expenses
5170	Depreciation
5180	Dues and publications
5190	Employee benefits
5200 (6200)	Employees' reimbursed expenses
5210 (6210)	Entertainment (see earlier discussion)
5220	Equipment leasing (nonauto)
5230 (6230)	Factory meetings
5240	Freight and delivery
5250 (6250)	Hotels, meals, and tips
5260	Insurance—general
5270	Insurance—group
5280	Insurance—officers' life
5290	Interest
5300	Licenses
5310	Maintenance and repairs
5320 (6320)	Management conferences
5330	Office supplies and expenses
5340	Outside services
5350	Parking
5360	Personnel agency fees
5370	Plane and train fares
5380	Postage
5390	Professional fees
5400	Rent
5410	Retirement plan(s)—contributions

(*continued*)

Chart of Expense Accounts *(concluded)*

Numbers **5000 (6000)**	*Description* **Expenses (master account)**
5420	Retirement plan(s)—fees and costs
5430	Salaries—office
5440	Salaries—officers
5450	Salaries—salespeople
5460	Salaries—warehouse
5470 (6470)	Sales meetings
5480 (6480)	Salespeople's reimbursed expenses
5490 (6490)	Selling expenses
5500 (6500)	Seminars
5510	Taxes—payroll
5520	Taxes—state income
5530	Taxes—others
5540	Taxicabs and car rentals
5550	Telephone answering service
5560	Telephone (including cellular and car phones)
5570	Temporary employment agency fees
5580 (6580)	Trade shows and booth displays
5590 (6590)	Travel
5600	Truck expenses
5610	Truck leasing
5620	Utilities
5630	Warehouse supplies and expenses
5640	Xmas expenses

In establishing a computerized bookkeeping system the following steps shoud be taken:

1. First choose a *tentative* Chart of Expense Accounts, using your best judgment and keeping in mind that it can later be easily revised, as often as needed.

2. At the same time, consider the IRS implications of your chart! It's always better to break down IRS audit triggers like *travel, entertainment, conventions, and auto* into as many different accounts as is practical. The IRS audit computer is always looking for *big* numbers (dollars *or* percentages), particularly in the travel and entertainment, conventions, and auto areas. Don't help their computer any more than honesty requires. So the smaller the category, the better (more on that later).

3. Train one individual in your office to simply enter the proper chart numbers on each check stub. (A little help may be needed in coding payroll checks, which is probably the hardest part.) Multiple breakdowns on a single check stub can be easily handled by assigning different account numbers to various amounts (e.g., payment of

one credit card bill with many charges). No bookkeeping experience is really required; if you can read and write and breathe, you qualify! (In the case of our clients, we train the selected individual.)

4. The check stubs with account numbers and amounts (usually photocopies), plus a figure for total commissions (and any other income) for the month represent the entire documentation for the bookkeeping system. In our firm, this data is input on our in-house computers.

5. If you want to add an important control, the bank statement and canceled checks should also be sent to the CPA firm doing the data processing. The bank reconciliation by an outside party provides assurance that all the figures are essentially accurate and complete (it won't necessarily catch fraud). For even better control purposes, many of our clients have each bank statement mailed *directly to* our office so that nobody else gets their hands on it. A nice safety tip.

From this modest input, you will get back the following output:

- A monthly and cumulative statement of income received (i.e., commissions) and expenses paid (with all entertainment at *100 percent*, as already explained).
- A monthly itemized listing of each check issued detailing payee, amount, check number, and the account charged.
- A monthly and cumulative general ledger showing each check for the month individually posted to each general ledger account.
- A monthly listing of any journal entries made.
- Monthly and cumulative employee payroll records (upon request).
- Quarterly payroll tax returns (both federal Form 941 "Social Security and Withheld Income Tax" and state); annual federal and state payroll tax returns (e.g., federal unemployment compensation Form 940 "Federal Unemployment Tax"); annual wage statements (Form W-2, "Wage and Tax Statement,"); payroll transmittal forms (Form W-3 "Transmittal of Income and Tax Statements") and the accompanying reconciliations; all comparable state reports; and so forth.
- As an option: annual federal (Form series 1099) and state information returns and their transmittals (Form 1096, "Annual Summary and Transmittal of U.S. Information Returns").

All this can be easily accomplished by the Chart of Expense Accounts and the computer input described. If you have the time, people, and equipment, you can do this at your own rep firm. A completely biased comment: Using an outside CPA firm for all this provides independent monthly reviews of your transactions for both tax, financial, and security reasons. Any suggested changes can be made monthly and any problems (even embezzlement) could be handled promptly. Finally, a CPA firm can monitor your approaching fiscal year-end and the zeroing-out tax process (see Chapter 16).

As a by-product of proper and detailed subclassifications of travel and entertainment expenses, it is your prerogative to avoid bunching these expenses into one or two accounts. At the same time, you can legally and fully disclose (and properly subclassify, for improved management analyses) every element of your travel and entertainment expenses. Don't get lazy and ignore these suggestions, or you'll later remember them during your frequent IRS audits!

You should also be aware of IRS buzzwords. These are words that instantly trigger negative feedback (very harmful to human beings who are taxpayers) on the part of every IRS agent and probably every IRS computer audit program! The worst buzzwords are likely "travel, entertainment, conventions, and auto." You can probably avoid using some of these entirely if you carefully review the chart.

As you examine the chart, you will find about 12 other account titles that could replace the "terrible four." For just plain psychological reasons, we recommend that you do *not* use the word "entertainment" at all. There are still too many old-time IRS agents who have ingrained prejudices against *anything* called entertainment. They mentally translate that word into "taxpayer stealing" every time they see or hear it. We simply don't use it in our clients' charts of accounts; there are many legitimate substitutes.

To summarize, the worst thing you can do is to *combine* those two terrible buzzwords into one account called: "travel and entertainment." The best thing you can do is to have a number of logically different accounts covering those categories, none of which includes the word "entertainment." These are just our own personal opinion, but formed over many years of dealing with the IRS and sales rep audits, so please consider this advice.

Here are some specifics to help you as you use the chart.

SALESPEOPLE'S REIMBURSED EXPENSES (ACCOUNTS 5480/6480)

Nobody else knows exactly what this account means, since we invented it. It's a catchall account for reimbursed salespeople's expenses that you *don't* choose to break down into the various other expense categories.

For example, assume an employee turns in an expense report from a trip, which includes hotel, meals, tips, plane fare, auto rental, postage, telephone, office supplies, and secretarial service. For whatever reasons, perhaps because it might take hours to sort the report into the various categories, you or your bookkeeper don't want to bother breaking the expense report down into the various categories. Instead, the entire reimbursement is charged to this *one* category, "salespeople's reimbursed expenses."

However, the entertainment portion of that account is only 50 percent tax-deductible. Accordingly, you must allocate even this catch-all account between the 100 percent deductible expenses (charged to 5480) and the 50 percent deductible entertainment expenses, which you must charge to 6480, as already explained. *Another reminder:* All charges to the 6000 accounts are entered at 100 percent during the year.

Two warnings, before you go charging off (i.e., accountingwise) everything in sight to this one easy-to-use account:

1. Never use this account for the *owner* of the company, since we are implying by the very account title that these are reimbursed expenses of nonowners. (Also, this will help cool the audit ardor of any IRS agent toward this account.)
2. Don't get so lazy that you use this account to excess and it becomes the *largest* expense account on your books. Resist temptation and use it judiciously. Remember, *no* travel and entertainment type account, including this one, should individually stand out in the eyes of the IRS or their audit selection computer program!

AMORTIZATION (ACCOUNT 5020)

This account now includes the mandatory 15 year amortization of Section 197 intangibles (Revenue Reconciliation Act of 1993). Such intangibles include goodwill and *every* covenant not to compete, *regardless* of the actual length of the covenant. Further, any *arrangement similar* to a covenant (for example, consulting fees, with no services actually rendered), is considered to be the *equivalent* of a covenant under this new IRS Code Section 197 (much more in Chapter 31).

AUTOMOBILE EXPENSES (ACCOUNTS 5030/5040/5050)

By all means split your auto expenses among these three accounts, following the rationale that many small accounts are better than a few big ones. The account for automobile expense reimbursements (5040) can include two kinds of payments:

1. If you exactly reimburse your employees for their auto expenses.
2. If you pay your employees the flat ("no questions asked") mileage reimbursement for every business mile (e.g., 29¢ in 1994).

However, flat auto allowances (e.g., $400 a month and no accounting) become *mandatory* additional compensation under IRS rules and *must* be added to "Salaries" (account 5450) and are then subject to payroll taxes. Flat auto allowances don't belong here at all, and the lack of any accounting for that allowance is costing you, the employer, 15–20 percent additional payroll taxes and related costs. We don't *ever* recommend such an expense arrangement (see Chapter 6).

BUSINESS GIFTS (ACCOUNT 5060)

The limit on tax-deductible business gifts is $25 a year to each individual, including a spouse. If you exceed that limit the excess does not belong in this account, as it is a nondeductible charge against retained earnings in the case of a corporation or the capital account of a proprietor.

CONTRIBUTIONS (ACCOUNT 5140)

Contributions are only tax-deductible by a corporation up to a limit of 10 percent of net income (i.e., net profit). However, if you follow our zero out procedures (Chapter 16) there may not *be* any net income, and accordingly any contributions are wasted (only taxwise, of course). In that event, consider whether any of those contributions were to buy space in ad books or for similar promotional reasons. If so, reclassify those expenditures to "Advertising" (account 5010) and you can legally avoid that 10 percent limit.

CONVENTIONS (ACCOUNTS 5150/6150)

Conventions; one of the IRS buzzword accounts that we try to avoid. Use one or more of the alternate accounts on the chart.

DUES AND PUBLICATIONS (ACCOUNT 5180)

Effective for tax years beginning *after* 1993, the tax deduction for club dues has been *completely* (not 50 percent) eliminated. That's *every* kind of club you can think of, without exception: country, city, athletic, airline travel, social, hotel, and so forth. Club dues have been clubbed to death! Any such payments from your business should be charged directly to #1300 as "officers' loans, if incorporated, or the "capital" account of proprietors #3300 but *never* to expense account #5180 "dues and publications."

NOTE

This new law does *not* affect the tax deduction for business dues other than clubs. For example, trade association dues paid the Electronics Representatives Association (ERA) and similar organizations is still usually 100 percent tax-deductible (except to the extent, if any, that lobbying expenses are paid for with a portion of the dues).

EMPLOYEE BENEFITS (ACCOUNT 5190)

We use this account as little as possible, primarily for educational and child care benefits paid by the company. Most other benefits can usually and properly be classified to "Insurance—group" (account 5270) and the rest can fall into various other accounts. This is probably an IRS semi-buzzword, particularly if it gets too large.

ENTERTAINMENT (ACCOUNTS 5210/6210)

Already discussed at length. A *super* IRS buzzword. Dump it!

INSURANCE (ACCOUNTS 5270/5280)

If your company has an uninsured medical reimbursement plan (which usually supplements regular group medical insurance), we recommend you also charge such payments to "Insurance—group" (account 5270). Similarly, if the company pays for group life insurance, up to $50,000 per individual (Section 79 insurance), it should be charged to that same account.

Any group life insurance over $50,000 per individual should be segregated and the excess premiums (under a special IRS table calculation) are considered additional compensation by the IRS. Thus, the excess premiums end up in "salaries" and subject to full payroll taxes/costs. As with personal use of business autos, discussed later, if you want to save payroll taxes and related costs you should have each individual *repay* the company for the excess premiums (see your insurance agent for the calculations and details).

Group life insurance policies permit the insured to name the beneficiary. "Officers' life" policies are those where the *corporation* is the beneficiary. Those annual premiums, net of the annual increase in cash values, belong in "Insurance—officers' life" (account 5280). This is a *non*tax-deductible expense eventually charged to retained earnings; however, any insurance proceeds are then received by the corporation free of *regular* income tax (although 75 percent of such proceeds may be subject to the corporate alternative minimum tax [AMT], which is a flat 20 percent).

OUTSIDE SERVICES (ACCOUNT 5340)

Charges to this account are about the first place the IRS will look in an independent contractor audit, while the second place they'll look is in "Commissions" (account 5090). Therefore, we are generally leery of this account and we analyze all the charges made to it. Use this account carefully; if an expense can legally fit into another expense account, you are advised to do so.

Independent contractor audits and employee classification problems are something you should be continually alert to, but they are outside the scope of this chart and discussion (see Chapters 8 and 9).

OVERVIEW OF MASTER ACCOUNTS

The complete set of master accounts is:

1000	Assets
2000	Liabilities
3000	Capital (net worth)
4000	Income
5000	Expenses
6000	Business meals and entertainment

An overview of how chart numbers dovetail will be helpful. Balance sheet master accounts are 1000, 2000, and 3000. The 4000 series is for income accounts, and, of course, the 5000 and 6000 series are used for the 100 percent deductible expense account and the 50 percent deductible business meals and entertainment account, respectively.

THE BALANCE SHEET

The *balance sheet* overall master numbers are assigned as follows:

1000	Assets
2000	Liabilities
3000	Capital (net worth)

Chart of Balance Sheet Accounts

Numbers	*Description*
1000	**Assets (master account)**
1100	Cash
1200	Commissions receivable
1300	Accounts receivable—others
1400	Inventories
1500	Prepaid expenses
1600	Prepaid taxes
1700	Property and equipment
1800	Accumulated depreciation
1900	Other assets
2000	**Liabilities (master account)**
2100	Accounts payable
2200	Accrued expenses
2300	Mortgages (trust deeds) payable
2400	Notes payable—banks
2500	Notes payable—others
2600	Notes payable—shareholders
2700	Taxes payable—income
2800	Taxes payable—payroll and others
2900	Other liabilities
3000	**Capital (master account)**
3100	Capital stock—common
3200	Capital stock—preferred
3300	Retained earnings (or capital)
3400	Paid-in capital
3500	Other capital (e.g., donated materials)
3600	Treasury stock

EXPANDING A BALANCE SHEET ACCOUNT

Let's use account 1300, "Accounts receivable—others," as our example. Here are various accounts you might select within the 1300 series:

1310	Accounts receivable—trade
1320	Loans or advances receivable—employees
1330	Due from officers/shareholders
1340	Due from related companies
1350	Installment receivables
1360	Foreign receivables
1370	Accounts receivable—previously written off
1380	Warehouse and other fees receivable
1390	Less: Provision for doubtful accounts

These subclassifications are easily handled by this flexible computer bookkeeping system. We can also utilize the last digit to attain further flexibility. For example, account 1330, "Due from officers/shareholders," can be further subclassified:

1331	Due from Jones
1332	Due from Smith
1333	Due from Brown

The system is indeed simple, easy to use, and flexible. It can be "big" for the big rep firm and "small" for the small! So give it a chance.

INCOME ACCOUNTS

Income accounts comprise the 4000 series.

Chart of Income Accounts

Number	*Description*
4000	**Income (master account)**
4100	Commission income
4200	Warehousing fees
4300	Sales (buy-sell, distributor)

4400	Less: Cost of sales
4500	Expense reimbursements (e.g., from factories)
4600	Interest income
4700	Dividend income
4800	Other income
4900	Personal use of business autos

EXPANDING AN INCOME ACCOUNT

This is the same concept used in expanding a balance sheet account. For practice, let's select account 4100, "Commission income." One alternative would be to control commission income by *principal*. Then the breakdown would look like this example:

4110	Commision income—Jones Co.
4120	Commission income—Smith Co.
4130	Commission income—Brown Co.

If you had a lot of factories you represent, you could sequence every number or every other number (4110, 4112, 4114, 4116, 4118, etc.) and have room for 50 to 99 factories. (We only know of a few reps with 50–99 lines—on a good day they collect three commission checks of about $50 each—and then a bunch of small ones!)

Assume that for some unusual reason 99 numbers were not enough and you needed further subclassifications, perhaps 500 or 1,000. The solution is simple: Enter an entirely new and unused *master* number, such as a 7000 series, and you'll have 1,000 additional numbers to use as you please. Our computer bookkeeping system easily accommodates such an expansion of the chart.

Alternatively, you might want to enter *territories* separately and then later relate them to *salespeople*. We can departmentalize by *both* territory and salespeople by using subdivisions of numbers (the first set of subdivided numbers is the territory):

4100-01	Commission income—Los Angeles area
4100-02	Commission income—San Francisco area
4100-03	Commission income—San Diego area
4100-04	Commission income—Phoenix area

Or, you can also use these subdivisions to enter categories such as commission income by salesperson.

EXPANDING AN EXPENSE ACCOUNT

Expanding expense accounts, the most commonly used area, uses the same concept as expanding accounts in any other sections of the chart. Simply use a *second* set of subdivided numbers. Let's select account 5450, "Salaries—salespeople," keeping in mind that we have already assigned the *first* set of subdivided numbers to territory. We now add a *second* set to identify salespeople and relate them to their territories.

5450-03-01	Salaries—Jones
5450-01-02	Salaries—Smith
5450-04-03	Salaries—Brown
5450-02-04	Salaries—Daskal

In this example, Jones is salesperson number 1 and is in territory number 3, which we earlier identified as San Diego. Smith is salesperson number 2 and is in territory number 1, which we earlier identified as Los Angeles. Brown is salesperson number 3 and is in territory number 4, which we earlier identified as Phoenix. As for that last salesperson, Daskal—I'd keep a close eye on him if I were you!

Almost *any* type of breakdown can be achieved because of the flexibility of the system we are using, and remember, a computer does not get even a little weary! If it gets overloaded, just increase its memory capacity. You could have thousands of accounts in this chart. Our firm has produced 50–60 page monthly computer financial statements for large and diversified rep firms.

We have a number of clients who keep track of each salesperson's compensation and expenses (as well as the commissions earned by each individual) through our system of subdivided numbers. In other words, each expense paid for or reimbursed to a particular salesperson is charged to the subdivided number of that person, including travel, entertainment, auto, and even telephone bills for car phones. This system provides management with an excellent handle on every salesperson. The computer printout provides a package of income earned, compensation paid, and direct expenses paid for *each* salesperson. Such bookkeeping is somewhat more expensive, but it offers an almost perfect way to supervise and to judge performance.

PERSONAL USE OF BUSINESS AUTOS (ACCOUNT 4900)

There are two reasons why this title appears as a separate category in the *income* accounts:

1. If your company is not charging each employee, including owners, for the personal use of every company-provided auto you are blatantly ignoring an entire set of mandatory IRS rules and regulations.

2. Assuming you are following the law as a matter of tax presentation (a virtual religion around our office) it is far preferable to highlight to the IRS that you are indeed conforming to the rules by charging and *collecting* for personal use of business autos. By being detailed as a *separate* income category on the company tax return, this account accomplishes that purpose.

However, if your bookkeeper is netting such amounts collected by deducting them from total auto expenses, you are losing the opportunity to *highlight* to the IRS the fact that you are conforming to the law. Why not let the IRS know what an honest taxpayer you are (i.e., one who hardly ever needs to be audited). Right?

The IRS offers two ways to handle the personal use of those company provided autos. Naturally, they recommend a way that will cost you an extra 15 to 20 percent or so in payroll taxes, workers' compensation, payroll fringes, and so forth. Naturally, we recommend *another* way, one that is perfectly legal but hardly mentioned by the IRS.

The IRS suggests you charge personal use as additional compensation to each employee. That treatment makes such sums subject to all payroll taxes, a combined hit of over 15 percent for Social Security and Medicare taxes alone, *plus* unemployment compensation, workers' compensation, and so forth. Don't do it!

Save that 15 to 20 percent by using the alternate method. *Collect money* from each employee for her share of personal use of a business auto and you eliminate the additional compensation factor and all those related payroll costs. An easy way for each employee to pay back the company for the cost of that personal use is by small deductions from *each* paycheck of *each* employee (some generous employers even give compensating raises to about cover these costs). The hard way is for each employee to write a repayment check to the employer, a virtual impossibility for most sales employees of most rep firms, since writing a check implies that they haven't already spent their entire paycheck!

CASH RECEIPTS INPUT PROBLEMS

Here is a warning about how to input income under this bookkeeping system. Usually commission income is reported as one figure for the month (unless you are keeping track of commissions by each principal). That single amount, or each reported deposit total, is fine as long as *everything* in such totals is indeed income. This is usually assumed. However, special items, such as loans from banks or other people, additional capital contributions, refunds of deposits, or refunds of taxes, must be segregated and your CPA must be advised of such. Otherwise, you will be paying taxes on *non*taxable items, something too terrible to even contemplate!

CONCLUSION

Here is a *flexible* bookkeeping system, especially and particularly designed by us for sales reps. Don't be afraid of the word "computer" or these many suggestions. Give it a try! Break down your expense accounts (particularly travel and entertainment) in sufficient detail to hopefully avoid that first IRS computerized audit sweep and perhaps a subsequent IRS audit. Study these suggestions and then establish your Chart of Accounts.

Also, use the subdivision breakdowns for income and expense charts as a management tool; get a little more sophisticated in your business operations than you thought you could be. Enter data intelligently, do it legally, and conform to the current IRS laws regarding such things as entertainment and personal use of business autos. Be the competent and capable business manager and successful entrepreneur who is buried inside almost every sales rep. You should know by now that to succeed you have to be a good executive *manager* of your agency and not just great at sales. All the thriving reps manifest excellent management abilities, and some of them really can't sell. They hire those who can sell, while they ably study and manage the numbers. Here are the tools to do just that!

Chapter Eighteen

Equipment Leasing and Expensing

The idea of business leasing has spread in the last decade. For example, in the area of computers, where a good rule of thumb is that computers have at most a three-year life and are then obsolete, it's a good idea to lease them for three years, turn them in, and then lease the next generation of computers. The lease payments are 100 percent tax-deductible unless the equipment is not used 100 percent for business or the lease is, in effect, an installment purchase of the equipment. Other prime lease candidates are copiers, fax machines, phone systems, and other high-tech stuff that gets obsolete fast. Leasing furniture, like desks and chairs, is usually not a good idea, since they last and last and don't go out of date.

Of course, you are paying *interest* as part of every lease payment, but you have the use of your money and are not stuck with the equipment at lease-end. Also, such leased equipment is not recorded on the books and accordingly, doesn't increase the total assets of your company (total assets are a primary IRS audit selection technique used for corporations; the higher that total, the more chance of an audit). Finally, since most reps have limited working capital, leasing offers an easy way to get needed equipment.

One of the biggest reasons for *not* leasing disappeared when the Tax Reform Act of 1986 eliminated the investment tax credit. This was the 10 percent credit for purchasing new assets. However, even in those days my firm was still pro-lease because most of our reps would zero out (see Chapter 16), and with no corporate tax to pay the investment tax credit was wasted. For the same reason, if the investment tax credit is reinstated (as is proposed from time to time), it will be of little use to most of our reps.

The other leasing attraction lies in the fact that because office equipment is only depreciable over seven years and computers over five years some of these items receive an unrealistically low tax deduction. So, short-term *leasing* of such assets (computers, copiers, fax machines, phone systems, etc.) increases the tax write-off to match the time span that these items will realistically be used.

Leasing autos is another topic with completely diverse rules and will not be discussed here (see Chapter 2). Nor will real estate be discussed.

EXPENSING EQUIPMENT PURCHASES

Before you get too intrigued with equipment leasing, there is another way for some businesses to claim even better tax deductions. This is the so-called IRS Section 179 election. This allows you, at your option, to deduct as an expense for tax purposes up to $17,500 for warehouse and office equipment purchased by your business each and every fiscal or calendar year, year after year after year. Of course, you must *buy* the assets each year to claim the tax deduction. Also, you cannot claim this tax deduction if you zero out your profits.

A few rules control this asset expensing:

• The write-off cannot exceed a yearly $17,500 spent for newly *acquired* (not necessarily new) equipment. It cannot be claimed for company assets purchased in prior years and it cannot be effectively claimed for autos.

• The total expense deduction for each year cannot exceed $17,500 *or* the net profit of the company, whichever is lower. Thus, you cannot use this expensing option to create a net operating loss, but you can use it to bring a profit of $17,500 or less down to zero.

• You can claim the $17,500 write-off (if you qualify) in a year of no profits, but it will simply become an expense deduction *carryover* to future years under the same rules as for current purchases.

• If the company purchases equipment in excess of $200,000 during its tax year, the $17,500 expense write-off is reduced dollar-for-dollar above that amount. Therefore, if you acquire $217,500 or more in purchases in any one year, you cannot claim any part of a Section 179 tax deduction in that business year.

This immediate tax deduction opportunity represents a virtual "can't lose" situation. For any rep showing an annual net profit (not many of ours do), here is a tremendous tax and accounting convenience! First, you eliminate all that complicated depreciation recordkeeping. Second, you immediately reduce your income taxes. We recommend the Section 179 election in virtually every applicable case, since this method is even better than leasing, deductionwise. However, do keep in mind that if you *buy* that computer and claim the Section 179 deduction, you may be wondering how to get rid of the bloody, obsolete thing three years later!

> *TAXTIP*
>
> If Section 179 expensing appeals to you, buy the first $17,500 of equipment and immediately deduct that amount as an expense. Then consider the option of leasing any *further* equipment needed in that same tax year.

Can you write off the $17,500 as part of a more expensive piece of acquired equipment? Yes, you can. For example, if for some reason your firm purchases a $25,000 computer installation, you *can* claim $17,500 of that equipment as your Section 179 immediate expense deduction (subject to the rules and limitations just discussed) and then depreciate the other $7,500.

WHAT TO EXPENSE

> *TAXTIP*
>
> You can save additional income taxes by expensing whatever assets have the *longest* depreciable lives. If you expense computer-based telephone central office switching equipment, you are achieving an instant write-off of equipment that otherwise must be depreciated over five years. However, if you expense almost any general category of office or warehouse equipment you are still getting an instant expense write-off for the same dollar amount, but it is of equipment that otherwise must be depreciated over seven years. You should get rid of (i.e., expense) the assets that otherwise would take the *longest* to depreciate. You thus increase your total tax deductions for depreciation *and* Section 179 expensing combined.

DEFINITION OF A LEASE

Just because they stick a piece of paper in front of you that is titled "lease" does not necessarily make it a lease in the eyes of the IRS. In fact, some leases may actually be conditional sale contracts. In such case, the IRS will consider the transaction a *purchase* of the equipment for tax purposes. If that happens, you will be right back where you didn't want to be: unable to deduct those high lease payments and limited to (usually) seven-year depreciation.

So please get this straight. You need a true lease to obtain leasing deductions from the IRS and to avoid the lease versus purchase trap. The kind of lease you want to obtain to preserve your lease payment tax deductions is variously called a "tax-oriented lease," a "true lease," an "operating lease," or a "guideline lease." Any other kinds are generally *not* such leases and usually will *not* qualify for the favorable tax treatment we are seeking. And, just having the correct name on your lease will not itself protect you from IRS disallowance.

There are guidelines to prove a lease to be a true lease, although they are not foolproof. Conforming to the following rules from various IRS pronouncements will generally defend your leasing deductions:

- The term of the lease should not exceed 80 percent of the useful life of the equipment at the beginning of the lease.
- Therefore, the residual value at the end of the lease should be 20 percent or more.
- Any purchase option at the end of the lease should be at fair market value and not at a fixed and predetermined price.

> ***TAXTIP***
>
> A final very low and *fixed* purchase price virtually assures that the contract is simply an installment sale and not a lease. Accordingly, those contracts that have an absurd final purchase price ($10 or so) are *never* leases in the eyes of the IRS.

- The equipment must be general use equipment that can be used by other businesses. It cannot be limited use equipment and there must be a market for the equipment.
- Neither you nor any related entity can pay for or guarantee payment of the price paid by the leasing company for the equipment.

WHAT KIND OF EQUIPMENT SHOULD YOU LEASE?

Earlier, we said that you should expense equipment with the longest depreciable life. Conversely, you should lease equipment that will not last as long as the prescribed lives you must use for depreciation.

In other words, lease equipment that will probably become technologically obsolete before it is fully depreciated, and lease it short term.

Who wants a purchase option anyway for that future junk? Instead, you should conform the lease to the IRS guidelines (with the help of your CPA, before the fact, not after) and currently deduct all the payments under a true lease! Lease it, and *give it back* at the end of the lease, with no "cutesy" minimal purchase options.

Again, the most obvious items to lease are computers, software, and peripheral equipment, telephone systems, copying machines, fax machines, and anything else involving *rapidly changing technology*.

ASSORTED LEASING COMMENTS

Leasing can help your cash flow because the lease payments are usually less than the payments to finance a purchase. Also, leasing normally provides 100 percent financing with no down payment required, another saving. What rep doesn't need help with cash flow?

The leasing company can usually obtain financing for transactions at considerably lower interest rates than you can. You should be able to lease at about the same interest rate factor as if you directly financed a purchase at your bank.

The leasing payments should reflect the residual sale value for the equipment at the end of the lease, but the leasing company keeps the equipment (we won't tell them how technologically obsolete all that high-tech stuff will be). Note that the *leasing company* gets the tax benefits of depreciation deductions while leasing to you.

Shop for leasing terms and conditions just as carefully and shrewdly as you shopped for the equipment itself. A major failing of most reps is they're too busy to shop, and they're too easily sold (just as they hope all the buyers they call on will be). Many equipment manufacturers offer favorable leasing terms as a marketing tool to help sell their product. By all means take advantage of any such opportunities you may encounter; again, consult with your tax adviser before you sign any papers.

Also, ask the leasing company to tell you the effective rate of interest being used in the lease, just as if you were borrowing money from the bank. Carefully consider all the additional options and conditions. For example, do you have the right to renew or extend the lease? Do you have the right to improve the equipment? What insurance must you carry on the equipment? Who pays any property tax? Can you cancel the lease early? If so, are there penalties? Is any security or guaranty required? What happens if the equipment is destroyed by fire or lost by theft? And so forth.

Leasing may help your company save its borrowing power for situations in which it *must* borrow. While a true lease has to be disclosed by footnote on the financial statements, it does not increase the actual liabilities shown on the company balance sheet, which in turn may make it easier for you to borrow. As noted, a true lease also does not show up as an *asset* on your tax return balance sheet and thus can lower your IRS audit profile.

For major equipment leasing, try to negotiate a lease termination clause if the equipment is severely damaged (or damaged beyond reasonable repair). There is usually a casualty value fee charged in such a case, but it is well worth considering.

Look for leasing companies that have been around a long time and have a reputation for integrity and stability. Leasing arms of major manufacturers (e.g., General Electric Credit or GMAC), major insurance companies, or major banks are logical places to begin your shopping. Also, as noted, some manufacturers offer favorable leasing as a method of selling their product (just like the auto manufacturers have been doing, on and off, for some years now).

LEASING TO YOUR OWN BUSINESS

This used to be a great tax idea! In the olden days (before the Tax Reform Act of 1986), there were humongous tax advantages if you personally bought equipment, autos, and so forth and leased them to your corporation. You got the 10 percent investment tax credit that was just like cash, you could claim double-declining balance depreciation on all the leased equipment, and you could use those deductions, without limit, on your personal tax return. For example, you could depreciate two-thirds of the cost of an auto in the very *first* year. All gone, bye-bye.

The investment tax credit is gone (although someday it may be reinstated in some form, possibly more limited than before). Depreciation on equipment is seven years, with a maximum of only six-months depreciation in the first year, which really stretches the deductions into the eighth year. (Depreciation deductions for owned autos are absurdly low, as discussed in Chapter 2.) And, as stated earlier, you must conform to various lease rules to avoid items being classified as purchases. Finally, the IRS has had considerable success in getting the courts to ignore even properly drawn leases if they were executed by an individual who *controls* the corporation. They have claimed that such leases are meaningless, since the individuals in control can cause them to be changed at any time.

For all those reasons, we generally recommend against leasing to your own corporation.

CONCLUSION

Begin by electing $17,500 of expensing in any year with a profit and when there is newly acquired equipment of that amount, or more. After that, consider the advantages of leasing further acquisitions in the same year. If you and your financial adviser decide that leasing is for you, select the equipment best suited (taxwise, financially, and technologically) to your particular needs. Lease those assets that would otherwise be subject to the longest (therefore the least) depreciation deductions, whenever possible.

Be sure to obtain a lease that will pass IRS scrutiny and thus preserve all your leasing tax deductions. *Shop* all the costs and terms and conditions as carefully as you shopped for the equipment itself. Consult your tax adviser at each step along the way.

Chapter Nineteen

Record Retention Guidelines

Business records proliferate at about the same rate as rabbits and, if left uncontrolled, they can make about as big a mess! Record storage expenses within your office are costing you whatever your monthly square foot rental may be. Even record storage costs off the business premises can exceed $1 a square foot per month in some US cities.

The loss of time and efficiency because of unnecessary records is hard to measure in dollars; however, there are substantial savings available for every business if you follow these two rules:

1. Use the ideas in the chapter to destroy unnecessary and outdated records and files now.
2. Adopt regular and logical procedures to constantly cull your records in the future.

In most rep firms records are destroyed on an irregular basis when someone notices the problem because the clutter and mess is getting completely out of hand. That's not the way to do it! You must have logical guidelines, and you must eliminate records on a regular basis.

RECORDTIP

My estimate is that one-third or more of your current records are unnecessary, obsolete, and should be immediately destroyed. Aside from any legal, and tax considerations, current opinion is that 90 percent of all business records are needed for less than 6 months and 98 percent are needed for less than a year!

Instead of an *alphabetical list* of everything, let's classify documents by the *length of time* you should keep them. Let's begin with those you should keep forever. Don't get discouraged by the size of the list on the following pages; this is the "guts" of a rep firm, but much of it will not exist for the average sales agency. After determining those records for your permanent file, you can begin to burn, shred, tear, cut, toss, and generally all have a swell time! First, however, is a list of records to preserve eternally:

RETAIN THESE RECORDS PERMANENTLY

Accounting records—all.

Actuarial reports.

Agreements for all retirement plans and trusts.

Annual financial statements—(see "financial statements").

Agreements and deeds.

Applications filed with regulatory and governmental agencies.

Appraisals of property.

Articles of incorporation.

Audit reports—(see "financial statements").

Bills of sale (for all important purchases).

Bonds (records of issuance).

Bylaws.

Canceled checks for important payments and major expenditures of any kind, federal, state, and local including income taxes.

Capital stock and bond records: applications and issuance.

Certificates ledger, transfer records, and anything else relating to stock issued and corporate indebtedness.

Charts of accounts (see Chapter 17).

Contracts, agreements, and leases (of major or current importance, e.g., employment, partnerships, government, union).

Copyright(s) registrations and records.

Correspondence (any important: legal, retirement plans, tax, and similar).

Credit history of the company.

Deeds and mortgages.

Easements.

Engineering and research projects.

Financial statements and reports:
- Annual.
- Audited (i.e., "certified").
- 401(k) plans—(see "retirement plans").

Insurance records (preserve upon advice of your attorney).

Ledgers and journals:

- Cash: receipts, disbursements, and related.
- Customer.
- General.
- Journal entries: year-end.
- Payroll.
- Plant.
- Private.
- Property.
- Royalty.
- Stock.

Legal correspondence of almost any kind, unless your attorney approves its destruction.

Licenses and licensing agreements.

Minute books:

- Board of directors.
- Executive committee.
- Shareholders.
- Other.

Mortgages and deeds.

Note register.

Patent(s): registrations and records.

Plant surveys.

Property appraisals.

Property records:

- Account ledgers.
- Appraisals.
- Deeds.
- Easements.
- Plans and specifications.
- Purchases.
- Sales.
- Surveys.
- Titles.
- Proxies.
- Purchases of property.

Retirement plans (pension, profit-sharing, 401[k] and others):

- Individual employee account records.
- Internal Revenue Service—letter(s) of approval and determination letters.
- Internal Revenue Service—all other correspondence.
- State and municipalities—letter(s) of approval.
- State and municipalities—all other correspondence.
- Virtually anything else relating to retirement plans.

Sale of property.

Securities registration documents.

Tax returns (along with all related documents, worksheets, agent's reports, canceled checks, etc.):

- Estate.
- Gift.
- Income (federal, state, and local: individual, partnership, C or S corporation, trusts).

Trust agreements.

Title papers.

Trademark(s): registrations and records.

Union contracts.

Unsolicited outside suggestions (check with your lawyer).

Warrants.

And a copy of this chapter for future reference.

ALL THE REST OF YOUR SALES AGENCY RECORDS

Almost everything else not contained on the preceding list *can be destroyed* over different time periods. Everything listed from this point on is to be discarded and destroyed after taking into account these conditions:

- Other tax returns of all kinds (e.g., sales, excise, business property, business licenses, etc.) are generally retained in accordance with federal, state, and local laws and their various statutes of limitations.
- Payroll records must frequently be retained for stated time periods under both state and federal laws. However, payroll records present a particular problem because of the increasing

potential for litigation with ex-employees or even current employees. So a special warning is in order for these records and you may want to let your lawyer decide.

- Speaking of lawyers, anything your lawyer tells you to keep, you keep! In any situation involving potential or actual litigation, forget any other guidelines and just take orders from counsel.
- The same comments made for payroll records should also be applied to records of payments to independent contractors. (See Chapter 8 if you have already forgotten those potential problems.)
- Finally, anything your CPA tells you to keep, you keep, in any situation involving taxes or matters financial.

As to all other records, nobody agrees and nobody is right. You will have to make some decisions based on logic, your own particular business situation, and with the advice of your attorney and CPA. For example, on published lists I have seen, the times to destroy canceled checks that are not on the permanent list are variously listed as seven years, nine years, and three years. Nobody is right and nobody is wrong! Aside from the permanent section of recordkeeping, everything else is subject to variable opinions and unsettled guidelines.

So from here on, we are totally involved in judgment calls, except for the special areas discussed above and the permanent list. As an example, general correspondence is frequently listed on either two year or three year retention lists. But how long should you keep a copy of a letter that says, "Dear Joe, Thanks for the nice birthday card," or, "Dear Angie, This will confirm our lunch date next Tuesday." Or a thousand similar and innocuous types of business letters? I suggest that in such cases an absolute *maximum* of six months will suffice and perhaps 30 days is enough.

On the other hand, a business letter regarding an important transaction, event, order, problem, situation might very well be kept two or three years, or longer if your attorney or CPA so advise. For example, in a recent case involving one of our rep-clients, his biggest principal terminated him on 30 days' notice. However, he produced a letter from the principal, written about three years earlier, which established different termination provisions. That letter got him almost $200,000 without going to court!

The following lists have been constructed with time *ranges* to force you to think about your business and make decisions within those confines. These ranges are not cop-outs, because we simply don't know the answers. Nobody knows but you!

Six months to three years

Acknowledgments.
Bank deposit slips.
Bank reconciliations.
Bank statements.
Bills of lading.
Budgets.
Canceled checks—general.
Canceled checks—payroll.
Claims—settled and company won.
Commission statements to salespeople.
Contracts—routine sales or purchases.
Correspondence—general.
Credit memos.
Delivery receipts.
Deposit slips.
Employment applications—not hired.
Equipment repair records.
Expense reports from employees.
Export declarations.
Financial statements—interim (and not audited).
Freight bills.
Freight claims—after settlement.
Garnishments.
Insurance policies—after expiration.
Inventory records.
Inventory tags—physical inventory.
Internal reports—miscellaneous.
Invoices—sales and purchases (issued or received).
Manifests.
Petty cash records.
Petty cash vouchers.
Production reports.
Proxies—shareholders.
Purchase contracts.
Purchase invoices.

Purchase orders.

Receiving reports.

Requisitions.

Sales contracts.

Sales invoices.

Sales reports.

Shipping reports.

Shipping tickets.

Stockroom withdrawal records.

Tabulating machine cards.

Time cards.

Travel records—employees.

Trial balances—monthly.

Waybills.

Now you have the two most important subdivisions of record retention lists. The first list (permanent) enables you to segregate what should never be destroyed, so get those records out of the way and outside of your consideration. The second list (six months to three years) is by far the most flexible, and here is where you have the opportunity to make judgment calls for your firm.

For example, as I scan the preceding list, I would generally advise keeping claims, commission statements, employment applications, expense records, freight bills, freight claims, insurance policies, and proxies for the full three years. You, however, must make decisions based on your own unique business situation. As another example, in our CPA firm, we keep most general correspondence about two years and income tax correspondence at least until the statute of limitations has expired. Yet in another type of business I might not consider keeping general correspondence a minute over six months or even less.

The biggest mistake you can make is to do nothing! If you insist on doing as little as possible, at least set up items on the preceding list for destruction at the end of three years (subject to exceptions already noted). You'll then accomplish the task of eventual and systematic destruction, even if you do keep most of those records longer than necessary. But *do something*, or eventually you are going to drown in records and paper! Then you'll never even be able to get out the door to sell something, and you'll waste a lot of time, money, and efficiency.

The lists that follow are even more subjective. Who is to say if you should keep something four years, rather than five or six? Apart from legal and tax requirements, we are again in the area of opinion, and *you* are the final arbiter. The following lists are therefore just for general guidance in making final decisions. Use them according to good business reasoning and your particular business needs.

Four years to five years

Canceled checks—dividends paid.

Canceled checks—payroll taxes paid.

Canceled checks—other taxes (except income).

Correspondence—employment applicants (not hired).

Cost accounting records.

Credit files.

Depreciation records.

Employees' tax withholding statements (Form W-4).

Employment eligibility verification—Form I-9 (see page 22).

Internal audit reports.

Leases—expired.

Maintenance records—machinery and equipment.

Tax returns—payroll.

Time reports—daily.

Six years to seven years

Accident reports—settled cases.

Accounts receivable—uncollectible.

Bond registers.

Claims—settled, but company lost.

Complaint reports.

Correspondence—credit and collection matters.

Damage reports.

Disability records—employee group.

Employee records—terminated.

Expense analysis and allocation schedules.

Equipment inventory records.

Fire damage reports.

Fire inspection reports.

Fixed asset records.

Independent contractor records (see Chapters 8 and 9).

Insurance—fire inspection reports.

Ledgers—see "subsidiary ledgers."

Maintenance records—buildings.

Notes receivable ledgers.

Payroll—bonuses.

Payroll—general.

Payroll—overtime.

Payroll—part-time.

Payroll—temporary.

Photographs—installations, plants, and so forth.

Plant acquisition records.

Plant cost ledgers.

Price exceptions and adjustments.

Purchase orders for capital expenditures.

Royalty computations.

Safety reports and records.

Sales sheets.

Scrap and salvage records.

Shareholder lists.

Specification sheets.

Subsidiary ledgers—accounts receivable, accounts payable, and so forth.

War contracts and all related records.

Eight years to nine years

Employees' job applications—hired.

Employees' disability claims.

Employees' compensation cases (closed).

Employees' correspondence—to and from.

Employees' earnings records.

Employees' individual earnings records.

Employees' payroll journal.

Employees' personnel files and records.

Employees' salary and wage changes.

Employees' unemployment claims.

Employees' workers' compensation claims.

Employees' W-2 forms.

Real estate tax bills.

Tax returns—business property.

Tax returns—sales and use.

You might as well put anything that you think that should be kept ten years or longer into the permanent storage category. You will probably never keep track of them and the division gets blurred between 10 years, 15 years, and forever! I wouldn't bother making ten years and over a separate category.

SOME GROUND RULES

To understand how to apply the suggested time spans, please study these rules:

- For all tax returns, the recommended retention period begins with the due date of the return, or the actual filing period, whichever is *later*. For example, tax returns filed delinquent, or under approved extentions of time, take the later date.
- For tax and related accounting records, the retention period begins at the *end* of the related fiscal year. Accordingly, file such documents conforming to the fiscal year of the company rather than the calendar year, so tax returns, financial statements, accounting records, and other documentation match time frames. Target your destruction program to begin after each fiscal year-end.
- Any federal, state, or local law will always override any of these suggested time frames. For example, California has a standard four year statute of limitations for income tax returns, Michigan, Nebraska, and Tennessee have six year statutes, while the federal statute is three years. Perhaps there is some local ordinance in your area with a 10 year recordkeeping statute for "waste disposal," "insecticide spraying," or "calling on purchasing agents." Whatever the law may be where you are located, follow it exactly.
- As mentioned earlier, anything your lawyer or CPA says to keep, you keep!
- Since payroll records are a particular problem, we have lengthened some of the suggested retention periods. They are discussed in the next section of this chapter.

The last thing we want to imply is that any of these guidelines represent legal opinion, or an absolutely safe cutoff period for retaining documents. This chapter is intended as a general discussion of what is being done by the average business, in an average state, under average circumstances. Legal (and your CPA's) opinions and instructions, governmental rules, regulations and laws, and management decisions should overrule any of these suggested guidelines.

PERSONNEL RECORDKEEPING

As a rep-employer, you are certainly aware of the potential problems that exist whenever you employ even one individual, let alone 5 or 20! We are currently seeing monetary awards against employers, no matter what the size of the workforce, for reasons such as:

- Discrimination based on age, sex, disability, race, color, religion, nationality, sexual habits and preferences, AIDS, pay differentials, failure to promote, and so forth.
- Job-related physical injuries, including lower back pain and headaches, which are impossible to verify.
- Job-related stress and other mental injuries and disabilities.
- Making employees perform "demeaning" or "unpleasant" tasks.
- For sexual harassment. Sexual harassment charges ranging from the Supreme Court hearings of Clarence Thomas, to the famous Navy Tailhook parties, to Senator Robert Packwood of Oregon have received national publicity. Every employment situation has the potential for constant problems in this area, which can include charges of both physical and mental harassment.
- Whatever else I have not covered, but is lurking out there waiting to attack rep-employers.

What happens when an ex-employee (or even a current employee) threatens or files a suit or claim? Your lawyer or a state or federal regulatory body asks for all your personnel records. Are those records complete? Honest? Current? Flawless? Well documented? Do they exist, or did you discard them too soon and foolishly? Notice the recommended periods for retention of various payroll records! I have been deliberately cautious, yet the time frame may be further extended by applicable laws, your lawyer, or even your CPA.

If you warn a nonperforming employee three times, before dismissal, is each and every time *documented* in your personnel records? If you terminate a minority person first (or take another action that might be construed as discriminatory), are the reasons recorded, documented, and explained in your records? If you don't hire a minority person, are those (nondiscriminatory) reasons clearly disclosed in your files? Or if you fire an employee for what you consider good cause?

In California, and particularly Los Angeles, an entire industry has been created to pander and encourage employees to file suit against their employers. Television ads exhort people to come for a free interview if they even *think* they might have a case. This, coupled with an absurd California law with minimal requirements to prove job-related mental stress, is one of the many reasons driving employers from California. (After even one workers' compensation award against an employer, they suddenly find their premiums doubled and tripled by a so-called surcharge.) Your personnel records may prove to be virtually priceless!

Obviously, the preceding discussion is impinging on the practice of law, and I cannot give information about federal and state laws and regulations. My best lay advice is to recognize that every employer is potentially the subject of attack by every employee and ex-employee, without warning. Keep complete, honest, and well-documented records with that thought in mind, and retain those records for at least as long as my suggested guidelines!

To protect yourself in advance of any possible trouble, a number of government and private publications have been written on the subject. Or, if you want to go even further, you can retain a specialist in personnel policies, procedures, and practices. I am told a written personnel manual for *every* firm, regardless of size, is essential.

EMPLOYMENT ELIGIBILITY VERIFICATION

A new record retention problem was created by the Immigration Reform and Control Act of 1986. In brief, the law says that you must only hire American citizens, or aliens who are *authorized* to work in the United States, and that you must verify that employment eligibility for every employee you hire and not just for aliens. And, you must complete and retain Form I-9, "Employment Eligibility Verification." How's that for a record retention problem, and how many of you have followed this law to the letter?

To be safe, this form is listed under our four years to five years suggested retention, but the legal rules are as follows:

- Retain Form I-9 for at least three years.
- If you employ a person for more than three years, you must retain the form until a year after the end of that employment.

To summarize some of the key provisions of the law, the form is in two parts. The first part is filled out by the employee, who certifies that she qualifies for employment. The second part is filled out by the employer, who certifies that one of the following documents verifying both employment identity and eligibility was examined:

- US passport.
- Certificate of US citizenship.

- Certificate of naturalization.
- Alien registration card.
- Unexpired foreign passport with employment authorization.
- Combination of driver's license or US military card with a Social Security card or birth certificate or INS employment authorization.

Failure to comply with the recordkeeping requirements is punishable by fines of $100 to $1,000 for each employee! Those requirements include completing and retaining Form I-9, and presenting the form when requested by Immigration and Naturalization Service (INS) or (DOL) Department of Labor officers (with three days' advance notice).

How many of you rep employers went through all that rigmarole when you hired someone you thought was an American citizen. That's the killer, because there are *no exceptions* to this law, except if any employee was hired before November 7, 1986. For every employee hired after that date, you had better have a properly completed Form I-9 in your files! It doesn't matter if you hired your own son, or a former U.S. president's son! That's the law! Finally, domestic employees working in your home are included and fall under the law's requirements. How many of you have a completed Form I-9 for your maid? Do it right and fill out and then retain Form I-9 if this situation applies to you.

CONCLUSION

You will achieve considerable savings in aggravation, penalties, fines, interest, litigation, lost time, and professional fees by following these guidelines discussed in this chapter.

Whether you use our system or another, you must set up regular, logical, and automatic procedures for both record retention and record destruction. Then, with a clear head, go out and sell something.

Chapter Twenty

How to Steal Money from Almost Any Rep Firm

"Embezzlement": "To appropriate dishonestly and fraudulently to one's own use; steal [money] by falsifying records"; "To take [money, for example] for one's own use in violation of a trust." Using either definition, it's stealing!

In the past few years, a disturbing number of incidents of stealing have been discovered within our own small business clientele. We have uncovered four cases in 1992 and 1993 alone, and the best estimates are that only 10 percent of all business frauds are detected! If we apply that factor to our own practice, we can postulate that some kind of employee fraud is occurring at about 10 percent of our client companies. What do you think is really going on in *your* business? If you think your sales agency firm is too small or immune from stealing, this chapter should open your eyes.

A first lesson is that employing a CPA does not provide the *slightest* guarantee that frauds will be detected! As you read the business news, you continually see stories about large CPA firms missing various kinds of frauds at types of businesses, such as ZZZ Best, Equity Funding, Lincoln Savings and Loan (and hundreds of other savings and loans), Phar-Mor, Bank of Credit and Commerce International (BCCI), and hundreds of real estate and tax shelter syndications. The CPAs were not necessarily incompetent or not doing their job. *None* of their professional services, including certified audits or reviews, and certainly not compilations and simple monthly bookkeeping services are designed or intended to catch fraud or embezzlement!

It's a sad business fact that normal audit and accounting procedures only occasionally uncover stealing. We catch fraud not entirely by accident, but usually when the person stealing is so dumb or so greedy that normal accounting procedures uncover the defalcation. That's true for any size accounting firm and every kind of accounting engagement. The average businessperson thinks so highly of his CPA that he thinks the CPA can find anything and catch everything. Unfortunately, that's simply not true.

However, there are things you can do and lessons to be learned from the sad experiences of others. The purpose of this chapter is to make you more aware and more knowledgeable about the dangers and tell you ways to avoid being a victim of embezzlement. We are not talking about the employee who steals office supplies (three ball-point pens and three pads of paper) or steals your time by always coming in late. Those occurrences, however, are an *indication* that they may later graduate to the kind of things we will be addressing in this chapter.

THE BLUNT FACTS ABOUT EMPLOYEE FRAUD

Consider these facts:

- It is estimated that 20 percent of all business failures are the direct result of employee theft, which stands to reason since the new, naive, and inexperienced businessperson in many cases virtually invites stealing by making it so easy and so tempting.
- One white-collar crime expert says that 25 percent of the employees will steal at any time they *can* and 50 percent of employees will steal given the opportunity and if the risk of being caught is minimal!
- One survey showed that the businesses most vulnerable to fraud are in the service (like reps) and retail sectors. Ironically, the particular businesses that were victimized were considered to be well managed and stable.
- Three factors, the experts say, contribute to fraud are: opportunity, financial pressure, and a rationale for the theft. If all three are present 50 percent of employees will probably steal. Rep-owners should realize that it is only the *opportunity* that they can do something about. The *rationale* is developed by the employee: "It's just a loan that will be repaid"; "The employer's so rich she won't miss the money"; or "I'm underpaid and really deserve a bonus." Of course, these rationalizations keep the employee from feeling guilty while stealing your money! (And of *course* you will be repaid—about 10 years after all your principals triple your commission rate, and their sales managers insist on picking up every dinner check!)
- Those who steal, steal *again!* The experts agree that once an employee begins stealing he rarely stops even though the immediate need for cash has been eliminated. In the beginning, they need cash fast, so they steal, hoping to pay it back before anyone notices. When no one notices, they steal again, and again.
- The average cumulative fraud reported in a recent study was just over $48,000, but 15 percent were over $100,000!
- While it is estimated that only 10 percent of business frauds are detected, of those detected only 10 percent are reported to law en-

forcement agencies or insurance companies. The employee is fired but not prosecuted, which turns a thief loose to pray upon other unsuspecting businesses!

• *Unprosecuted* employees almost always commit fraud again! They have the highest rate of recidivism of all criminals! The worst thing you can do to other businesspeople is *not* prosecute each and every case, but 90 percent of employers are too embarrassed, or fall for the arguments of "have sympathy," or "it was the first time," or "it won't happen again." Sheer nonsense!

PETTY CASH

Story Number 1

Your petty cash is undoubtedly being maintained under the imprest system, which is an exact reimbursement system for petty cash expenditures. If you begin your petty cash fund with $200 and pay out $134.67, you reimburse petty cash for $134.67 and attach those bills to the petty cash slip. Two hundred dollars is again in your petty cash fund and you can back up the expenditure in your files.

Because you are reimbursing petty cash for *actual expenditures,* what are the odds that petty cash checks would repeatedly be written for even amounts, say $100 or $200? How often would petty cash payouts total an *even* $100 or $200? That was our first employee fraud situation. Many of the petty cash reimbursement checks were indeed for even amounts of $100 and $200 (we do this particular company's computer bookkeeping *monthly,* or we might never have noticed!). On further investigation we found that the rep-owner had no idea of how the petty cash fund was really run. When the sole office employee said "we need more money for petty cash," the rep thought that perfectly reasonable and signed checks without hesitation. After all, everybody knows you need more money in petty cash from time to time.

The owner should have insisted on seeing the actual bills previously paid out of petty cash, and should have always questioned *even* ($100 and $200) reimbursement amounts. Now he knows, but we really don't know how much was stolen or if there were other kinds of stealing as well. The rep-owner didn't prosecute the employee and the employee is still out there, maybe working for *you!*

Story Number 2

One of our clients (a medical practice with gross income in the low millions, but it could have just as easily been a large rep firm) always had a rather substantial volume of petty cash expenditures. A number of the doctor-owners were reimbursing themselves for various business expenses from the petty cash fund, a *terrible* tax and business practice, but one we were not aware of (owners should turn in complete expense accounts and get reimbursed by separate check, but *not* use the petty cash fund).

Suddenly, both the number and amount of petty cash checks increased noticeably. Investigation revealed both questionable reimbursements and numerous checks for flat amounts with no backup at all. Since using petty cash was good enough for the owners, some other employees had decided to use petty cash for their own purposes! In this case, the owners had set the example for the others to follow! I can just hear the employees' rationale: "Well, if they can take money from petty cash, as rich as those doctors are, why not poor underpaid me?"

Remember, if the dollar volume or the number of petty cash checks steadily—or suddenly—increases, someone is probably stealing from you! For both tax and financial control purposes, always limit petty cash to those minor expenditures that cannot be charged or easily paid by check. Don't use petty cash as a slush fund, as these owners were doing.

PAYING BILLS

Who signs the checks in your office? Even if you do, what real *controls* do you have over bill paying? If you have a gasoline credit card with the XYZ Oil Company and your trusted office employee brings you a check for $386.42 payable to the XYZ Oil Company, are you sure you're not being cheated?

We recently discovered a trusted employee of a client company writing one business check for the gasoline charges of the company *and* his personal use! The employee simply opened an account with the same gasoline company the business used! You (or another person signing) *must* see the bills being paid at the time you sign the check!

In the identical vein, consider your foolishly signing a large check to Visa, MasterCard, or American Express! Your company check is really paying the personal bill of your employee as well (what a generous person you are)! Again, the fact that a check is made out to a company you do business with does not mean it is the correct amount, or only in payment of company bills!

Of course, if your trusted employee is the one who signs the company checks, okays the bills, and reconciles the bank statement, you have indeed created all the elements of *opportunity*. Then, we only need *financial pressure* (very common) and *rationale for the theft* (easy to justify)!

CREDIT CARD CHARGES

We are all aware of some of the dangers implied in buying by phone and by credit card. But what if an office employee orders from a catalog using the company credit card number (easily available) and the company address for shipment, which the catalog house correctly verifies?

As in most fraud cases, we discovered this one primarily by accident. When the merchandise she had ordered arrived, the employee simply took the packages home. When the credit card statement arrived she simply approved it, and in this case had the authority to sign a company check in payment. This fraud was virtually undetectable, until (as always!) the amount of the charges grew and grew to noticeable amounts. There is no question in my mind that the stealing probably extended to other areas (there were many checks to cash for "travel advances") and for even larger sums of money. Our rep-client could not understand why his new business could be so successful and, at the same time, always short of cash.

SALARY CHECKS AND SALARY ADVANCES

Even if the individual making out the payroll does not sign the payroll checks, there are a number of opportunities to cheat:

- Calculating his own paycheck too high.
- Obtaining double paychecks, each one signed by a different officer of the company.
- Calculating vacation pay incorrectly, for example, at the wrong rate or for too many days or weeks.
- Drawing a check to a nonexistent employee and cashing that check.

Of course, if that same individual can sign on the account, all the preceding can easily happen!

In one case (not at our firm), the controller of a manufacturing company, a 10-year trusted employee (employees you don't trust, don't get the chance to steal!) transferred sufficient funds to the payroll account to pay nonexistent employees and had the checks deposited into bank accounts he set up. His girlfriend was the payroll clerk! The amounts were small at first, but as his confidence and greed increased (as always!) more and more nonexistent employees were added to the payroll. In the third year of the scheme, during a certified audit of the company, the payroll account had grown so large that it was questioned by the auditors. An actual count of employees uncovered this very substantial payroll fraud.

Salary advances represent a sneaky way to steal money. We've discovered this type of fraud in many of our cases. Any employee can usually get some kind of salary advance and if a regular repayment arrangement is not set up, that money may never get repaid. If you lose track of it, or if the employee leaves, you probably won't get your money back!

> ***TAXTIP***
>
> At least write off salary advances and get a tax deduction (and tax the employee or ex-employee) by reporting additional income on Form W-2 (wage statement) or Form 1099 (information return), when the advances are truly uncollectible. Remember, advances later reclassified as forgiveness of indebtedness by your company become taxable income to the employee forgiven, as do advances later recharacterized as additional salaries or commissions.

STEALING COMMISSION INCOME

"Impossible," you say, "We get our commissions from our principals, entirely by check, and every check is made out to the corporation. No one can cash a corporation check, it can only be deposited!" All of which is generally true, but still not complete protection. Would you really know if one *single* commission check in one *single* month was not deposited in your company account? You might possibly know whether it was *received*, but I doubt you would know every deposit detail.

As a generalization, the more checks the company receives each month, the less noticeable it will be if some of them are missing. The classic method is for the employee to go to a different locality or a different bank and open a company account. The employee has the federal identification number of the employer company, as well as company letterheads, and perhaps even corporate minutes or the corporate seal (borrowed for a few hours, although corporate seals are used less and less).

The employee represents that she is an owner or officer of the company and is opening another account for any one of a number of reasons. The account is opened with just one signature required, that of the trusted employee. Most banks will welcome any new business account with open arms!

Then checks are deposited into this new account. Since most rep books are cash basis, it's easy to cover up the thefts of income. However, in some cases the commission income is entered in the books in case the owner should check, but the bank balance is later adjusted to cover the missing commissions. Commissions receivable (if any are recorded on the books) can also be adjusted by journal entry, credit memo, or misposting. In a very sloppy bookkeeping situation, the bank balance or commissions receivable may simply be left out of balance for months or years.

The employee eventually begins drawing checks on this special account and paying personal bills such as credit card changes, insurance, utilities, auto repairs, and similar categories that would *appear* to be perfectly legitimate and reasonable payments from a typical company account. In a recent case (involving a nonclient, but heard firsthand), the employee had not withdrawn any of the money from the extra corporate account; he was saving all the funds until there was enough to buy an $80,000 Porsche! That's class.

SUMMARY, SO FAR

Remember the three elements of employee fraud: opportunity, financial pressure, and rationale for the theft. If *you* provide opportunity, the other two will follow! Remember, 50 percent of employees will steal given opportunity and minimal risk. Also remember that employing a CPA firm, in and of itself, affords you little protection against employee fraud. And remember that those who steal *always* steal again!

Now let's shift our focus from "what they do to you" to "how to stop them from doing it." A minimum of financial sense, and much common sense, is all that's required.

INTERNAL CONTROLS

"Internal controls" is fancy accounting terminology for setting up some kind of system of checks and balances. For example, something as simple as not signing checks without the actual bills in front of you is a basic internal control.

For those involved with larger rep firms, separation of functions and a system of checks and balances can easily be arranged with the help of your accountants. I advise larger firms to use the functions of various employees as cross-checks against each other and let your own advisers take it from there.

The small rep firm, however, cannot adequately separate the various financial functions because of too few employees. Let's try to help small- and medium-sized rep firms devise some clever alternatives. Here are some basics:

- Never sign blank checks.
- Never sign a check in which all the lines are not filled out.
- Never sign checks unless you have the bills being paid in front of you.
- Whenever possible, have somebody who does not prepare the checks OK the presented bills.
- Whenever possible, you (or your partner) should sign the checks.
- If employees sign the checks, require two signatures by two different employees.
- Watch petty cash fund checks (see earlier discussion) in both amounts and frequency.
- Have only one individual sign payroll checks and spot check calculations (see earlier discussion).
- Examine credit card bills with extra care (see earlier discussion).
- Whenever possible, make the deposits yourself (my partner and I still do!) or at least open the incoming mail yourself (we still do) to get an idea of incoming checks.
- Restrictively endorse or stamp all incoming checks as soon as received so they cannot be cashed or deposited in another bank account. This procedure, plus the previous suggestions can forestall a lot of trouble!
- Look at your monthly financial statements with an eye for any expense that looks out of line, and then investigate.
- Watch your cash balances closely, for example, if you are making money, why are the balances dropping? Is that bank account reconciled by someone you trust (ha!), or yourself, or your outside CPA firm?

BANK STATEMENTS

Bank statements are probably the number one method of internal control for a small rep firm, but *only* if you use them properly! In even the smallest of businesses, the bank statement should *never fall first* into the hands of any employee who signs on the bank account! The business owner should see the bank statement *first,* in every case, before there is a chance for any kind of employee chicanery with canceled checks and such. Two infallible methods to prevent this possibility are to have the bank statement sent directly to the home address of the owner, or to have the bank statement sent directly to the office of the company CPA firm.

If you, the owner, receive the bank statement first, quickly look at every check, both front and back. That's only about a 10-minute job, but a priceless procedure! You may find almost anything: forged checks, altered amounts or amounts that look too high, payees you never heard of, unusual endorsements (double or triple endorsements from one payee to a second or third unknown company, one employee endorsing a paycheck over to another [an indication of loans, gambling, or drugs], or employees cashing paychecks in bars and other unusual places), double payments to an employee or creditor, a check issued to a corporation that was cashed rather than deposited, and so forth. Incidentally, that last item can, unfortunately, apply to your own incoming commission checks as well. We have seen many cases where friendly bank tellers cashed checks made out to corporations even though the law says not to. You (not necessarily your CPA!) can spot most of these unusual items, and all for about 10 minutes a month!

As you look at your monthly statement, glance at your deposits and your daily balances to see if anything looks out of line. Was an overdraft shown on the bank statement, even for one day? *Should* there have been? *Could* there have been? Are the daily balances lower than your checkbook balances? Generally your checkbook balances should be *higher* because of checks not yet cleared. Once a month, try to act a little bit like Dick Tracy; then bring the statement into the office and have an employee reconcile them with the bank or (still better) send it to your CPAs but mail it to them yourself.

Having the bank statement sent *directly* to your CPA firm gives them the chance to both scrutinize and reconcile the bank statement. We found one case where two paychecks signed by two different officers were issued to the same employee for the same week's pay, but only one was recorded in the checkbook (the other paycheck was taken from the back of the checkbook and the stub marked void). For small reps, the additional cost of having a CPA do these bank reconciliations would be approximately $25–$50 a month (tax-deductible!), depending on the size of the account.

I'd recommend using both the described procedures, that is, the owner reviews the bank statements at home and then they are sent *directly* to the outside accountants (bypassing the owner's office completely).

SCREENING

Everybody *hates* to screen job applicants and it is not always easy, but the alternative is to leave yourself open to a considerable number of people who intend to steal from whomever hires them! I just read about the case of a busy dentist who signed blank checks in batches for the office manager, many of which were used to pay the employee's personal bills.

Remember, we have learned that stealing continues—and increases—if the employee is not caught. In the case of the dentist, the first month's theft was $400, the second $800, and the third $1,200. In one year, the total was $20,000, and during the final nine months $54,000 was stolen. The three year total before the thief was finally caught was $90,000!

The point of this story is that the office manager was on parole for embezzlement and had used a false name and Social Security number. The dentist, who could just as easily have been a rep, never checked any of the purported references because he was "too busy." You simply *must* do some screening for every employee. (Also, consider how quickly and easily our suggested bank statement procedures would have caught these thefts.)

INDICATIONS OF POSSIBLE EMPLOYEE FRAUD

Certain patterns develop that are frequently clues to stealing. I'm sure you have all heard about the dedicated, hard-working employee who *never* takes a vacation. Frequent, voluntary overtime and refusal to take vacations are considered to be extremely suspicious behavior by companies that insure against employee fraud (vacations are mandatory at banks!). Complicated fraud involves juggling various sets of records and bank accounts, a lot of (daily) hard work, and almost no time off because someone might stumble on the scheme. Therefore, from every owner's standpoint, compulsory vacations are a must!

Here are more employee indications of possible stealing:

- A high standard of living, compared to income.
- Frequent rewriting of records to make them "neater."
- An overly protective attitude toward the records ("they're mine, don't fool with them").
- Maintaining a constant backlog of entries to hamper keeping records up to date ("it's a big job and I'm very busy with so many different matters").

- Commission and other accounts receivable details not up to date and not balanced ("it's a big job and I'm very busy with so many different matters").
- Accounting records in general not up to date ("it's a big job and I'm very busy with so many different matters").
- Excessive gambling or drinking, or drug use.
- An extramarital affair (such affairs put a strain on the employee's money and time).
- Frequent borrowing from fellow employees, or excessively generous and repeated treating of fellow employees to lunch, dinner, drinks, and so forth.

There are also accounting indications of possible stealing:

- Cash storages or overages.
- Unusual fluctuations in accounts, particularly travel, entertainment, interest, taxes, or petty cash.
- Missing documents that are "here somewhere," but somehow never located.
- Unusual second or third endorsements on checks (mentioned earlier).
- Old checks outstanding and other stale items in bank reconciliations (easily used to cover up fraudulent *current* transactions).
- Unexplained adjustments to commissions and other accounts receivable (or too many credit memos, refunds, or returned merchandise if you have a buy-sell operation).
- Stealing merchandise from a buy-sell operation or samples from a rep firm (although an accounting entry was rarely required in most such cases).

Also mentioned earlier, check for alterations, duplications, or even forgeries.

FIDELITY INSURANCE

Standard property insurance coverage excludes employee dishonesty. However, such coverage is available in the form of a fidelity bond. The costs are generally low. In California, a $50,000 bond for five or fewer employees is about $250 a year, while a $1 million bond for the same number of employees costs less than $1,000.

There are essentially three kinds of fidelity bond insurance policies in most states. The first, the *position* bond, covers all those working in a certain *position* in the company (e.g., bookkeeper, controller, treasurer, vice president, etc.). The second, the *blanket* bond, covers ("blankets") *everybody* in the company. The third, the *individual* fidelity bond, is specifically written to cover *individuals* in the company by name (this individual policy is usually written after an insurance company investigation of the person or people being covered).

Some states (including California) offer a multi-coverage dishonesty policy (called "3-D" by one insurance company) that insures three possible situations: employee dishonesty, money on or off the premises, and credit card and depositor's forgeries. Consult your own insurance agent, but you are well advised to carry as much of this insurance as you ever may need in the worst conceivable situation.

TAX TREATMENT OF EMBEZZLED FUNDS

In the case of employee fraud, there's a tax break! The loss from embezzlement is generally deductible in the tax year in which the loss is *discovered*. Consider the alternative: You would have to retroactively determine in which years the stealing took place and file amended tax returns for those years (just think of the accounting fees alone!). If the statute of limitations had expired, you would lose those deductions forever!

As far as the dishonest employee is concerned, a tax rule says *embezzled proceeds are taxable income*, which may be some small consolation for the employer. However, since we are already dealing with a liar, cheat, and thief, the odds are good that if the employer doesn't report the embezzlement to the IRS the crooked employee never will!

Given the predilection of employees to sue employers and further given that you are in an adversarial situation with the dishonest employee, the employer had better be careful exactly how and how much he reports as embezzlement proceeds to the IRS! If you report nothing, on the other hand, you're encouraging theft, (plus you would have overreported your taxable income and tax liability as well). You will have to take the advice of your attorney, having supplied her with information obtained from your CPA.

In the rare and simple case in which there is only one theft, for say $5,000, and the employee admits to that theft, the solution is easy. On the employee's Form W-2 (wage statement) in the year of discovery of the loss, add $5,000 to total compensation (box 1), and also put the $5,000 in the box used for memo items. Insert next to the $5,000 memo item the words, "embezzlement proceeds." That ought to get some attention from the IRS!

If the employee is long gone when you discover the theft but the amount is inarguable and perfectly established, you might consider filing either a Form 1099 (information return) with the same description or a separate Form W-2 with just that single amount on it. I always suggest the Form W-2, since the IRS verifies virtually 100 percent of all Forms W-2 filed, but only about 90 percent of Forms 1099.

A serious reporting problem occurs when the total amount of the theft is either in doubt or being disputed by the former employee. Then you must follow the lead of your lawyer or be prepared for probable litigation with the ex-employee (who hates you anyway because you caught him!). However, you should still notify the IRS and claim a tax deduction! In some cases, I have seen 1099s or W-2s filed with estimated amounts of embezzlement income, and in some cases, the attorney has written a letter to the IRS detailing the facts and circumstances and employee name, Social Security number, and so forth.

SEX

Why would an owner not notify the IRS of an embezzlement and take a tax deduction? Sometimes the owner is embarrassed or doesn't want to call attention to the company by the IRS. But surprisingly often doing nothing is the result of a romantic involvement between the owner and the employee. After all, if the employee is going to steal from the company, a sexual involvement with the (preferably married) business owner is better insurance against prosecution than you can ever buy from any insurance company! The dangers implied in a combination of adultery, embezzlement, and possibly blackmail may make a great movie script, but it is about the single dumbest and single most dangerous thing that any owner (male or female) can do! Enough said, but this warning is meant to be taken very seriously.

ALWAYS ASSUME THEY ARE VERY SMART!

Always assume that an employee who steals is smart! The thieving employee has eight hours a day to plan and steal, a knowledge of your books and internal controls, and a dishonest mind-set already bent toward fraud. I always shudder when one of my clients says, "I know my rep business so well, I would know the instant anybody was stealing." Wrong! If I worked for any of you for about a year, I could have half your money and maybe half your entire rep business, and you wouldn't know it until your checks start bouncing and you found out how much money you really owe. About that time you'd get a "having a wonderful time" postcard from Brazil!

IF YOU STEAL, THEY STEAL!

As mentioned earlier, if the owner "steals" in any noticeable form (expense accounts, cash, or anything similar), some employees will quickly take that as a license to follow in the boss's footsteps. Then you have created a company atmosphere where dishonesty permeates the entire attitude of the employees toward the business and you! Instead of the James Bond "license to kill," you have granted a "license to steal." Not only will the employee think, "If he can, I can!" but "If he can, I can do it *better!*" The owner will always lose *that* contest! Please heed my advice.

Finally, it bears repeating that the dishonest boss is wide open to blackmail by the dishonest employee and can never safely report that employee for any kind of stealing. Don't break any laws and maybe, just maybe, they won't either.

CONCLUSION

Employees are stealing from every fifth firm right now! Study this chapter and immediately take some positive steps. *Don't* think it can't happen to you: if you think that way, you are probably the one it is happening to!

Chapter Twenty-One

Loans to and from Shareholders

LOANS TO SHAREHOLDERS (FROM THE CORPORATION)

If you will refer to a corporate income tax return, Form 1120, on page 4, Schedule L, line 7 (on the 1993 tax form, and consistently appearing year after year), you will find "loans to shareholders." Why do you think the IRS uses up one of its lines on the tax return to require *separate* disclosure of this particular information? Because such transactions between a closely held corporation (99.9 percent of all rep corporations qualify for that description), and its shareholders are always subject to special IRS scrutiny.

Of all transactions, probably the most suspicious are the shareholders' expense accounts and loans to shareholders. It's absolutely true that a shareholder can borrow money from the corporation, but a great deal of care is required to keep the IRS from calling that transaction either a taxable dividend or additional compensation.

FORMALITIES: TOP HAT, WHITE TIE, AND TAILS!

The absolute key to protecting the status of shareholder loans lies in the observation of a series of *formalities*. Now, the average rep generally enjoys formalities about as much as I enjoy an audit with a tough IRS agent, representing a rep-client whose records range from minimal to incomprehensible to mythical to none! But the courts have consistently held that "facts and circumstances" determine whether a shareholder loan is truly that, rather than a taxable distribution, and the appropriate formalities are really the *key* to setting the stage and winning the facts and circumstances test.

A special defense is available in a situation where similar loans are made to nonshareholders who are employees of the corporation. For example, if the corporation has a written and established policy of making loans for medical emergencies to employees, your own loan for a medical emergency is much more likely to be accepted. Much greater credence is given in such a situation and, of course, the IRS can never claim that a nonshareholder was paid a "dividend."

If, however, at the time a loan is made it is called a dividend or compensation, a later and retroactive recharacterization as a "loan" can be easily brushed aside by the IRS. At the time a loan is made, there must be a clear intention for the money to be repaid and that intention must be clearly documented.

IRS GUIDELINES

Shareholder loans are another IRS test area where the more evidence the better, and the more formalities you meet, the safer you are:

- The transaction must be recorded on the books as "loans receivable—shareholder" or a similar *receivable* title. Such recordation is *prima facie* evidence that the corporation expects to be repaid, and represents the *first* basic essential of every loan transaction.
- The loan must be evidenced by an interest-bearing note.
- Was there obvious intent, initially and in every way possible, by both the corporation and the borrower to regard the payment as debt? Was repayment intended to be with regular repayment of interest?

The borrower must make regular interest payments to the corporation in conformity with the terms of the note. The IRS definition of "regular" is "quarterly or more often." Many borrowers flunk this major IRS test: How could this be a loan if you never or sporadically pay interest?

My recommendation is to record the granting of such loans in the corporate minutes (a very telling piece of "formality"). Approve the loan and recite all the terms of the loan including interest, repayment of principal, and other provisions.

IRS AUDIT ATTACKS

Of particular peril is a loan to a 100 percent shareholder who has unlimited authority to call the withdrawal anything she chooses. The IRS will much more closely question that type of loan transaction, and therefore the facts and circumstances had better support the loan characterization in every way and in every detail.

In the event of an audit adjustment, the IRS will invariably try to call the loan a "constructive dividend" if the corporation has retained earnings that equal or exceed the loan. This affords the IRS the best of both possible worlds: the loan is a taxable dividend income to the shareholder, but such dividends do *not* represent tax deductions for the corporation.

The IRS is in a weaker position if the corporation has little or no retained earnings (because of losses, annual zeroing-out, etc.). Since you cannot pay dividends if no retained earnings exist, their next mode of attack is to classify the loan as additional compensation. However, this would be more difficult to prove than a constructive dividend paid from retained earnings, and if they do win, the additional compensation determination would provide the corporation with a tax deduction for the same amount. In either case, however, the borrower gets taxed.

Here is a quote, which speaks for itself, from the IRS *Audit Technique Handbook:*

> Consideration should be given to shareholder's loans . . . Loans to shareholders, particularly when they are noninterest open account loans, may frequently be taxed to the borrower as constructive dividends. Of prime importance are the intent and ability to repay.

SUMMARY: LOANS TO SHAREHOLDERS (FROM THE CORPORATION)

Properly record the loan on the corporate books from day one, observe all loan formalities, execute an interest-bearing note, pay interest frequently (quarterly or more often) and exactly as called for, repay the principal on time, and enter the loan and all the details in the corporate minutes.

LOANS TO THE CORPORATION (FROM SHAREHOLDERS)

Refer to the 1993 corporate income tax return, Form 1120, page 4, Schedule L, line 19, "Loans from shareholders." Each year, the IRS uses one of their valuable lines to make you reveal this information as well. Obviously, loans to the corporation from shareholders are also subject to special IRS scrutiny. But this comes as a great surprise to most reps, who wonder "What do they care if I put more money in the business, I'm only trying to help the agency? I'm not trying to fool the IRS in any way at all. What difference does it make to them?"

Loans to the corporation seem completely innocuous to most of you, but obviously not in the suspicious eyes of the IRS. Of course their motive, as usual, is to collect additional income taxes. Here's how they do it.

THE IRS DOUBLE-BARRELED ATTACK

If you are not as equally careful with loans *to* your corporation as with the loans *from* your corporation, a fast IRS one-two punch will hit you with added income taxes. If the loans are made to your business on a casual, indefinite, and informal basis, the IRS will come along, after the fact, and reclassify them as additional permanent capital you have put into the corporation rather than loans. If your first reaction is, "So what?" Here's "what."

When business improves and you repay those loans you so casually and informally dumped into the corporation, you will want to treat those loan repayments as tax-free ("I loaned the money in, then I took it out"). And you probably forgot about charging interest. Why bother when it's your own corporation, right?

But the IRS, after the fact and after an audit says that since you really put the loans in as additional permanent capital, there were no moneys owing you. So, when the company eventually did make a repayment of your loan, the IRS says you really paid yourself a taxable *dividend!*

Of course, if line 19 on the corporate tax return hardly decreases from year to year, that's further *proof* to the IRS that you gave permanent capital and that any subsequent repayments are taxable dividends. Isn't that a neat IRS snare?

WHAT TO DO?

The same formal procedures should be followed as if you took a loan *from* your corporation: minutes, signed notes, accounting entries, interest, and so forth. Refer to the first part of this chapter for the details. However, in giving a loan *to* your corporation, there is a *further* IRS trap.

IRS LOAN RATIOS

Even if you follow each and every procedure suggested, the IRS can still run roughshod over your so-called loans and classify them as additional permanent capital if the ratio of those loans to capital stock gets too high. From court cases and common usage, the rule of thumb is that your loans to the corporation should not exceed a 4:1 ratio. In other words, if your issued capital stock totals $10,000, your loans should not exceed $40,000 no matter how perfect your documentation and formalization. Otherwise, on that basis alone, the IRS has a great chance of winning the reclassification to capital of your "excess ratio" loans, again creating a taxable dividend situation for the owner when loans are repaid.

SUMMARY: LOANS TO THE CORPORATION (FROM SHAREHOLDERS)

You must follow all the loan procedures of the preceding sections. You also must make regular loan repayments (or similar), and finally, you must watch the loan ratios. As you now can see, loans to (as well as from) your own rep corporation carry concealed tax dangers that you probably never dreamed of.

Chapter Twenty-Two

Unreasonable Compensation

Most reps are probably aware that the IRS can challenge your compensation as being "unreasonable." If their challenge is successful, your agency will usually suffer severe financial penalties, additional accounting and legal fees, plus some terrible aggravation! So, let's all learn about the ins and outs of being "reasonable."

THE VAGUE GUIDELINES

The determination of reasonable compensation is highly subjective because the guidelines are so vague. Final determinations have been left to the courts, and from those court cases the more definitive rules have slowly developed. Not a good situation.

Internal Revenue Code Section 162 says that "ordinary and necessary" deductible business expenses include a "reasonable allowance for salaries or other compensation for services actually rendered." The related IRS Regulation 1.162 is supposed to explain what Section 162 means, but it simply blathers on about "whether the payment is reasonable in relation to services performed" (the so-called amount test) and "whether the payments are solely for services rendered" (the so-called purpose test).

The regulation also gives such a vague definition of reasonable compensation that it has served only to support many lawyers (and their families) and many accountants (and their families) over many years. The definition: "Reasonable compensation is the amount that would be paid for like services under like circumstances." What a big help!

Here are guidelines derived from that unhelpful explanation:

- Your total compensation (and that of your employees) must be "reasonable." This includes and aggregates your salaries, bonuses, commissions, retirement plan contributions, group insurance premiums, and all other fringe benefits. "Reasonableness" has been defined (in one of the many court cases) as: "Reasonableness is determined by comparing the amount of compensation paid to an individual with the value of services performed. This determination is made on an individual employee basis and not in terms of aggregate compensation paid to all employees."

- The services must actually be "rendered." For example, your children, your spouse, or even a friend must only be paid compensation for *genuine services* they carry out for the company.

THE COST OF ANY DISALLOWANCE

Understand how serious any disallowance of compensation can be. Disallowed salary payments become *nondeductible* dividends. Your corporation thus owes federal and state income taxes on the amount disallowed plus interest. Conceivably, a portion of your retirement plan contributions related to that part of the salary could also be disallowed (although I have rarely encountered this). And, don't forget all the related accounting fees and legal fees!

COMPARABLE COMPENSATION

If the IRS does question the reasonableness of your total compensation, one means of attack is evidence of compensation being paid by *comparable* rep firms (one of the few guidelines specifically mentioned in that IRS Reg. 1.162). If you can show that a competitor, similar in size and nature to your agency, pays as much or more for similar services, you have probably quashed any IRS challenge.

The compensation paid other employees, who are *not* owners, may also provide you with major IRS ammunition. If you pay yourself $90,000 as president of your agency and pay your vice president and top salesperson $60,000, your compensation looks right in line. However, if that vice president (and nonowner) is being paid $60,000 and you are paid $275,000, don't raise this defense.

SPECIAL QUALIFICATIONS AND ABILITIES

Here is the area where you can personalize your defense. Anything special in the way of talent or position is a feature that can earn the right to higher (yet still "reasonable") compensation. For example, holding office in a trade association demonstrates that you are highly regarded in your industry; industry awards, recognition, leadership, and publicity also prove higher worth.

Special abilities or expertise in one or more corporate areas, such as finance, marketing, production, product design, or distribution, also justify a higher salary. Some reps even help their principals with product design, product innovations, and production problems. Companies *do* pay more for highly talented and multitalented individuals. Remember, once the IRS questions your total compensation, modesty goes out the window and bragging becomes the order of the day!

Another situation justifying higher compensation and rewards would be if you were the founder of the business, the one who built the business, and the one primarily responsible for the profits, growth, and success of the company. In two cases I have studied, the fact that the controlling stockholders *developed* the business and their services were regarded as *indispensable* won the day for their claims of reasonable compensation. (But maybe if they had been better prepared, and they had proved those assertions to the IRS agent, they would not have had to go to Tax Court to win.) In the opposite vein, the fact that your father owns the company and gave you the best accounts and the best territory does not really make you a star, and is not justification either saleswise or compensationwise.

Almost *everything* can help your case: hours worked, education, serving in more than one capacity. Remember, the IRS agent does not have the slightest idea of your duties, position, function, and what you really do for a living. It's up to you and your CPA to do a selling job when you present your case to the agent. Factor in the scope of your business, its complexity and size, the extent and nature of your work, and your resultant duties. In some cases, a comparison of your compensation to both the gross and net income of your corporation may be helpful. Advance preparation and lots of documentation are the best suggestions.

YOU ARE OPERATING A PERSONAL SERVICE CORPORATION

Sales reps are in a service business. The services they render are "selling" services. Their corporations are personal service corporations *not* in the technical sense of certain personal service corporations with special tax restrictions by the IRS and a *flat* 35 percent tax rate, as explained in Chapter 12, and therefore the earnings of the agency depend primarily on the personal services rendered by the owners. In general, the courts have been quite generous in reasonable compensation cases involving personal service corporations and their owners. They seem to agree that the *personal efforts* of owners/officers are directly responsible for the earnings of the corporation and that invested capital has little to do with creating or affecting such earnings.

In most of these cases, your defense is simply that your personal efforts as owner were the primary and direct cause of the earnings. Therefore, compensation in direct ratio to those earnings is not unreasonable. This argument will frequently convince any IRS agent, particularly after she studies all the favorable cases on service businesses.

WARNING

The preceding position is far more defensible in the case of a *small* rep firm (say up to five individuals) than a larger one. In the small sales agency, the owner is responsible for virtually all the earnings. However, the larger the corporation and the more employees, the less directly responsible that owner is for direct income and the more he is involved in administration, supervision, finance, personnel, and other matters. In such cases, it is more difficult to prove a direct relationship between the owner's compensation and the corporate income.

As a practical matter, the IRS is aware of the difficulties in attacking personal service corporations, and a challenge will generally be raised only with the larger rep firms. However, nobody is invulnerable to attack; the more you know about this problem, the better prepared you can be. It would be just your luck to get a stubborn IRS agent who insists on fighting the point in a three-person sales agency.

If you have recently incorporated your business, you can take corporate compensation equal to your earnings in the last *un*incorporated year (and you are about as safe from attack as you ever can be!). The logic is obvious: Why should you be worth any less just because you now are incorporated?

THE WRONG WAY TO ZERO OUT

Despite all that cheery news, compensation problems can easily be created when you're zeroing-out your fiscal year-end.

One of the worst things you can do is to pay year-end bonuses *in proportion to the stockholdings* of the owners. In other words, the 10 percent owner would receive a $10,000 bonus, the 60 percent owner a $60,000 bonus, and the 30 percent owner a $30,000 bonus. In the eyes of the IRS, this represents a clear attempt to *distribute profits*, rather than compensate individuals for services rendered. Those payments would therefore be unreasonable compensation and thus nondeductible dividends by the corporation. However, if every shareholder received the same or fairly similar dollar bonus, regardless of the ownership proportion, a potential attack from the IRS arsenal is thwarted. Don't ever pay bonuses in the exact ratio of stock ownership.

Another mistake is to simply clean out the corporate account with a last minute bonus that almost equals the net profits of the corporation. The IRS views this as an attempt to drain off profits and can argue that the bonus had little relationship to reasonable compensation, since it was simply calculated to equal the remaining profits of the corporation. This IRS attack is even more damaging if no dividends were paid (more on that later).

As a safer alternative, consider adopting or amending your corporate retirement plan so you can increase the fiscal year plan contributions. This represents a better way to zero out the net profits of the average sales agency. Instead of grabbing that last minute bonus, let the same funds go into your tax-deferred retirement plan and you will get the *same* tax deduction without the danger.

Even if your rep corporation files on the cash basis of tax reporting (I certainly hope so!), any retirement plan contribution can be deducted for tax purposes at the end of the fiscal year. Actual payment is not required, however, until the due date of the corporate income tax return, including an extension of time to file. Thus you can deduct the retirement plan contribution now and not pay it for 8½ months after the end of your fiscal year (the regular 2½ months, plus a six-month extension of time to file). A major loophole in cash basis tax reporting and deducting!

TAXTIP

Some pension-type retirement plans can be amended to allow a higher contribution than in the past, and thus a higher income tax deduction. Retirement plan contributions are a simple and low-profile way to zero out small corporations. Additionally, the contributions are not current taxable income to the owner (that dangerous bonus certainly is!).

DIVIDENDS

A very sophisticated attach can sometimes be launched by an IRS agent: If your company does not pay *any* dividends, then some portion of your compensation is (impliedly) a return on your invested capital and thus represents a dividend. A dividend, of course, is *not* deductible by your corporation, while compensation is deductible. This is another attempt to disallow part of your salary even when your total compensation *is* reasonable.

One defense against this attack is that the invested capital in your rep firm is minimal—a 5 percent return on invested capital of $982.74 is $49.14—and you will be happy to pick up that amount as dividend income. A second defense is that there is absolutely no relationship between invested capital and earnings in almost any sales agency, anyway: you are in a service business and not in a capital intensive enterprise.

After many court cases, the IRS has backed down on their automatic presumption that any time a corporation does not pay *any* dividends, part of the owner's compensation must include a dividend by *implication* (their changed position is memorialized in IRS Rev. Rul. 79-8). Frankly, I have not had such dividend challenges in the case of sales rep corporations. Further, since we zero out almost all our rep-clients, they have virtually no retained earnings and any IRS dividend attack is moot.

CORPORATE MINUTES

From time to time, I have had an IRS agent state that the corporate minutes of a small business were self-serving since the owner could *control* exactly what they said. Be that as it may, the courts frequently give great weight and credence to corporate minutes. Don't forget, self-serving or not, they are the *only* minutes that exist. You are throwing away a great opportunity to defend reasonable compensation (and your dividend policies) if you don't take advantage of them. You have nothing whatsoever to lose.

IRS agents first ask to see the corporate minutes when beginning an audit; the *content* of those minutes can set the tone and be essential to the eventual outcome of the audit. If you throw away a major advantage that is yours for the taking, you deserve what follows!

From the IRS *Audit Technique Handbook*: "Establishment of compensation toward the end of the year is sometimes an indication that . . . an element of profit distribution [i.e., 'dividend'] is involved." So to help protect you, here are my essential instructions:

- Always write your annual salary in the corporate minutes.
- Always do so at the *beginning* of each fiscal year.
- Always make your annual salary *high enough* to include any possible year-end bonus, back salary, and so forth. (If you set it high and don't reach the stated amount, so what? But if you have a great year, the money was *preapproved* and is safely yours.)
- Recite in the minutes all reasons and circumstances leading to any increase in your compensation.
- Avoid any appearance of trying to match your compensation to the net profits of the corporation (this problem is easily avoided by determining your salary at the beginning of the fiscal year).
- Always maintain at least annual (and formal) corporate minutes. I understand that every rep hates paperwork and paying legal fees, but this one is essential!

PRIOR COMPENSATION

In this area, you can launch a devastating attack or counterattack on any IRS challenge of unreasonable compensation. You can measure reasonableness of compensation over the *whole period* of your employment and not just over the year subject to audit. This concept can represent a great defense if your present salary is intended to compensate you for the low salaries of earlier years. If so, document those facts in your corporate minutes, preferably in each and every year of low salaries.

HEDGE AGREEMENTS

Hedge agreements are used to protect against the possibility of an IRS disallowance. The two major areas where hedge agreements are often used are compensation agreements and expense accounts. The act of the IRS disallowing part of your compensation as unreasonable can (as you have learned) convert a corporate tax deduction for salary into a nondeductible dividend. A hedge agreement requires that the employee *repay* any portion of the salary disallowed as unreasonable (and any portion of expenses disallowed as unsubstantiated). The individual will receive a major tax deduction, since the repayment of the salary and expenses results in an individual income tax deduction in that year (or sometimes retroactive to the actual year of the unreasonable salary and unsubstantiated expenses).

Well then, why doesn't every business in the United States use hedge agreements? Because of an IRS catch-22 philosophy: The very fact that a hedge agreement *exists* is frequently considered by the IRS as evidence in and of itself that you were indeed aware that compensation or an expense really *was* unreasonable!

Many tax attorneys and CPAs believe that the hedge agreement *increases the risk* of compensation and expenses being disallowed. Others, while recognizing the danger, say signing a hedge agreement is worth the gamble. I personally think the hedge agreement is a toss-up; I simply call it to everyone's attention for the record with no final opinion.

S CORPORATIONS

As you will remember (Chapter 13), an S corporation is a special kind of corporation that is treated like a partnership for federal income tax purposes. It pays no federal income taxes, since all taxable income flows through to the shareholders of the S corporation. Electing to be treated as an S corporation will instantly *eliminate* all questions regarding reasonable compensation.

We are not in love with S corporations (again, see Chapter 13), and we use them for reps only in one of the following situations:

- To avoid any challenge of unreasonable compensation (and then only when salaries are very high).
- To avoid being forced to accrual basis reporting if commission income exceeds $5 million annually.
- If the rep firm is in a loss situation and that loss is better deducted on the personal tax return of the owner than at the corporate level.
- If there is a problem with excess retained earnings over $250,000. S corporation treatment prevents any further accumulations since all future earnings are distributed to the shareholders.
- To avoid the corporate alternative minimum tax (AMT) of 20 percent in certain situations.
- In conjunction with a stock bonus plan to employees (see Chapter 33).

CONCLUSION

Follow the clear-cut rules and suggestions. Remember, the special protection for most service businesses! When in doubt, consult this chapter again and don't forget those minutes!

Chapter Twenty-Three

Estate Planning

"Estate planning" is the process of transferring property at death and *maximizing* the estate by *minimizing* estate taxes, gift taxes, income taxes, administration expenses, excise taxes, and other costs. Such planning is intended to achieve the goals of the decedent and to provide for the financial needs of the family and other heirs.

To accomplish these goals, three significant estate planning ideas are:

1. Lifetime gifts, which reduce the eventual estate.
2. Life insurance in an irrevocable trust or owned outright by the children, which when properly arranged, can pay the entire insurance proceeds to the beneficiaries free of both estate and income taxes.
3. Lifetime transfers of business interests to avoid future appreciation and to reduce the remaining interests that may be taxed in the estate.

The gross estate includes the *fair market value* of any interest held in any property by the decedent at the time of death. Community property laws (only in the states of Arizona, California, Idaho, Louisiana, Nevada, New Mexico, Texas, and Washington) have a major affect on the amount includible in the estate. Generally, only one-half of any community property shared with the surviving spouse will be included in the estate of the deceased.

As you can see, we are quickly getting to matters of law, and it is impossible to write about this topic without becoming continually entwined with legal discussions. Many readers will assume that this chapter contains most of the necessary legal information to do your estate planning. That impression is absolutely wrong; the purpose of this chapter is to simply give enough information to persuade you to run, not walk, to a competent estate-tax attorney, your own CPA, your insurance agent, and possibly an investment adviser and a bank trust officer as well. That's your estate planning team.

It does little good to work all your life, accumulate some money (usually by virtue of a retirement plan, some life insurance, and perhaps the sale of your agency, and then have the IRS take over half of it away! They get *two* chances to do that: sometimes when you die, but almost always when the surviving spouse passes away.

Unfortunately, the typical sales agent assumes that estate taxes only hit the very rich and, besides, he's too busy selling to think about the worst combination in the world, death and taxes. Salespeople are optimists by their very nature and never want to consider or ponder such grim facts of life. However, if you want to double, triple, or quadruple the amount that ultimately passes to your spouse and then to your children, you should pay close attention to this chapter.

Let's study a few estate facts and discuss the rules and regulations in detail. Again, don't stop reading here because you think your estate is too small to worry about taxes. If you'll read on, you'll find out how rich the government will say you are, and how it can take most of it away.

ESTATE FACTS

The highest federal tax rate is the *estate* tax rate, which effectively begins at 37 percent, peaks at 60 percent, and then drops back to 55 percent (the highest federal income tax rate is 39.6 percent, and only on any taxable income in *excess* of $250,000). So the estate tax rate *begins* close to where the top income tax rate ends.

Everything in your estate will be valued at *market value* for estate tax purposes: your home, sales agency, other real estate, other investments, and sometimes even life insurance proceeds. This market valuation rule is the killer that frequently boosts the small estate into the taxable area.

UNLIMITED MARITAL DEDUCTION

Most reps say they don't have to worry about estate taxes because all property, of unlimited amount, will escape estate taxes if left to a surviving spouse. However, leaving everything outright to your spouse will increase the total estate taxes that will *eventually* be paid when the surviving spouse dies. It is a foolish thing to do (taxwise) and is probably the most common estate planning error of all. It can cost as much as an extra $330,000 in estate taxes! (This extra tax can be simply and easily avoided by using a bypass trust as explained later.) But if you don't have a will, your spouse will not inherit everything (in most states), or if there is a common disaster (both spouses dying near the same time), there might even be two estate taxes levied in a row.

WARNING:

If your will was drawn up before 1981, probably only one-half of your estate will pass tax-free to your spouse, instead of an unlimited amount.

Your retirement plan accumulations are considered part of your estate for estate tax purposes and are *also* subject to income taxes as the money is withdrawn by the surviving spouse, or sometimes immediately if left to anyone else. Further, there is a special 15 percent excise tax on excess retirement plan accumulations at death, which can put the three taxes combined (estate, income, and excise) at about *80 percent* of the total retirement plans in the estate.

Life insurance proceeds if the beneficiary is *not* your spouse, may be taxed as part of your estate. Such proceeds are *income* tax free, but not necessarily *estate* tax free. It primarily depends on how carefully you arrange the ownership of the policies. Jointly-owned property with anyone other than your spouse will still be taxed in your estate in direct proportion to your investment in that property, not necessarily just one-half.

Living trusts (i.e., revocable until death) are generally the right way to hold ownership of everything you own. However, this will only save you *probate* costs, but not a dime of estate taxes (although there are other advantages as well).

THE $600,000 EXEMPTION

When you die, all your property is valued at market value, and any debts and expenses are subtracted from that figure. The result is your *net* estate, from which a $600,000 exemption and all bequests to your surviving spouse and to charity are subtracted to arrive at your *taxable* estate if any. Estate taxes on that taxable estate are levied at a beginning tax rate of 37 percent, going up to 60 percent, and then dropping to 55 percent.

Obviously, if you leave everything to your surviving spouse, there are no estate taxes to pay, but one $600,000 exemption has been wasted as follows. Assume your net estate is $1.2 million, and you leave it all to your spouse tax-free. Further assume that your surviving spouse lives off the income of your estate and eventually dies, again leaving an estate of $1.2 million.

When the surviving spouse dies there is again a $600,000 exemption for that second estate, but the remaining $600,000 would be *taxed* with a total estate tax (in this example) of about $195,000! That entire $195,000 tax can be easily and legally avoided. (Further, in a larger estate, the extra tax on the second $600,000, at 55 percent, is the amount of $330,000 mentioned earlier.) So instead of leaving every-

TABLE 23–1
Sample Estate Tax Rates (After Deducting the $600,000 Exemption)

Taxable Estate	*Tax Rate*
$500,000	37%
$750,000	39%
$1,000,000	41%
$1,500,000	45%
$3,000,000	55%
$10,000,000 to $21,000,000	60%
Over $21,000,000	55%

thing outright to your spouse, you should instead leave $600,000 directly to your spouse and the other $600,000 in a bypass trust for the benefit of your children! That would save $195,000 or ($330,000)!

The surviving spouse can *still* get income from the trust and can invade the trust *principal* under certain circumstances, but when the surviving spouse dies, the $600,000 in the trust passes directly to the children estate tax-free. Why? Because the bypass trust assets were sheltered from tax by the other $600,000 exemption of the *first* spouse to die.

This arrangement leaves only $600,000 in the taxable estate of the surviving spouse, which is then sheltered from tax by the $600,000 exemption. To sum up, we used two $600,000 exemptions to shelter $1.2 million from estate taxes (one at the death of each spouse), instead of wasting one exemption (and, in this example, $195,000 in needless estate taxes) by leaving everything *outright* to the surviving spouse. Some difference!

GIFTS

A great way to reduce estate taxes is by annual gifts to your children (or anyone else). You and your spouse can jointly gift up to $20,000 annually or $10,000 individually in cash or property to as many individuals as you want. There are *no* gift or income taxes to pay. Ten grandchildren can be gifted (in a trust, if necessary) an annual $200,000 (10 × $20,000). Four children and their four spouses can receive an annual $160,000 (8 × $20,000), three CPAs can be gifted an annual $60,000 (3 × $20,000), and so forth. This technique is regularly used by the very rich, although there is some talk in Congress about an overall annual or perhaps lifetime limit on tax-free gifts.

One of the slickest legal methods of transferring money to your children tax-free is for the children to use your annual gifts to pay the premiums on life insurance on your life. At your demise, if the children *own* the policies outright or indirectly through an irrevocable life insurance trust, the gifts are eliminated from the estate of the donor and the insurance proceeds are received completely tax-free. You have transferred money to the next generation *without any income or estate tax costs at all!*

Gifts of *unlimited* amounts for educational tuition and medical expenses for the benefit of *any* individual are tax-free if paid directly to the institution. There are no carryover provisions for these annual gifts; if you don't make them in any particular year, the tax-exempt gift opportunity for that year is lost forever!

TAXTIP

I would suggest that you gift property that is most likely to appreciate in value! Although the present value of such a gift might not be great, the potential appreciation will be in the hands of the donor and escape your estate taxes.

This particular technique can also be used in cases where your adult children work in your agency; annually gift them minority stock interests in the company. When gifting stock in your sales agency, be sure your CPA and lawyer follow the *very favorable* IRS Revenue Ruling 93-12. This ruling concedes that a "minority discount" can be applied to such gifts of stock even when you gift a *majority* of the stock to two or more children and even though the stock remains within the family unit. These discounts can cut the ostensible market value of your stock gift by as much as *50 percent*. Also, consider the following taxtip.

TAXTIP

The $600,000 exemption described earlier is actually a combined estate and gift tax exemption. You can use up this $600,000 by making *excess gifts* over and above the annual limit during your lifetime. Your estate will no longer be able to claim that exemption. However, if you have large amounts of sharply appreciating assets (e.g., real estate, stocks, or ownership of the business) it may well pay you to gift them now and get them (and all further appreciation) out of your estate forever. As mentioned earlier, some tax experts are betting that the $600,000 exemption amount may be reduced in the future, and they are recommending that you use it up while it's still at that figure. Of course, you will need expert advice to do this (and of course you must file a gift tax return).

LIFE INSURANCE

Life insurance proceeds are usually not subject to *income* tax, but they may be subject to *estate* tax. If the proceeds are payable to your spouse, they are estate tax free under the unlimited marital deduction. However, if the proceeds are payable to anyone else, including your children, they may be subject to estate tax, depending on the *ownership* of the policy.

If the proceeds are not payable to your spouse, you can still avoid the estate tax but only by giving up all "incidents of ownership" of an existing insurance policy more than three years before your death. Such incidents include the rights to legally own the policy, name the beneficiary, borrow against the policy, and convert to another policy.

A basic misunderstanding is that life insurance proceeds are completely tax-free, but now you know this is usually true only as it applies to income taxes, and not necessarily estate taxes. If the spouse is not the beneficiary and the deceased retained incidents of ownership in the policy, the entire policy proceeds will become part of the estate of the deceased for purposes of calculating the *estate* tax liability! Therefore, see your insurance agent and your estate planners to get this arrangement exactly right; it's simply a matter of rearranging incidents of ownership to avoid all estate taxes. Or, consider the next very popular idea.

THE (IRREVOCABLE) LIFE INSURANCE TRUST

Another and even more sophisticated way to keep insurance proceeds out of the taxable estates of both spouses is by setting up a life insurance trust to own the insurance on your life, pay the premiums, and distribute the proceeds at your death (according to the provisions of the trust instrument). Then you (the insured) usually gift the premiums to the trust each year, or you can transfer income-producing property to the trust.

This irrevocable trust is commonly used to hold life insurance policies that will eventually pay the insurance proceeds to your children. The purpose of the trust is to avoid estate taxes at the death of both spouses yet still maintain some measure of informal control during your lifetime by using a "friendly" trustee (do not appoint your spouse, but your CPA or attorney is fine, and a sister or brother is usually OK). Your lawyer must set up this trust and will advise you, under your own state's laws, who can be the "safe" trustees.

If you gift an existing policy to the trust, you must outlive the gift by three years or the insurance proceeds will *still* be considered part of your taxable estate. However, if the *trustee* applies for a *new* policy, you then avoid that rule (sometimes the IRS fights this, but they usually lose).

Under this trust arrangement, the insured has no powers over the insurance policy or the trust such as the rights to change beneficiaries, select settlement options, or to borrow against the policy. Only the trustee (who cannot be the insured or the spouse) has the power to borrow. Since the trust is irrevocable, nobody has the right to change the beneficiaries that are specified in the trust instrument. So don't use this insurance trust if you later want to disinherit your children, although you can change your mind and stop making annual gifts to pay the premiums and let the policies *lapse* (if the beneficiaries don't pay the premiums). I have seen this situation more than once.

The life insurance trust can hold not only conventional life insurance policies on the life of either parent, but it can also be used as a vehicle to own the special "second-to-die" insurance (described in the next section). Using that so-called survivorship insurance and the life insurance trust, it is quite possible to pass the entire amount of your entire estate to your children intact without any reduction for payment of estate taxes. Read the next section and tie it to this insurance trust idea for the best way in the world to avoid all estate taxes. Of course, as with most good ideas, it has been grossly overdone by many insurance agents.

SECOND-TO-DIE (SURVIVORSHIP) LIFE INSURANCE

Virtually a whole new life insurance industry has been created to sell and deal with these new insurance policies and their applications. The basic idea is to leave a tax-free estate to the children. For example, if a surviving spouse leaves a $5 million taxable estate, the taxes will be about $2.4 million, and the kids will only get the remaining $2.6 million.

But if $2.4 million of second-to-die (survivorship) life insurance was purchased while both spouses were alive, the proceeds would be kept out of either estate by use of a life insurance trust or by direct ownership of the policies by the children. At the death of the *surviving* spouse, the children would receive tax-free life insurance proceeds of the same $2.4 million.

The wonder of it is that for as little as 10 percent (a single $240,000 premium in this example), you can buy $2.4 million of life insurance (depending on your age, the age of your spouse, the health of both of you, how you pay the premiums, what kind of policy, etc.). So, in this example, the children received a net (after estate tax) inheritance from the estate of the second spouse to die of $2.6 million, plus $2.4 million from the second-to-die life insurance. A total of $5 million, which was indeed the complete estate! And that's how you do it.

This rather new life insurance product is *cheaper* than life insurance on either spouse *individually*, because two people have to die before the insurance company must pay off. The policy only pays when the second spouse dies, but that is exactly when there is an estate tax to pay (at the first death, the unlimited marital deduction avoids all estate tax). To say it another way, at the second death, this policy pays your children (tax-free, if properly arranged) the approximate amount that is being taken from them in the form of estate taxes, and they end up with about the same total as your entire pre-tax estate!

If you can afford it, the best buy is to purchase a single-premium insurance policy since it has the lowest net cost of all. Using single-premium, second-to-die insurance, many of the examples an insurance agent will show you are indeed at a cost of about 10 percent of the face amount the children will receive (and thus many insurance agents claim, correctly, that you can "reduce your estate taxes by up to 90 percent"). How would you like to be selling a line where you could claim that the product will save the consumer 90 cents for every $1 spent?

A lot of life insurance is being sold this way, and properly arranged it makes all the sense in the world for most of you with estates of any size at all. However, see the following discussion about being sold *more* insurance than is really necessary.

HOW THEY SELL YOU TOO MUCH LIFE INSURANCE AND WHY YOU FALL FOR IT!

Nobody is easier to sell than a salesperson. You're the pushovers of the world, because you gladly treat every salesperson the way you would like to be treated, so you buy and buy! The average life insurance salesperson is in hog heaven when calling on the typical sales rep.

You will recall that at date of death, everything in the estate is valued at (and potentially taxed at) current market value. The down side of that is the possibility of higher estate taxes on higher values. The up side is that the inheritors receive the property at that higher tax basis. For example, if a stock cost $1,000 and is now worth $8,000, it will be valued (and potentially taxed) in the estate at $8,000. However, if the heir sells the stock the next day for $8,000, no income tax is due since her inherited tax basis is $8,000, the same as the selling price. With those ideas firmly in mind, let's return to our life insurance salesperson and how much insurance you should buy.

Consider the common second-to-die policy, sold while both spouses are alive. The *higher* the estimated market value of the estate at the death of the second spouse, the *higher* the potential estate tax liability and the *higher* the amount of the survivorship insurance you should buy. So, it is to the *absolute benefit* of the insurance agent to make each and every assumption to *increase* the estimated value of the estate at the death of the second spouse.

What is your sales agency worth after your death? In truth, it may never even survive your death! My position is that in a single owner agency, at the very date of death, most rep firms are worth zip! At date of death, there is absolutely no assurance or even probability that the majority of the lines will remain with the company, and if they do it will be the result of *subsequent* actions, at a later date, by the people who are *then* running the company. But at the date of death (unless there is a funded buy-sell agreement) the agency probably has little or no value.

But along comes the insurance agent and he says, "According to rep guru Mel Daskal, the average sales agency is worth one- to one-and-one-half times a year's commission income, plus the tangible net assets of the company. So I figure your agency will have a fair market value, at death, of $800,000." Your first reaction is to *sell* the bloody company! Your next reaction is to puff up your chest and contemplate how much richer you are than you ever thought, and not to argue with that nice insurance sales agent who just made you rich.

In similar fashion, the insurance agent values your house and everything else as high as possible. It's a big ego trip for you, and you seldom object as the figures grow and grow. Even those limited partnership investments you got sucked into get valued at original cost, which is probably a 1,000 percent overstatement. But boy, are you rich, and boy oh boy do you need a lot of life insurance to cover the eventual estate taxes at the second death. So you have been sold, just as you dream of selling every purchasing agent your every line. Can *you* puff up the purchasing requirements of *your* customers as was just done to your own life insurance requirements?

The final con is their basic assumption that the surviving spouse will never dip into capital. Therefore, whatever you leave your surviving spouse is assumed to still be there *intact* when the surviving spouse dies. What if she spent it all? What if the surviving spouse remarries and gains another unlimited marital deduction? What if the market value of certain assets decreases in future years? As a generalization, you should assume that the smaller your estate will be, the more likelihood the surviving spouse will dip into capital and may spend it all. In that event, there will later be no estate taxes or any need for insurance to pay them.

Now let's make a different assumption. Your spouse and children have been actively working in your sales agency, and there is continuity and virtual assurance that your principals will stay with the company in the event of your death. Now the IRS might make the case that there is a major jump in market value when the surviving spouse dies and the children smoothly continue the operation. The insurance agent (also smoothly) says, "In this case, for sure, we must value the agency at $800,000, and we sure need a lot of insurance to cover those estate taxes at the second death."

Not necessarily! What if, after the first death, the surviving spouse promptly begins a systematic program of gifting the stock of the company to the children ($10,000 a year, per child, using the minority discount formula, plus the same for their spouses if she so chooses)? Certainly up to 49 percent of the agency could be comfortably gifted and with an iron-clad compensation contract for the surviving spouse (and maybe even a voting trust for the stock) conceivably 100 percent of the stock might be given away and thus be *completely* out of the second estate. How much life insurance do you need then?

Now take the real worst case. At the death of the second spouse, the children have none of the stock but they are smoothly operating the company; the IRS comes in and says $800,000 is indeed the fair market value of the stock. Now for sure the insurance agent says you will need that big policy, and for sure he doesn't mention Code Section 6166. So let me mention it to you.

Code Section 6166 provides that the estate tax attributable to a closely held business interest (defined as over 35 percent of the adjusted gross estate) is entirely deferred for four years after death and then is payable over the next 10 years in equal annual installments. Annual simple interest is charged on this deferral at 4 percent on the first $1 million in valuation. Thus you have 14 years to pay the estate tax in such circumstances, which rather weakens the need for immediate insurance cash, wouldn't you say? However, I cannot recall an insurance agent *ever* mentioning this fact when advising how much second-to-die insurance is needed.

By this time, you have certainly assumed I am against life insurance. *Au contraire*, I absolutely *love* the uses of life insurance in many business situations, and I think second-to-die insurance for estate tax purposes is the greatest invention since sliced bread! What I don't want and can't stand is when we give an insurance agent the opportunity to sell a big policy to one of our clients, and he promptly attempts to *over*sell using all the tactics I have just described. As a result, our firm limits our recommendations to just a few select insurance agents who have earned our trust and respect.

The concept of second-to-die insurance is both viable and valuable; just be careful about the amount that agents attempt to sell to you and take the following precautions as well. To keep any insurance agent honest, get competing quotes from two or three agents and have your CPA review and monitor all the proposals. I know this is more effort and cost, but big money is involved in premiums for those big policies. So do it!

RETIREMENT PLANS

Retirement plans are not necessarily the best assets to leave to your spouse (and almost never to your children) as far as taxes are concerned. Your retirement plan assets may be subject to three different taxes after you are gone. These taxes are:

1. Estate taxes. When retirement plan assets become part of your taxable estate they can be subject to estate taxes unless the surviving spouse inherits. Estate taxes are usually due and payable in cash, exactly nine months after the date of death.

2. Income taxes. If someone other than the surviving spouse inherits the retirement plan, the total benefits are subject to income taxes, sometimes in the year of death of the participant as well as possible estate taxes. Therefore, the traditional advice is to not leave retirement plan(s) to anyone other than your spouse and, as we will later discuss, you *possibly* may be better off using up some or all retirement plan assets while you are still alive, because of the special tax penalties and adverse tax treatments.

3. Excise taxes. Depending on the size of all qualified retirement plan accumulations at death (including even IRAs and rollover IRAs), there may be an additional 15 percent excise tax levied on the excess of retirement plan accumulations. (While the definition of excess accumulations vary with your age, an average figure is that any amounts exceeding $1 million or so will be subject to the 15 percent excise tax.) If applicable, the excise tax is then payable in *all* cases, regardless of whether there is a regular estate tax liability. The three taxes (excise, estate, and, sooner or later, income), can eventually reach about 80 percent of the total retirement plan assets in an estate!

Here is an illustration from our favorite retirement plan administrators, National Benefit Services, Inc., of Westlake Village, California. It illustrates a situation where there is no surviving spouse and, of course, is a worst-case scenario. But it does make the point:

> Roger had worked many years to salt away money in his retirement plan on a tax-deferred basis. A total of $1.5 million had been accumulated that might ultimately pass to his heirs. He died before the benefits were distributed.
>
> The regular estate tax bite was $825,000. There was an additional penalty estate tax of $112,500 because the plan balance was so large. The income tax hit was $175,150. Thus, the total tax bill

was $1,112,650, leaving $387,350 (26 percent) for the heirs. Clearly a tax tragedy!

Roger could have reduced the tax nightmare by getting off the deferral train and accelerating well-planned distributions to himself. The accelerated payments, although subject to income taxes, could have been repositioned to avoid or reduce the estate tax hit. The old adage that continued tax deferral is always the best course of action just isn't true.

COMMENT

Of course, this example is rigged to show maximum possible tax costs, but an important point is that poor Roger was not married and therefore there were full estate taxes and income taxes at his death. As a married individual, both estate and income taxes could have been deferred at the time of his death, and perhaps the estate taxes avoided altogether.

So one recommendation (but *not* universally approved—see later) is that *if* the combined tax bite is going to be anywhere near that 80 percent, the owner of the plan could begin withdrawing the retirement plan benefits in annual installments the minute he reaches age 59 (the age when you first avoid the penalties for premature withdrawal). Up to about $150,000 can be withdrawn each year without penalty (the exact amount changing with "indexing," "grandfathering," etc.), but if an excess amount is paid out it is subject to the 15 percent excise tax.

Up to that approximate $150,000, you pay income tax on the annual distributions, and you can then use the money for any purpose including living expenses, annual gifting, funding an insurance trust, buying tax-exempts, and so forth. By so doing, you can avoid two of the three taxes (estate and excise).

However, one of the smartest insurance agents we work with, as well as an expert tax attorney, both adamantly insist that you should *never* voluntarily take out one cent from your retirement plan between ages 59 and 70½ if your spouse will inherit the retirement plan assets! The insurance agent has worked out a math and computer module to prove that the tax-deferred earnings will always *exceed* the penalty-tax costs of any increased accumulations. His exception is if someone other than the spouse will inherit the plan. But take the advice in the preceding and following paragraphs with a grain of salt. There is certainly no consensus in this matter, and naturally any advice tied to the purchase of life insurance should be viewed with skepticism and some degree of mistrust! Surely run all these alternate ideas by our own tax advisers.

To be taken with a large grain of salt: Some estate planners even go one step further. They suggest that if you have other substantial assets to live on, you cash in your entire retirement plan at one time! Up to approximately $750,000 (the exact amount again varying with "indexing," "grandfathering," etc.) can be withdrawn at one time without being subject to that 15 percent excise tax. Generally, you will only pay income taxes on the entire lump-sum distribution and will avoid the other two taxes. Further, you can (at this writing, but maybe not much longer) use 5-year or 10-year averaging in computing the income taxes you will owe.

These estate planners recommend that you use the *entire* after-tax distribution from your plan to buy a huge single-premium, second-to-die policy, using an insurance trust that will avoid all taxes upon the second death. Your children eventually inherit an enormous amount of tax-free money, the insurance agents earn humongous amounts in insurance commissions, and you have completely avoided two of the three potential taxes on retirement plans. In some limited circumstances, this may be a good idea, that is, if you have enough other assets to live comfortably the rest of your life. I have personally *never* seen this done, perhaps because most of our clients are not that rich, or perhaps for other reasons.

Of course, this startling idea is tied into the sale of *tons* of life insurance, but if you fit this financial profile, those ideas are perhaps worth (with a grain of salt) considering. If so, shop for the lowest insurance premiums and the safest insurance companies. Another idea in these times of financial insecurities is to split such policies among various life insurance companies to spread the risk. Even insurance companies have been getting into financial difficulties and this is an extra safety play.

To reiterate: Conventional wisdom in the past was to never touch your retirement plan for as long as possible, since it was growing and compounding tax-deferred. A new (grain of salt) suggestion (not at all universally accepted) is to sometimes use up retirement plan money *first,* since eventually the retirement plan accumulations may be subject to higher combined taxes (80 percent) than anything else in the estate.

ON THE OTHER HAND, TAXES SCHMAXES!

Other retirement plan experts (besides the noted and notable insurance agent and tax lawyer) insist that all the preceding ideas are nonsense! Their overriding consideration is that the retirement plan assets are compounding tax-deferred until withdrawn. They state that in most situations, that incredible growth over long periods of time will *more* than offset any taxes that may be assessed.

> ***TAXTIP***
>
> The same insurance expert also recommends a tax-free rollover of the retirement plan by the surviving spouse to continue even *more* tax-deferred growth, without income taxes, at the time of death. The surviving spouse is entitled to roll over the retirement account into her *own* IRA. By doing so, she becomes a participant rather than a beneficiary and can then establish her *own* joint life expectancy distribution pattern with the children. (Perhaps the outstanding expert and proponent of what he calls The Family IRA concept is Bernie Weinberg of Shadur, Weinberg & Associates in Encino, California, who has done this with *great* success for a number of our clients.)

Some retirement plan experts also make light of the 15 percent penalty tax on excess accumulations at death and believe that the strategy of many tax advisers has erroneously focused on the management of the penalty tax, because the penalty may only result in a net tax of approximately 7.5 percent (because it is *tax-deductible against the gross estate*). This seems to be the planning area that generates the most heat and the most conflict.

Some people think that many of the fancy suggestions are really just intended to sell life insurance, and that the miracle of tax-deferred compounding of the earnings will offset all other drawbacks. As another expert said, "Taxes, schmaxes, just keep the money earning tax-deferred as long as you can, don't touch a dime, and don't worry about a thing!"

Yet another retirement plan idea is to purchase life insurance through your retirement plan, thus using tax-deductible dollars to pay the premiums. However, the proceeds may be subject to estate tax (unless left to the surviving spouse), and will be partially subject to income tax as a retirement plan lump-sum distribution, but only to the extent of the cash surrender value, *less* the annual PS 58 insurance costs (the cost of the current annual life insurance *protection* [i.e., the death benefit portion of the premium], *not* that portion of the premium that goes to increase the cash value of the policy equals PS 58 costs reported as income each year by the decedent. In other words, the difference between the face amount of the policy and the cash surrender value is tax-free income, but the cash surrender value of the policy *less* the PS 58 costs reported is taxable.)

> *TAXTIP*
>
> It is a serious mistake not to report PS 58 income each year. If you omit such reporting there will eventually be a much greater tax due on such insurance proceeds!

An aggressive planning technique to keep such proceeds completely out of the estate is to create a special subtrust amendment to the retirement plan and have a special trustee named as owner and beneficiary of the retirement plan insurance policy. The special trustee then pays the insurance benefits to your spouse or children. The IRS has not approved, commented, or disapproved this idea, but it has virtually no *downside* risk and costs little to create. If it works, it might save considerable taxes.

THE LIVING (REVOCABLE) TRUST

The purpose of this trust is *not* to save estate taxes or income taxes, but to save probate costs, fees, delays, and publicity. It's intended to avoid the hassles of probate administration. There is not a *dime* to be saved in taxes, but plenty to be saved in those other ways. The main reason for these trusts is the big cash saving in probate fees.

This kind of trust (also called grantor trust, inter vivos trust, or family trust) is simply a legal fiction to hold title to your assets. You are the trustee and you are the beneficiary (until you die). You can change the terms of the trust at any time during your life, and the management of the trust is only a minor inconvenience during your lifetime. If all your assets really were in the living trust, your estate would completely avoid the costly, cumbersome, and public probate process. There would be no delays in settling the estate and no public record of your assets or details of your estate. In addition to avoiding the inconvenience and expense of probate, living trusts allow privacy, ease of transition from disability or incapacity to death (no need for a conservatorship), and the opportunity to correctly value estate assets.

The successor trustee (usually the surviving spouse) simply distributes the assets of the trust according to the trust's instructions and those distributions are not subject to any delays (they could be done the day after death, or the day after the funeral!). The entire process is cheaper, faster, and much more private! The most expensive and complicated probate states are reportedly Connecticut, Massachusetts, New York, and Rhode Island. California is not far behind.

The trust can further provide for management of assets if the grantor becomes unable to handle his affairs, and thus avoids the appointment of a court-appointed conservator and related court supervision costs. Also, assets for a minor beneficiary can be managed within the trust, eliminating the need for a court-appointed guardian and the related court supervision costs.

Conservatorships are expensive, time consuming, and administratively cumbersome. All actions and a mandatory financial accounting are subject to court supervision and review. Conservatorships are to be avoided whenever possible, and the living trust can do just that.

In California, for example, the cost (attorney, executor, and appraiser fees) to probate a $600,000 (market value, remember?) estate is at least $30,000, and the court *freezes* the estate assets for four months. During that period, anyone can contest the will without even hiring a lawyer. To contest the living trust is difficult and expensive, and plaintiffs must hire a lawyer and file a civil suit; and as mentioned previously, the assets of the trust are not frozen at all and could be distributed immediately. A disgruntled heir would then have to sue each and every beneficiary individually.

Again, using California as an example, the executor's statutory commission *and* the estate's statutory attorneys' fees are *each* computed as follows, for, say, a $2.7 million (market value) estate in probate:

The first $15,000 @ 4%	=	$ 600
The next $85,000 @ 3%	=	2,550
The next $900,000 @ 2%	=	18,000
The balance @ 1%	=	17,000
		$38,150

Thus, the minimum probate costs in this example are $76,300 (2 × $38,150), as the same fee is paid to the executor and *also* to the lawyers. Now add in the costs of appraisers, referees, and extraordinary legal costs that are frequently requested on top of the statutory fees (and usually granted by the court). I hope you are convinced that avoiding probate is the only way to proceed!

YOUR WILL

Without a will, no estate planning is possible and no tax savings are possible. The laws of your state will control who inherits and in what percentage. If you don't have a will, there is no sense in even reading all this. For shame!

Assuming you do have a will: While the will is generally intended to dispose of all your property at your death, keep in mind that certain property does *not* pass under the will but goes to the person so named. Understand that such property may be part of your estate for *estate tax* purposes, but who then inherits the property is not controlled by your will, nor can it be. Jointly owned property with right of survivorship (bank accounts, real estate, securities, or anything else held in this manner), life insurance proceeds payable to a named beneficiary, and qualified retirement plans payable to a named beneficiary are excluded from provisions of a will.

CHARITABLE BEQUESTS

Anything you leave to charity under your will (in unlimited amounts) comes right off the top and reduces your taxable estate dollar-for-dollar. There are, however, some very sophisticated plans involving charitable income trusts, remainder trusts, and retained life tenancy trusts; gifting appreciated property to charity while living; the capital gains and estate tax bypass trust; and many others. Your own tax attorney and CPA can explain. In general, the wealthier and more charitable you are, the more you should explore these particular ideas.

JOINT TENANCY

There is an old story that lawyers tell: "The deceased held everything in joint tenancy, so nothing was left to pass under his will, the fool!" Anything you leave in joint tenancy (i.e., to the other joint owner) avoids probate but does *not* avoid estate taxes and, as indicated, is not subject to the terms of your will. What joint tenancy really accomplishes is to act like a second will that bypasses all your careful estate planning.

Joint tenancy means that only one-half that property will usually receive a step-up in basis (to market value) at death, while in California (a community property state) the same asset held as community property will usually qualify for a 100 percent step-up in basis. Further, jointly owned property with anyone other than your spouse is still taxed in your estate in direct proportion to your ownership interest at death, and not just one-half. Joint tenancy does not save you taxes! It's just an easy way to pass property at death to someone else, but rarely is done with any thought to overall estate planning or the difficulties presented if you later change your mind.

TAXTIP

Property left to a joint owner could just as easily be left that person in your living trust or in your will. That way you can easily *alter* your wishes at any time, while joint tenancy can be difficult to revoke. A highly significant point if you are even slightly inclined to modify your bequests at a later date.

You are foolish to arbitrarily select joint tenancy for your home and other assets without consulting your advisers first! If you are putting *everything* in joint tenancy with your spouse, you are probably wasting one $600,000 estate tax exemption, as explained earlier, and you may be inadvertently disinheriting your other heirs as well, since there will be nothing left in the estate for them to inherit!

THE QTIP TRUST

A number of sophisticated trust arrangements can be used in estate planning. We have already discussed living trusts and life insurance trusts, and mentioned the bypass, or credit shelter trust, to make sure that *each* spouse's estate fully utilizes each $600,000 exemption. Also in common usage is the qualified terminable interest property (QTIP) trust, which provides the surviving spouse with the *income* from the QTIP trust assets, but at the death of the second spouse the assets go to the heirs named by the *first* spouse (who set up the trust).

The QTIP trust enables property to qualify for the marital deduction but does *not* allow the surviving spouse any control over the ultimate disposition of the property. Thus the donor spouse (now deceased) controls that final distribution of the trust assets when the surviving spouse dies. This is a significant and oft-used arrangement when the final beneficiaries of the QTIP trust are the children of the first deceased from a *prior* marriage. The surviving spouse is provided for during her lifetime, but the children of the former marriage are also assured of an ultimate inheritance.

The QTIP trust requires that all income must be paid to the surviving spouse and the principal is also for her benefit until her death. The QTIP trust may be the ideal way to leave control of your agency to your spouse and at the same time assure that your children will inherit the agency on the death of the surviving spouse.

CHARITABLE REMAINDER TRUST

A charitable income trust pays income to a charity for a fixed period of time after which the property is distributed to specified heirs. A charitable remainder trust is the reverse. The income goes to the beneficiaries (generally the donors) and the principal (property) belongs to the charity when the trust ends.

I also call this trust the "capital gains and estate tax bypass trust." It's where (preferably) highly appreciated assets are contributed to charity during your lifetime, thus forever removing them from your estate. In return, you and your spouse get a lifetime income from the charity, equal or sometimes higher than the income you were getting from the assets before the donation. Since the charity is a tax-exempt entity, it can sell the assets and use 100 percent of the sale proceeds as an investment to pay the donors a lifetime income. The charity, of course, keeps the donated assets or the sale proceeds therefrom, that is, the principal.

The donors also get a current charitable contribution deduction equal to the present value of the property gifted to charity. Such tax savings can be used to pay the premiums on a life insurance policy that will pay the heirs an amount equivalent to the property gifted (and which they will no longer inherit). (Of course, those insurance proceeds can be kept out of the estates of the parents and passed tax-free to the children, using the life insurance trust techniques we have already discussed.)

Alternatively (and my personal choice), the charity buys life insurance on the donors' lives with the children as beneficiaries, and in a sufficient amount to compensate them fully for those assets they never inherited. Even if the donors' life income is accordingly decreased because the charity is paying the premiums, it's a "cleaner" arrangement in my opinion. If this one fits, by all means consider having a talk with your lawyer, your CPA, and your insurance agent, and the (no charge) lawyers for the charity.

OTHER DOCUMENTS

There are other documents to discuss and prepare relating to health and similar problems. They may prove extremely valuable when you least expect it:

- Durable power of attorney for health care.
- Durable power of attorney for asset management.
- Living will (directive regarding heroic life support measures).
- Burial instructions.
- Anatomical gifts.

A LETTER TO YOUR SPOUSE

Always assume worst case! Assume there will be no lingering illness, no time to ask questions, supply information, and then rearrange your financial affairs. Always postulate the sudden fatal heart attack, that the plane will go down, the building will collapse, the fire will quickly spread, or the terrorist bomb will go off without warning. Disaster can strike suddenly and without warning. The most intelligent, essential, loving, and caring thing you can do is to create a letter to your spouse. This is not a legal document and you can write it as informally as you want. The point of such a letter is to provide as much information as possible in case of sudden death! This may be one of the biggest gifts you can leave behind to help your grieving spouse in a time of great need!

Create a letter that will inform and lead your spouse through virtually every situation you can think of. Add to my list as you see fit and to fit your particular circumstances.

Perhaps the best way to begin is to make a simple and informal list of all assets, liabilities, and related documents. Use that list for reference and keep adding to it as you think of additional items. When you have that completed list and the following hypothetical questions in front of you, you can construct this immensely valuable letter to your spouse. I will phrase all the following fourteen questions in the first person, as if I were the spouse asking the questions.

1. What is the plan for succession of the business in the event of your death? Who are the individuals involved and what are their

home phone numbers? Which one should I call first? Where is the agreement kept? What's the name and number of the lawyer who drew it up? Is the CPA familiar with it? What's her name? Do I know her? Where do I reach her? Is there business life insurance involved, or a formal buy-sell agreement? Where are all those documents located? Who has copies? Where are my copies? What happens first and how soon does it take place? Who do I rely upon and who should I distrust? Any other information I should have?

How do I get by at first? What do I do? What about medical insurance coverage for me, now that you are gone? What about any other payments I will get from the business? How much? How often? How sure? Will the business continue to pay auto and other business expenses? For how long? Is the business car leased or owned? If we own it, where is the title? Can I get money from the business in the first 30 days for funeral and other expenses? Who do I ask for it? How much? Have you made advance arrangements for me to get that money? What else should I know about the business and the business plans for the future?

COMMENT

I could write 50 pages on this topic alone. In my opinion, this is the most complicated and most essential information to supply. Sit down and write an answer to every one of the preceding questions! Do it *now*. How do you know you will still be alive after lunch?

For example, I recently had a woman tell me after an estate planning seminar, "All I know is that there's some life insurance carried by the business. But I don't even know how much, who gets it, or what other arrangements my husband has made. He just keeps telling me that I'll be well taken care of, whatever that means. I feel terribly insecure, and I hope he listens to your suggestions. He has already had one heart attack."

Hey, that's no kind of business planning! You wouldn't leave your business partner in that kind of a mess! Why do it to your spouse and children? This is the only place where I get "preachy." I have dealt with sudden deaths of clients, including one where the sales agency was gone in six months (the two top lines left with the two top salesmen!) and the widow was left in serious financial trouble. No insurance, no plan for succession, no advance instruction letter, no guidance at all! We had to go in and play detective, try (but failed) to save the rep firm and negotiate after the fact. The end result was still terrible, and needlessly expensive. Perhaps the letter will also force you to think about an orderly business succession plan now.

2. The obvious: Where is our will? Does the attorney who drew it up have the original? If so, his name and number? If not, where is the original? Where is my copy? Any comments about what's in the will? What does it all mean and intend? Give me some direction. For my sake and the sake of the kids, I need some ideas of about how much money and other assets will be involved in your estate. Any other helpful comments are more than welcome!

3. Who are the people I can most rely on, who do you trust the most, who do you feel are both our consultants and friends? I need the name and number of the CPA, lawyer, insurance agent, banker, stockbroker, investment adviser, trustees of any trusts, and so forth. Give me a ranking on these people. Who are the "good guys"? If two of them disagree in their advice, who should I listen to? Who do you favor? Who do you feel close to? Who do you barely trust? Who do you think is marginal at best? Were you about ready to get rid of any of them? If so, who? Should I? Do you feel at this time that the lawyer who drew up the will should now be the lawyer for the estate? Or, do you have a different name for me to select? Or, should I get three names from our CPA? Guide me!

4. Please tell me where everything essential is. Begin with the most basic: the bank checking accounts. I don't even know where the checkbooks are for all our bank accounts (I only have the household checkbook). Tell me each bank name, account number, title on the account (joint, separate, trust, etc.), and the location of the checkbooks. Do I sign on each account? Approximately how much do you keep in each account? Anything else you think I should know about checking accounts? Remember, this will be my first source of immediate funds, and the day after you are gone there will be bills to pay.

5. Please give me all the specifics for savings accounts, money market accounts, brokerage accounts, stocks, bonds, mutual funds, titles and details of real estate owned, partnership investments, trusts, S corporations, and anything else that may be an asset. Names, numbers, locations, everything! Are there particular investments (a special stock, a special building, etc.) that you consider unusually valuable and that I should never consider selling? If so, give me an idea of their true value and information on why I should hold on to them.

6. Where are the life insurance policies, how much is the coverage, who is the insurance agent, who are the beneficiaries, what are the settlement options? Were any loans taken against the policies? I have the same questions for policies paid for and owned by the business. Is any business buy-sell agreement funded by insurance? Or is there a key person or split-dollar insurance? Are there loans against the business insurance policies?

Is there any group life insurance, fraternal organization life insurance, government (e.g., military service) insurance, or similar? Did we carry any second-to-die insurance on both our lives (if so, this insurance will later be on my life only)? What do I do and who do I turn to for advice if the insurance agent now tries to sell me new life insurance or new annuity policies (a very common practice after death of a spouse)? Is there any life insurance payable directly to the children or to any trust? Was any life insurance carried as part of a divorce decree from an earlier marriage?

7. Speaking of trusts, was a living trust set up to avoid probate? Where is a copy of the trust instrument? Who is the successor trustee when you are gone (is it me)? Are you trustee of any other trusts? Do we have assets in any other trust? I need to know all details: locations of trust documents, assets, beneficiaries, successor trustees, and so forth. Which CPA or lawyer has all that information? Trust me, I need to know all about the trusts!

8. Do we have a safe deposit box? Does the business also have a safe deposit box? Please write down the location, number, the keys to the box(es), who can get access, and so forth. What's in those boxes? Securities, papers, jewelry, money, stamps, coins, other valuables? In our state, will the box be sealed at your death or not? If so, should some papers, such as insurance policies and your will, be kept out of the box?

9. What about retirement plans? Any business retirement plan(s), including pension, profit sharing, IRAs, Keoghs, rollover accounts, SEPs, or others? Please list all the details, including location, account numbers, beneficiaries, approximate amounts, trustees, and terms.

10. What do we owe? Mortgages, bank loans, investment debt, loans from relatives, loans from friends, credit card debt, business debt with personal guarantees (not only for business loans, but also on a business lease), any other personal guarantees (or contingent liabilities) you have signed? Or anything else? Please supply all the details for each of them: payment terms, totals, guarantees, and so forth. Am I also personally obligated on any of that debt? Are there any obligations resulting from a former marriage owed by your estate under the terms of that divorce decree?

11. Who owes money to us? All the same details and the same information are needed as for the above. Some individuals will never come forward and admit they owe any money, and will hope I don't know about such loans!

12. Are there legal documents, business agreements (e.g., buy-sell), partnership agreements, S corporation agreements, investment documents, and similar? Where are they? What do they mean? What do I do with them? Who should advise me? As in all cases, I need all the facts about them.

13. Do you have burial instructions? Is there a family cemetery plot? Is it fully paid for? What funeral parlor should be called? What kind of service? Who should conduct it? Who should speak? Who are

the pallbearers? Do you wish to be cremated? If so, discuss the disposition of the ashes.

14. Do you wish to note bequests not in the will? This letter is a perfect place to express your wishes informally to friends and family.

> ***TAXTIP***
>
> You can possibly even save estate taxes by noting bequests in this manner. Say you leave $50,000 in jewelry to your surviving spouse, which passes tax-free under the unlimited marital deduction. She later gifts $10,000 of that jewelry to each of your five children and again there is no tax under the annual gift tax exclusion. However, if that $50,000 had been left directly to the children in the will, it would have used up part of the $600,000 estate exemption, or might even have been subject to estate tax!

Every family has disparate problems, diverse needs, various kinds of assets and debts, and divergent motives and ideas that require dissimilar solutions. You certainly got the idea from this long dissertation! I beg you to begin immediately! We are all mortal! Do it, and do it now!

THE SHAPE OF THINGS TO COME

There are more proposals in Congress to make changes in the general area of estate taxation than in almost any other part of the tax laws. Here are some of the ideas presently being discussed, and you should monitor future developments to see how they may affect your estate plans:

- A proposal to decrease the estate tax exemption from $600,000 to $200,000. Some wealthy (and concerned) taxpayers have already completed gifting $600,000 in assets with all due haste to beat any such change in the law. I personally don't think the law will change.
- A tax (at capital gains rates) on the *increased* values of all assets in every estate. This would mean that while the assets would still receive a step-up in tax basis to market values, the difference between the decedent's original cost basis and the market value at death would be subject to capital gains taxes just as if each asset had been sold (at present the step-up is entirely tax-free).
- A lifetime cap on the amount of gifts you could make tax-free, say, $300,000.

• An annual cap over the amount of gifts you could make each year, say, $60,000. (Under present law, you and your spouse can jointly gift $20,000 a year to an unlimited number of individuals.)

CONCLUSION

This entire discussion is, of necessity, just a simplified overview of an enormously complicated legal area. Do not try to implement any of these ideas and plans without expert legal advice. State laws vary considerably, and I have glossed over many complexities buried within these general ideas. However, this overview should give you a general knowledge and many ideas about smart estate planning. Remember, it's your hard-earned money, made over a lifetime, that's at stake. It can go to the IRS or be preserved for your own family. The choice is yours!

Chapter Twenty-Four

Business Insurance

Insurance is simply the method by which you pay in advance to cover the risk of future losses. You are shifting the risk from you, the insured, to the insurance company. We commonly find reps either underinsured or not insured at all, particularly for some segment or other of their business risks. And the risks are many, frequently not understood, and often unanticipated.

LIABILITY INSURANCE

A fire, earthquake, hurricane, tornado, or other disaster will seldom put a rep out of business, because reps have a *service* business and property damage does not represent a primary threat. You can pick up and move from one location to another with your business in your briefcase. In my experience, however, the most unanticipated business loss for the average sales agency is in the liability area of their business operation. Liability exposure is the one place where a rep with, say, $300,000 a year in commissions could conceivably have a liability suit against her for $5 million! There is no particular relationship between the size of the agency and the potential amount of liability. None whatsoever!

Think about this: If you insure a car, office equipment, jewelry, or furniture, any potential loss and any insurance coverage is in an approximate one-to-one ratio. For example, you lose $5,000 in equipment and you get paid (give or take) $5,000 from the insurance company. Potential liability risk, however, has no such relationship. An accident in your office, an error in business, an omission (i.e., failure to act when you should have), or unsafe working conditions, among other reasons, could result in multimillion-dollar liability awards for negligence (particularly for accidents resulting in lifetime disablement or death at an early age). In my opinion, this is the most essential business coverage of all for the average rep, and perhaps the least considered in the average sales agency.

TYPES OF LIABILITY INSURANCE

Liability insurance is unlike any other in that it pays a third party the liability damages (bodily injury, personal injury, property damage, etc.) resulting from your *actions* or *inactions*. It does not pay *you* for a loss *you* have incurred, and this is quite different from all other kinds of insurance. There are various kinds of liability coverages offered (in descending order of interest to reps): general liability, product liability, excess liability, directors'/officers' liability, errors and omissions liability, and malpractice and professional liability.

GENERAL LIABILITY INSURANCE

General liability policies cover bodily injury to people or damage to property. Virtually any (noncriminal) business action that results in a liability award can be covered. My advice is to consider the maximum amount of coverage you can carry. You will usually find that increased amounts of liability coverage cost proportionately less as coverage increases.

Most people never explore the minor added cost of higher liability coverage and don't realize how little the additional premiums may be. In these days of multimillion-dollar awards and supergenerous juries, you should rethink your liability coverage and ask a few searching questions of your insurance agent. This advice applies equally to every kind of liability coverage that you may carry.

PRODUCT LIABILITY INSURANCE

Injury or property damage arising from the sale of a product represents an eternal trap for the average rep, who assumes that responsibility lies with the principal and that the principal carries all the insurance necessary. Completely false! In about 98 percent of all product liability cases, the rep gets sued, as well as the principal, because lawyers sue *everybody:* the principal, the sales manager, the president of the company, the individual (and company) who sold the product to the injured customer, perhaps the company that delivered the product to the ultimate seller, *and the rep and rep-owner!* Lawyers sue everybody, because they are, well, lawyers.

Legal fees *alone* could break the average rep! The rep could easily be out $10,000, $25,000, or $150,000 in legal fees before the case is settled, and even if the lawsuit completely fails. Product liability insurance, however, usually pays all legal fees, sometimes with a deductible.

What to do? First, you should immediately ask that each and every principal endorse you and your sales agency as an "additional insured" on their product liability policy (and find out how much they carry). Almost invariably, one or more of the factories you represent will refuse to do so, for some "legal" reason or other, or you will be horrified to learn they don't have such coverage ("too expensive"), or you will find out their coverage is minimal (e.g., $500,000 for any given product or only a few million for a manufacturer of explosives or guns).

Whatever factories agree to cover you, well and good, but your primary defense should be your *own* product liability policy. Even if the principal covers you this year, what if you lose the line next year? Or the factory later drops the policy? Or they switch insurance companies and forget to add you to the new policy? Or the policy is canceled for nonpayment of premiums? Or the principal goes out of business or is acquired?

Every sales agent *must* carry product liability insurance to cover potential legal defense costs, although that's far from the only reason. I'm sure you realize, no product is totally safe and all can cause injury or death through either use or misuse. Infants—and even adults—can choke to death on anything and injure themselves with everything.

The first place to look for liability insurance is usually a trade association. Compare coverages and costs with those quoted by your own insurance agent, and remember my comments about decreasing costs per dollar of increased liability limits.

AUTO LIABILITY POLICIES

Auto liability is one of the most obvious policies for a sales rep to own. Auto liability exposure for nonowned and hired cars is frequently unanticipated, or again, your limits are probably too low. If any of your employees use their *own* car on company business (probably 70 to 95 percent of all rep-employees) and cause bodily injury or property damage to another party, you, the employer, can get sued as well. Question: What liability insurance protects you in that event? Answer: None, unless you take the trouble to obtain this special safeguard! If you don't have such coverage you are liable for actual liability damages and, of course, legal fees. Another hidden way to break your sales agency!

Nonowned and hired auto coverage can be added to the existing company policy by an endorsement, a normally rather inexpensive procedure. If you don't have company-owned autos, then you should add this coverage to the general liability policy of the company. In either event, you must take action or you will have no such insurance protection. Excess liability (umbrella) policies do *not* cover you unless you have *primary* liability insurance coverage for that particular situation, that is, you cannot fall back upon your excess liability protection if you have not added the necessary endorsement to your other policy.

Hired auto coverage covers you for all car rentals so that you do not have to buy their absolutely outrageous liability coverage. The use of certain credit cards also provides some liability coverage when renting cars, but I would never rely on that coverage *alone,* since they keep changing the terms, conditions, and amounts of coverage.

Most reps have the wrong amount for their auto insurance deductible. Just as an insurance company charges less for higher liability coverage, they charge more for lower deductible amounts, since they can get nickeled-and-dimed to death. For most businesses, at least a $500 deductible—not the usual $250—is realistic, and you will be surprised at how much you can save. However, for any except the smallest businesses, we recommend $1,000 to $2,500 as the auto insurance deductible. Just watch your premiums drop! Remember, if your business pays a $1,000 deductible arising from an auto accident, that deductible is tax-deductible!

WORKERS' COMPENSATION INSURANCE

Another familiar liability insurance is workers' compensation insurance. As far as I know it is mandatory in every state, but even if it were not you would be crazy not to carry it. Workers' compensation laws vary from state to state as do the premium costs. Claims, abuses, and outright fraud have become a major problem in California, and the problem is so bad that many companies (particularly manufacturers) are moving to other states, primarily to reduce the outrageous costs of such insurance. In the end, we *all* pay for fraud and abuse in the form of higher insurance premiums and higher product cost.

EXCESS LIABILITY (UMBRELLA) POLICIES

Excess liability (umbrella) policies cover you for liability exposures that exceed your primary liability limits. They're a safety net that pays when other (primary) coverage has been exhausted. Umbrella policies should be carried by both your business and yourself personally (you can be held personally liable for many of your nonbusiness actions). The insurance company will determine how much and what kinds of primary liability coverage you have; the more and better primary protection you have, the less you will have to pay for an excess liability policy.

Excess liability policies are perfect illustrations of my earlier comments about the decreasing cost per dollar of insurance as the amount of coverage increases. I have seen personal umbrella policies for $1 million (with excellent primary coverage carried by the individual) with annual premiums of $600, but the premium for $5 million of coverage was $1,200! In this case, the insurance agent never thought to mention the higher coverage alternative to our client. In these litigious days, consider these policies a necessity and consider buying higher liability limits than ever before. Cheap "peace of mind" insurance.

DIRECTORS'/OFFICERS' LIABILITY

Directors and officers will get sued by shareholders, creditors, and anyone else who feels damaged by their actions. If you are a company owner, no matter how small your agency, seriously consider this insurance. Even in a one-person corporation, you could get sued by a creditor for improper actions as the director/officer of your agency.

If you are asked to serve as an outside director of another company, my best advice is to refuse *unless* you are covered by ample amounts of their liability insurance. I extend similar advice to those of you asked to serve on boards of public charities, trade associations, and civic, educational, and similar organizations. While I strongly approve of public-spirited service, you should have their liability insurance protection covering you.

OTHER LIABILITY INSURANCE

Special policies or special riders (endorsements) on your regular liability policy can be used for unusual situations not otherwise covered. Two examples that come to mind are injuries arising from serving liquor at a company party, or having a company party on a boat. The best advice is to always check your insurance coverage before any kind of unusual company event.

Errors and omissions and malpractice insurance are generally for doctors, lawyers, and CPAs. Check with your own insurance agent (who undoubtedly carries errors and omissions insurance for her own business) to see if any further liability protection is needed.

OCCURRENCE AND CLAIMS MADE LIABILITY COVERAGE

Coverage on an occurrence basis means that claims are paid by the policy in effect at the *time* when the event occurred. For example, if someone is injured on your premises in 1992, but does not file a claim until 1995, it is your 1992 insurance that covers that incident.

To eliminate uncertainties—who was the insurance carrier, are they still in business, what were the policy limits, and so forth—the insurance companies have pushed for claims made policies and coverage, that is, the insurance policy *in force* at the time the claim is made or reported is usually responsible for the liability coverage. In our same example, a 1992 injury first reported in 1995 would be the responsibility of the insurance company that issued coverage for 1995.

Problems are inherent with claims made insurance: gaps in coverage when changing from one type of policy to the other, the need for tail coverage at the very end of your career, and so forth. See your insurance agent for further details.

PROPERTY INSURANCE

A broad form insurance policy will protect you against fire, lightning, wind, hail, explosion, riot, smoke, aircraft, vandalism, water damage, glass breakage, falling objects, and so forth. The comprehensive form usually adds theft, collapse, sewer backup, electrical damage, and chemical spills. Obviously, you are better off with comprehensive coverage, but check your own policies with your own agent for exact coverage, costs, deductibles, and so forth.

You really can be insured against almost everything but IRS audits (what an idea!). However, the amounts of such coverage should be examined and updated as needed.

COVERAGE AMOUNTS

"Actual cash value" is not what you think, and is not the best coverage to have. This coverage only pays for the replacement cost of the property *less* the drop in value because of age and normal wear and tear. Think: How much would you get if a 50-year-old building you own burned to the ground? About $88.45?

Replacement cost insurance, however, covers the cost of replacing the property *without* any deduction for that decline in value (as in the preceding). You must, however, carry insurance for *80 percent or more* of the actual total value. For example, if a building is valued at $100,000, the replacement cost insurance you carry *must* be $80,000 or higher. If you fulfill that condition, this insurance will rebuild, replace, or repair the property with like materials and labor. If you do not replace the property, you will receive the actual cash value (i.e., $80,000 in my example). Inflation-guard coverage provides for automatic increases in the amounts of that insurance to keep up with inflation. This option can be used for whatever insured assets that increase in value, especially real estate. For example, my own jewelry floater offers a flat 5 percent increase in stated values every year or so with no new appraisals required. Consider inflation-guard coverage in light of your own particular situation.

In general, if you do not insure business property for at least 80 percent of fair market value, you will not receive full payment, but only a prorated percentage. Said another way: If your coverage is for less than 80 percent, you are self-insuring a portion of the property if there is a loss. That may be OK if you fully understand what you are doing. If not, ask your insurance agent to explain co-insurance, how it is figured, and how much any insurance recovery would be. You should understand this long *before* there is any loss.

Buildings and other property must be appraised. One way to avoid disputes is to buy agreed-value insurance. An appraisal is made and the insurance company agrees to insure for that value. In the event of a loss you get that *exact* amount, no questions asked! The typical (expensive!) jewelry floater policy is similar; whatever the individual stated amounts may be are *exactly* what is paid in case of loss.

I owned a car over 20 years old, and the blue book value was far less than the worth I placed on this treasure, which had many improvements and extremely low mileage. After an appraisal, I obtained agreed-value auto insurance for about three times the blue book value. If the car had been stolen or totaled I would have received the exact agreed-value amount, just like a jewelry floater.

TAX-DEDUCTIBLE INSURANCE

You can claim business tax deductions for the following kinds of insurance premiums, as long as they're ordinary and necessary expenses in carrying on your trade or business:

- Fire, theft, flood, or other casualty insurance.
- Liability insurance.
- Merchandise or inventory insurance.
- Auto and other vehicle insurance.
- Credit insurance to cover losses from unpaid debts.
- Group health and accident insurance.*
- Disability insurance.*†
- Group life insurance up to $50,000 per employee.
- Malpractice insurance and errors and omissions insurance.
- Workers' compensation insurance.
- State unemployment compensation insurance.
- Use and occupancy and business interruption insurance. This insurance pays for lost profits if your business is shut down by fire or other causes.†
- Overhead insurance. This insurance pays for business overhead expenses if your business is shut down by your injury or disability.†
- Employee fidelity insurance.

WHEN TO DEDUCT PREMIUMS

The IRS says you can usually deduct premiums in the tax year to which they apply. In other words, you cannot prepay insurance premiums for future periods and deduct them in the current period. As the IRS explains (emphasis mine):

> If you make an advance payment of a premium for an insurance policy that covers *more than one tax year,* you cannot deduct the entire premium in the year you make the payment, *even if you are a cash basis taxpayer.* You can only deduct the part of the premium that applies to the current tax year. In each later tax year you deduct the part that applies to that tax year.

That's pretty easy to understand. Any insurance paid for future tax periods is set up as an asset ("prepaid insurance") and then charged to expense in the later applicable tax year. However, for all manufacturers of *any* size or for distributors or retailers grossing over $10 million a year, the UNICAP (uniform capitalization) rules apply (IRS

*Subject to certain limitations on deductions, unless you are operating as a "C" corporation.

†Will result in taxable income when received, if the company paid and deducted the premiums.

Code Section 263A), and part of what would otherwise be insurance expense becomes part of the cost of inventory.

INSURANCE BONDING OF EMPLOYEES

Employee fidelity bonds cover losses due to dishonesty, fraud, forgery, stealing, and the like. As with all insurance, your losses are only covered up to the amount of your policy. Again, I urge you to consider your total coverage realistically and carefully. As you learned in Chapter 20, those who steal eventually steal big (except when they are caught early)!

However, it's more difficult to collect under these policies. You cannot simply claim that money has disappeared or inventory is missing. These policies are subject to the following three conditions, or you *don't* collect:

1. A reasonable certainty that the stealing was by an employee (i.e., not a customer stealing from a retail store).

2. Proof of loss, and not just unsupported statements such as "I'm sure we had a lot more inventory that the new count shows," or "Somebody must be stealing, or we wouldn't be losing money," or "We've been showing a profit, but the bank balance is much lower than it should be, so we've been robbed." (In my experience this requirement has been the killer that has lost many businesses their insurance recovery.)

3. Once dishonesty is discovered, the employee must be fired, or your fidelity insurance coverage is ended immediately (the limited exception is if the employee has promised to repay and is kept on the job, but then there is no further insurance coverage for *that* individual).

There are four kinds of fidelity bonding policies:

1. Individual bonds. Insure only the individuals specified by name.
2. Position bonds. Insure whoever has the position as treasurer, controller, bookkeeper, chief financial officer (CFO), and so forth.
3. Blanket bonds. Cover all employees with the premium generally based on the number of employees who have access to money or property.
4. Combination crime policies. This excellent policy combines fidelity bonding with crime coverage for such things as robbery, burglary, disappearance or destruction of cash money, and disappearance or destruction of securities.

Fidelity bonds normally cover regular employees. You can cover independent contractors or other nonemployees but *only* by a special endorsement added to the policy. So, if your CPA signs on your bank account and pays your bills, but is acting even more nervous and twitchy than most CPAs usually do and has recently left his wife, grown a beard, is driving a red Porsche convertible, has a new 19-year-old girlfriend, and is collecting brochures about castles in Spain, it may be time to prudently consider this extra endorsement.

SPLIT-DOLLAR LIFE INSURANCE

The 1993 tax law's lower $150,000 limit on retirement plan compensation, plus higher income tax rates for some taxpayers have made split-dollar insurance arrangements more attractive than ever before.

The Arrangement

Split-dollar insurance is an excellent fringe benefit for employees, particularly younger employees, and will certainly help hold key individuals in your company. However, every employee of *any* age will love this plan!

"Split-dollar" refers to a method of *premium payment* in which the employer and employee share the premium payments in a way that is advantageous for the *employee*. The insurance is purchased on the life of the employee under a written agreement that the employer will pay that part of the premium equal to the guaranteed annual increase in the cash value. The company also pays the balance of the premium for the employee as a taxable economic benefit but under favorable tax rules (see next section). Alternatively, the employee personally pays the small and decreasing *remainder* of the premium, equal to the annual term insurance value.

As co-beneficiaries (in effect), the employer is entitled to a *return* of all the cash value payments, either from a portion of the proceeds at death or when the employee cashes in the policy or takes a policy loan. The employee's beneficiary receives the remainder of the proceeds in the event of death. Or, part of the policy dividends can be used to buy *additional* term insurance. In that situation, the employee's beneficiary will receive the *entire* face amount of the policy in the event of death, and the employer will still receive a refund of the full cash value payments.

As the dividends and cash values increase, the amount due from the employee will decrease and, for most of the policy years, the employee will have little or *nothing* to pay. Most insurance companies have designed special policies to provide large cash values in the *early* years of the policy and thus quickly decrease the employee's share of the premium.

The Advantages

Under the split-dollar plan, younger employees will obtain a *large* amount of life insurance when they need it most and could not otherwise afford it. The employer will get back all the money invested and grateful, loyal, and permanent employees. In effect, the employer has made a no-interest *loan* to the employee with secured and guaranteed repayment assured! At the employee's retirement age, the policy could be used to fund a private pension plan (see Chapter 10), a buy-sell agreement, or a deferred compensation plan. However, a split-dollar insurance plan can be offered on a *discriminatory* basis to selected employees.

COMMENT

The cash value of the policy is an *asset* of the employer company that dresses up a balance sheet very nicely; if need be, the cash value can even be borrowed back by the company on short notice and at favorable interest rates.

The Tax Factors

Premium payments are *not* tax-deductible by the company, but the eventual return of those cash value premiums is a nontaxable return of capital. If the *employer* pays the entire premium, the employee is liable for income tax on the economic benefit, *but* that taxable amount is computed by using the lower of the IRS annual renewable term PS 58 rates or the one-year term life insurance rates of the insurance company. The amount the employee must pay is usually *less* than the actual cash benefit to the employee (and overall but a small share of the total premium, which, as noted earlier, quickly disappears). If the *employee* pays the balance of the premium (the less typical arrangement), there is no tax effect on either the employee or the employer. Insurance proceeds to the employee's beneficiary are, of course, income tax free and often can be arranged to be estate tax free as well.

IRS approval is *not* required to establish a split-dollar plan; however, a formal agreement *must* be drawn between the employer and the employee as required by the Employment Retirement Income Security Act (ERISA). Don't use just anyone to draw up this document, as it requires an expert.

TAXTIP

The IRS has *not* applied their imputed interest rules to these no interest loans, and thus, in effect, has given its tacit approval to these arrangements. If they should change their mind about the interest-free loan involved in this plan, I feel that all *existing* split-dollar plans would be left alone and "grandfathered."

Unfortunately, a split-dollar insurance plan could be dangerous for majority *owners* of a company. The IRS *can* take the position that if a corporation controlled by any individual has an ownership interest in his insurance policy, the insurance proceeds are *includible in the estate* and subject to estate taxes (but see the rollout solution in the next section).

The Split-Dollar Rollout Solution

Some of these plans are cleverly set up so that after about 6 to 10 years the policy is "rolled out" (i.e., given outright) to the employee and the employer *forfeits* the right to recover its cash value premiums. In this case, company *owners* could also be included in the arrangement.

One illustration goes like this: A $500,000 policy on a 36-year-old owner is set up as a split-dollar plan for 10 years. Then the policy is rolled out to the owner, at which time the policy is *paid up* and has a cash value of $100,000. The individual is supposed to report the $100,000 cash value as taxable income, but despite this fact, the overall economic benefit to the *individual* is sensational! You and your financial adviser should think this scenario through with your own numbers.

Alternatively, just before the rollout, the corporation can *borrow* an amount equal to its cash value premium investment and *then* roll out the policy to the individual. In this situation, the IRS takes the position that the only taxable income to the individual is any remaining cash value *less* any cumulative premiums paid by the employee (generally very little or nothing). However, in this instance the employee doesn't receive a paid up policy or one with substantial cash values, so, particularly for owners, I generally favor the first option.

Finally, if the employee leaves the company, she can simply buy the policy for the amount of the cash value (borrowed from the insurance company if need be) and then continue to pay the premiums. No tax liability is incurred in this kind of transaction for either side.

Policy Illustrations

It is wise to remember that life insurance illustrations presented by an insurance agent are nothing more than projected *estimates* of what *may* happen in the future! If interest rates drop, so will the return on the policy and all the assumptions as to cash value, dividends, and so forth will change. Of course, the higher the projected interest earnings rate, the easier it is to sell a policy, since the *apparent* cost is lower!

In today's economic world, *don't* accept any interest rate earnings projection of more than five or six percent. If the illustration you are given is based on a higher assumed interest rate, ask that it be recomputed at 5 percent and also at 6 percent. Then, review it with your tax adviser.

GROUP-TERM LIFE INSURANCE

Group-term life insurance is frequently referred to as Section 79 insurance, because that's the IRS Code section that controls this plan. It's a great idea! Group term is an absolute win-win for every employer and employee!

Tax Rules

Group-term offers a tax-free fringe benefit and an interesting option to benefit your favorite charity. Here are the guidelines:

• For group-term insurance coverage of up to $50,000 per employee, the payment by the employer is *tax-deductible,* but the insurance benefit to the employee is *tax-free* (further, the cost of each policy is cheaper than for individual term policies).

• The coverage must be offered on a *nondiscriminatory* basis, but it can vary as a percentage of compensation or by other reasonable formulas such as years of service or job classification. Even companies with less than 10 employees can adopt this plan (but in such cases all employees must be covered).

INTERESTING OPTION

This coverage can be extended to company commission salespeople, *regardless* of whether they are considered employees or independent contractors (Rev. Rul. 56-400).

• As with all life insurance, the proceeds are income tax free to the beneficiary. If necessary, ownership of the policy can usually be transferred, which may also avoid estate taxes.

Charitable Exclusion

If the company buys coverage for an individual employee in *excess* of $50,000, that extra coverage is *not* taxable to the employee if the beneficiary of the group term policy is a recognized *charity*.

TAXTIP

Consider the tax angle: Assume we have a very charitable owner who wants to leave $250,000 to her church. Properly arranged, the premiums on a group term policy for $250,000, with the church as beneficiary, will be tax-deductible by the company and not result in *any* taxable income to the individual.

Other Exclusions

Excess coverage over $50,000 is generally tax-exempt for any retired or disabled former employee.

CONCLUSION

I seriously believe that the richer you are, the less you need insurance. Very wealthy individuals frequently don't have life insurance or jewelry insurance because they can stand the loss. Similarly, if a General Motors plant burned down and the company had to suffer millions in underinsurance or co-insurance, they would hardly notice the loss (and they might celebrate if it were an old and obsolete factory). However, the opposite is also true for the poor rep; you had better have PU-LEN-TEE of insurance! By all means consider the favorable business life insurance options explained in this chapter. Finally, I cannot emphasize enough that *liability* insurance is essential for the average sales rep, and the lack thereof may put you out of business faster than losing your lines!

Chapter Twenty-Five

How to Avoid an IRS Audit

Surprisingly, preparing an income tax return for the average sales rep involves a certain amount of *selling*. You (and your accountant) have to sell your business tax return to the IRS, that is, sell them *not* to audit your return.

Your sales pitch to the IRS simply involves methods of presentation and disclosure. It does *not* involve fraud, misfeasance, misstatement, misclassifications, lies, or violating the Internal Revenue Code. How you present information and how you disclose information may make the difference between your tax return being quickly passed, or quickly selected for an IRS audit. As we usta' say on the South Side of Chicago: "Da cherce is yers."

CORPORATIONS

If you will get a blank corporation income tax return, Form 1120, we will go through this together. Remember—this is about *selling* and not about (boring) accounting.

Principal Business Activity Code (Page 3, Schedule K, Line 2a)

If I had to pick just one piece of advice, this would be it: Make *sure* you have supplied the correct business code number on your tax return! The IRS has different audit parameters for different kinds of businesses, and although those audit guidelines are a top IRS secret, common sense and a lot of (friendly) IRS feedback has lead me to an inescapable conclusion: Once you supply the business code number of the tax return, the IRS audit computer "pulls up" *specific* guidelines for that particular kind of business! Any misstatement or misclassifications of the business code will cause the IRS computer to compare apples to oranges, and guess what happens then?

Corporations have a different *set* of business activity code numbers than proprietorships or partnerships (we'll be discussing corporate classifications). I have seen reps misclassified under "wholesale trade," "retail trade," and "manufacturing." The truth of the matter is that you are in a *service* business and the service you render is "selling." The fact that you sell is what matters, *not* the product. You belong in the corporate classification section (the 7000 and 8000 series) called "Services."

Consider what an incorrect classification number does to you. Many times, an electronics rep is classified under 5060, "Wholesale trade—Electrical goods." Why? Well, the accountant looks over the entire list and can't find the word electronics on it at all (which is true). He knows that you don't sell at retail (to the general public), so apparently you are selling at wholesale, and "electrical" is somewhat similar and the closest word to "electronics." Classification 5060 is as close a fit as he can find, so he writes that down and gets on with the tax return.

The IRS audit computer checks your return and pulls up the secret 5060 guidelines for a wholesaler (i.e., distributor or buy-sell operation) of electrical goods. From the first moment, the return doesn't match the IRS profile! Page 1, line 2: there is no "cost of goods sold." How can a wholesaler not have a product cost? Page 2, Schedule A, lines 1 and 7: there are no inventories reported. How can a wholesaler not have any beginning or ending inventories?

According to the secret IRS guidelines, perhaps 0.5 percent of sales is the average amount of entertainment expense for this business code category. But this rep claimed 4.7 percent—over nine times the average for this category! Also, why would a wholesaler of electrical goods not have any freight-out to customers? And no returns or allowances? Or bad debts? Why is trade show expense for a wholesale distributor so high? Why are auto expenses so high? Why isn't there any warehousing expense for the goods? And on and on and on, until: *Tilt!*

So that tax return gets pulled for an IRS audit, for no other reason than a *wrong* principal business activity code number! I call that *negative* selling or putting your *worst* foot forward. It's bad enough to do that with a customer or a principal, but to needlessly cause an IRS audit can be deadly and expensive. After all, what rep has perfect records?

What business code number should you use? The answer is: *8980*. This number is in the principal business activity code section for "Services." If you review the list of service categories (from 7200 on), there is no mention of anything like "selling," "agent," "broker," "commissions," or similar categories. The only possible fit is "*Miscellaneous* services" (8980).

Logically, the one category where the IRS audit computer *cannot* have predetermined guidelines is "miscellaneous." At least this way, computer guidelines can't select your tax return for an audit! Of course, a human may still do so, but at least you're past that first *computer* hurdle!

Business Activity (Page 3, Schedule K, Line 2b)

We know that the IRS computer can read and deal with the business code number. But we must now postulate the worst case, that the computer pulled your return for further scrutiny by an IRS reviewer. Whether your return now gets selected for audit or is passed, is usually up to this IRS individual. So we have to *sell* this individual on what you do, how you do it, and why it probably would be nonproductive for the IRS to audit your return.

We must now begin the process of persuading the agent that your travel and entertainment and other expenses are justifiably high. What is the most descriptive word we can use to portray your business activity? The answer is a one word characterization of your business: "Selling." An IRS agent knows that people engaged in the business of selling normally have higher than usual auto, travel, entertainment, and similar expenses, which is what we want to accomplish!

Just use the one word: "Selling." That's your answer and it also follows two highly recommended principles: KISS (*K*eep *I*t *S*imple *S*tupid), and never answer more than you have been asked.

Product or Service (Page 3, Schedule K, Line 2c)

To answer this question as to your product or service, we follow the rationale developed in the discussion of the business activity code number. It does not matter what product you sell; your activity is *selling* and you are in a *service* business. So, the answer is not "electronic components," or "automotive accessories." The answer should again describe your business in general (KISS) terms and again slip in the fact that you are in sales.

Given the space limitations on the form and keeping our goal in mind, the best answer is: "Mfrs. Sales Agency." That accomplishes everything we possibly can in one short line.

Other Income (Page 1, Line 10)

Here's a last chance to describe your business to the IRS reviewer. We do not report the income from the rep firm on line 1 ("gross receipts or sales") of the tax return. Instead, we report the agency income on line 10 ("other income"), which states that you must attach a descriptive schedule. We gladly do so, and our schedule will state, as a description of the income, "Sales commissions." Gee whiz, we got the word "sales" in front of the IRS reviewer, *again!* Further, we really have given the best description of exactly what you do for a living: you are in sales; you are paid on a commission basis; by implication, you therefore pay all your own expenses; and by inference, your travel and entertainment and auto expenses will be much higher than normal. That's a whole bunch of selling!

That's not all we put on that schedule for line 10. In Chapters 2 and 17, we discussed personal use of business autos and income inclusions. Following the logic that you should always highlight (sell!) that you are *exactly* following the law, we now include a second and separate income item for the line 10 schedule called "personal use of business autos." We never net this amount against auto expenses or hide it from the IRS. We proudly advertise what we have done!

So we have "sold" the IRS person twice: first, in the way we reported the commission income and second, in the scrupulously honest way we reported personal use of business autos. Nothing illegal about it: just "presentation" and "selling," and you *do* know about that, don't you?

Total Assets (Page 1, Box D)

The primary way the IRS selects *corporation* tax returns for audit is by "total assets." This number is entered at the top of page 1; the bigger the number, the more chance of the return being selected for audit. Now, of course reps aren't reporting $50 million or even $1 million in assets, but this is an area where smaller is better, and it's one more place to lower your "audit profile." How do you legally do this? It's simple: spend all your cash paying bills just before fiscal year-end and, whenever possible, lease equipment, computers, autos, or anything else that makes good business sense. Both of those moves *reduce* total assets.

Assume one rep has $25,000 in the bank at fiscal year-end. That $25,000 becomes part of the total assets reported in box D. Another rep spends the whole $25,000 paying tax-deductible bills *before* the fiscal year ends. The total assets reported in box D are $25,000 *less* than our first rep and a lower audit profile results. Assume also that the first rep bought a computer installation on time for $20,000, and the second rep leased the same equipment and software. Again, the first rep will show $20,000 more in box D, but the amounts for leased equipment will not be reflected in box D by the second rep. In conjunction with these ideas (particularly about spending all your cash before fiscal year-end) you should also refer to Chapter 16 on zeroing out.

Personal Service Corporation? (Page 1, Box A[3])

No, you are *not* a personal service corporation, and that box should *not* be checked or your tax return is wrong. See the discussion about the special categories of personal service corporations in Chapter 12. Sales agencies are *not* one of them and a checked box here could cause some real IRS problems.

Other Deductions (Page 1, Line 26)

The schedule to attach for this line contains all the expenses not individually itemized on the preprinted lines 12 thru 25. Here is where our Chart of Accounts (see Chapter 17) comes into play. Reread Chapter 17 for the rationale and explanations of how to split and present the various expense accounts, particularly travel and entertainment. You are well advised to follow all the suggested procedures and *sell* those expenses to the IRS reviewer! One way is to always alphabetize that list of expenses. Doing so implies a degree of precision in your books and records that can impress the IRS classifier that you have accurate, logical, and complete records. Ha! Only you and I know how many of those expense amounts were recorded on the inside of matchbook covers.

> ***TAXTIP***
>
> You will never know which of the presentation suggestions will win an IRS "pass," so I'd strongly recommend *all* the ideas in this and related chapters.

Page 1, Lines 28, 29 and 30

If you followed the suggestions in Chapter 16 to zero out your tax return, line 28 ("taxable income") is showing a small loss, line 29a is showing a net operating loss deduction carryover from prior years, and the last line, line 30, is showing the cumulative loss figure. Those negative numbers are powerful IRS audit deterrents! This is prime advice; consider it carefully!

Paid Preparer's Signature (Page 1)

If I were an IRS reviewer, I would look askance at *any* corporate tax return that was not prepared and signed by a CPA or other tax professional. Corporate tax returns are tricky, and I doubt that the average sales agency can adequately prepare a corporation tax return unless the agency is so large that in-house accountants are employed.

Compensation of Officers (Page 2, Schedule E)

Never give the IRS more information than is required (just like in the Army, never volunteer!). The instructions state to complete Schedule E only if the corporation's gross income is $500,000 or more, so if it isn't, don't!

Now refer to page 1. You will see that line 12 is "compensation of officers," while line 13 is "salaries and wages" of others. The reason these two lines are at the very top of the expense listing and next to each other is so the IRS can quickly compare how much the owners and officers were paid compared to employees. They are looking for unreasonable compensation. Read Chapter 22 for background information.

My advice is to list *just* the owners of the company if they are the chief operating officers, and not all the others who may legally be vice presidents or assistant VPs, but just as a matter of public image, ego, or reward. More is *not* better when it comes to filling out this schedule.

Loans to and from Shareholders (Page 4, Schedule L, Lines 7 and 19)

Chapter 21 covers the topic of shareholder loans in detail. In brief, any amounts entered on these lines is potential trouble. The fact that the IRS uses 2 of only 27 total available lines on the balance sheet to highlight these figures speaks for itself.

Total Assets (Page 4, Schedule L, Line 15)

This figure is copied from page 1, box D of Form 1120 and is used as a major IRS audit selection parameter. See the earlier discussion in this chapter.

Travel and Entertainment (Page 4, Schedule M-1, Line 5c)

The 50 percent nondeductible portion of travel and entertainment expenses must be entered on line 5c of Schedule M-1 (see Chapter 1).

It can certainly be an audit trigger if the line is left blank or if the amount bears no relationship to the expenses claimed in these categories. For example, if these deducted expenses total $20,000 (at net 50 percent) and the amount on this line is only $1,800 (instead of *also* $20,000), you might very well have just gotten yourself an audit!

There is one loophole. As the note to Schedule M-1 states, if your total company assets are under $25,000, you do not have to complete either Schedule M-1 or Schedule M-2. Once again, *don't volunteer!*

Form 4562 (Part V, Sections B and C, Lines 27 thru 38)

Form 4562 ("Depreciation and Amortization") is used for depreciation and amortization, but Sections B and C of Part V request information regarding the business use of vehicles, so this form is applicable to virtually *every* sales rep's tax returns.

The IRS instructions state, "Always complete this section for vehicles used by a sole proprietor, partner or other 'more than 5% owner,' or related person," that is, all corporation owners of more than 5 percent of the company stock as well as the others listed. Time after time, however, we have seen tax returns prepared by other accountants with Sections B and C left blank. Trust me, the IRS doesn't like that!

Section B primarily asks for the business and personal total miles of each business vehicle, while the remainder of the section and all of Section C contain general questions about business autos. We *always* answer these questions, if need be, with estimates or approximations, but we *always* fill in Form 4562 for sales reps.

Who knows what the irritation level of the IRS may be when Form 4562 is ignored or incomplete, but large amounts of auto expenses and reimbursements and auto leasing is claimed? I don't care to find out, do you?

SOLE PROPRIETORSHIPS

I went into considerable detail on how to avoid IRS audits of sole proprietorships in Chapter 15, and you should absolutely refer to that section of the chapter. But I'm going to go over proprietorships again with some different and some similar comments; after all, any reiteration that may help avoid an IRS audit is reiteration well spent, right? So, if you are a proprietor, read both sections for maximum protection. Obtain a blank Schedule C ("Profit or Loss From Business"), which is later attached to Form 1040, U.S. Individual Income

Tax Return, to follow the discussion (I'm using one dated 1993, but any current year will do).

Business Activity Code (Schedule C, Page 1, Box B)

The principal business activity code list for sole proprietors (who file Schedule C) is *not* the same as the code listing for corporations. Interestingly enough, in this case the IRS has recognized that sales reps do indeed exist and they have provided two code numbers for you to use, albeit in the wrong section of the list.

While we know that you are in the service business, as I have explained in these chapters, and especially in the first part of this chapter, the IRS classifies sole rep proprietors under "wholesale trade" (as if you took title to the goods you sell, which you don't). But at least there are codes to use, so select them accordingly. Under "wholesale trade," there are two categories: 2634 (durable goods) and 2675 (nondurable goods). The description for both categories is "Agent or broker for other firms—more than 50 percent of gross sales on commission." So the description is right, even if the general category is wrong. Although most of our rep-clients are incorporated (see the many reasons in Chapter 12), we do use these two numbers for sole proprietors.

Methods of Valuing Inventory (Schedule C, Page 1, Box G[4])

Since you don't have any inventories, be sure to check the fourth box, "does not apply," instead of skipping the question completely (so as to not build up the IRS irritation factor).

Other Income (Schedule C, Page 1, Part I, Line 6)

The "other income" line is used exactly as the one described for corporations, so please reread that information.

Car and Truck Expenses (Schedule C, Page 1, Part II, Line 10)

At this point, the note to Schedule C states, "attach Form 4562." Reread the discussion about Form 4562 ("Depreciation and Amortization"), and then do as suggested. In some limited circumstances, you can enter this information on page 2, Part IV instead, but the point is to enter it *somewhere* and not irritate the folks at the IRS.

Interest (Schedule C, Page 1, Part II, Line 16)

If you want to save a lot of IRS aggravation, you will be very careful about what you list on line 16a ("mortgage interest"), as opposed to line 16b ("other interest"). The IRS has a new computer audit program in which they *match* any amount claimed on line 16a with information return Form 1098, "Recipients of Mortgage Interest," (this is the form on which the financial institution reports to the IRS the mortgage interest you have paid to them).

So if the mortgage interest you claim you paid on line 16a does not match up to the amount reported to the IRS on Form 1098, you can expect to receive a computer audit letter asking you to explain the discrepancy. Never claim any interest deduction on line 16a unless you have a copy of Form 1098 to back it up. Otherwise, claim all business interest paid on line 16*b*, which is not (yet) subject to computer audit.

Vehicle Leasing (Schedule C, Page 1, Part II, Line 20a)

The instructions for this line warn about "income inclusions" for leased autos. Chapter 2 will tell you all about that strange item. We recommend you show income inclusions separately on line 6, "other income."

Travel, Meals, and Entertainment (Schedule C, Page 1, Part II, Line 24)

Again refer to our Chart of Accounts and explanations in Chapter 17. If these expense amounts are large (as for most reps), we prefer to skip all entries on this line and use line 27, which is detailed on the open lines of page 2, Part V ("other expenses"). It is there that you may list all your travel and entertainment accounts, giving the breakdown as required (see Chapter 17). On a separate line, you will list the reduced number for "50% of travel meals and entertainment." What you have accomplished is to avoid the computer audit pattern, which undoubtedly exists for line 24. We prefer this presentation, particularly when large travel and entertainment amounts are involved.

Other Expenses (Schedule C, Page 1, Part II, Line 27)

Line 27 expenses are entered on page 2, Part V. Again, refer to Chapter 17 and list your accounts accordingly. Don't forget to alphabetize the list for reasons discussed on page 294.

Home Office Expenses (Schedule C, Page 1, Part II, Line 30)

You *must* attach Form 8829, "Expenses for Business Use of Your Home," if you claim any expenses on this line, or you are really asking for trouble! See Chapter 4 for everything you ever wanted to know about home office expenses.

CONCLUSION

If you violated every one of these suggestions, your chances of an IRS audit are virtually guaranteed. The *more* of these ideas you can implement, the *less* your audit chances will be. For those of you who always wondered why you are audited year after year, the truth may very well be in this information. Sole proprietors should reread Chapter 15 on IRS audits.

Finally, bear in mind that you will never know when adding just one more of these sales ideas will tip the balance from "audit" to "pass"! So start selling the IRS! It probably pays better than most of your other lines!

Chapter Twenty-Six

Dealing with Your Banker

Most bankers understand the rep business almost as well as most IRS agents: minimally to zero. You have to educate them what it is you *do*. We found one good banker at a suitable bank and started referring our rep clients to her. She now has about seven reps for customers, and she understands their business and our financial communications.

WHY BORROW?

In a service business like yours, you are not borrowing to expand your plant and equipment. You should borrow money and pay interest when the present or future potential return on the money *exceeds* the cost of that money considerably, and only in certain circumstances, such as:

- A prospective principal says if you will hire two more salespeople for certain territories, you will get the line. You have the potential to make a lot more money, but it will be at least six months before you see any profit on those two individuals. If you borrow money to carry that added payroll for six months or so, that makes sense.
- If you borrow money because a principal is three months behind in commissions but is about to get a major infusion of new capital and you should get paid up to date, that makes sense.
- If you borrow money to carry your existing payroll even though three individuals are not generating adequate commissions but you are negotiating for additional lines, that make sense.
- If you borrow money to buy out another rep firm and the line fit, future prospects, and synergism are all sensational, that makes sense.
- If you borrow money because your business is terrible, but you don't want to let anyone go, even though there are not any good line or customer prospects, that usually does not make any sense. However, there is a fine line to walk: if you let too many people go,

you will lose further lines as a result. (There is no easy answer to that one.)

• If you borrow money because business is down and *you* are faced with taking a pay cut, although the salespeople are profitable, that doesn't make any sense at all! Borrowing money to save the owner a reduction in pay is foolish indeed. The *first* step when business is poor would be for the owner to take a pay cut. After all, when business is great most of the increased net profits go directly to the owner. The sword cuts both ways! Further, where is the return on that 10–15 percent loan interest cost? And how will the loan principal

As we have slowly worked our way through a recession, the arguments about reducing owners' pay have been bitter. A typical statement from a rep-owner is, "I simply couldn't live on one dollar of less pay. We just couldn't make it!" I am in complete sympathy. However, how does that change the facts? Borrowing to pay the owner's compensation is a sure way to eventual failure, unless sales quickly improve or new lines are quickly obtained. But unfounded optimism is a quick way to the poorhouse!

So get your head on straight about when to borrow and when not to. Sometimes it's as foolish a solution as increasing the unpaid balance on your credit card and continuing to pay 19.6 percent interest.

THE CASH BASIS PROBLEM AND SOLUTION

Hopefully you have received good accounting and tax advice and your books are maintained and tax returns are prepared on the cash basis (reflecting commissions actually *received* and expenses actually *paid*). That's the way it should be (see Chapter 12). *Until* you want to borrow some money.

Once you have decided it does make sense to borrow money and approach your banker for a loan, the invariable comment is, "Let's see a copy of your last two corporate tax returns and financial statements, and a current financial statement as well."

WARNING

The wrong move here and you will bury your loan prospects.

You or your CPA must begin the education process with your banker. Your response should be something like this: "You know, we are in a sales service business: we don't take title to the goods, we don't carry inventories, and we just earn commissions on the products we sell by acting as sales representatives for various factories. So, we are allowed to exercise the valuable right to file our tax returns and keep our books on the cash basis. That way, we never owe taxes until we actually receive our commissions, and even then we can legally avoid paying corporate taxes by zeroing out our profits at fiscal year-end through year-end payment of bonuses, bills, and retirement plan deductions. In that way, we can increase our cash flow enormously. I'm sure you are familiar with this practice from your dealings with law firms, CPA firms, and medical practices, all of which do the same, according to our CPA." The banker replies, doubtfully and nervously, "Er, yes, I think so."

Then you or your CPA continue: "So our cash basis books do not reflect the true value of the company, since all sales commissions earned and legally owing our sales agency, but unpaid, are not shown on our books or tax return. Further, our exclusive sales contracts with the various factories we represent (called 'principals' in our jargon) are a very valuable intangible asset and not shown on our books at all; some even include vesting provisions in the event of termination. Finally, since we zero out at fiscal year-end by paying all our bills, we have no payables, but lots of receivables. Do you understand?" The banker replies, queasily and querulously, "You mean your books aren't correct?"

At this point, you give the banker your last two corporate tax returns. He quickly scans them, looks at the bottom line, and says, "This looks like you're losing money and going broke!" Then he looks at the balance sheet on the tax return and says, "The company only has assets of $8,243! Based on these figures, but only because of our longstanding banking relationship, we can only loan you up to $2,000."

At this point in the conversation, using your best sales voice you reply, "You see, that's why my CPA is going to prepare an *accrual* basis financial statement, right up to date, so that you will have a true and accurate picture of the company." The banker replies dubiously, "Maybe that will help." So you desperately tell your CPA to rush preparation of an accrual basis financial statement.

SUGGESTIONS FOR YOUR ACCOUNTANT

In preparing that accrual statement, the following are my suggestions for your accountant:

1. Commissions receivable are figured like this: Determine commissions for goods actually *shipped* from the factory by balance sheet

date that are still unpaid at that date and book those as "commissions receivable." If your client has no financial controls over those figures, trace subsequent collections and determine which of those can be accrued at balance sheet date. Then determine if there are still further unpaid commissions to be added to the collected amounts.

If none of this is practical, use 1½ times the last month's commissions collected as a generally accurate ballpark amount, since there are always the previous month's commissions earned and not collected (30 days), plus the usual 45–60 day accounts. If collections from principals are really slow, use 2 times the last month's figure. Discuss the proper multiple with your client to get the best feel for what this number accurately should be. Don't just guess high.

2. You absolutely *cannot* accrue commissions receivable for unfilled orders. The rep has no legal claim of right on those funds at balance sheet date. This transaction belongs in future periods and can no more be recorded than you would book a company sale for unshipped goods still in inventory (what if the goods are *never* shipped because the order is canceled or the factory burns down?). However, if the rep has a huge backlog of unfilled orders, you could footnote the approximate total and approximate commissions.

3. Although we do not do so in preparing our accrual basis rep financial statements, you could consider recording some of the costs paid for obtaining those unfilled orders as prepaid expenses. In so doing, you are really matching income and related expenses in the same accounting period in accordance with generally accepted accounting principles (GAAP).

4. Accounts payable will really be only accrued expenses for the typical sales rep. In most rep firms, this figure ranges from insignificant to none. Scan the following month's cash disbursements to see if there are any significant items that might be applicable to the prior month. Accrued payroll is frequently the only major item in accrued expenses, depending on the timing of those payments at month-end. Also, adjust your payroll tax liability to the actual accrued amount payable.

5. The income statement is a little trickier. You cannot simply add the commissions receivable amount to the commission income of the current period. You can only add any *incremental increase* (or subtract any decrease) in commissions receivable to current cash basis revenues. To determine the figure you need, you must first establish how much the commissions receivable were at the beginning of the income reporting period. Use the same techniques described in step 1, but the job should be easier since you are doing a retrospective analysis of existing data.

6. Depreciation is generally not a major expense factor in most rep

firms. We prefer to use a flat approximation (e.g., $3,000) to tell the reader it is exactly that. Remember, you do have the right to use longer depreciation lives for financial reporting than those arbitrarily dictated by the income tax code (i.e., MACRS, ACRS, and all that nonsense, have nothing to do with *realistic* asset lives).

7. For "provision for income taxes," we again use a rounded amount to put the reader on notice that this figure is an approximation. After all, this liability varies upward by percentage as income increases and no one knows what the final liability may be at fiscal year-end. A reasonable estimate should be so signaled by the financial statement presentation (e.g., $10,000, $20,000).

8. The balance sheet classification of the income tax provision presents a problem. If the rep is consistently zeroing out year after year, there is in all practicality no tax liability by the corporation. However, as required by GAAP, you simply cannot omit that entire liability from the balance sheet. Our compromise treatment is to show the tax obligation on the balance sheet, but not as a current liability. Our usual title is "Deferred Income Taxes," and we give a footnote explanation of why we do not consider them current (they certainly aren't going to be paid within 12 months and perhaps never). Of course, this classification legitimately improves the current ratio of the company, which should somewhat please the banker.

9. Speaking of footnotes, the first one (under "Summary of Significant Accounting Policies") concerns the fact that these financial statements have been prepared on the accrual basis. Another one (under "Income Taxes") is that the company income tax returns are prepared and filed using the cash (receipts and disbursements) method of tax reporting, which leads into the explanation of why there is only a deferred income tax liability on the balance sheet (as explained in point 8). Finish up with all the other common and usual footnotes as necessary. We omit about half the footnotes to reduce our time and fees. Because rep financial statements are so simple, the bankers don't care, and our reps are a little bit happier (feewise, that is).

TRUE STORY

While going through this entire exercise for one of our clients, the exasperated banker, who just wasn't getting it at all, finally blurted out in frustration, "Why don't you file the tax returns the *right* way, on the accrual basis?" Our client repeated this question to us and we advised him that the IRS would *gladly* let him change to the accrual method, but he would then owe an additional $30,000 in income taxes! He resolutely decided not to do so.

So, the rep pays all this money to have this accrual basis financial statement prepared and proudly delivers it to the banker, who, with wrinkled brow and puzzled demeanor states, "Why, this financial statement doesn't even match the tax return. There's something wrong." Restrain yourself once again and repeat the explanation we provided earlier. Hopefully, it will finally sink in, and hopefully you will eventually get the loan. To repeat an overused line in this book: "It ain't easy."

PERSONAL GUARANTEES

The bank will usually insist that you personally guarantee their loan to your sales agency. This is usually unavoidable and essential. Before you execute the personal guarantee, you will be asked to submit a personal financial statement that will be used to determine if your personal guarantee is worth anything (which sometimes poses a further problem, given the proclivity to acquire debt faster than assets).

BIG TIP

The personal financial statement is supposed to show all your assets at current market value rather than actual cost. My tip concerns the way you value the stock in your company. I have seen many personal financial statements where the rep put down the $1,000 that was paid for the stock as the value of the agency. The correct answer is to value the stock in your rep firm at 100 percent of one year's commission income (the traditional "goodwill"), plus the commissions receivable (see earlier), plus the tangible net worth (i.e., shareholder's equity) as shown on the cash basis books of the agency. This advice holds true if you are preparing a personal financial statement for any *other* purpose, for example, to obtain a home mortgage, to refinance an existing mortgage, or to obtain a personal loan.

Here's an example. Your firm is doing $600,000 a year in commissions; the commissions receivable are $71,844, and a cash basis financial statement shows shareholder's equity (i.e., net worth) at $15,232. On your personal financial statement you should value the stock of our company like this:

Goodwill	$600,000
Commissions receivable	71,844
Shareholder's equity	15,232
Total value	$687,076

CORPORATE ALTERNATIVE MINIMUM TAX

The alternative minimum tax (AMT) for corporations is a flat 20 percent tax levied on alternative minimum taxable income (AMTI), after deducting a $40,000 exemption, which phases out at higher income levels: If the AMT is *higher* than your regular corporate tax, you pay this higher tax instead of your regular corporate tax.

The *very act* of preparing a financial statement can subject your sales agency to the AMT! Included in AMTI is 75 percent of the difference between the income reported on the corporate tax return and the adjusted current earnings (ACE) of the agency. What can be used by the IRS to determine those earnings and profits? Why, a *financial statement* as fiscal year-end, which shows a *different* net income than the tax return. But we just issued an accrual basis financial statement to get that bank loan!

For example, assume our rep exactly zeroed out for the fiscal year on the cash basis corporation tax return. Further assume that to get a bank loan an accrual basis financial statement was prepared at fiscal year-end, which showed a net profit of $100,000. Finally, assume (worst case) that there is an IRS audit and the agent asks for and gets a copy of that financial statement. (After all, you and your CPA are not going to commit perjury and deny the financial statement even exists. Besides, the IRS could easily get one from the bank.)

Says the IRS agent: "First of all, you owe an AMT of $7,000. I have taken your ACE of $100,000 from that accrual basis financial statement, used 75 percent of it ($75,000), subtracted the AMT exemption of $40,000, and your tax is 20 percent of the net $35,000, or $7,000. Additionally, based on a random test of your travel and entertainment records, I am disallowing 92.7 percent of all those expenses. Your total bill is $22,753, plus interest and penalties."

That bank loan, with the necessary accrual basis financial statement, just cost you an extra $7,000 in (AMT) taxes! And they only loaned you $2,000! And assume you had already repaid the loan (with interest) before the IRS audit. What should you do in this situation? We beg the bankers to accept *interim* (i.e., not at year-end) accrual basis financial statements. That way, they cannot legally be used by the IRS to hang you with the AMT. This is one of our biggest problems and hardest sells to the typical banker. A frequent response is, "Oh, we must have a year-end financial statement for our credit files. We simply must."

You have two possible ways to avoid the AMT. Explain the AMT potential to your bankers and see if they will accept only interim accrual financials, or cash basis financials at fiscal year-end and accrual basis interim financials. Either way, there will not be a fiscal year-end, accrual basis financial statement in existence, which should avoid the AMT.

THE THREE Cs

Just for the record, every banker looks to the following in deciding if you are a creditworthy and reliable borrower:

- *Cash flow.* Is it sufficient to repay the loan, including interest?
- *Collateral.* Do you have a major stake in your business?
- *Character.* Is your reputation and past performance worthy of the loan?

CONCLUSION

Perhaps you should share this entire treatise with your banker. It may help explain your business, clear the air, justify cash basis tax reporting, rationalize accrual basis financial statements, and avoid the AMT.

Chapter Twenty-Seven

The Right Way (and the Wrong Way) to Take Money Out of Your IRA

Almost every reader will need the advice in this chapter eventually, and always *before* age 70½. At age 70½, every IRA owner *must* begin taking money out of her Individual Retirement Account or pay a *50 percent penalty* on any *under*distributions. Since many IRAs contain rollover amounts (e.g., from corporate retirement plans), I'm talking about *big* money and *major* decisions! Here are some key points:

- Whoever you select as beneficiary of your IRA *must be so designated to the financial institution managing your IRA,* and not just in your will. That designation must be made *before age 70½.*
- Two basic methods, "recalculation" and "term certain," are used to calculate life expectancy and your minimum annual IRA distribution. IRS Publication 590 (Individual Retirement Arrangements") doesn't clearly tell people they even *have* a choice of two methods, let alone how to make a required election.
- Many banks and virtually all stockbrokers either tell you to make your own calculations (using IRS Publication 590), or they use the more common recalculation method that may *ultimately* be less favorable for some individuals.
- To choose the term certain method, the more unusual option of the two, you must *make an election, in writing, before April 1 of the year after you turn 70½,* or you lose this chance forever.

SIX MAJOR SCENARIOS

Assuming you *have* made the elections just noted *before age 70½,* here is what can happen if you should die *before* age 70½:

1. Your *spouse* can roll over the IRA to her account and begin the payout election process all over, or leave the IRA alone and distribute over the *surviving spouse's* life expectancy beginning

in the year when the *decedent* would have been 70½, or continue to use the term certain method (explained later) if it was previously elected.

2. Any *other heir* can distribute over the heir's life expectancy, beginning in the year after the decedent's death, distribute all proceeds after five years from the decedent's death, or continue the term certain method if it was previously elected.
3. If left to the *estate,* the funds must be entirely distributed five years after the decedent's death (not a great idea).

If you should die *after* age 70½:

4. Your *spouse* can roll over the IRA to her account and begin the election process all over, leave the IRA alone and distribute over the *decedent's* life expectancy, or continue to use the term certain method if it was previously elected.
5. Any *other heir* can distribute over the *joint* life expectancy of the heir and the decedent, or continue to use the term certain method if it was previously elected.
6. If left to the *estate and if the recalculation method was used,* it must be distributed by December 31 of the *year of death.* If the term certain method was previously elected, then annual distributions can continue for the fixed term of years.

TAXTIP

Leaving the IRA to your estate *and* using the recalculation method is probably the worst alternative! In *this* situation, the experts suggest the term certain method!

THE RECALCULATION METHOD

The recalculation method will be familiar to almost all of you who are actually receiving IRA distributions. It works like this: An individual turning age 70½ divides the total IRA account balance by her life expectancy (using IRS tables) to determine the minimum amount that *must* be withdrawn each year. You have the option of using a table for your own *single* life expectancy, or you can use a *joint* life expectancy table for you and your beneficiary (who is usually your spouse, but selecting your spouse may not always be the best choice).

Each year, the required distribution is *recalculated* (hence the name given this method). This process takes into account that each year total life expectancy increases somewhat. For example, a 70-year-old husband and a 67-year-old wife have a joint life expectancy of 22 years. A year later, the same couple at age 71 and 68 have a life expectancy of 21.2 years (not 21 years). In other words, your life expectancy drops *less* than one full year for each year you live. Similarly, for an individual who turns 70½ in 1993, the IRS life expectancy table shows 16 years; in 1994, it's 15.3 years, in 1995 it's 14.6 years, and so on. Again, the life expectancy drops by less than a full year each time.

> ***TAXTIP***
>
> If you want the *lowest* legal distribution under this method use the *joint* life expectancy tables, which produce a higher life expectancy and thus a lower annual required distribution. For example, at age 65, the single table shows a 20 year life expectancy, while the joint table for a man at age 65, with say, a 55-year-old spouse or other beneficiary, is 30.9 years (and even with a 65-year-old beneficiary, it's 25 years).

EXAMPLES

For that married couple ages 70 and 67, assume the IRA account was $100,000. The first year they divide $100,000 by the joint 22 year life expectancy and the annual distribution is $4,545. Assume the remaining balance in the IRA of $95,455 earns 5 percent, or $4,773. The IRA now has $100,228 ($95,455 + $4,773 earnings). So the second year the distribution is $4,728 ($100,228 divided by the 21.2 year life expectancy).

For the single table user described above, the first year distribution is $100,000 divided by 16, or $6,250. The second year, assuming 5 percent earnings, its $98,438 divided by 15.3 years, or $6,434. One of the magical things these examples illustrate is that if the *earnings* in any retirement account are high enough, the balance in the account will remain about the same, or even increase, depending on the level of earnings. If my examples had used an 8 percent earnings assumption, all the IRA account balances would be *growing*, despite the annual distributions.

The withdrawal method is initially appealing since the time over which you can take the distributions is always increasing because life expectancy drops less than one year for each year that goes by. Thus, taxable distributions using the joint table are as minimal as possible, and the IRA balance remains about the same or even continues to grow. However, the operative words are "initially appealing," depending on how long you actually do live.

The problem with the recalculation method is if death occurs after age 70½ and if:

- You are single, or your spouse dies before you, and your estate receives all money from the IRA account, the estate must pay income taxes on the entire balance that year.
- Your surviving spouse is the beneficiary and places the IRA in a rollover IRA, which avoids current taxation, the minimum distribution must be calculated on the life expectancy of the remaining spouse *only*, which will boost each year's annual distribution. For example, if the surviving spouse is then age 75, under the single table that then must be used, the life expectancies are 12.5 years at age 75; 11.9 years at age 76; 11.2 years at age 77; 10.6 years at age 78, and so forth.

CAVEAT

A surviving spouse should usually choose a spousal rollover IRA for the deceased spouse's IRA account. By so doing, any existing recalculation election can be *broken* and a *choice* made between it and the term certain method. However, the surviving spouse would now be much older and have a shorter life expectancy than if the couple had *first* chosen the term certain method.

THE TERM CERTAIN METHOD

Under this method, the term of the payout is determined up front and for a *fixed number of years that never changes,* not even when one spouse dies. With the spouse as beneficiary, the joint life expectancy table can be used to set the *fixed* term of the payouts as of April 1 of the year after the IRA owner reaches age 70½. Using this joint table decreases the required minimum distribution.

EXAMPLE

Using the same couple with the 22-year life expectancy, the first year the payout would be 1/22 of the IRA account balance, the second year 1/21, the third year 1/20, the fourth year 1/19, and so forth. The advantages occur with the death of the first spouse and continue with the death of the second spouse as follows. Upon the death of the first spouse, there is *no recalculation of benefits* and the *same* payments can continue to the surviving spouse. Upon the death of the surviving spouse, there is *no change in distributions* and the payments for the *original fixed term* can continue to the estate (or heirs) of the second-to-die spouse. Thus, by using the fixed term arrangement, you are *assured* that payments will be made for that term (22 years in our example) no matter who lives or who dies. Payments are only taxable as received and are *fixed term* distributions.

> ***TAXTIP***
>
> While the minimum withdrawal amount is slightly larger initially, there is *no risk* of having the IRA income accelerated when either spouse dies! *Taxes are lower because only a small amount of the IRA is subject to tax each year, and* the growing balance of the IRA account continues to earn tax-deferred income until the end of the *fixed* term of years. As I mentioned earlier, most financial planners recommend the term certain option as their choice (of course, your own financial planner or retirement plan expert should decide in your particular case). Assuming you are convinced that term certain is best, you *must* make a *timely* election or lose the chance to select this option!

THE ELECTION

You only have until March 31 of the year *after* you turn age 70½ to make the election. IRS Publication 590 is not only unclear that you *have* a choice between two withdrawal methods, but it also does not tell you *how* to make the choice!

Many accountants, tax lawyers, insurance agents, and financial planners are unfamiliar with the method of making the election. A *written* election must be made. Some sophisticated banks have an election form that allows you to choose between the recalculation and term certain methods. However, many banks and stockbrokers do not have such a form. When no election is made, you default to the recalculation method, which is not where you may want to be. To avoid that, you should send a timely *certified* letter to the financial institution holding your IRA, in these approximate words:

> I, ______________, am holder of IRA Account #________ at your financial institution. I hereby elect the term certain method of making withdrawals from the aforementioned IRA account, based

upon the joint life expectancy of myself and my spouse. I do not choose to use the recalculation method. The term certain period that I elect is ______ years, which period does not exceed our joint life expectancies, as determined in the year that I, ______ attained age 70½, using the official tables in IRS Publication 590.

A COMPARISON OF THE TWO METHODS

In the event of death of the IRA owner and spouse in their late 70s or 80s, the recalculation method may cause the payment of taxes on the IRA far too soon! The reason, of course, is that the recalculation method ends with the death of the second spouse, and the IRA then could become entirely *income taxable* in the estate in the year of death. With the term certain method, however, the annual periodic payments can *continue unchanged* even after the death of both spouses. Thus, the payments are only taxable over the remaining *fixed* term of the payouts.

Consider this example using our same couple ages 70 and 67. Using the recalculation method, if they both die 10 years later, the IRA, including annual earnings, will still be approximately $100,000, possibly all taxable as income in the estate. Using the term certain method with a fixed 22 year life expectancy, if they die after 10 years, the *payments will continue annually for another 12 years* and will only be taxed on an annual basis as distributions are made to the eventual heirs. The overall income tax bite could be far less under the fixed term method.

CONCLUSION

To minimize your annual IRA payouts and potential income taxes:

- Consider the term certain method.
- *Never* leave your IRA to your estate, but to your spouse or preferably to younger heirs. Actually *name* your beneficiary with your IRA administrator (as *well* as in your will), *before* age 70½.
- Always use the *joint* life expectancy table if you want to *lower* the required annual payout.
- Reduce the minimum payout by selecting a *younger* individual as your IRA beneficiary if you can afford to bypass your spouse because of other assets in your estate, because you can use that age in the joint life expectancy tables. Example: At age 70, the joint life expectancy with a 65 year old spouse is 23.1 years. At

age 70, the joint life expectancy with a 45 year old child is 38.3 years.

Study the *six major scenarios* one more time. Consider each one as it applies to your particular situation. Then study the differences between recalculation and term certain options. Even if you are confused by all this, at least you have a *reference* to keep and ponder as you make your decision (*before* age 70½) or meet with your own advisers.

Chapter Twenty-Eight

Assorted Taxtips

HOW TO SAVE SOCIAL SECURITY TAXES ON DEFERRED COMPENSATION

If you elect to defer a portion of your compensation in any particular year to future years, the IRS jumps right in and says that Social Security taxes must be paid in the current year when the compensation is *earned* (the services performed) and *not* in the year when it is finally paid.

However, in some situations this may provide a major tax advantage. If, in the year you elect to defer part of your compensation, you have already *reached* the maximum Social Security limit, there will not be any additional Social Security tax due on that deferred compensation. Then, in years when you actually *receive* the pay, Social Security taxes will not be due. Thus, in certain situations, you can legally avoid payment of Social Security taxes on deferred compensation in both the current and future years.

Setting up a legally impeccable deferred compensation plan is a job for professionals only. If you are interested, get expert advice on reporting and other requirements.

DISCOUNTS IN GIVING CORPORATION STOCK AND SIMILAR ASSETS TO FAMILY MEMBERS

If you are contemplating a gift of stock in your corporation (or similar interests) to your children or other family members, there is extremely good news from the IRS. In IRS Revenue Ruling 93-12, the IRS *concedes* that a "minority discount" can be applied to such gifts even when you gift a *majority* of the stock, partnership interests, and so forth and even though the stock remains within the family unit.

Before this ruling, the IRS resisted this valuation approach in the circumstances just mentioned. What does the ruling mean? For example, you could gift 30 percent of your company stock to each of two children and still claim a sharply discounted value for the stock. *Two* valuation discounts are now available: when each *individual* gift of stock represents a minority interest and when there is a lack of marketability of the gifted interests. Typical discounts from full value are about 25–35 percent for gifts of minority interests and *another* 25–35 percent for lack of marketability of the stock or other interests. The two discounts, aggregated, can run 40–60 percent of full market value.

Assume you have a small family business with a total fair market value of $500,000, and for estate planning purposes you have gifted 30 percent to each of two children. At full value, each gift is worth $150,000 (30% × $500,000); however, by applying the two referenced discounts, at say a combined 50 percent, each gift is only valued at $75,000 ($150,000 × 50%). This cuts in half the amount of your estate tax exemption (currently $600,000) that you are using up by these gifts. A key point to understand in this example is that although a *majority* of the stock ownership was gifted (60 percent), the *minority* discount can still be applied to each stand-alone gift of 30 percent. This is a *very big deal*, as your own tax adviser will confirm. Why did the IRS suddenly become so generous? For the usual reason: they have been stubbornly losing case after case on these issues for almost 20 years, so they have finally recognized reality.

Consider the tax planning possibilities: you can simply gift interests outright, as already discussed, or you can get even more sophisticated by gifting to family limited partnerships and certain kinds of trusts. This new and desirable estate planning tool is not limited to the rich. You can also transfer real estate, S corporation stock, and virtually any other assets that can qualify for these valuation discounts.

WITHHOLDING, WITHHOLDING, WITHHOLDING!

Both the IRS and most of the states have come to the realization that it is easier, more foolproof, and faster to collect income taxes by mandatory withholding than by waiting for voluntary compliance at a later date. Some people think this tactic is a little like robbing a bank instead of just asking for the money that is your due. In any event, it's a very successful technique and its use is spreading rapidly.

Effective January 1, 1993, the rate of backup (i.e., compulsory) withholding was increased from 20 percent to 31 percent, and it will undoubtedly increase to 36 percent (or 39.6 percent) for 1994. Backup withholding is ordered by the IRS in cases where incorrect Social Security numbers are supplied financial institutions, dividend and interest income are repeatedly not reported by a taxpayer, Social Security numbers are not supplied to a financial institution upon request, and similar violations. Of course, this rate change represents a boost of over 50 percent in the withholding rate. Similarly, mandatory withholding on gambling winnings of over $5,000 was increased from 20 percent to 28 percent for 1993, and is expected to increase in 1994 as well. If you want more information on this subject, obtain IRS Publication 1679, "A Guide to Backup Withholding," and Publication 1281, "Backup Withholding on Missing and Incorrect TINs."

There is now a *mandatory* 20 percent withholding from retirement plan distributions paid directly to any *individual*. Only direct rollovers from the retirement plan to a financial institution (or IRA distributions) are exempt from this withholding requirement.

California has a 7 percent withholding rate for all *nonresident independent contractors* who perform services within the state. Originally, this withholding law was limited to certain industries (like the entertainment industry), but now applies to all industries. For *nonresidents* of California who sell real estate located within California, there is a mandatory 3.5 percent withholding of the *sales price*. For *nonresident* partnerships operating in California, there is an 11 percent withholding rate on the income allocable to *nonresident* partners, *whether distributed or not*. For California partnerships with *nonresident* partners, there is 7 percent withholding on any actual distributions of profits. The state of California can give the IRS a few withholding lessons! Even if you don't live in California, these ideas are sure to spread to many other states.

California is one of the few states (as well as New York) aggressively chasing retirees who have moved to other states but whose retirement benefits were *earned* while they were residents. Their rationale is that if the benefits were earned in California, then a California employer got a tax deduction for the retirement plan contribution. And when the benefits are paid out, no matter where the individual is living, the piper must be paid! I think it's just a matter of time before California institutes compulsory withholding on retirement benefits paid to *nonresidents* to avoid having to hunt, locate, and chase retirees for the tax money; mandatory withholding would be much easier.

BUSINESS TAX DEDUCTIONS FOR TOTAL WAGES PAID

The General Accounting Office has reported that small business corporations and proprietorships have overstated their expense deductions for total wages paid by *billions* of dollars! Naturally, the IRS has announced a tax compliance check of such deductions. The IRS intends to do "reverse matching," in which they will compare the total wages reported on all W-2 forms to the deductions claimed by employers on their business tax returns. Even if the employer reports on a fiscal year they could estimate the figures or pull Form 941 ("Employer's Quarterly Federal Tax Return") for an even closer check.

> *TAXTIP*
>
> One of the first things IRS agents do in business audits is tie payroll reports filed on Form 941 with the total wages claimed as an expense. At our firm, we do such a wage reconciliation *before* the tax return of the business is prepared, and so should you.

BUSINESS EXPENSE REIMBURSEMENTS

Two interesting IRS private letter rulings involve expense reimbursements. In the first ruling, sales employees were receiving commissions and paying all their own expenses. Perhaps after considering the drawbacks to such an arrangement (including the waste of excess payroll taxes and related costs), they changed their compensation arrangement. The employees *elected* to reduce their commissions by a *stated* amount, and the company would pay their expenses but only up to that *stated* amount. The IRS letter ruling *denied* this new arrangement and said the sales employees were "assigning future income to the company *in exchange* for expense reimbursements."

COMMENTS

I never would have adopted their original compensation arrangement, never would have offered this new arrangement as an elective *option* or with a *stated* expense amount, and I never would have requested an IRS letter ruling.

In the second ruling, a sales manager received an expense *allowance* based on an *estimate* of his business expenses. He did not submit any expense documentation to his employer, and he did not have to return any excess payments. The IRS ruled that this expense allowance was a "nonaccountable" plan and had to be included in his gross income. He could only deduct his actual expenses as a miscellaneous itemized deduction on his individual income tax return.

COMMENT

I could have told them that! Any *flat* (nonaccountable) expense *allowance* paid to an employee is additional taxable income to that individual.

HOME OFFICE DEDUCTIONS TEST

Ms. Smith is a sales rep with her *only* office in her home. She never meets customers in that office, but she spends about 15 hours a week writing orders, doing paperwork, talking to factories, and phoning customers. She spends about 30 hours a week in the field, calling on customers and selling, selling, selling.

What so-called home office expenses can she deduct? Absolutely nothing! Under the new Supreme Court decision, since she spends the bulk of the workday in the field, her home office does not qualify as her "principal place of business" for any deductions, even though it is her *only* office! If she had met with customers on a regular basis, or if the offices were in a separate structure from the home, she probably would have been able to sustain a home office deduction.

FREQUENT FLIER WARNING

The IRS is both interested and frustrated over frequent flier awards, free trips, and similar perks. They feel that when you earn such awards in connection with a *business* trip and then use them on a *personal* trip they are cheated out of appropriate income taxes on that personal benefit. Their frustration lies in the fact that it would be impossible to try to determine each case of personal benefit in relation to business miles. After all, you also earn frequent flier miles on personal trips, and you can use the awards for either personal or business travel. Further, you might let the awards expire unused, give them away, and so forth.

Because of that recordkeeping nightmare the IRS is instead after those individuals who *sell* their *business* mileage awards for cash. They have launched a test program in the Orlando, Florida, IRS office and are taxing such payments as a taxable fringe benefit.

NO FREE PARKING

While tax law permits an employer to pay up to $155 a month for employee parking as a tax-free fringe benefit, that change for 1993 does *not* apply to partners in partnerships or 2 percent or more shareholders of S corporations. For those individuals, *any* parking paid for them will be taxable income.

AUTO MILEAGE

For 1994, the IRS has increased the "no questions asked" business mileage allowance from 28¢ to 29¢ a mile. There is generally *no limit* on the number of business miles that can be reimbursed in this manner; however, the IRS does not approve this reimbursement method for *leased* cars. The allowable deduction when using your car for charitable purposes remains at a measly 12¢ a mile. How charitable.

THREE IN A ROW!

Sometimes the taxpayer hits the jackpot. Since personal interest is no longer tax-deductible, the IRS likes to call any interest it possibly can "personal." Among other things, the IRS took the immediate position that *all* interest on *all* tax deficiencies was personal interest. That position has been declared invalid by a US District Court in North Dakota. That court ruled that when the interest paid relates to *business* income, the related interest is *business* interest and fully deductible.

• In a similar vein, the IRS took the position that income tax preparation fees relating to the preparation of Schedule C ("Profit or Loss From Business—Sole Proprietorship") were not deductible as a business expense. After a number of court losses, they finally conceded that such fees are fully deductible as a *business* expense.

• After losing a Tax Court case, the IRS has agreed that an individual who did not file a timely tax return is *not* liable for the failure-to-file penalty *if* the withholding tax credits are greater than or equal to the tax liability on the delinquent return filed.

HANDLING FORMS 1099 AND W-2 TO YOUR BEST ADVANTAGE

W-2 ("Wage and Tax Statement") and all applicable 1099 forms must be sent to the individual *payees* by January 31 of each year; however, they do *not* have to be mailed to the *IRS* until the following February 28.

> ***TAXTIP***
>
> Do not, under any circumstances, send these forms to the IRS *before* the February 28 due date. Businesses have a 30 day "correction window" after these forms have been sent to the individuals in which the individuals can notify the business of a possible *error*. As long as you have *not* sent the forms to the IRS, you can simply make any necessary corrections internally, in your records and on these forms, and then mail a perfect set to the IRS. However, if you do *not* allow for this 30 day correction period and mail *early* to the IRS, you may later find yourself busy filing *corrected* W-2 and 1099 forms (and calling a lot of attention to yourself!). Save yourself trouble and *don't* file early.

Form W-2 is now one-half of an 8½ by 11 page, larger than ever before and comes only two to a page. The IRS finally made some intelligent changes to the form:

- The primary information of "wages, tips, other compensation" is now box 1, at the head of the parade, where it always belonged, instead of box 10.
- All state tax information is now at the extreme bottom of the form, boxes 16 through 21, nicely segregated from all the federal information.
- The sub-box information regarding statutory employee, pension plan, and so forth has been dropped to box 15 (near the bottom) where it doesn't clutter up the numerical reporting.

> ***TAXTIP***
>
> In virtually all but a few exceptional cases (e.g., allocated tips in box 8) the amount in *box 1* is the *only* sum you should report as taxable income on your tax return. For example, the following are *included* in box 1 even though they may be detailed in *other* boxes of your Form W-2: flat and unaccounted for expense allowances, deferred compensation or payments from nonqualified retirement plans, cost of group term life insurance *in excess* of $50,000, and dependent care payments of *over* $5,000. If you *add* amounts in those memo boxes to the income in box 1, you are overreporting income, and overpaying taxes, and we have yet to see a case where the IRS corrects such an error.

The IRS uses Form 1099 information returns (along with the Form W-2 wage statement) as their *primary* method of verifying the accuracy of individual income tax returns. Business filers should *always correct any errors immediately* or the individual will be involved in a costly tax nightmare with the IRS. You will generate ill will beyond belief from the person involved, and maybe an IRS audit as well.

The primary Form 1099 involving most reps is Form 1099–MISC (Non-Employee Compensation and "Miscellaneous Income"). Form 1099–MISC reports annual payments of $600 or more to individuals (*not* required for payments to *corporations*) for "business services," as well as payments for rents, prizes, awards, and so forth. Not only are there penalties for nonfiling of these forms, but you can hang yourself where independent contractors are concerned. Additionally, reps have required reports for such payments as dividends, interest, rents, securities sales, real estate sales, gambling winnings, retirement plan distributions, and mortgage interest.

FAILURE TO FILE 1099 FORMS

The IRS almost invariably will rule that nonfiling of an information return was due to an *intentional disregard* of the filing requirements. In that event, the penalty for *each failure to file* (i.e., *each* Form 1099) is the *greater* of $100 or 10 percent of the aggregate amount of the items required to be reported correctly. So if you miss just a few payments to independent contractors, for an aggregate of $100,000 or so, the penalty could be $10,000! Expensive errors!

TAXTIP

If you have made some borderline judgments in classifying certain individuals as independent contractors rather than employees, the *nonfiling* of 1099 forms for those individuals will murder you if there is an IRS audit! To even *begin* to argue with the IRS that a certain individual is in fact an independent contractor, you *must* have filed a Form 1099–MISC reporting payments to that person. Also, there are *penalties* for not filing any required Forms 1099.

TAXTIP

If your employee possibly qualifies as a statutory sales employee, it can be a *big* tax help to any employee claiming unreimbursed business expenses if

(continued)

you check box 15 on Form W-2. (However, if the employer reimburses *all* expenses there is no tax advantage to the employee.)

The IRS defines a statutory salesperson (see Chapter 7) as an *employee* who works full time for one firm or person getting orders from customers. The orders must be items for resale or use as supplies in a customers business, and the customers must be retailers, wholesalers, contractors or operators (of hotels, restaurants, or other businesses dealing with food or lodging). This definition certainly covers the salespeople employed by *food brokers* and really excludes only those salespeople selling to *manufacturers*. You might, however, have an employee who calls on manufacturers *and* wholesalers, in which case the employee might qualify as a statutory sales employee.

IRS Nonfiler Program

The IRS has an aggressive nonfiler program in place and estimates that more than $47 *billion* in tax revenues are lost *each year* by individuals who don't file income tax returns. (I'm sure there is big money at stake, but their estimate probably includes drug money, illegal gambling, and prostitution.) By the end of January 1993, more than four million delinquent returns had been filed under this program, and nearly 45 percent of those filing received *refunds!*

The IRS estimates that four million *1992* individual income tax returns have still not been filed. The best explanation is that the reduced withholding rates instituted in 1992 by the Bush administration made it impossible for many individuals to pay their balance due at filing time, so they just dropped out of the system. In the past six months more than 100 individuals were charged with failing to file tax returns. The unreported income in those cases ranged from $10,000 to more than $1 million.

The IRS offers free assistance to those nonfilers who come in *voluntarily*. By the law of averages, some of our readers are nonfilers. Call the IRS at 1-800-829-1040 to find out where this help is available or get publication WR 92-31F about the nonfiler program, or see your friendly CPA.

But note! The IRS estimates that about one-third of all *nonfilers* of income tax returns are entitled to *refunds!* In our limited experience in filing delinquent tax returns for individuals, the percentage of refunds was more like 70 percent, although late filing and other penalties usually wiped out any refunds.

Offers in Compromise

When you don't have enough income *or assets* to pay the IRS in full you can make an offer to settle for less than the full amount. Despite IRS claims of a new and cooperative attitude by the IRS (in which "all taxpayers are treated similarly and fairly"), the *acceptance rate* of these offers varies widely.

In Missouri, the IRS accepted 79 percent of offers, while in Laguna Niguel, California, they were *dead last nationwide* at 19 percent. Idaho was 77 percent, while Los Angeles was 34 percent. Albany, NY, was 73 percent, while Manhattan and Brooklyn were 33 percent and 32 percent, respectively. Not exactly a uniform standard. For additional information on offers in compromise and installment agreements read Publication WR 92-31F.

INDEPENDENT CONTRACTOR HORROR STORIES

A sole proprietor misclassified his employees as independent contractors. He was audited by the IRS *more than three years* after he filed Form 1099 MISC. information returns that reported payments made to the supposed independent contractors. The US District Court in Missouri ruled that he was *not* protected by the three-year statute of limitations because "The information provided on the Forms 1099 (MISC.) was not sufficient (for the IRS) to determine how much tax was due since it was not evident to the IRS agent that the workers were employees."

COMMENT

If this decision holds and spreads to other courts there might not be a statute of limitations protecting *any* business entity that similarly misclassified and reported regular employees!

We have heard of one case where an operator of a trucking business classified all his drivers as independent contractors. Upon audit, it was determined that they were all really employees. He lost all the protection of the safe harbor provisions (IRS Code Section 530 Chapter 9) about "innocent misclassifications" because *he did not file any 1099 forms covering those payments!* If you *do* insist you are employing independent contractors, you *must consistently file* information returns!

However, understand that while *not* filing 1099 forms can lose you this protection, the act of *filing* these forms is but one small piece of evidence of independent contractor status and not any kind of automatic protection against the IRS changing that classification.

IRS RETIREMENT PLAN AUDITS

The IRS is engaged in an audit initiative of small business retirement plans over about a five year span. Their main audit thrust is to *retroactively* challenge the assumed earnings rate and age of retirement. They have lost case after case after case but are *appealing* those decisions from the lower courts.

In the first major *appeals* court ruling, the IRS lost again! The court held that 5 percent annual earnings estimates and age 62 retirement date targets were reasonable. The Tax Court has previously decided against the IRS on these same assumptions.

In a different case, the Tax Court ruled that owners cannot make loans *to* their company retirement plans. Loans to company retirement plans were ruled "prohibited transactions" subject to excise tax and even though reasonable interest was being charged.

Those who *receive* Form 1099 should guard it with their lives! If not correctly reported, about 18 months later a computer form letter from the IRS will be received, stating in *impossibly confusing terms* that the employee has neglected to report all income. Usually included is a bill for additional taxes, interest, and penalties.

Have I made myself clear? Preserve, protect, guard and report every information return you receive! Our firm requests that our clients simply give us *every* form received, and *we* interpret and enter these reports for them. This is a much safer procedure, since many of them (e.g., stockbrokers' statements) are quite difficult to comprehend.

IRS PROPOSALS

The IRS has deftly slipped some major proposals into the national health care programs (which are not law at this writing), some of which have little to do with health care:

- Repeal of the safe harbor provisions of IRC Section 530, which they hate with a passion, relating to independent contractors versus employees (see Chapter 9).
- Treatment of all S corporation earning of all *service* businesses as self-employment income, whether actually distributed to owners or *not* (see Chapter 13).

- Elimination of all medical benefits from cafeteria plans.
- Elimination of all company plans that pay *unreimbursed* medical expenses.

Also, from proposed IRS regulations being bandied about, they want to eliminate the option of company directors adopting Keogh retirement plans if they are 5 percent or more owners, and possibly for *all* director-employees.

TYPE OF TAX RETURN AND IRS AUDIT ODDS

The 1992 audit percentage figures are in: The two winners continue to be Schedule C filers and individuals with incomes over $100,000.

Individuals (no Schedule C)	*1992*	*1991*
Under $25,000	0.84%	0.80%
$25,000–$49,999	0.59	0.64
$50,000–$99,999	1.01	1.11
$100,000 and over	4.92	5.26
Individuals (with Schedule C)		
Under $25,000	1.49	1.45
$25,000–$99,999	1.99	1.85
$100,000 and over	3.95	3.63
Corporations (by total assets)		
Under $250,000	1.23	1.05
$250,000–$999,999	4.04	2.60
$1,000,000–$4,999,999	10.04	5.59
$5,000,000–$9,999,999	18.95	13.31

I consider the percentage for the individual with an income of $100,000 and over, with no Schedule C, to be almost meaningless. There is no breakdown between an individual with $100,000 income and one with $5 million. Or between an individual with a $150,000 salary and another with $150,000 in investment and rental income (and matching expenses). Or a person with huge itemized deduction or a person with minimal deductions.

Schedule C audits show an *increasing* percentage trend in all categories, which comes as no surprise, and is confirmed in our own accounting practice. We also note huge jumps in audits of smaller corporations and *particularly* those with assets of $250,000 up. Those trends will probably continue.

GEOGRAPHY AND IRS AUDIT ODDS

Here are 1992 IRS average audit percentages for individuals in various US cities:

Highest Chance of Audit		*Lowest Chance of Audit*	
Las Vegas	1.89%	Milwaukee	0.24%
Los Angeles	1.39	Philadelphia	0.31
San Francisco	1.30	Chicago	0.38
Anchorage	1.28	Honolulu	0.40
Laguna Niguel	1.08	Boston	0.43
New Orleans	1.05	St. Louis	0.43

Chapter Twenty-Nine

Your Family Working in Your Business

There are two decisions to make about family members working in your rep firm. The first is personal: Do you want them to work for you at all? For example, I would probably kill my wife after two or three weeks if she worked in our accounting firm, so she never will. But that's my personal problem, personal hang-up, and personal decision. Similarly, I would not want my children working for me, and I find it simply incredible that many other companies actually want to hire them and pay real money for their services!

The second decision, the one we will discuss in this chapter, is a financial one and based on payroll tax considerations, income tax, marital concerns, and retirement deliberations. There are different rules for children, married couples, unincorporated businesses, incorporated businesses, and so forth. So we will take it a bit at a time and get all the rules clarified for you.

PAYROLL TAX RULES

If you are *not* incorporated and a sole proprietorship:

- Your children under age 18 are exempt from Social Security/ Medicare taxes when paid a salary (tax-deductible by the proprietorship).
- Your children under age 21 are exempt from the federal unemployment tax when paid a salary (tax-deductible by the proprietorship).
- Your spouse is *always* subject to Social Security/Medicare taxes and is always exempt from the federal unemployment tax when paid a salary (tax-deductible by the proprietorship). However, keep in mind that the spouse's salary will usually be reported on

the joint income tax return of the husband and wife, so although the business gets a tax deduction for that salary, the same amount is reported as income from wages on the joint income tax return.

If you *are* incorporated (in which case it doesn't matter if one spouse is the sole shareholder, or even if both share in the ownership):

- Your children at *any* age are subject to both Social Security/Medicare taxes and the federal unemployment tax.
- Your spouse is always subject to both Social Security/Medicare taxes and the federal unemployment tax.

If your business is a partnership consisting *only* of the two parents:

- Your children under age 18 are exempt from Social Security/Medicare taxes when paid a salary (tax-deductible by the partnership).
- Your children under age 21 are exempt from the federal unemployment tax when paid a salary (tax-deductible by the partnership).
- Each spouse is subject to Social Security/Medicare taxes on net earnings as a self-employed individual partner, but not subject to the federal unemployment tax.

If your business is a partnership in which only *one* spouse is a partner with other individuals:

- Your children at *any* age are subject to both Social Security/Medicare taxes and the federal unemployment tax.
- Your spouse is always subject to both Social Security/Medicare taxes and the federal unemployment tax.
- The spouse who is a partner is subject to Social Security/Medicare taxes on net earnings as a self-employed individual partner but not subject to the federal unemployment tax.

In any estate, even if it is the estate of a deceased parent or a deceased spouse:

- Children at *any* age are subject to both Social Security/Medicare taxes and the federal unemployment tax.
- The spouse is always subject to both Social Security/Medicare taxes, and the federal unemployment tax.

THE OTHER SPOUSE AS AN EMPLOYEE

Now that the ground rules are out of the way, here is the most commonly asked question of all: "My spouse also works in the business. Am I better off paying a salary, or not?" Like most of these questions, the answer is more than a simple yes or no.

With the combined Social Security/Medicare tax cost at a very high 15.3 percent of annual salary (plus all the other payroll tax and related costs), you are frequently better off *not* paying any salary to a spouse. By not receiving any salary at all, your spouse is entitled to the higher of 50 percent of your Social Security benefits or her own benefits. Without ever paying a dime in payroll taxes, your spouse can draw up to one-half of whatever your ultimate Social Security benefits may be. In many cases, this will indeed be a higher amount than any benefit that could be earned by your spouse.

You will need help from your own CPA, because there are major exceptions to the rule. The reverse advice may be true if, by paying your spouse a salary, your spouse can attain any combination of the following benefits:

- Substantially higher Social Security benefits from her own account at retirement.
- Substantial company retirement plan benefits as a result of contributions made to either a corporate or a self-employed retirement plan.

CAVEAT

Family members, including the spouse and children under age 19, are considered as *one* employee for purposes of the annual compensation limit for retirement plan contributions. This annual compensation limit is $150,000 (reduced from a high of $235,840 by the 1993 tax act).

- Various substantial fringe benefits, including individual coverage under the company group medical insurance (if for some reason that is important, e.g., to double the policy maximum).
- The right to tax-deductible travel *with* the other spouse, since the 1993 tax act *limits* such travel deductions to bona fide *employees* of the company *and* only for a bona fide business purpose.

If you don't have a company retirement plan or if you are contemplating a low salary for your spouse in relation to your own, the answer would be to not pay your spouse any salary at all. A high salary and high retirement plan contribution may make it worthwhile, however, for your spouse to be on the payroll. With these facts in mind, consult with your own tax adviser.

Finally, here are a few other Social Security facts to also consider when making your decision:

- A surviving spouse can claim survivor's benefits, based on the deceased spouse's earnings, when she becomes 60 years old, instead of having to wait until at least age 62, unless disabled.
- An ex-spouse who was married to an individual for 10 years or longer and who has not remarried can draw the higher of 50 percent of the ex-spouse's Social Security benefits, or her own (if any).

DIVORCE, OR EVEN CONTEMPLATION THEREOF

The possibility of divorce can negate everything said in the preceding section! Whichever spouse is considering giving up a salary, Social Security coverage, retirement plan contributions, and fringe benefits had better be sure that the marriage is solid. If there is even a hint of marital problems on the horizon, the advice for the second working ("other") spouse is exactly opposite. Take your fair share of salary, even if your spouse must take a cut. Go for the maximum allowed in the retirement plan contributions and take every possible perk and fringe that is legally allowable.

THE CHILDREN AS EMPLOYEES

It *always* pays to put your children on the payroll, regardless of whether you incur payroll tax costs or not. Always! Understand that no matter what their age, their *earned* income is always taxed at their lower tax rates (only investment income is subject to special tax rules).

Assume you pay one of your dependents, for reasonable services rendered, a moderate annual salary of $5,700:

- The child will pay absolutely no income taxes on that money after claiming the individual standard deduction (1993) of $3,700 plus putting $2,000 into an Individual Retirement Account by April 15 of the following year. Deductions will equal salary!

- If $2,000 is put into an IRA each year (with the magic of tax-free compounding of the earnings), the child will have about $1 million at the end of 30 years, or $2 million in about 50 years! Encourage them to take advantage of this option every year! And encourage them to begin IRA contributions as early as possible (10 year olds could invest income from baby-sitting, cutting grass, delivering newspapers, shoveling snow, etc.). Don't get confused by the so-called kiddie tax levied on children under 14 years of age. That only applies to *investment* income and not to earned income such as salary. Children of any age, when providing reasonable services to your company, can be paid a moderate salary without any adverse tax effects. Further, if they *are* exempt from payroll taxes (see the section on payroll tax rules), that's frosting on the cake.

  Now that they get a salary, you can cut their allowance or let them save for their college education, or they can use part of the salary to pay for anything you are now paying that is not tax-deductible.

- The salary you pay your child (and any related payroll tax or other related cost) is tax-deductible by your company (your children will be in low tax brackets, while you, of course, are in a higher bracket). If they are old enough and work enough, each child (no longer a dependent) could be paid a tax-deductible salary of *$30,150* by your business and still remain in the 15 percent tax bracket. How's that for "income shifting"? Using 1993 tax rates, here is the calculation:

Total salary		$30,150
Less:	Standard deduction	(3,700)
	Personal exemption	(2,350)
	IRA contribution	(2,000)
	Total tax deductions	(8,050)
	Taxable income	$22,100

- The *15 percent* tax bracket for singles goes from $0 to $22,100. What a coincidence! (Of course, new tax laws and rate changes may occur, but the *concept* holds. Don't get hung up on slight dollar or percentage variations.) But again, these payments must represent *reasonable* wages for the work actually *performed* and not just some slick tax sleight of hand (but consider cutting your salary at the same time your children go on the payroll for $30,150 *each!*).

SHAM TRANSACTIONS

This great idea only works with *great difficulty* if at all! Assume these facts: you are drawing a salary of $75,000, you just reached age 65, and your spouse is 10 years younger, works in the business, and has a salary of $10,000. You now "retire," and your spouse will run the business. You will not receive any salary, since you are "retired." However, your spouse is now running the business (you say), and receives an annual salary of $85,000! The total family income stays the same as before ($75,000 + $10,000), but you now apply for Social Security and receive about $900 a month for life!

Unfortunately, the Social Security Administration knows all about that ploy, and they have the right to investigate your claim, examine your books, hold up payment, or even refuse payment. In our experience, the preceding example is exactly the one they try to claim as a sham transaction; they realize that your spouse received a big raise at the same time you took a cut. We've seen similar problems when a father "retired" from the business and the son then received a big raise. The Social Security Administration seems to challenge those kinds of family-related interactions.

However, if you are incorporated and your spouse is *not* in the business (or is in the business but did *not* receive a raise), there is a real and legal loophole. A corporation is a separate legal entity, and the Social Security Administration does not have the authority to reallocate corporate earnings. So, if you choose to work for your corporation from age 65 to 70 for little or no pay (but expenses, of course), in our opinion you can indeed claim your Social Security benefits. Then, at age 70, when there is no longer any earnings test, you can draw as much salary (including back salary) as you wish.

For someone directly engaged in a trade or business (therefore not incorporated), there is an additional problem: A "substantial services" test is used to determine if you have reduced your activity to the point where you can be classified as retired. An individual is not considered retired if he continues to provide substantial services and is either actively or constructively paid for them. "Substantial services" are defined as 45 hours (or more) a month in a trade or business or 15 hours (or more) a month if the service requires a high degree of skill (for example, a doctor). The substantial services test is used *only* for the year of retirement and *only* for an unincorporated individual in a trade or business. After that, the only test before you begin to lose some of your Social Security benefits is the amount of earned income you are allowed, which increases each year. However, after age 70 you are no longer subject to this penalty, regardless of how much you earn.

To sum up, shifting your salary to your spouse (or child) so you can claim Social Security benefits will usually be challenged by the Social Security Administration. However, if you are incorporated and do not engage in that gambit, you have every right to reduce your salary and claim full Social Security benefits at age 65. If you are not incorporated, you must face a "substantial services" test in the year of your retirement (only), as well as the earned income test that everyone must pass until they reach age 70 (earned income can be defined as wages plus other self-employment income).

BOARD OF DIRECTORS' FEES

Your spouse and adult children can be paid fees for serving on the board of directors of your corporation. Such fees are considered self-employment income, and the recipient is therefore liable for full Social Security/Medicare taxes. However, each board member has the right to set up a Keogh plan and pay in a tax-deductible 20 percent each year, *regardless* of whether she is covered by another retirement plan.

Since fees are earned income, your child can claim the standard deduction of $3,700 (1993) plus her personal exemption of $2,350 (if not your dependent) when filing her own individual tax return in addition to claiming the 20 percent Keogh plan contribution deduction.

So here is another way to divert income to your children, who are assumedly in lower tax brackets, or to provide additional retirement plan contributions for your spouse, albeit at the cost of Social Security/Medicare taxes (but see page 326 for proposed changes).

CONCLUSION

It will generally pay to place your children on salary (and on the board of directors if they are old enough). It is generally not worthwhile to pay a salary to your spouse unless higher retirement plan contributions and higher Social Security benefits will result, than from your salary alone. If there is a chance of divorce on the horizon, the other spouse should receive a salary and establish retirement benefits.

If you are incorporated, Social Security benefits are easily attained if you are age 65 and do not switch your approximate salary to your spouse or adult child. If unincorporated, the "substantial services" and "constructive" receipt of earnings tests are additional problems.

Finally, paying board of directors' fees to your spouse will always permit a new Keogh plan contribution but at a cost of paying the Social Security/Medicare taxes on those fees.

Chapter Thirty

The Revenue Reconciliation Act of 1993 and Year-end Tax Planning in General

Most of the provisions of the Revenue Reconciliation Act, passed on August 10, 1993, will be with us for many years to come. This chapter is a perfect preamble to Chapter 31, which describes how this tax law has forever changed the rules for selling a sales agency. Also, this chapter will give you the flavor of year-end tax planning in general (until the tax laws change again).

THE NEW TAX RATES

Much of the publicity and pronouncements about the 1993 tax bill were political statements and "much ado about nothing." The repeated statements that the tax burden would fall heaviest on the middle class are simply not true. The fact is that of 116 million tax filers, no more than the top 1.2 percent end up in higher tax brackets than in 1992, and the higher levies on Social Security only affect the uppermost 13 percent.

The top tax rate, retroactive to January 1, 1993, was increased to 36 percent from 31 percent for couples with *taxable* income *above* $140,000 and for singles with taxable income *above* $115,000. Factoring in average itemized deductions and exemptions, which are claimed before taxable income is calculated, this new top tax rate will affect *gross* income above $180,000 and $140,000, respectively. If your income doesn't exceed those figures, there is *no change* in your tax rates or total tax!

For *both* couples and singles a new 10 percent surtax on *taxable* income *above* $250,000 (*gross* income of perhaps $325,000–$350,000) was enacted, for a marginal rate on that excess income of 39.6 percent. The Treasury Department says about 400,000 joint filers and

100,000 individual filers reported taxable income above $250,000, and they represented only 0.4 percent of all tax filers.

Keep in mind that these two new rates *only apply* to that *portion* that *exceeds* the amounts previously listed.

EXAMPLE

Your joint gross income is $160,000, and you have itemized tax deductions of $25,000 (after phaseouts). Your taxable income is $135,000 ($160,000 – $25,000); there is *no change in your tax* because you are under the new $140,000 tax rate amount.

EXAMPLE

Your joint gross income is $200,000 and you have itemized tax deductions of $35,000 (after phaseouts). Your taxable income is $165,000 ($200,000 – $35,000). Only the *excess* over $140,000, or $25,000, is taxed at the new rate of 36 percent. Thus the *additional* tax is only another 5 percent of that $25,000, or $1,250, for a couple with gross income of $200,000.

EXAMPLE

Your joint gross income is $400,000, and you have itemized tax deductions of $80,000 (after phaseouts). Your taxable income is $320,000 ($400,000 – $80,000). The *excess* over $140,000 to $250,000 is taxed at 36 percent and the *excess* from $250,000 to $320,000 is taxed at 39.6 percent. The *additional* taxes would be $5,500 for the first tier and $6,230 for the second tier, or a total of $11,730 more than would have been paid under the 1992 tax rates. That's certainly a substantial increase, but it really affects only 0.4 percent of all those filing tax returns.

Finally, a taxpayer may elect to pay any *increased* tax resulting from the 36 percent rate in three equal installments, *without interest*, on April 15 of the following three years.

CAUTION

This payment plan is only for any *additional* tax specifically caused by the 5 percent increase from 31 percent to 36 percent and *not* the total balance of any tax you may owe.

INCREASED TAX ON SOCIAL SECURITY

Effective January 1, 1994, up to 85 percent of Social Security benefits *may* be subject to tax, but only if gross income (*including* tax-exempt income and one-half of Social Security income) exceeds $44,000 for joint filers or $34,000 for all others *except* married, filing separately (for those filers, *all* Social Security income from the *first dollar* is 85 percent taxable!).

Below those new threshold amounts, the old rules apply: Social Security benefits are 50 percent taxable for joint incomes of $32,000–$44,000 and single income of $25,000–$34,000. Below $32,000 for joint filers and $25,000 for single filers, Social Security is not taxable at all (as in the past).

TAXTIP

Investing in growth stocks that don't generate dividends or in US Savings Bonds, which don't produce taxable income until they mature, can reduce your income threshold for figuring the tax on Social Security.

TAXTIP

Married taxpayers who are considering filing separately for 1994 and after should first study the income tax effect on Social Security benefits, since *every* dollar of Social Security income then becomes 85 percent taxable.

TAXTIP

If in 1994 or later you receive any Social Security lump-sum payments *applicable to prior years,* you can use the tax formula of the *prior years* to figure the tax on that payment. In many cases the taxable amount of such benefits can be reduced from 85 percent to 50 percent, or less.

MEDICARE TAX LIMIT REMOVED

Effective January 1, 1994, there is *no limit at all* on the Medicare portion of the FICA tax deducted from wages or applicable to self-employment income. Employees will pay 1.45 percent Medicare tax on *every* dollar of salary, and their employer will pay another 1.45 percent. The self-employed will pay 2.90 percent (and get a 50 percent deduction for self-employment taxes).

EXAMPLE

Under prior law, the Medicare tax ceiling was $135,000 of salary. The tax law will skyrocket on the really big salaries! For example, the old law limited the maximum deduction to $1,957.50 (1.45% × $135,000), even if your salary was $300,000 or more. For 1994, the Medicare tax deduction on $300,000 would be $4,350 (and the employer would pay *another* $4,350). On a $1 million salary, the deduction would be $14,500 (and the employer would pay *another* $14,500).

ESTIMATED TAXES

The new law simplifies the prior provision that forced many taxpayers to refigure their estimated taxes quarterly and amend each tax payment accordingly. The accounting fees for refiguring and amending the estimates four times a year exceeded the potential penalties for not doing so, so many people were ignoring this regulation. Thankfully the law has been changed.

Individual's tax estimates for 1994 and after can *avoid all penalties,* regardless how high income may be if they are figured as follows:

- If 1994 adjusted gross income (AGI) was $150,000 or less, the 1995 estimate must be based on *100 percent* of 1994 total tax liability.
- If 1994 adjusted gross income was *over* $150,000, the 1995 estimate must be based on *110 percent* of 1994 total tax liability.

A refreshing and sensible alteration in the law, but as always, all 1995 payments must be made *evenly, timely, and in full* to avoid the underestimate penalty.

QUALIFIED RETIREMENT PLANS

Effective for retirement plan years *beginning* in 1994, the amount of compensation that can be taken into account for any one individual is reduced from $235,840 to $150,000. This means that owners of small businesses will have to contribute more for the employees to keep their own contribution at the same level (this also applies to Keogh and SEP plans). It is quite likely that this change will simply accelerate the number of small businesses that have been dropping qualified retirement plans ever since the Tax Reform Act of 1986.

EXAMPLE

In 1993, if a business contributed 10 percent of salaries to a qualified profit sharing plan, the owner received credit for $23,584 of the contribution (10 percent of the maximum of $235,840, assuming his compensation was over that limit). In 1994, the same 10 percent contribution for all employees will only credit the owner with $15,000 (10 percent of the new maximum of $150,000). A total contribution of *15 percent* of salaries would get closer to the old number (the owner would receive a $22,500 credit).

In other words, the owner would have to increase the *total contribution by 50 percent* (from 10 percent to 15 percent) to keep his personal amount about the *same*. Not many small business owners can afford to do that, or would want to increase employees' benefits by 50 percent. For some, this is a *major* change!

TAXTIPS

(1) Consider a defined-*benefit* pension plan that disproportionately rewards the older and highly compensated. (2) Consider *nonqualified* plans, such as a private pension plan funded by insurance, which can allow you to discriminate. (3) Consider deferred compensation plans for the top executives. (4) Consider dropping your qualified plan completely under certain circumstances and with expert advice. (5) Consider adding a 401(k) plan; the employees pay in most of the money (the maximum employee contribution in 1994 is $9,240) and reduce their *taxable* salary by the amount they contribute. Above all, *please* get some expert advice.

HEALTH INSURANCE DEDUCTION FOR THE SELF-EMPLOYED

The 1993 law restored the 25 percent health insurance premium deduction for the self-employed, retroactive to July 1, 1992, but it may or may not be continued in the future.

TAXTIP

If you did *not* claim the 25 percent tax deduction for the last six months of 1992, you can file an amended tax return within three years and claim a refund.

BUSINESS MEALS AND ENTERTAINMENT

The rules regarding deductions for business meals and entertainment are probably the most serious change in the law for sales agencies and other service businesses with a high *percentage* of expenses in this area.

Effective for tax years *beginning* after 1993, entertainment, business meals, and travel meals are only 50 percent tax-deductible instead of 80 percent.

TAXTIP

Be aware that your fiscal year-end will determine when this new rule applies. If, for example, your corporate year ended September 30, 1993, this law is only effective for your fiscal year *beginning* October 1, 1994, since that's the first year to begin *after* 1993.

TAXTIP

Get in the habit of saving each receipt you get your hands on and record each minor (under $25) expenditure that doesn't require a receipt (the more the better!). From now on, entertainment bookkeeping pays more than ever! The new tax change is too big to ignore, so spend extra time on your entertainment records.

TAXTIP

The new law has no effect on employees who are 100 percent reimbursed for expenses in this category; that reimbursement continues to be completely tax-free. It is the *employer doing the reimbursing* (and the self-employed) who will have the 50 percent tax deduction. If, however, the employee is *not* being reimbursed she can only claim a 50 percent deduction.

CLUB DUES

Effective for tax years *beginning* after 1993, the deduction for club dues is eliminated. That's *every* kind of club you can think of, without exception: country, city, athletic, airline travel, social, hotel, and so forth. Club dues have been clubbed to death!

SPOUSE'S TRAVEL EXPENSES

Effective January 1, 1994, the travel expenses of a spouse, dependent, or friend accompanying the taxpayer on a business trip can only be deducted *if:*

- The accompanying person is a bona fide employee.
- A bona fide business purpose for that person's presence on the trip exists.

> ***TAXTIP***
>
> You will have much more trouble convincing an IRS agent that you should be allowed a travel expense deduction for your spouse or companion. The IRS will make it a *lot* more difficult to win in such situations and, of course, if the individual in question is not a *true* employee, the tax deduction is lost in any event.

INCREASED EXPENSING DEDUCTION

Good news! Retroactive to January 1, 1993, the maximum amount of office equipment (furniture, computers, and the like) that can be immediately deducted as a current expense has been increased to an annual $17,500 from $10,000. As under prior law, these deductions phase out as purchases exceed $200,000 in any one year.

> ***TAXTIP***
>
> Here is a perfect opportunity for year-end tax planning. By all means buy that new computer, machinery, desk, copier, fax, or phone system before December 31 of the tax year and get an immediate tax deduction *that year* of up to $17,500.

CHARITABLE CONTRIBUTIONS

Effective January 1, 1994, you must have *written substantiation from the charity* for every contribution of $250 or more. A canceled check is *not* considered substantiation; you must have a *written* acknowledgment or receipt *from the charity* that confirms the amount of the contribution.

> ***TAXTIP***
>
> Contributions are *not* aggregated throughout the year. Thus, if you contribute $2,250 to the same charity in payments of $225 at 10 different times in one year, you do *not* need their written acknowledgment (however, I would be wary of writing multiple checks on the same day).

Effective for contributions made after June 30, 1992, the new law eliminates the alternative minimum tax (AMT) on charitable contributions of appreciated property, whether intangible (i.e., stocks and bonds), real, or personal. This change applies to both individuals and corporations.

> ***TAXTIP***
>
> Whenever possible, make *every* charitable contribution in the form of *appreciated* property. You get a tax deduction for the full *market* value of the property without an AMT to worry about. On the other hand, if you have property that has decreased in value (e.g., a stock), always sell it yourself so *you* can claim the tax loss, and *then* contribute the cash proceeds from the sale.

ANNUAL GIFTS

Every year you can make tax-free gifts of $10,000 to as many individuals (not just family) as you choose, and with the consent of your spouse, that limit doubles. These gifts reduce your ultimate estate; however, there is *no carryover* of these gift exclusions from year to year. Make them by December 31 of each year or lose the benefit for that year.

BAD DEBTS

If you have worthless or nearly worthless securities, have your broker *sell them* for $10, $5, $1, or whatever and establish a loss this year. You then have a bona fide *sale* to report on your tax return instead of a nasty argument in the future about "establishing worthlessness" and in what year it can be claimed. If you cannot accomplish an actual sale, build up a file to *document* your attempts to sell, collect, or recover, and all possible evidence of worthlessness.

> ***TAXTIP***
>
> Always claim a bad debt deduction in the *earliest* possible year. Then, if the IRS disallows the deduction in *that* year, your claim simply rolls over to the following year.

If you have any worthless Section 1244 small business stock (the stock of most small privately owned corporations), you can claim an ordinary loss (i.e., *fully* deductible from all your other income) of up to $100,000 a year on a joint income tax return. I have seen individuals walk away from a losing corporation and never even *think* about claiming this possible (huge) tax deduction!

YEAR-END TAX PLANNING

Defer Income to Next Year

Since 1993 and 1994 (and probably 1995 and 1996) tax rates are identical, many of you can make arrangements to defer December bonuses, salaries, commissions, and fees until January. If you are self-employed, postpone sending out bills until January (when possible). Don't cash savings bonds until next year. Delay all legally possible retirement plan distributions or dividends and stay the exercising of stock options until next year.

Buy US Treasury bills, notes, or bonds with the first interest payment due the following January. Buy a certificate of deposit (CD) with a maturity of less than one year that does *not* credit interest until next year's maturity. Switch income investments to US Savings Bonds, with the interest only reported at maturity, or growth stocks that pay little or no dividends.

Accelerate Tax Deductions to This Year

Accelerating tax deductions to the current year has the same effect as deferring income to next year, since it *decreases* your net taxable income by the amount of the increased deductions. The most obvious ones you can control and accelerate are charitable contributions (see earlier discussion about contributing appreciated property), real estate tax installments, and state income tax payments. However, since those last two tax deductions can help trigger the AMT, don't overdo them without some expert advice.

> ***TAXTIP***
>
> You can easily increase your state income tax deduction if you simply pay next year's state withholding tax in the last pay periods of the present year. We have had some clients triple and quadruple their end of the year tax withholdings, and a few desperate individuals have even applied *100 percent* of their December salaries as withheld income taxes!

"Bunching" Certain Tax Deductions

In two special cases, certain expenses are only deductible *above* a stated limit (floor), an amount that represents a percentage of adjusted gross income (AGI). For medical expenses, the floor is 7.5 percent of AGI, and for miscellaneous itemized deductions, which include unreimbursed business expenses unless you are a statutory sales employee, the floor is 2 percent of AGI.

In those two instances, you must ignore the general advice to accelerate deductions into this year and *only do so if these added deductions will permit you to exceed the floors.* If you are approaching the 7.5 percent medical limit, pay all additional expenses in this year and have elective surgery, dental work, eye exams and prescription glasses completed by year-end. If you are way under the 7.5 percent floor, defer all remaining payments and elective procedures to next year when they *may* provide a tax benefit.

Follow the same method for miscellaneous itemized deductions and the 2 percent floor. "Bunch" into this year or defer into next year, depending on whether you can exceed the 2 percent limit in the current year or not.

OTHER PROVISIONS

I have already discussed the changes most applicable to our average reader. The following are some other changes that could be discussed further with your tax adviser:

- Net capital gains are still taxed at a maximum 28 percent. The new spread from this top of 28 percent to the new 39.6 percent maximum rate for ordinary income makes capital gains more attractive than ever. *However*, if your top tax rate is 28 percent or 31 percent, the fact that capital gains are taxed at 28 percent makes them less attractive.
- Tax rates on income *retained* by trusts continue to jump and are now 15 percent (to $1,500); 28 percent (to $3,500); 31 percent (to $5,500); 36 percent (to $7,500); and 39.6 percent (over $7,500). It rarely pays to accumulate income in a trust anymore!
- The luxury tax was repealed for everything but autos (retroactive to January 1, 1993).

> *TAXTIP*
>
> You can apply for a *refund* if you paid luxury tax in 1993 on anything except a car.

- If you hold qualified business stock for over five years, you can exclude 50 percent of the capital gain when you sell it.
- The top 55 percent and 53 percent estate tax rates were retroactively restored to 1992 levels and made permanent.
- Moving expense deductions are now a deduction from gross income.

- The earned income credit was increased and simplified for low income (generally under $30,000 a year) families.
- *As discussed at length in Chapter 31*, effective August 11, 1993, intangible assets such as goodwill and going-concern value must be amortized and charged to expenses over 15 years (under prior law they were not deductible at all).

> ***TAXTIP/WARNING***
>
> All *covenants not to compete*, regardless of their *stated* length of time, *must now be amortized over 15 years!* A covenant no longer produces a better or faster tax deduction than the stated purchase of "goodwill"!

- The depreciation period for nonresidential realty acquired after May 13, 1993, was increased from 31½ years to 39 years.

> ***TAXTIP***
>
> For AMT purposes, the write-off period is 40 years. For the one year difference (39 versus 40), you are probably better off using a 40 year life for *all* purposes.

- The top corporate rate (above $10 million) went from 34 percent to 35 percent, effective January 1, 1993.
- Effective January 1, 1993, the AMT for individuals is a two-tier tax of 26 percent (to $175,000) and 28 percent above that.

MORE YEAR-END TAX PLANNING

Discuss these additional ideas with your CPA and see how they apply:

- Shift income to your children: family partnerships and S corporations are two neat vehicles. So is putting them on your company payroll.

- Contribute every possible dime to every kind of tax-sheltered retirement plan. Don't forget 401(k) plans as well as all the others. The more, the better!
- Pay any *back* alimony you may owe this year; it's tax-deductible when you actually pay it (you cannot prepay future alimony and get a deduction).

Chapter Thirty-One

Selling Your Rep Firm: IRS Background

If you read my 1988 book on this subject, *The Valuation and Sale of a Manufacturers' Sales Agency*, you will quickly determine from this and the following chapters that the old book is completely out of date and obsolete. Since 1988, the tax laws have changed more than once, and the times as well as my ideas have changed. In order to intelligently sell your agency, you *must* understand the IRS rules and how they affect the seller and *particularly* the buyer. If you get bogged down in the details of this chapter, at least make sure your tax advisers are up to speed. If they never heard of IRS Code sections 197 and 1060, *you* have a real problem!

At this writing, my involvement over the years in sales and mergers of rep agencies has topped 100 firms. As the rep business gets tougher and as reps get older (and more tired), there are more and more ownership transfers. As a generalization, I have probably seen the most *mergers* among rep firms in the automotive industry and the most *sales and transfers of interest* among rep firms in the electronics industry, but both sales and mergers of rep agencies in all industries continue unabated and seem to be increasing.

BACKGROUND INFORMATION AND IRS DEVELOPMENTS

For many years, there was a constant struggle between the IRS and tax advisers whenever the *sale* of *any* business took place. Until August 10, 1993 (with the passage of the Revenue Reconciliation Act of 1993), goodwill or going concern value of any business sold was completely and permanently *nontax-deductible* by the buyers. Therefore, every tax adviser tried to structure every purchase of a business to reflect the *least* amount of goodwill and a maximum of every other tax-deductible category of purchases. Naturally, the IRS took the *opposite* approach.

So, particularly in the sale of a service business, such as is the typical rep firm, tax advisers ascribed as much of the purchase as possible to such items as consulting fees, a covenant not to compete, subcommissions, and similar, and left a minimal amount, usually about $200, for goodwill. The IRS didn't like that at *all*, since they never like anyone to obtain a tax deduction for what is most likely nondeductible goodwill.

In the early years, the only chance the IRS had to raise objections was when auditing the books of a company that coincidentally was involved in a purchase or sale of another business. They reclassified many payments and dollars at audit to goodwill. But they still weren't satisfied, because they had no way of *knowing* exactly *when* a business was sold and the *details* of the sale. All they could count on was the occasional audit that, by happenstance, stumbled over a purchase or sale of a business.

To improve this situation, the IRS instituted an *automatic reporting requirement* effective in 1988. Code Section 1060 provided that whenever a business was sold and *any assets* of a company were also sold, a mandatory report had to be filed by *both* the buyer and seller on IRS Form 8594 ("Asset Acquisition Statement"), and the two reports had better *match*. This form required a great deal of information about the company sale, so the IRS knew when a business was sold and could decide whether or not to audit.

That satisfied them temporarily, but what the IRS expected to be invariably called nondeductible goodwill (carefully defined, with the *exact method of calculation* mandated by Code Section 1060), instead was frequently (cleverly!) allocated to such things as customer lists, information base, licenses, permits, franchises, and any other category that could possibly be *deducted* (amortized) over a period of time. Of course, the IRS knew this was happening because of the Form 8594 reports.

The final nail in the coffin was when the IRS audited and challenged such allocations and *lost* some major cases! For example, the courts ruled that costs could be written off as they occurred: a customer list *as* the customers were *lost*, or a license or permit as it expired, or an information base as it became obsolete, and so forth. Our firm had great success in arguing that if the purchase of a rep firm did include goodwill (really the *lines*), then if a principal was *lost* a portion of the goodwill allocated to that line was tax-deductible!

This brings us to the present. Rather than continue losing significant court cases and having to litigate every clever tax allocation involving the purchase or sale of a business, the IRS reluctantly agreed that goodwill *and similar intangibles* could *always* be deducted, but only in equal amounts over 15 years! They gave in on the goodwill write-offs but asked for some other "clarifications" (trade-offs).

Perhaps the most significant change in *favor* of the IRS relates to covenants not to compete. *Regardless of the actual length* of any covenant, it must be amortized ratably over 15 years, just like goodwill. *Code Section 197,* which makes these drastic changes, *has forever changed the way you will structure the sale of your rep agency.*

IRS CODE SECTION 197

For all transactions *after August 10, 1993,* the costs of what are now called "Section 197 intangibles" *must* be amortized (i.e., written-off and tax-deducted evenly) over a 15-year period beginning in the month of acquisition, *regardless* of the actual (or stated) useful life of such intangibles. No *other* depreciation or amortization can be claimed for any such section 197 intangibles. These intangibles are defined to include in *all* cases:

- Goodwill and going-concern value.
- Covenants not to compete: "or *any other arrangement* to the extent that the arrangement has substantially the *same effect* as a covenant not to compete, entered into in connection with the direct or indirect acquisition of an interest in a trade or business (or substantial portion thereof). For this purpose, an interest in a trade or business includes not only the assets of a trade or business, but also stock in a corporation that is engaged in a trade or business or an interest in a partnership that is engaged in a trade or business" (House-Senate Conference Report).
- Workforce in place.
- Information base.
- Know-how.
- Any customer-based intangible (e.g., a customer list).
- Any supplier-based intangible (e.g., your lines).
- Any license, permit, or other right granted by a governmental unit or agency.
- Any franchise, trademark, or tradename.

The *good* news for buyers is that goodwill can now, for the first time, be written off over 15 years. Therefore, in a worst-case scenario, if all payments were classified (or reclassified under audit) as Section 197 intangibles, the buyers would *still* get a complete tax write-off but spread over 15 years. The *bad* news is that all covenants not to compete (and "other similar arrangements"), also fall into the 15 year category regardless of their *actual* length. That "other similar arrangements" provision is going to cause a *lot* of trouble, particularly considering the following explanation from Congress.

FROM THE HOUSE-SENATE CONFERENCE REPORTS: COVENANTS NOT TO COMPETE AND OTHER SIMILAR ARRANGEMENTS

Whenever a new law needs interpretation, one of the key authorities to refer to for enlightenment are the congressional reports on that subject, since they disclose "the intent of Congress." *Please pay careful attention* to the exact quote regarding the second bullet in the preceding list (emphasis mine):

Covenants not to compete and other similar arrangements

For purposes of this provision, an arrangement that requires the *former owner* of an interest in a trade or business to *continue to perform services* (or to provide property or the use of property) that benefit the trade or business is considered to have *substantially the same effect as a covenant not to compete to the extent* that the amount paid to the former owner under the arrangement *exceeds the amount that represents reasonable compensation for the services actually rendered* (or for the property or use of property actually provided) by the former owner.

As under present law, to the extent that the amount paid or incurred under a covenant not to compete (or other similar arrangement) represents additional consideration for the acquisition of stock in a corporation, such amount is not to be taken into account under this provision, but, instead, is to be included as part of the acquirer's basis in the stock.

Thus hath Congress spake and my translation followeth:

- Any payments to the seller *that exceed* reasonable compensation for *services actually rendered* will be *reclassified* to a covenant not to compete and thus can only be written off over 15 years. The current tax deduction would be lost.
- Any payments to the seller as *rent* for the use of property that *exceed* reasonable payment for the property will be *reclassified* to a covenant not to compete and thus can only be written off over 15 years. The current tax deduction would be lost.
- Any compensation paid the seller that *is* currently classified for a covenant not to compete (15-year write-off), but really part of the payment for the stock of the corporation, will be *reclassified*

to the (nondeductible) basis of the stock. The 15-year tax deduction would be lost entirely.

Undoubtedly the largest amount of audit problems will occur in the area of "other similar arrangements." Buyers will want to structure the sale so that essentially they pay subcommissions to the seller. If the IRS audits and says those payments are *really* a "similar arrangement" to a covenant not to compete, only a 15-year write-off will be allowed, rather than the immediate tax deduction being claimed by the buyer. Of course, our firm would insist that these payments are for *current services actually rendered* (thus currently tax-deductible).

> ***TAXTIP***
>
> When you pay for a covenant or "other similar arrangement," you are paying the seller to do *nothing* (i.e., to *not* compete). When you pay for current services actually being rendered, you are paying the seller to do *something* (i.e., supervision, consulting, administration, training, principal contacts, customer contacts, etc.). Keep this difference in mind if you want *immediate tax deductions* under Code Section 197 upheld and structure the purchase or sale of the agency accordingly. I cannot emphasize this enough! Finally, understand it is the *buyers* who are at risk; the seller is picking up the payments as current income regardless, but it's the *buyers* who may lose an immediate tax deduction!

WHAT TO DO?

About the only *immediate* tax write-off left for buyers are payments for *services actually rendered*. As you will learn in this and the following chapters, we always recommend that the seller actually sell three to five years *before* retirement; this dovetails beautifully with the seller staying on and continuing to *render actual services* such as administration, supervision, principal contacts and customer contacts, and consulting, training, and advising the buyers. For such *services actually rendered* we feel the buyers can still claim an immediate tax deduction regardless of whether the payments are made to the seller or to the seller's corporation. Probably the best way to pay for and characterize those services is to pay them to the seller's corporation as subcommissions. However, if those services are only a *sham* and there are no reasonable services being rendered, the IRS will wipe out the deductions at audit.

CAVEAT

When a section of the Internal Revenue Code is *amended*, the exact intent of Congress is usually clear. When a *brand new* section of the law is added, as was Code Section 197, it may take years before the law is completely clear. The IRS will issue explanatory regulations (always slanted in favor of the IRS), a process that may take three to five years. Then, some parts of the regulations will be challenged in court, and some of those challenges will be successful (thus changing the interpretations of the law). Perhaps 10 years from now we'll know all the connotations and implications of Code Section 197 with more certainty. Until then, take your best shot and follow the *apparent* meaning of the law and study the "intent of Congress" in the congressional conference reports.

IRS CODE SECTION 1060

As mentioned earlier, Code Section 1060 was added to the law to define goodwill (nontax-deductible at *that* time) and exactly how it should be calculated and to mandate Form 8594 *reports* to the IRS whenever a business (i.e., the assets) was sold. It is still the law and now works in tandem with Code Section 197, so you must learn about it as well.

The reporting requirements of Section 1060 can present major problems unless we carefully and legally try to skirt the pitfalls. The Code Section 1060 reporting issue arises whenever the old corporation sells *assets* to the new corporation. This reporting requirement (on Form 8594) became effective for tax returns due on or after September 13, 1988.

Here is the essence of Code Section 1060; keep in mind the *method for determining goodwill* as described in this section *is still the law* (emphasis mine):

> If a trade or business is sold, generally each asset of the business is treated as being sold *separately* in determining the seller's gain or loss and the buyer's basis in each of the assets acquired. The purchase price must be allocated among the assets, other than goodwill, according to their fair market value and *the remainder is assigned to goodwill.*

Congress updated instructions to the IRS concerning Section 1060 as it now relates to new Section 197 (emphasis mine):

> *Modification of purchase price allocation and reporting rules for certain asset acquisitions*
>
> It is expected that the present Treasury regulations which provide for the allocation of purchase price in the case of certain *asset* ac-

quisitions will be amended to reflect the fact that the bill allows an amortization deduction with respect to intangible assets in the nature of goodwill and going concern value. It is anticipated that the residual method specified in the regulations will be *modified* to treat *all amortizable section 197 intangibles* as Class IV assets [e.g., goodwill] and that this modification will apply to any acquisition of property to which this bill applies.

Section 1060 also authorizes the Treasury Department to require the transferor and transferee in certain *asset* acquisitions to furnish information to the Treasury Department concerning the amount of any purchase price that is allocable to goodwill or going concern value. The bill provides that the information furnished to the Treasury Department with respect to certain *asset* acquisitions is to *specify the amount of the purchase price that is allocable to amortizable section 197 intangibles* rather than the amount of purchase price that is allocable to goodwill or going concern value. In addition, it is anticipated that the Treasury Department will exercise its existing regulatory authority to require taxpayers to *furnish such additional information as may be necessary or appropriate* to carry out the provisions of the bill, including the amount of the purchase price that is allocable to intangible assets that are not amortizable section 197 intangibles.

Thus hath Congress spake once more and again my translation followeth:

Congress has now instructed the IRS to *change* reporting Form 8594, so that section 197 intangibles are reported *separately,* and to require whatever *additional* information they feel they may need in light of Code Section 197.

BAD OLD IRS FORM 8594

Regarding the filing of Form 8594, here are selected quotes from IRS Regulation 1.1060 and IRS Code Section 1060 relating to asset acquisition reporting requirements:

> The seller and the purchaser each must file asset acquisition statement on Form 8594 with their income tax returns . . . that include the purchase date . . . State whether in connection with the acquisition of the group of assets, the purchaser also obtained a license or a covenant not to compete or entered into an employment contract, a lease agreement, management contract or similar arrangement with the seller . . . State the maximum amount of consideration. [IRS Reg. 1.1060.]

Thus, when *assets* are sold as part of the sale of *any* business, we must put the IRS on notice by filing Form 8594, which is like extending an invitation for them to come in and audit! Says the IRS (emphasis mine), "The buyer and seller may agree in writing to allocations of . . . the consideration involved in the transaction and the fair market value of any *assets* transferred. The allocation generally will be given effect if both parties are bound by the agreement unless the IRS determines that the allocation is inappropriate." [IRS Code Section 1060.]

It's a given that we would all prefer to legally *avoid* filing Form 8594. In a sale of a retail, wholesale, or manufacturing business, the sale of business assets are absolutely material, essential, and unavoidable. In the case of the average rep firm, they frequently are *not*, so try to arrange matters in such a manner that filing Form 8594 is legally *not* required. Here are some ideas, subject to your lawyer's approval, as well as that of your CPA or other tax adviser. They must make the final call:

- *Don't* sell any *assets* at all to the new corporation, which should eliminate the Form 8594 filing requirement. There are other ways to compensate the seller for the fact that there is no cash down payment arising from a purchase of assets.
- If absolutely necessary, *lease* the appropriate assets to the buyer corporation. Again, there would be no asset sale to report (unless you make the lease the equivalent of a purchase, in the beady eyes of the IRS).
- *Gift* fully depreciated assets to the buyer corporation.
- Allow the buyer to have use of the assets *free* (continue to share office space, as is the usual case).
- Sell the assets in a later fiscal year when the sale is disassociated from any consulting or other agreements or the actual sale of the agency. (This is my last choice.)

Of course, I have seen some transactions in which both the buyer and seller simply ignored the Form 8594 reporting requirement, even though they were carefully advised of the requirement by our firm. In one case, the attorney took the position that the asset sale was "too trivial to report," although I cannot find *any* such exception or authority in the law. Read my later discussion of the potential penalties (that could break any rep firm) before you or your lawyer brush aside the Form 8594 filing as inconsequential. You will need some expert advice if you intend to avoid, legitimately and lawfully, the tax law relating to Form 8594. Remember, it's the sale of *assets* that triggers the reporting requirement.

If you do file Form 8594:

- Report the transaction exactly as structured and pray you are not audited. In the event you are audited, use the arguments I present in the next section.
- Allocate some relatively small amount of the consulting or similar contract to goodwill ($25,000 or $50,000 is a frequently used figure). In the event you are audited, use the same arguments plus the fact that there was an arm's-length negotiated goodwill allocation.

Here is a quote from a problem section of Form 8594 (Part II, Section 3).

> To be completed by the buyer only: in connection with the purchase of the group of assets, did you also purchase a license or covenant not to compete, or enter into a lease agreement, employment contract, management contract or similar arrangement with the seller (or managers, directors, owners, or employees of the seller)? Yes____No____. If "Yes," specify (a) the type of agreement, and (b) the maximum amount of consideration (not including interest) paid or to be paid under the agreement.

About this time, some of you are saying, "Forget the bright idea of a new corporation. I'll sell the stock of my old rep corporation to my buyer for a very reasonable figure and get paid out with a consulting contract for the big bucks. Then we don't have to file Form 8594 and get audited to death." Sorry, that won't get you off the hook. IRS Code Section 1060 also says that, effective on or after October 10, 1990, Form 8594 must be filed "If . . . a person who is a 10 percent owner with respect to any entity transfers an interest in such entity, and . . . enters into an employment contract, covenant not to compete, royalty or lease agreement, or other agreement with the transferee, such owner and the transferee shall . . . furnish such information [to the IRS]". And, that 10 percent ownership test is figured on actual or constructive ownership under IRS Code Section 318, which includes any stock ownership by a member of the family.

You had better read on to learn why keeping the corporation is a much better idea than selling it. You must be completely aware of IRS Code Section 1060, related Form 8594, and the interplay with the new Code Section 197 as well.

PENALTIES FOR NOT FILING FORM 8594

I would be less than honest if I were to tell you that I have never seen the sale of assets in a rep firm where everybody simply ignored Form

8594. Of course I have! In such cases, although they were advised to file correctly, clients were simply playing "audit roulette." I must also admit that I have reviewed a number of such sales of rep agencies by nonclients (structured by their own CPAs and lawyers) where nobody had ever heard of Section 1060 and Form 8594 (or so claimed). In such cases, they were also playing "ignorance of the law is an excuse," which it ain't!

So before you make a dangerous decision, you should understand the potential penalties involved. For your tax adviser's reference, the penalties are detailed in IRS Code sections 6721–6724. Any one of three penalties may apply, but the third one is the killer! Here they are:

> Failure to File Correct Information Returns. There is a penalty for failure to file correct information returns. The following types of returns or statements are subject to penalty: . . . reporting requirements of transferors and transferees in certain asset acquisitions. [This refers to Form 8594.]
> Amount of penalty. $50, if a correct return is not filed by August 1 of the calendar year in which the due date falls. [Note: That's just penalty 1.]
> Intentional disregard of filing requirements. If any failures are due to intentional disregard of filing requirements, the penalty is generally $100 for each failure without regard to when correct returns are filed. [Note: That's just penalty 2.]
> The penalty may be greater in three situations: . . . In case of a return other than . . . (certain nonapplicable ones), the penalty per failure is the greater of $100 or 10 percent of the total amount of the items required to be correctly reported. [Note: That's penalty 3, the one to worry about!]

Let's take a worst case example. Assets of the old corporation are sold to the new corporation for $5,000 along with a consulting agreement for $600,000 (payable over five years—not that it matters). No Form 8594 is filed. The IRS subsequently audits the new corporation because of seemingly high travel and entertainment expenses, but the agent quickly discovers the transaction involving the sale of as sets and the consulting agreement payments being made by the new corporation.

The agent promptly researches the applicable penalties. He asserts a penalty in the amount of $60,500 for "intentional disregard of the filing requirements" of Form 8594. As he explains, the penalty is figured at 10 percent of the amount that should have been correctly reported. You shriek, "That should be only $500, 10 percent of the $5,000 asset sale that wasn't reported. Where did the other $60,000 come from?" "Well," he replies, "It's *also* 10 percent of the $600,000 consulting contract, which is another $60,000. The buyer must report the consulting contract on Form 8594, and you intentionally didn't do so. $500 plus $60,000 equals $60,500. Ignorance of the law is no excuse. Of course, if you disagree you can appeal my findings to my supervisor or even appeal higher up, that is, if you can afford the huge legal and accounting fees that will be involved."

Then he might disallow 68.27 percent of your travel and entertainment expenses (missing matchbook covers for three months and no "business purpose" explanation for most of the expenses), 15.81 percent of your auto expenses (personal use of business auto and leasing income inclusions not recorded), and 16.76 percent of some other expenses (no documentation, or paid bills). The $60,500 penalty plus the other disallowances and interest, add up to a total bill of $87,413.88! That's a worst case, of course, but far from impossible.

KEY POINT

The bottom line is that Form 8594 is required if there is an *asset* sale and asset acquisition (the very title of the form is: "Asset Acquisition Statement") or, in certain cases, when there is a sale of some of the capital stock of the company accompanied by a consulting or similar contract (we ignore this alternative, since we *don't* recommend selling the old corporation). So, if you don't purchase or sell *assets*, the form need not be filed (in our example, if another $5,000 was added to the consulting fees, an asset sale could have been avoided).

CONCLUSION

Keep in mind that Form 8594 is a two-edged IRS sword:

1. If you *do* file the form, you may trigger an audit and a subsequent reallocation of tax-deductible future payments to 15-year deductible goodwill.
2. If you *don't* file the form (and you should have), you could get a 10 percent nonreporting penalty and a goodwill reallocation in the audit.

As I said before, *don't* sell any *assets*.

With all this IRS background behind us, we will now turn to the complete sale of a rep firm in the next chapter. But remember at all times, that from now on, under the 1993 tax law: Old Engine 197 is a comin' down the track—clickety, clack, clickety, clack.

Chapter Thirty-Two

Selling Your *Entire* Rep Firm

When selling out completely, the idea of keeping your existing corporation while the lines go to another (usually newly formed) corporation has virtually swept the rep industry. Today this technique is used in almost every such situation. Why? The advantages are many and the drawbacks are about zero. Both the buyer and the seller will benefit from a clever arrangement of this kind, so read on.

SPECIAL NOTE

However, because of the new problems raised by IRS Section 197, a newer alternative may completely avoid the mandatory 15-year write-off requirement. This arrangement still involves the buyers forming a new corporation, but with the *seller* corporation keeping the lines and then paying the *buyers'* corporation around 85–90 percent (or so) of the commissions for servicing the lines! First read about the usual method and then study this *new* option before you make up your mind. Both sides may be better off with this latest twist.

THE NAME GAME

Assume the owner's name is John Jones and the existing rep corporation is called "John Jones Sales, Inc." Jones is going to sell the business to his long-time top sales employee, Jane Smith. Here are the steps that should all be detailed in a contract and executed in advance of the purchase:

1. Jane Smith forms a new corporation with any temporary name, say, "Buyer, Inc."
2. John Jones changes the name of his existing corporation to: "JJ Corp."
3. At the same time, JJ Corp. (and John Jones) grants permission to Buyer, Inc. to use the corporate name of "John Jones Sales, Inc."

4. Buyer, Inc. promptly changes its name to John Jones Sales, Inc. (Is that slick or what?)
5. With the agreement of the principals (discussed later), all the lines are transferred to the new corporation, and Jane Smith is now the owner of a rep business.

Now we have the buyer (Jane Smith) in place with a new corporation but using the old name that is familiar to customers and principals. In addition to some tax advantages, we are offering "continuity in the marketplace," something that every customer and every principal responds to in a highly favorable manner. An established name is usually respected and carries with it the cachet of marketing clout, integrity, experience, knowledge, performance, and so forth. So Jane Smith has acquired a very valuable commodity, but so far (outside of minor fees to incorporate) Jane hasn't paid a dime for that valuable name and all those lines!

TAX TREATMENT OF THE PAYMENTS

Of course, Jane Smith is going to pay John Jones for the business, but the beauty of our suggested arrangement is that the new *corporation* is going to make all the payments to the old *corporation*. Hopefully, assuming payments are properly arranged in light of IRS Code Sections *1060 and 197*, all future and recurring payments made by the new corporation will be currently tax-deductible by the new corporation, while receipt of those payments by the old corporation may be partly sheltered from income taxes in various legal ways.

Future and periodic payments to the old Jones corporation characterized as, and in fact for, any of the following, should hopefully be currently tax-deductible by the new Smith corporation:

- Consulting fees, but only if services are *actually rendered* by John Jones Sales, Inc. (or John Jones as an employee provided by that seller corporation to the buyer corporation).
- Sales commissions (or subcommissions) paid on a percentage-sharing or any other arrangement by the new Smith corporation to the old Jones corporation. Again, services must *actually be performed*, or Code Section 197 will kick in.

In days gone by, the down payment usually represented a purchase by the buyer corporation of some of the physical assets of the seller corporation. If you wish to continue this practice (despite Code Section 1060 and the preceding discussion), assets such as furniture, office equipment, computers, autos, and so forth can be sold. Such payments can be deducted over time in the form of depreciation and possibly a Code Section 179 immediate deduction as well (of up to $17,500 a year, depending on net profits and the annual total of other acquisitions of similar assets).

KEY POINT

As explained repeatedly, we are simply not inclined to have any sale of assets. We recommend instead that there be no beginning sale of assets but instead an *initial lump-sum payment* for future consulting fees or subcommissions. Or the total for the contract payments could be higher overall and nothing up front need be paid. Either way, those payments hopefully should be currently tax-deductible by the buyer corporation (but they of course are taxable income to the seller corporation). As the Code Section 1060 discourse explained (Chapter 31), mandatory Form 8594 reporting is required for any kind of sale of any kind of *assets* from one corporation to another, so again, avoid any such *asset* sale if at all possible.

Despite Code Section 1060, if there *is* an asset sale, the seller corporation (Jones) generally will not pay full income taxes on payment received. To the extent that the original John Jones Sales, Inc. has an undepreciated basis in those assets, that amount can be offset against the selling price and only the difference represents income. However, if the sale price is less than the undepreciated tax basis, the seller corporation (Jones) has an ordinary loss deduction (depreciable property used in a trade or business and sold at a *loss* results in an ordinary, not capital, loss). The tax impact of asset sales on the seller is frequently minimal, none, or even tax beneficial, but the real tax cost may lie in a Section 1060 reallocation of the buyer's payments from currently tax-deductible fees/commissions to only 15-year and tax-deductible goodwill.

COVENANT NOT TO COMPETE

Of course, the buyers may still want a covenant not to compete for legitimate business reasons. They should simply understand that whatever cost is allocated to the covenant, regardless of its *stated* length, will only be tax-deductible over 15 years (Code Section 197). That's not to imply that a covenant is not helpful in many situations and essential in some, but be aware of the tax cost and the *mandatory* 15-year tax write-off.

SELF-EMPLOYMENT TAX AND THE COVENANT NOT TO COMPETE

The IRS classifies more and more items of income as subject to "self-employment tax" (i.e., subject to Social Security/Medicare taxes). They have continually broadened the definition of self-employment income to include such items as flat expense allowances, group term life insurance in excess of $50,000 in coverage, awards for back pay, tips (of more than $20 a month), expense reimbursements exceeding "reasonable," many scholarships and grants, severance pay, directors' fees, domestic help pay, the first six months of sick pay, residual commissions to life insurance salespeople *after* retirement, and virtually anything else they can think of.

As these tax rates and maximums have steadily risen (e.g., under the 1993 tax act there is no longer *any* wage ceiling on the 1.45 percent Medicare tax), the IRS keeps looking for and expanding their self-employment classifications for such tax purposes. Of course, commissions and consulting fees are considered self-employment income (if paid to an individual), but what about payments for a covenant not to compete if paid to an individual? For many years, I took the same position as most other accountants: payments for a covenant were *not* self-employment income because the individual was paid to do *nothing* (i.e., to *not* compete), while self-employment income was payment for doing *something*.

However, the IRS announced about two years ago that it was their position that payments to an individual for a noncompete covenant were absolutely considered self-employment income and subject to full Social Security/Medicare taxes. Their "logic" is that you are self-employed to *not* compete, if you can follow that. In other words, payments for a noncompete covenant are treated as compensation *not* to perform services, and of course "compensation" is indeed subject to self-employment tax. So, first the IRS said that "consulting" is self-employment income, even if you render *no* services to the company that is paying you and don't, in fact, consult; then they added any payments for a noncompete covenant, again for rendering *no* services.

If you presently are being paid as an *individual* for a noncompete covenant, you are now alerted to the twin dangers of being liable for self-employment taxes *and* perhaps losing any Social Security benefits (until age 70) because your self-employment (noncompete) income is too high. However, payments for a covenant when paid to another *corporation* are not self-employment income, since only an individual can be "self-employed." By the seller keeping the old corporation and funneling all payments to that corporation, the seller may or may not *ever* pay self-employment tax on the moneys received from the buyer corporation.

THE ADVANTAGES TO THE SELLER

Let me enumerate the many advantages of keeping the old corporation:

- The seller keeps the commissions receivable (owing but unpaid) at the date of sale.
- The seller keeps all assets, such as cash in bank, prepaid expenses, loans receivable, and his auto.
- The seller probably keeps the office furniture and equipment because of IRS Section 1060.
- All payments from buyer to seller go to the seller's corporation and may be sheltered from income taxes by operating expenses (including travel, entertainment, auto), retirement plan contributions, depreciation, fringe benefits, net operating loss carryovers, and expenses for new business ventures or new lines or territories. Thus, the seller draws a lower taxable "earned income" salary than the *gross* amount of commissions and consulting fees or other payments made to the seller's corporation.
- If the seller is receiving Social Security, she may even let the corporation pay income taxes on any net income and protect Social Security income from a disallowance because of self-employment income being too high. But remember, after you reach age 70, there is no disallowance for self-employment income, even if you take back salary after that time. See Chapter 29 for more on that idea.
- In many cases, our rep-clients have 5–10 years of net operating loss carryovers (there is an allowable maximum of 15 years) that will shelter substantial amounts of payments received from the buyer corporation in the future (see earlier Chapter 16 about zeroing out and Chapter 25 about avoiding IRS audits). Thus, the payments received are possibly tax-free!
- If there is the usual commission and consulting agreement between the seller corporation and the buyer corporation, the seller (if actually rendering services) can incur and deduct continuing expenses for auto, travel, entertainment, and similar expenses in future years. A situation eagerly welcomed by most rep-sellers!

> ***TAXTIP***
>
> If the seller is *not* going to render any services to the buyer's new corporation, consider structuring a major sale of *goodwill* (i.e., the lines). The seller can then go for favorable capital gains treatment and the buyers will have a 15-year write-off period no matter *what* the purchase is called!

We've had sellers who kept certain noncompeting territories for the same principals with the agreement of all parties (Hawaii is a favorite pick for California seller-reps), sellers who went into a buy-sell distributor arrangement with the same or different principals, and sellers who then went into completely different kinds of business, using their old corporations as the vehicle. And some sellers did absolutely nothing but consult and protect the lines for the buyer, so that the seller was assured of full payment.

Eventually, the seller can liquidate the corporation or continue it for the next generation, or merge it, or sell it. The flexibility is sensational! To sum up, the uses of the old corporation are only limited by the ingenuity of the seller and his tax advisers. The advantages are many, and the drawbacks are few or none.

THE ADVANTAGES TO THE BUYER

Let me enumerate the many advatages of starting a new corporation:

- The biggest advantage of the buyer starting a new corporation is that the *down payment* from buyer to seller drops from big to almost nothing! In the olden days, the buyer had to come up with enough money to acquire the old corporation that had cash in the bank, commissions receivable, furniture, equipment, and so forth. Frequently the down payment was well over $100,000.
- Now that the buyer is *not* buying the assets, those assets are being retained by the seller corporation. The cash requirements for the buyer now drop to about 45–60 days' operating expenses (before the first new commissions arrive) and whatever other "down payment" (perhaps an accelerated consulting payment), if any, must be made to the seller in that 45–60-day period.
- If the buyers can forgo their own salaries for 45–60 days, and if the seller will forgo any payments for 45–60 days, sometimes the buyers can swing the whole deal for peanuts.

- Customarily, the two corporations will share the premises of the old (seller) corporation. Then the buyers don't have to pay moving expenses or lease deposits, and can use the same office equipment and furniture (without actually buying assets, remember?). Of course, the new corporation could pay "rent" (to cover various "obligations") to the old corporation, if required. The changeover is virtually "seamless."

Another win-win for the good guys!

THE PERSONAL HOLDING COMPANY DANGER

A personal holding company (PHC) is a special kind of corporation that can be subject to an *additional* 28 percent federal income tax. You don't ever want to be one! Personal holding company income, as defined by the IRS, is for:

> Amounts received by the corporation for contracts for *personal services* . . . if (a) some person *other* than the corporation has the right to designate (by name or by description) the individual who is to perform the services, or if the individual who is to perform the services is designated (by name or by description) in the contract and (b) at some time during the tax year 25 percent or more in value of the outstanding stock of the corporation is owned, directly or indirectly, by or for the individual who has performed, is to perform, or may be designated (by name or by description) as the one to perform such services. [Emphsis mine.]

The usual way we have seen lawyers avoid the PHC tax danger is by carefully drawing the consulting contract to *never* name individuals, but simply state that one corporation (seller) will provide the other corporation (buyer) an (unnamed) individual "acceptable to both corporations," to render vague consulting and selling services on behalf of the corporation. This is an approximation of what I have seen, and it could further be affected by various state laws. So please remind your lawyer of this danger and let her take it from there.

Out here in California, where most of the entertainers are incorporated to obtain the many advantages we have discussed, the PHC danger is routinely avoided by their knowledgeable entertainment lawyers. They form so-called "loan-out" corporations, in which the corporation "loans-out" an *unnamed* individual "acceptable to both corporations" to a movie studio to make, say, a movie. Of course, both sides know in advance exactly who that individual is, just as you know in advance exactly who the individual is that will render future consulting/selling services to the new (buyer) corporation. But you have to carefully follow the exact rules, or the old (seller) corporation could get *killed* with an extra 28 percent PHC tax on all the income received from the buyer corporation!

Now you have been warned—and you're welcome. . . .

THE NEW OPTION, OR THE SECTION 197 SWITCHEROO

As indicated by the special note at the beginning of this chapter, there is another variation that may completely avoid Section 197 and the 15-year write-off problem. It works like this:

1. The buyers still form a new corporation, but the *seller* keeps the lines and the corporate name as before in the old corporation.
2. The old corporation (seller) contractually hires the buyers' new corporation to perform the actual sales services on the lines and with the customers. Thus the buyers will be acting in the same position as intended.
3. The *old* corporation continues to collect the *total* commissions.
4. The old corporation pays subcommissions to the new corporation of somewhere around 85–90 percent of the total commissions actually *received* to compensate them for their sales efforts. These payments should be *fully and currently tax-deductible,* since they are for sales services actually being rendered.
5. The balance of the commissions actually retained by the old (seller's) corporation (say 10–15 percent, or a fixed amount, or whatever), is geared to the actual buy-out agreement. Thus that "retention" is equal to the monthly amount the seller is supposed to receive under that agreement.
6. Note that the seller *controls* the commission income from the principals and *controls* the payments to the buyers. Under the more usual (older) method, the reverse was true. Interesting point?
7. The old (seller's) corporation reports 100 percent of the commission income and has an offsetting tax deduction for the subcommissions paid (say 85–90 percent or so).
8. The new (buyers') corporation reports as income only the subcommissions actually *received* from the old corporation of the seller (say 85–90 percent or so). This lesser amount already

gives effect to the retention/override/buy-out payment to the seller.

9. There do not *appear* to be any Section 197 tax problems.

While Section 197 is untried in the courts, this new arrangement seems to completely avoid the aim and provisions of 197. Note that there are *no payments* for consulting, goodwill, a covenant not to complete, or any other Section 197 intangible. Instead, we simply have a subcommission arrangement where the buyers' corporation is just being paid *entirely for services actually rendered*.

The seller, on the other hand, is simply retaining what amounts to an override on the lines. Note that there are *no payments from the buyers to the seller,* and it was *such* payments that raised the Section 197 deduction problem to begin with. This may really solve the 197 issue and still accomplish that aims of both parties to the agreement. Further observe that the buyers are actually getting an immediate tax deduction for the retention by the seller, since they only report as income the *net* subcommissions they receive and not the full commissions from the factories.

CONCLUSION

This is a *key* chapter, so let's first summarize the main points under the older and more typical method (until now):

• Of course there are exceptions to everything, but it is virtually inarguable that keeping the old corporation when selling your entire rep agency is the way to go. Proof positive, 100 percent of all recent sales to employees that we have been involved in have been exactly that way. Study the reasons why and you should agree.

• Avoid any sale of assets in order to avoid being required to file Form 8594. By not filing Form 8594, you are avoiding a possible audit and thus a potential reallocation to only 15-year tax-deductible (by the buyer) goodwill. As explained, there are other ways to compensate the seller. My favorite is to simply increase the *other* time payments of commissiion and consulting fees, and perhaps include some payments for rent (then let the buyers use the assets, free). Refer to Chapter 31 for more on substitute downpayments.

• Establish a nominal amount for the purchase of goodwill or take the position that no goodwill exists until after the date of transfer of the lines (unless *no* services are to be rendered and the whole sale can be structured as goodwill; see my earlier TAXTIP).

• Establish a covenant not to compete in the light of necessity and in view of Section 197. (Consider another idea of a *penalty* provision in the compensation agreement, *reducing* remaining payments if the seller does in fact compete in the future. Naturally I am very fond of this idea, since I invented it and I have seen it used successfully.) However, I strongly urge your consideration of the alternative arrangement, wherein the seller corporation continues to collect the total commissions, pays a high percentage as subcommissions to the buyers' (new) corporation for sales services actually rendered, and keeps a retention amount equal to the intended buy-out. I'm getting very fond of this latest variation.

If you are presently selling all (or part) of your agency, by all means buy this book for your lawyer, your CPA, the buyer's lawyer, the buyer's CPA, and all your other advisers. You should not attempt to verbally describe or relate all the facts in these chapters 31–38.

Chapter Thirty-Three

Selling Only *Part* of Your Rep Firm

Now clear your minds completely; in one sense this is an entirely new topic. Many times we have had rep-owners who come to us with a comment like this: "Key employees are asking these questions now, even though they understand we have no present plans to retire and are far too young to do so":

- When can they acquire *some* ownership in the company?
- How can they be assured of *eventual* ownership of the entire company when we finally do retire?
- Therefore, how can they *now* obtain some job security and assurances for the future?

The three variations that follow are suggested solutions to a *partial* sale of your rep firm.

VARIATION 1

Sell More and Get Company Stock Free!

The traditional profit split between salespeople and owners in a rep agency was 40 percent of the commission income to the agency (that pays all the company overhead) and 60 percent to the salesperson (who pays *all* expenses of travel, entertainment, auto, and so forth). Sometimes the split is 45–55 percent, sometimes 50–50 percent. This *same idea* can be used to reward key salespeople with stock in the company long before your retirement.

Let's assume, for this example, that 55 percent is going to the employees *and* the company is paying expenses. Here is how it works:

1. Each selected salesperson receives company stock as a *bonus for performance* above her present (or a target) level of sales.
2. On commissions collected by the agency above the existing performance (or a target) level of each salesperson involved, that

employee is credited with, say, 55 percent of those "excess" earnings.

3. Stock is issued for *part* of the earnings as calculated in point 2 and the rest is paid as a cash bonus computed as per the following point 4. That stock is appraised at full market value (probably based on a total valuation of 100–150 percent of annual commission income, plus the hard assets of the company; see Chapter 34 for more on sales agency valuations).
4. A *cash* bonus is paid to the employee for the balance of the earnings that were figured in point 2 sufficient to cover the income taxes due on both the cash bonus received *and* the bonus paid in stock. In effect, the employee has received the stock as if it were a tax-free gift. All she did in return was: sell!
5. Alternatively, the cash bonus may be sufficient to pay the tax on the stock received, plus the tax on the cash received, *plus* an amount of cash the employee retains as a net cash bonus amount. So the employee receives *both* a cash bonus and a stock bonus, yet will not owe taxes at the end of the year.

   For example, an employee earns a $10,000 bonus and gets $2,000 in cash. The other $8,000 is split between $3,500 withholding (to pay the taxes on the *entire* $10,000 at a 35 percent tax rate) and $4,500 in stock (market valued per point 3). The employee's bonus consists of:

Cash bonus, after taxes	$ 2,000
Witholding tax paid	3,500
Company stock received	4,500
Total bonus	$10,000

6. There are no potential problems with the IRS, since the stock is being valued at full market and the employee is reporting all stock received as taxable income at that full market value.
7. The rep company obtains a *tax deduction* for the *full market value* of the stock and, of course, for all the cash paid as well ($10,000 in the preceding example).
8. The rep *corporation* has no taxable income resulting from issuing company stock above par value (a corporation never has taxable profits or losses from selling or buying its *own* stock, at any price).
9. Key employees who are not salespeople can be added into this plan on some kind of a performance pool arrangement, in which they receive a portion (fixed or variable percentage) of salespeople's stock bonus earnings. The key employees' stock bonus can either be a portion of the salespeople's earnings or

an additional percentage over and above the percentage usually allocated. This system creates a team effort effect between key salespeople and other key employees, since the more the salespeople earn in stock, the more the other key people earn.

Restrictions and Safeguards

Of course, rep-owners are not going to in effect give away a major portion of the company without protection against employees who do not perform, do not stay with the company, are dishonest, or are potential future competitors. Therefore, a number of prudent, sensible, and mandatory restrictions on this stock bonus arrangement are suggested:

• The total additional stock issued should *never* aggregate more than 45 percent of the total outstanding stock until the owners retire. Thus, 55 percent stock control is always in the hands of the original owners for as long as they are still actively operating the company.

• While the stock bonus is issued in the name of each employee from day one, their unlimited and unfettered ownership of the stock is restricted by a vesting schedule. Stock only becomes their own according to an annual vesting percentage (something like retirement plan contributions, which are fully paid on behalf of each employee, but only become *entirely* their property with the passage of time). A suggested vesting schedule is 10 percent a year, so that every employee must be with the company 10 years to fully "own" the stock.

• If an employee *for any reason* leaves or is fired, all stock *must* be sold back to the company under a fixed-sum repurchase agreement (e.g., whatever was paid for the stock, plus 5 or 10 percent for each year of ownership, not compounded). Thus, you never have a disagreement over how much the stock is worth at the time of repurchase.

• As an alternative to a vesting schedule, or in combination therewith, a secular trust can be used to actually hold the stock of the employees and then only issue it when an employee is fully vested, or sometimes not at all, until the principal owners retire.

• The participating employees sign a covenant not to compete. At least in California, such a covenant between *owners* of a private company is considered strictly enforceable as these employees are indeed bona fide "owners."

What's in It for the Owners?

The owners now have "partners" who work to help the agency succeed! An entirely different work ethic pervades the entire company. The salespeople will sell like crazy, or you have picked the wrong individuals in the first place! (Who would turn down a deal where they can acquire a percentage of ownership of a growing company both dollar cost-free and tax-free?) Other advantages to the owners include:

- The owners have a smaller and smaller piece of a bigger pie as the employees sell and sell and sell! In effect, the owners are getting 100 percent of the base earnings of the company, plus 55 percent (much more in the early years) of all increases in the earnings of the company from the time the plan begins. (However, they pay all increased overhead out of that 55 percent.)
- The owners can easily continue to draw their same compensation, or more, since all costs of cash bonuses come out of increased earnings, and the cost of the newly issued stock is actually *nothing* (but engraved paper). The actual cash profits available for the owners should increase if the plan is successful.
- The company reduces its income tax liability without an accompanying outlay of cash to the extent each bonus (perhaps 45–50 percent of each earned total) is paid with corporate stock. (This is similar to what the public companies often do, but you reps never thought you would ever play in that league. Well, step up to the plate!)
- After a few years (certainly after five or so), the successful sales (and other key) employees simply cannot leave! They would be crazy to do so, as they acquire more and more of a larger and larger (and more successful) rep firm each year. Their increasingly vested interest holds them to the agency, somewhat similar to the way retirement plans do (but in this case with the much stronger incentive of permanent ownership!). True, they can leave with cash from selling back their stock, but also with an uncertain future and restricted by a covenant not to compete.

Switching to an S Corporation

This variation suggests one additional reason to consider electing S corporation status (see Chapter 13). In a regular corporation, the employees receive the stock as described above but don't really share in any excess earnings over and above their stock bonus, since the rep corporation rarely pays out such profits in the form of dividends.

However, an S corporation is really a corporate variation of what is essentially a partnership. To the extent of S corporation stock ownership, each owner automatically is credited with a share of the net profits, just as in a true partnership. Therefore, in addition to acquiring corporate stock based on performance, each share of stock thus acquired is credited with a pro rata share of corporate earnings. Employee ownership accounts will grow and grow in this compounded manner:

- The employee is awarded stock, based on performance, in the first year.
- That initial stock ownership interest is then credited with a share of the S corporation's net profits.
- The employee is awarded additional stock in succeeding years.
- Each additional share receives credit in each succeeding year for an added portion of earnings.

The employee sees his account growing in two ways: increasing amounts of stock and S corporation earnings credited to the increasing amounts of stock (a classic case of compounding of earnings). These provide even stronger incentives for key employees than the C corporation stock bonus plan, but a major drawback lies in the numerous disadvantages of the S corporation (see Chapter 13) compared to the advantages of the C corporation (see Chapter 12). You and your tax adviser will have to make that judgment call.

At Full Retirement

When the owners finally reach retirement age, or sooner if they choose, their remaining stock interests (now about 55 percent in our example) can be purchased in similar manner to the general discussions of valuations, purchase techniques, safeguards, and so forth in these final chapters of the book. The major differences in this case are that no new corporation will probably be formed, since the employees already own about 45 percent of the existing corporation, and the payments by the corporation for the remaining 55 percent or so of the stock will probably be with after-tax dollars (also, the purchase price for this stock may be reduced, since the corporation cannot deduct the payments). Also consider the following chain of events before making a final valuation decision.

Note that as the original owners' stock is finally redeemed and canceled, the 45 percent stock held by other employees suddenly becomes *100 percent* of the then remaining outstanding stock with no added income tax cost to the employees or the corporation! This wonderful circumstance may very well fully offset the fact that the corporation is buying that stock with after-tax (i.e., nondeductible) dollars. On the other hand, if there is a total redemption of the owners' stock and the related redemption rules are followed, the owners will be only taxed at capital gains rates on their total sale of the stock. Other alternatives are to use life insurance to eventually buy out the principal owners at their death or to have the corporation buy enough stock to reduce their interest below 50 percent and use life insurance to eventually purchase the remainder. Study the life insurance discussions in Chapter 38.

VARIATION 2

Sell More and Buy the Owners' Stock with Part of Your Bonus (and It's Still "Free")

The only drawback with Variation 1 may be for the owners. True, they are getting a good portion of the increased earnings on increased sales, but the stock going to the employees is from the unissued stock of the corporation. Thus, the *owners* are not selling any of *their* stock each year, so they are not receiving any annual cash payments.

The essential change in Variation 2 is that the employees first receive an *all cash* bonus (less the 35 percent or so withholding), and then use a portion of the remaining cash to buy stock *directly from the owners*. Let's use our previous example of a $10,000 bonus, but distributed as follows:

Cash bonus, after taxes	$ 2,000
Witholding tax paid	3,500
Cash used to purchase stock from owners	4,500
Total bonus	$10,000

As you can see, the *employee* ends up in the identical position as to stock, cash, and taxes paid. The advantage to the owners is that they are getting more cash each year as they sell their stock. The disadvantage is that the bonuses to employees are now being paid in *all cash* and the corporation is not getting a tax deduction for new stock being issued. The owners are trading more cash available in the corporation for more cash being paid directly for the stock. You should have your own CPA push around the numbers.

VARIATION 3

Another Arrangement to Buy the Owners' Stock with Your Bonus

This variation is based on an actual case study of a large rep firm. It is a sophisticated refinement of Variation 2 and resulted from numerous meetings and conferences with the key employees, the owners, lawyers, and CPAs (and it cost a lot of money to develop). The following information was distributed in writing to the key employees (emphasis mine):

Announcement to the Key Employees

The basic concept of this plan is that the owners of the company want to bring in you key employees to move the company to a new level of performance, and allow you to share in the *control, profits, and ownership* of the company. The existing revenue base of the company remains with the current owners. The key employees, after a 40 percent overhead allocation, receive *all* the increases in gross commission income over the current base. From these increased commissions, the key employees will receive both current income and ownership of the company.

Overhead Allocation

Current financial data indicates that the overhead of the company is about 40 percent of commission income. Therefore, any *increases* in commissions over the current (base) commission income will be split 40 percent to pay overhead and 60 percent to the key employees' group. Essentially all the profits generated, in excess of the existing base, will go entirely to the key employees' group.

Cash Payment Allocations

The 60 percent allocated to the key employees will be split into *two* categories, current cash compensation and common stock purchases. Current cash compensation will be equal to 20 percent of the additional commissions earned (i.e., 20 percent of the allocated 60 percent) and is subject to regular income tax withholding. Whenever the stock purchases reach their maximum level (see the following paragraph), the entire allocated amount will then revert to cash compensation.

Stock Acquisitions

The other 80 percent of the moneys allocated to the key employees will be for the purchase of stock. The stock acquisitions will *also* be currently taxable to you (it's as if you first received a second cash bonus and *then* used it to purchase the stock), and thus we will allocate 35 percent of the stock purchase portion to cover your approximate federal and state income taxes. The 65 percent after-tax balance will be used to purchase stock *from the existing company owners.*

Stock Trust

The stock purchased by the key employees will be held in *trust* for the sole benefit of the key employees. The trustees of the trust will be the key employees and the present owners.

The stock trust instrument provides that each beneficiary (the key employees) will be *vested* in that stock at the rate of 10 percent a year. This means that at the end of 10 years each individual is 100 percent vested and fully owns the stock. If one of the key employees leaves the company during the 10-year period, that employee will be paid for the *vested* portion of the stock valued at their cost. Payments to any such individual will be made equally over 10 years with interest at the current prime rate (although the company has the right to accelerate such payments at their option).

Each new owner will have the right to vote the *vested* stock interest in the shares held in the trust. Company income will be additionally allocated to each owner, based upon the *vested* percentage of stock ownership. This income allocation will *also* be used to buy additional stock. The maximum overall percentage that can be purchased under this plan is *40 percent* of the outstanding stock for the *entire* key employees' group.

Covenant Not to Compete

Every key employee in this group must sign a three year covenant not to compete, which will provide for both monetary damages and injunctive relief in the event of a violation. You are cautioned that such a covenant involving *owners* can be strictly enforced.

Value of Stock

For both purposes of this stock purchase plan and also for a final buy-out of the remaining 60 percent of the stock (see the following section), the same valuation method will be used. The value for *100 percent* of the company will be set at the net assets of the company (assets less liabilities), plus the gross commission income *received* by the company during the 12 months preceding any valuation date (i.e., 100 percent of one year's commission income). Both order backlog and commissions receivable will be *ignored* in these calculations. Appropriate percentages will then be applied to that 100 percent valuation figure to arrive at the value per share of stock.

It should be noted that by using this combined valuation method, the owners cannot manipulate the valuation. For example, if they were to withdraw an extra $50,000 in cash, their net asset valuation would also decrease by $50,000.

Final Buyout

At the end of the 10-year period for acquiring the first 40 percent of the stock, the owners would like to turn over the entire operation to the key employees and sell the remaining 60 percent of their stock. As noted, we continue to use the already established valuation formula. There are two options to consider:

1. An *Employee Stock Ownership Plan* (ESOP) set up in similar fashion to the current company retirement plan trust. The remaining 60 percent of the stock could be purchased in a tax-deductible manner by the ESOP since the company contributions to the ESOP trust *are* tax-deductible. Typically, the ESOP *borrows* the money to make the stock purchase and then repays the loan with the (tax-deductible) contributions received from the company.

The key employees would be the *sole* trustees of the ESOP trust. The *beneficiaries* of the trust would be *all* the employees of the company in a percentage equal to company contributions made on their behalf. Such contributions are allocated to participants in the same manner as contributions to the existing retirement plan. It should be noted that the owners selling the 60 percent to the ESOP *can defer all taxable gain* by reinvesting the proceeds of that sale in listed securities.

2. An *installment sale* of the remaining 60 percent stock interest directly to the key employees' group. They would pay 10 percent of the purchase price at the signing of the documents; the balance would be paid over 10 years, plus interest at the current prime rate. The promissory note would be secured by a Pledge and Security Agreement of the 60 percent of the stock until the note is *fully* paid.

CONCLUSION

Which variation do I prefer? Variation 3 is my favorite, particularly since I was intimately involved in both the design and successful implementation of that plan! However, you can certainly *combine* whatever ideas appeal to you, from any and all of the variations. Then you can implement your plan (and please send me a copy!).

Chapter Thirty-Four

Selling Your Rep Firm: Valuation

"Value" and "goodwill" are not identical concepts. There are three ideas to keep in mind when valuing the typical sales agency:

1. You operate a *service* business, just like lawyers, physicians, or CPAs (one more time: your service is "sales," while the product belongs to your principal).
2. The "value" of the agency when sold to your employees (or partner) is *not* the same as an IRS or other "goodwill" valuation, as in the event of death or divorce. I take the position that the average rep firm has no goodwill at the date of transfer, death, or divorce, because of the unique concentration of principals and adverse contract termination provisions. Don't use the words "goodwill" and "value" interchangeably.
3. What you can sell to your employees is the *probable* continuity of the business and the *probable* retention of lines through their future efforts and your careful advance planning. You are selling the employees something with potentially significant value, but it really isn't goodwill in the typical or IRS sense.

THE MOST TYPICAL VALUATION (WHEN SELLING TO EMPLOYEES)

In the most classic case, the value of total agency lines is usually one to one and one-half times a year's gross commission income. The variation is based on three factors:

1. The *longer* the payout to the seller, generally the *higher* the multiple. At a most common payout of five years, the multiple of one (i.e., 100 percent of a year's gross commissions) is the probably the most usual. At 7–10 years, that multiple customarily creeps up to 1.5 (i.e., 150 percent of a year's gross commissions). These variables cover both risk of default and implied interest (i.e., the "present value of money," discussed in Chapter 35) in the longer payouts,

because risk *increases* with time and the present value of money always *decreases* with time.

2. The security of the line and the value of the line are also factors. A firm with three major lines held for 20–25 years, with no indication of current trouble, is vastly different than one with no line older than three years or a firm with known major problems with a principal. Only the seller and buyer are able to evaluate this delicate judgment call; obviously, a stronger line position could command a somewhat higher multiple.

3. An additional factor in the overall valuation should be substituted because you did not sell the old corporation or the furniture, equipment, and other assets (see Chapter 31). You can also include something for the fact that the signed but unfilled orders (i.e., unearned commissions) are of greater or lesser value, but certainly worth something. Further, if the buyers are getting free use of the premises, figure in the total extra valuation (or consider charging rent, as I suggested in Chapter 31).

By following the reasoning of points 2 and 3, we have taken away the down payment that the seller received in the olden days. To compensate, you may now exceed the usual 1–1.5 times annual commissions valuation formula to some degree. Further, the payouts to the seller over the fixed time span can now include larger beginning payments to substitute for the down payment.

Here's an example of the valuation process:

> Seller will receive $490,000 in commissions and consulting fees paid equally over seven years, at the rate of $70,000 a year ($70,000 × 7 = $490,000). Further, the first year's payments shall also include an additional $30,000 in commissions and consulting fees, for a first year total of $100,000; therefore the entire consulting agreement is for $520,000 ($490,000 + $30,000 = $520,000).

In this example, the $490,000 was the figure agreed upon for the lines and the $30,000 extra is for the other items, as discussed above. The $30,000 could be paid in various ways: in the first month or in some other month during the first year, $10,000 a month for three months, or equally over the first year and so forth.

GIVE AND TAKE

I cannot emphasize enough that the valuation of a rep firm is not a fixed, mechanical, or purely numerical process. In *any* negotiation there is plenty of give and take. But particularly in this case, you are into a subjective judgment area that cannot be solved by absolute formulas. In a principal's business, the hard assets are valued by outside appraisers, the net income is established by past ("certified") audits, and the future of the company is reasonably predictable. Smart investment bankers, CPAs, and lawyers can easily establish and negotiate the value of a principal's company. But in the case of the average sales agency, this simply is not so.

In our case, we have a rep firm: here today, maybe gone tomorrow, uncertain growth, unpredictable losses, dangerous principal concentrations, lousy contracts, erratic future employee management performance, chancy product obsolescence, capricious customers, plus wars, earthquakes, fires, plague, and famine! You are never going to reach an agreed-upon value by using investment bankers and other consultants, except to sketch the broad outlines (as I have just indicated).

The final number must be determined by you, the seller, and I urge you to adopt a give-and-take posture. Employees will agree to virtually *anything* to get a chance to own the company, so a foolish, cunning, or greedy seller can arrange the sale under terms, conditions, and valuations that are ultimately impossible to meet. Let me assure you, however, that the seller is damaged financially by eventual default as much or more than the buyers! This advice is based on over 100 negotiations, sales, ownership transfers, and mergers of rep firms. It's hard-won knowledge that I am giving you, and I urge you to listen.

ESTATE VALUATIONS

I take the firm position that there is no goodwill left when a rep-owner dies. If a buy-sell agreement assures the surviving spouse a set sum of money, the exact value or payment specified in that contract should be reported as the fair market value in the estate of the deceased.

Absent a buy-sell agreement, there is simply no goodwill at the date of death and any *ultimate* goodwill is generated in the *future* by the *subsequent actions* of the successors to the firm. But further, the death of the owner will present the worst possible situation: lines are up for grabs, employees or competitors are actively seeking those lines, management is in shock, and principals may terminate.

A few years ago I shared the podium with Chicagoan David Fisher, who was the attorney for the Electronics Representatives Association (ERA) and a speaker at their management conference. Dave had many clients among both principals and sales reps in that industry (his experience in the valuation and sale of rep firms was about equal to mine). He spoke first on death and succession and took the *identical* position on goodwill that I have just explained. At the break he asked me if I agreed, and I showed him my virtually identical notes. We just smiled at each other: two rep experts in complete agreement.

INTERNAL REVENUE SERVICE VALUATION GUIDELINES

Here are the various factors the IRS (IRS Rev. Rul. 59-60) tells its agents to consider in valuing the goodwill of any corporation if a binding and legitimate buy-sell agreement does not exist:

- The nature and history of the business.
- The economic outlook in general and the outlook for the industry in particular.
- Book value of the company (i.e., total assets less total liabilities) and its financial condition.
- Earning capacity.
- Dividend-paying capacity.
- Goodwill or other intangible value.
- Prior sales of stock of the corporation.
- Comparison to similar publicly traded companies.

If the rep agency is being inherited by the surviving spouse, no estate tax liability exists (regardless of what the dollar value may be) because of the unlimited marital deduction. In that case, the IRS immediately loses interest in the entire process since there is no possibility of collecting any estate taxes.

However, keep in mind that whatever value is placed on the sales agency (and all other estate assets) becomes the tax basis for the surviving spouse if there is a subsequent sale. This basis will determine any future taxable profit or loss from any future sale. Remember, every asset in an estate is valued at market value at the date of death, so see your tax adviser before you assign any value to the rep firm no matter who inherits the agency. Refer to Chapter 23 for more on this subject.

DIVORCE VALUATIONS

Death is unavoidable. Selling the agency to employees is optional. But the *forced* valuation of a sales agency for purposes of divorce is probably the most traumatic valuation experience of all, since it takes place under adversarial conditions. The nonowner spouse is looking for the highest possible valuation of the rep firm, but since most rep firms have little in the way of tangible assets (modest cash, equipment, furniture, autos, and not much more), the valuation invariably settles on the goodwill of the sales agency. In this context, one of the best definitions of goodwill is "the commercial advantage of any business, due to its established popularity, reputation, patronage, advertising, location, etc., over and beyond its tangible assets."

The operative phrase is "commercial advantage." To begin with, obviously not every business can have a commercial advantage, since that advantage must consist of business superiority over some *other* competitor who does not have the upper hand in the business. So goodwill only exists in the above-average business that has above average profits and above average expectations for the future. (Above average profits are defined as "the quantified expectation of future profits from some source other than mere dollars at work," that is, from goodwill.)

In defining goodwill for divorce valuation purposes, the major problem we have encountered is that invariably some outside valuation "expert" can always find goodwill for *any* company, of *any* size, in *any* competitive position, with *any* amount of earnings, *regardless!* Note this well: Goodwill is not the *automatic feature* (i.e., trait, characteristic, property, mark) of *every* business! Only certain and especially successful businesses really qualify.

The most unfair valuations seem to land on the shoulders of the smaller reps. For example, if a rep is grossing $100,000 a year in commissions and netting $65,000, where is the goodwill? That individual can usually get a job with a competitor for $60,000–$75,000 (and perhaps more if the lines follow her). If that same individual were an *employee* in the process of getting divorced there would be *no discussion* of a goodwill valuation. Now stay with this example.

In comes a valuation "expert," who says, "I know all about valuing rep firms. I read in Mel Daskal's book that 100 percent of annual gross commissions is the most typical valuation, so that's $100,000 for goodwill. Or, if I figure three times the net profit (before compensation) of $65,000, I arrive at $195,000 for goodwill. So my recommendation to the court will be in the range of $100,000–$195,000 for goodwill, say $150,000." Of course this is utter nonsense!

There are two considerations in defining goodwill:

1. Does the particular rep firm *even qualify* as having any goodwill under the general definitions discussed above (commercial advantage, etc.) that are applicable to all types of businesses?
2. If so, then the particular and peculiar *characteristics* of every sales agency (adverse contracts, concentration of principals, etc.) must be further considered.

This is not to say that not many rep firms have goodwill, but generally only those at or near the top of each particular industry—the biggest, the best, the most profitable, the most secure in their lines and market positions—evidence goodwill associated with their sales agencies. However, these firms are in the *minority* while goodwill valuations are frequently applied to the *majority!* In our example, the rep flunked both of our goodwill conditions: there is certainly no commercial advantage over competitors evidenced within a minor rep firm below-average earnings, and the appraiser didn't even *consider* the special conditions that exist in every rep firm (principal concentrations, adverse contract conditions, etc.).

To summarize, both general and particular circumstances factor into any divorce valuation of a sales agency's goodwill. Admittedly goodwill valuation usually exists in top performing rep firms in each and every industry, but it is the *automatic* valuation of goodwill in all cases that you must resist, particularly in *small* rep firms where the owner's net earnings are *no more* than she could earn as a salaried salesperson.

After all, what does the average appraiser know about factories going direct, commission cuts, territorial cuts, house accounts, 30-day termination clauses, sales managers, military and aerospace procurements, line switching, principal mergers, principal failures, and so on (I deliberately won't explain these topics, and while all you reps will know exactly what I mean, those "expert" appraisers won't know what I'm talking about!)

Most of the "experts" think that a "principal" is someone who heads up the local high school, a "line" is something you dare someone to cross, a sales manager is a completely reasonable individual, and a "house account" is where you keep money to pay your mortgage.

Anyway, if you are going through a divorce, perhaps it will make you feel better to know that nobody ever really "wins," except the divorce lawyers. When it's all over, the *best* you can hope for is to be a little less dissatisfied than the other side.

MERGER AND SALE VALUATIONS

While the subject of mergers of agencies gets separate treatment in Chapter 37, let's just brush over the valuation techniques in the case of mergers. The lines of each party to the merger are generally valued at the same multiple for all the merging parties. For example, if Firm A is grossing $600,000 a year in commissions and Firm B is grossing $300,000 a year in commissions, the merger has a 2:1 commission ratio. That 2:1 ratio may be used to establish stock ownership in the new company or the difference in compensation, in other payments, or *something*. But obviously, Firm A has brought twice as much to the table as Firm B. Note that it does not matter what multiple of commissions are used; the *ratio* usually stays the same.

Having said that, there are always exceptions if the lines of one company are far more established and secure than those of the other firm. In that or other circumstances (perhaps different *qualities* of salespeople or owners), the ratio may be varied to suit those particular circumstances. In our example, if the lines of Firm B were far more valuable (for whatever reasons) than those of Firm A, the final ratio might be 60:40 or 55:45. (Understand the *idea;* don't get hung up with the numbers in the example.)

In the case of a true *sale* of one rep firm to another (even if disguised for public consumption as a merger), there is only one set of lines to value, that is, the lines of the seller. The valuation is usually like the one used when selling to your employees (see earlier). However, in an outright sale even lower valuations are sometimes used, like 90 percent or 80 percent of a year's commission income, because many times an outright sale indicates a *weaker than typical* sales agency. Perhaps the sale is motivated by illness or loss of a major line. Valuations are individual matters, but I have noted the general parameters we have seen used.

FAMILY VALUATIONS

Family valuations have less to do with accounting than with estate taxes and familial relationships. The transfer of ownership to the next generation within a family is nothing like the sale of a rep firm to the employees!

The parent is obviously not going to squeeze the children for every possible dime. In fact, the most common family technique is to transfer ownership by *gifts*. As detailed in Chapter 23, a married couple can jointly give $20,000 each year to as many individuals as they choose without any gift tax, income tax, or estate tax liabilities. Of course, many reps choose to transfer only a minority interest as long as they are still active in the business, but probably an equal number eventually transfer 100 percent ownership in this manner.

An alternative is a one-fell-swoop technique, in which up to $600,000 in additional transfers can be made, free of all taxes, by using up the combined gift and estate tax exemption of $600,000 for each individual (or the combined $1,200,000 of husband and wife). If the value of the agency stock is rapidly appreciating in value, it's a smart thing to do, since it gets that rapidly appreciating asset out of the estate and all future appreciation is passed on to the next generation tax-free. It's also a valid idea if you are afraid that the current $600,000 exemption is going to be cut drastically in the future (only a slight possibility, in my opinion, but not impossible).

Needless to say, nobody wants a sky-high valuation where family transfers are concerned, but we are careful to assign reasonable and defensible values that can be justified before the IRS.

GOOD NEWS: IRS REVENUE RULING 93-12

Of particular importance in gifting stock to family members are the major concessions by the IRS in their Revenue Ruling 93-12 (February 16, 1993), issued as the result of many IRS *losses* in court cases on this very subject. The IRS finally conceded that the value of the stock being gifted to each individual family member, if less than 50 percent of the firm's stock, can be decreased by a "minority discount," even though the stock is staying within the family group. These minority discounts can be applied even in cases where all or most of the stock is being gifted to the next generation, as long as *each* child's stock gifts are individually of a minority interest (i.e., less than 50 percent). The IRS also concedes that the percentage of stock being gifted to each child should *not* be aggregated with the percentages being gifted to other children to determine if, in fact, a majority interest is being transferred.

For example, if you were to transfer 20 percent of your sales agency to each of your five children, you may now apply a minority discount to the valuation of *each* 20 percent gift to each child as if the other gifts did not even exist and as if each recipient was not a member of the same family. You could give away 100 percent of your rep firm and *still* apply a minority discount to the value of each individual 20 percent gift!

TAXTIP

Since minority discounts in the range of 20–25 percent of actual fair market value are not uncommon, be sure your tax adviser is aware of IRS Revenue Ruling 93-12, and uses it to your maximum advantage. Also, keep in mind that there has *always* been a valuation concept that stock of privately owned companies should be discounted because the stock is not publicly traded and is, therefore, illiquid. This affords the opportunity to apply a *second* discount; perhaps *another* 20 percent?

TAXTIP

Another technique: Issue stock to your children at the time of incorporation when the value is usually minimal, and they can actually pay for the stock themselves, or they can be gifted a few thousand shares. Think about this idea if you are just forming a sales agency or just incorporating. Most rep firms, in my experience, are usually incorporated in the $1,000 to $10,000 range, with a few exceptions up to $25,000 or so. A final idea: You can also incorporate with two classes of stock: voting stock for the parents and nonvoting stock for the children. The voting stock can have a much lower *value* but still control the corporation.

CONCLUSION

As you are beginning to learn, the sale and valuation of a rep firm is a rather complicated matter. Let's continue, next, with necessary information about the actual payments.

Chapter Thirty-Five

Selling Your Rep Firm: The Payments

CLASSIFYING THE PAYMENTS

We should all be in agreement that the payments for your rep firm will not include a purchase of assets. If need be, you can reread my reasons and the alternate solutions I have already discussed (see Chapters 31–32).

The characterization of the payments as either "commissions" or "consulting fees" (always payable to the old corporation of the seller) is the ideal way to structure payments *if you can justify the fact that they are for current services actually being rendered* (see Chapter 31 regarding Code Section 197). If not, the buyer only gets a tax-deduction amortized over 15 years *no matter what the payments are called,* and this includes any covenant not to compete (Chapter 31 again).

Assuming you can meet the Section 197 requirements, I prefer to simply call the payments commissions rather than consulting fees, since that strengthens the position that the old (seller) corporation is still operating as a sales agency. It also helps avoid the taint of a personal holding company (see Chapter 32).

LENGTH OF PAYMENTS

Payments are usually made over a period of 5–10 years; in my opinion, anything over 10 years is too long. Anything under five years is usually quite difficult for the buyers, since you are then asking for payments of more than 20 percent of total annual commissions. As explained in Chapter 32, the multiple is one times gross annual commissions (i.e., 100 percent, for a five-year payout to one and one-half times gross annual commissions (i.e., 150 percent) for a 10-year payout. Intermediate years generally call for anything between 1 and 1.5

as the multiple. All choices are the result of the negotiations and final valuations.

DOWN PAYMENT

Since we eliminated the traditional down payment (to avoid IRS Section 1060; see Chapter 31) that usually covered office equipment, furniture, computers, and autos, my suggestion is to add that figure to the overall commission contract, with perhaps extra or higher payments in the beginning.

PERCENTAGE PAYMENTS: THE 10–15 PERCENT SOLUTION

We have had increasing success using a buyout formula that calls for a percentage of commissions *collected*, the most typical being 10–15 percent of the actual cash receipts. If commissions equal the past performance of the agency, the total payout will be in the 7–10 year range, depending on the percentage selected. We have found that a figure higher than 15 percent puts a serious strain on the average rep operation, since that 15 percent may easily represent one-third to one-half of the entire net profit that is available to pay both the new owners and the seller.

Here is an example of how to arrange payments: Assume the total contract amount is $350,000 in commissions payable to the old (seller) corporation. Of this amount, $25,000 is to be paid within 30 days of the signing of the contract and another $25,000 within 60 days. The $300,000 remaining balance is to be paid monthly as 15 percent of commissions actually received, beginning with the third month of the contract (based on present annual commission volume of $300,000 a year).

The first month the seller's corporation gets $25,000 in commissions; the second month, another $25,000; the third month, 15 percent of commissions actually received that month. Assuming the new owners (the former employees) continue the firm at the same level of commission income, in the third month (after 60 days of serious selling!) approximately $25,000 in commissions will be received by the new corporation. The payment to the old (seller) corporation will then be 15 percent of that amount, or $3,750. If the volume remains at the $300,000 level, the seller will be paid off in a little under seven years. If the volume goes up, the payoff will be faster; however, if it goes down, we need a minimum.

THE FLOOR

Percentage payment is one of my favorite ideas, but the danger lies in a sharp drop in commissions received. Without fixed minimum payments, the seller can be left with little or nothing for the month! So, continuing with the same example, we put in a floor (minimum) that provides that "the monthly commission payments (to the seller corporation) shall be 15 percent of commissions actually received, or $2,500, whichever is *higher*." In this example $2,500 is the floor, but of course you should pick your own. It's all a matter of judgment and negotiation.

What if the new owners cannot even make the minimum payment? It's time for the seller to think about taking back the company, since it's obvious that major lines have been lost and the company is deteriorating.

THE CEILING

I no longer recommend a ceiling when using a fixed sale amount coupled with the percentage payment idea. Think this through: If the buyers' commission income skyrockets, they will simply pay off the seller faster, will have their own needs met, and will get out from under whatever restrictions, provisions, and guarantees are involved in the contract (see Chapter 38). Of course, the seller should also be thrilled, since all the payments were made, and even early!

In the more unusual case, however, where the seller says no fixed dollar amount will be involved but *only* a percentage of collections for a fixed period of time, both floors and ceilings may be required. An example in this situation would be to still provide for a $25,000 payment in the first month and again in the second month. Beginning in the third month, the seller (corporation) could be paid commissions each month equal to 12 percent of those collected (by the new buyer corporation) for eight years; no dollar is mentioned.

In this example, however, either the buyer or seller could incur losses without some limits on that contract. If the buyers' monthly commissions run from $25,000 to $100,000, they really don't want to pay 12 percent of that sum (i.e., $12,000) to the seller each month for eight years. If the buyers' monthly commissions fall from $25,000 to $4,000, the seller really doesn't want $480 a month (12% × $4,000) for eight years. So, with some give-and-take, both floors and ceilings should be negotiated. In this kind of contract there will be some upside and downside risk to each side. The seller is gambling on increasing success for the new operation when she waived a fixed contract price for a percentage price; therefore, without a potential extra reward in the deal, it was a foolish thing to do. The buyers, however, don't want to share their increased success without limit. We can therefore craft something like this: Pay the seller 12 percent of commissions collected each month, up to a maximum of $6,000 (i.e., maximum monthly commission income received of $50,000 [the ceiling], since 12% × $50,000 = $6,000). Above that amount, nothing further is payable. Or, a sliding percentage of 12 percent, 10 percent, 8 percent, 6 percent, and so forth could be paid at higher and higher amounts of commissions received by the buyers' firm.

If the operation is not a success, the seller will want some downside protection, so perhaps they set a minimum (floor) payment of $2,500 a month, or $2,000, or whatever. The variations on these ideas are almost infinite, but the basic ideas are well proven and useful in almost any situation.

ROLLING AVERAGES

Here is another possibility. If you have used the 10–15 percent concept, you have automatic built-in payments that vary with the fortunes of the company. However, if you are using a fixed monthly payment, one idea is to vary them on an annual basis (you will get your total payments over a lesser or greater period of time as the income of the agency fluctuates).

For example, annual payments to the seller could be one-seventh of the average yearly commissions of the previous three years, and such annual payment amounts could be recalculated at the first of each succeeding year, using the latest (and newer) three-year average. That's an example of a three-year rolling average for a seven-year payment contract, which is where the "one-seventh" came from. Or, following the same idea, you can use the single previous year or the two most recent prior years as your base and still adjust annually for your recalculations. In any event, the averages and payments vary until the contract total is paid. Again, there is usually a floor on the monthly payments.

However, you are achieving the same result in a cleaner and easier way by simply adopting the 10–15 percent idea. That payment plan adjusts *monthly* for the actual performance of the rep firm instead of cumbersome annual calculations and recalculations. In my opinion, the percentage arrangement is the most practical method.

INFLATION AND INTEREST FACTORS

While not commonly used, I call your attention to two other ingredients that you may want to consider for the payment stew: substantial inflation and sharply rising interest rates, either or both occurring during the payout period. In effect, you may want to ask for a cost of living adjustment to the total payout.

The reference for an inflation adjustment is the Consumer Price Index (CPI) and a reference for the interest factor is the prime rate (or some other money index). However, keep in mind that if you keep packing in too many of these additional provisions (as logical as they may seem), you will gradually lift the total payments toward the point of failure. If you are in love with these two ideas, you might want to give somewhat on another point.

FRINGE BENEFITS AND COMPENSATION POOLS

In my previous book, I spend considerable time trying to make sure that the seller could still receive all the usual fringe benefits, particularly health insurance, life insurance, autos, and retirement plan coverage. That discussion is now moot by the simple arrangement of the seller keeping the old corporation (see Chapter 32). The *seller* can arrange for all those benefits and no further manipulations need be involved in the contract to sell. Times have changed.

In my last book, I devoted an entire chapter to the idea of paying the seller under my compensation pool idea, whereby the seller's expenses are all paid or reimbursed *first* and then a variable commission is paid for the balance of each monthly payment. Again, because the seller keeps the old corporation, that plan can be arranged between the seller and the old corporation, and the buyers and their new corporation are not involved at all. (See Chapter 32.)

RISK

As I mentioned earlier, the *longer* the term of the payments, the *higher* the risk. For that reason, plus the fact that the present value of money decreases as the length of payments increases, you will want a higher multiple with the longer payment periods.

I should not have to tell the average rep anything about risk, but just for the record, remember you have new worries: Will the buyers keep the lines, handle the money, run the agency efficiently and effectively? That's in *addition* to the usual market shifts, product obsolescence, principals going direct (or broke), production delays, order cancellations, principal mergers, sales manager problems and changes, and so forth. You're not selling a shoe store and taking it back if the buyers don't make the payments; in your case, what you take back may not even resemble what you sold!

THE PRESENT VALUE OF MONEY

You should understand just a tad about this concept. If I repay you the $100 I borrowed an hour ago, you got back exactly what you loaned me. But if you lend me $100 and I don't pay you back for a year, you have lost the earnings on that $100 for 12 months. If you can earn 8 percent a year on your money, what you really got back was only equivalent to $92 (rounded), since you have lost the interest that you *could have earned* plus any interest earned on that *interest* during the year (if the interest were earned daily and compounded monthly, like a money market fund).

Following the same logic, if you sell your agency for $300,000, payable over five years, you are not getting the same dollar value as if you were paid $300,000 *today*. You do not have that $300,000 to invest and earn a yield on for a full five years. Instead, each month you are only receiving one-sixtieth of the amount, which is all that you can invest. This concept is called "the present value of money." In our first example, the present value of that $100 was only $92.

To pick an extreme example, if you can earn 8 percent on your money and you were to sell your rep agency for $300,000 with just one single payment due at the end of nine years, you have really sold your rep firm for only 50 percent, or $150,000. That's because the present value of $100, at 8 percent, for an entire nine years is $50. Don't kid yourself about how much you are getting when you sell your business; consider the actual value of the money with extended payments.

Don't jump to conclusions! Some readers' first reactions will be, "Now that I understand what I'm really losing, I'm going to double the asking price for my agency!" Wrong! The formula of 1 to 1½ times annual commissions has evolved because that valuation *takes into account* the present value of money. If all rep firms were sold for one all-cash *immediate* payment, the most typical valuation might be 50–75 percent of a year's commission income. Said another way, if you were selling your rep firm for $300,000, payable monthly over seven years, and I offered you a single cash payment of $200,000 right now, would you take it? You had better grab the $200,000!

Just for reference, here are some present value calculations to consider and reflect upon (note how the *more* you could have earned, the *less* the present value and the *longer* the term, the *less* the present value):

TABLE 37–1
Values for $100 at Various Rates of Earnings

Year	*8%*	*10%*	*12%*
1	$92.26	$90.90	$89.30
2	85.70	82.60	79.70
3	79.40	75.10	71.20
4	73.50	68.30	63.60
5	68.10	62.10	56.70
6	60.00	56.40	50.70
7	58.30	51.30	45.20
8	54.00	46.70	40.40
9	50.00	42.40	36.10
10	46.30	8.60	32.20

THE REPOSSESSION TRIGGER

After you sell a shoe store, you could look to inventory, fixtures, and perhaps accounts receivable if you had to take the business back. In retaking a rep firm, you will generally end up with only the unpaid bills! Of course, there will be far fewer lines remaining or you would not have had to repossess.

My advice is to understand how fragile and unique the rep business is that you are selling, and to be prepared to move fast if you must take it back. Accordingly, I recommend that you have another commission floor *not* for purposes of your monthly payment, but for purposes of taking the business back from the buyers. Let me emphasize that this may not necessarily be the same figure as the previous monthly payment floor; it may even be a higher number!

This second floor is really a "repossession trigger" amount. If you continue to wait after commissions have dropped, say, 50 percent, *even if* the buyers continue to make the monthly payments (perhaps from borrowing or personal resources), the less you will end up with when they eventually default. Set a realistic and not too low trigger amount (maybe 50 percent or 60 percent of present commissions), and if the business drops below that point (for perhaps a straight 90 days or so), you have the right to repossess the agency. By then you would be able to judge that the employees just couldn't make it as owners, operators, and entrepreneurs, but you would still have a somewhat viable business and a fighting chance to bring it back up to where it was. If you wait until commissions drop 98 percent from the time of the sale, you could indeed end up with no lines but a great collection of unpaid bills!

Now let's turn to probably the key idea of all: when selling your rep firm, advance planning the sale.

Chapter Thirty-Six

Selling Your Rep Firm: Advance Planning

YA GOTTA' DO IT!

The average Japanese company has business plans that span at least the next 20 years, while large American companies plan about one to three years in the future. (Unfortunately, the average rep-owner's future business plans are usually about where to have lunch!) If I had to select the single biggest reason why reps are not able to sell their firms or why they sell them unsuccessfully, it's because they did not start the process of sale and succession *soon enough*. By now we should all agree that a rep business is a special kind of service business, with special problems and a fragile business structure. You cannot wake up on a Wednesday morning, decide you've had enough, call in your top salesperson and declare, "Hey, kid, ya wanna' take over the business starting next Monday? I've had it, and I'll be leaving next Tuesday." The "kid" will gladly take over the business next Monday, but within about 120 days you probably will have to take back the pitiful remains of a once successful rep firm.

A number of factors enter into a successful sale of your agency. The most important rule of thumb is to actually sell the agency about five years before you want to retire. You simply must stay around after the sale and remain *partially active through most or all the payoff period*. This in turn might require you to begin your advance planning, negotiations, and discussions about seven years before you plan to completely retire. (And, by actually remaining and *rendering services*, the buyer can still obtain *immediate* tax deductions for payments to you despite Section 197.)

In the first few years, the seller must maintain high visibility to both principals and customers. Further, particularly in the first year or two, you absolutely must guide and counsel the buyers. The buyers must be trained to *manage:* they already know how to sell.

It's virtually impossible to sell your sales agency to anyone but your employees or your partner. You can merge with another rep firm, or you can sell to another rep firm if you stay on, but except for the rare case you cannot simply sell to strangers and walk away. Why? Because, to quote an old line of mine, "The principle problem is the principal problem."

The principals must be sold on the ownership change, even more carefully than a major customer. You must reassure them and tell them the only two things they ever want to hear about: *continuity and the prospect of higher sales.* You can reassure them of continuity by saying something like this: "You already know Joe, who is buying into the agency. He's been our top salesman for the past eight years, and you have dealt with him many times. Of course I'll still be around, working with Joe for many years to come." And, as for higher sales you can say: "There are significant prospects for higher sales, since Joe is now an additional and major owner. Not only will he work harder, but he will probably start adding new salespeople, and it looks like the agency will expand."

If *you are still there* and they already know and have been dealing with the individuals that will eventually own the company, the principal won't be frightened by a change in ownership. They'll also figure Joe is pumping new money into the company, which is certainly a plus for future expansion and increased sales. There will be no principle problem at all if you sell your principals!

But note, *principals won't accept inferior people as the new owners!* You, the seller, must develop some strong middle management individuals as candidates for the buyout. These people should have broad experience dealing with the major principals, they should be officers of the company, they should have demonstrated management ability, and they should be trained in supervising others. It's a given that they already know how to sell, but don't ever forget those most important principal contacts.

Understand that the purchase price will really come from the future earnings of the agency; therefore, you must help safeguard the future of the company in every way possible! With this statement in mind, both the purchase price and the time span for the payout must be *reasonable,* or you have set the deal up for future failure. It does no good to structure a sale for 300 percent of a year's commissions, payable over 24 months, when the buyers can never make those payments. Or to structure a sale so that the buyer loses all or current tax deductions for payments to the seller (e.g., for the capital stock of your corporation or the 15 year deductible goodwill) when payments should have been mostly made with currently tax-deductible dollars.

CASE STUDY #1

An unusual individual, who had previously bought two sales agencies at different times, structured a deal to sell out to his employees and brought it to us to critique (he was not a client). Mostly I just reviewed it with admiration.

The agency was valued at one time annual commission income, which was $720,000 in this case. The buyout was 10 years. The seller only wanted to stay around two more years, and he felt that he had already taken care of evident continuity. He also felt that the transition, as far as the principals were concerned, was already in place. For services that truly were to be rendered over the next two years, he would be compensated as follows. His current salary was $7,000 a month. For the next year he would work four days a week, and his salary would be $5,600 a month (80% × $7,000), plus normal expenses. In the second year, he would work three days a week, and his salary would be $4,200 a month (60% × $7,000), plus normal expenses.

The buyout would begin immediately, rather than at the end of two years (this is an optional decision that you may or may not want to follow). To prevent too large a cash drain, his buyout payments were to be on a sliding scale as a percentage of commission income actually collected (very clever): Year one, 5 percent, Year two, 7 percent, and Years 3–10 at 11 percent or another 88 percent. (This totals 100 percent.)

He also provided for floors, ceilings, and a repossession trigger (see Chapter 35). The ceiling for the entire 10 years was 25 percent over existing commission income. Since the existing commission income was $60,000 a month (one-twelfth of $720,000), this meant that if monthly commissions increased to $75,000 (25 percent more) that year's percentage rate of payment would apply, and he would be paid more than was originally anticipated. If commissions exceeded $75,000 a month, he would not receive any of that excess, but any higher payments to him on collections between $60,000 and $75,000 a month were an extra bonus and did not reduce the base purchase price of $720,000. Thus, if business was sensational for the entire 10 years, he could be paid up to 25 percent more than $720,000, or another $180,000. His rationale was that if the business in fact increased up to 25 percent it would be substantially due to his efforts over the next two years and the existing goodwill with principals and customers that the company had built up in the past.

The floor was 15 percent less than the existing $60,000 a month for the entire 10 years. Any such lower payments between $60,000 and $51,000 a month ($60,000 − 15% = $51,000) were accepted in full as a lower purchase price for the business, and the $720,000 would be adjusted downward. Thus, if business was terrible for the entire 10 years, he would only be paid $612,000 ($720,000 − $108,000 [15%] = $612,000) as full payment. So, he shares in the good times, and he shares (somewhat less) in the bad times. There is a good argument for less penalty on the downside (15 percent) than reward on the upside (25 percent). If the sales agency was steadily growing until the employees took over, any substantial drop in commission income is probably their fault to a considerable extent, so the seller takes the hit up to 15 percent and no further.

To sum up, he could receive total payments of up to $900,000 maximum ($720,000 + 25% [$180,000] = $900,000) if things were sensational. He could receive total payments of $612,000 if things were dreadful. Or, he probably would be paid somewhere in between.

Both the floors and ceilings were calculated on an annual basis and there were *no carryforwards* of money owing into the next year. It was felt that 12 months was long enough to average out monthly variations in collections and sales, while to carry these figures forward for a full 10 years would get very cumbersome and complex (this was one way to do it but of course not the only way; you could incorporate these formulas over the full 10 years, 5 years, or whatever you choose).

The repossession trigger was a 20 percent drop in commissions collected for three months in a row. In other words, if the monthly collections were less than $48,000 ($60,000 − 20% [$12,000] = $48,000) for a consecutive 90 days, the seller could take back the business.

A final clause was to the effect that any lines lost in the first six months of the buyout period would be used to reduce the total buyout figure, valued at one time annual commissions. The rationale was that any lines lost that *quickly* were probably the fault or result of the seller's previous operation. Very clever!

We added the following ideas to the proposed arrangement:

• We easily convinced the seller to add our idea of establishing a new corporation for the buyers (we gave him all the details from Chapter 32). He was not familiar with this idea, and he loved it!

• We suggested an increase in his monthly salary equivalent to now be paid as "commissions" from the new corporation to the old corporation for the next two years because his travel, entertainment, and auto expenses would not have to be paid by the new corporation, and the new corporation would be saving all Social Security/Medicare taxes and other payroll tax costs that otherwise would have been paid by their buyers' corporation. The two sides settled on an additional $1,500 a month for that initial two-year period.

CASE STUDY #2

One of the most successful sales of a rep firm that I have ever encountered went like this. The sale was planned about seven years before it took place. The sole buyer was the top salesperson in the company. Five years before the sale he was made president of the company, and the owner moved up to chairman of the board. For those five years, the buyer not only ran the company on an increasing basis, but continually enlarged his dealings with all the principals. At the end of the five years, the sale actually took place. The sale was structured with a new corporation for the buyer and the old one was retained by the seller, and they used my idea of transferring the old name to the new corporation. It was announced to the principals that the president of the company was *a* new owner of the company (*not* that his ownership was total; that came out gradually over a few more years), and that the seller was, of course, remaining with the company in his present position as chairman of the board. All the principals and customers just yawned and said, "So what else is new? That's not really any kind of a change."

In spite of all the advance planning, the seller did indeed stay on even after the sale was completed. He swapped offices with the new owner so the buyer was now seated in the largest "power" office, but the seller stayed around and continued to be visible to principals and customers. Then, about two years after the sale the seller really started cutting down his time at the rep firm. Today he tells me that he just stops in about once a week to get his mail and see what's new. Every principal and customer probably says now and then, "Whatever happened to good old what's-his-name?"

Consider this: The sale was planned about seven years before it took place, and the buyer stayed around on a significant basis for about two years after the actual sale. So the highly successful changeover took about nine years from planning to execution to actual retirement. Oh yes, the firm was a very large rep firm when sold but under the new owner it is about 25–40 percent larger than before, and the seller easily got all his money.

CASE STUDY #3

I would like to use my own personal experience as another example of how to sell a service business. This story has a twist in that I did not retire, but rather sold 50 percent of my CPA firm to another person, so I'll tell you how to take in a partner rather than make a total sale. All the facts are true, and nothing has been changed.

About 10 years ago, I was the sole owner of a small but very successful CPA firm. I was far from thoughts of retiring, but the firm was too large for one owner: vacations were almost impossible, going out of town for a few days to give a speech was a major trauma, and the thought of possible illness on my part for any time kept me in terror of the consequences. So, I decided it was time for a partner. After a serious executive search and many interviews, I selected Morry Spector, who is my partner to this day.

How did we structure things? We spent a lot of money in legal fees, most of it covering eventualities if the deal did not go through, and the rest covering future arrangements (I had had a bad experience in Chicago with a 10 percent partner). Then, as further protection, we had a sixth-month "engagement," during which time Morry was simply an employee of the firm. Throughout that six-month period, either of us could cancel the deal without giving cause or reason, but simply because we had changed our minds or just because we felt like it. Neither of us did so, although I confess I really had to make some early ego adjustments in sharing my practice (since virtually all the clients were mine).

After the six months, we went forward with the deal. I sold Morry 50 percent of the stock of the company for a reasonable amount (I practice what I preach and zero out the corporation each year, so the net worth was nominal). The smartest thing we did was to structure a 5-year "buy in," during which time our salaries were disproportionate. However, instead of using a fixed *dollar* amount, we used a *ratio*. In our case, we used 2:1 as the salary ratio, no matter what the dollar amounts might be. In other words, if $1,500 in profits were to be distributed as salary, I got $1,000 and Morry got $500. This arrangement went on for five years.

At the end of the five-year period, I was supposed to cut my hours back (I wanted more time to write), and our salaries would then be equal. The firm would essentially be run by my partner, just as I had run it alone, but we would provide back up for each other and I would have a nice income for less work. But it didn't work out that way! At the end of the five years, the billings of the firm almost exactly doubled, and we were *each* as busy as I had been five years earlier! No complaints, but we never dreamed that this could happen. No doubt part of that growth was because I had more freedom to prospect for new clients because existing business was always covered by my partner. The same thing might happen in your case.

We now rewrite salary arrangements annually. Compensation is still a *ratio*, but based approximately on each individual's billings of the previous year. After 10 years, we now have more than 100 current rep clients, and Morry knows everything about the rep business and more about sales agents than any other CPA in the country (except possibly yours truly). But we are already close to a dead heat, and he's still *gaining* on me every day!. To quote Jesse Owens, "Don't look back, because somebody might be gaining on you!" But in this case, it makes me proud.

So, if I were to leave tomorrow, the firm would continue as in the past. Our rep clients are perfectly comfortable dealing with my partner, and today he and I are virtually interchangeable in the eyes of most of our clients. By now we think alike, talk alike, counsel clients alike, and tell the same jokes. In fact, Morry has even taken over some of my speaking engagements. (I gave him all the speeches in Detroit, Cleveland, Pittsburgh, St. Louis, and Milwaukee, while I only kept Hawaii, Palm Beach, Acapulco, London, Paris, Scottsdale, and Palm Springs.) Morry is more than 20 years younger than I am, which of course is another assurance of future continuity for our clients (just as you reps must offer the promise of continuity to your principals).

I can't tell you the end of this story, since there are no present plans for either my retirement or a third partner. However, if I am suddenly called to that great CPA roundup in the sky, it will be with the sure knowledge that the firm will continue on into the far, far future, and will surely prosper as long as there are sales reps and the IRS!

CONCLUSION

Here are some of the lessons of this chapter. Follow these rules so you'll be able to *get your money from the sale of your agency:*

- You'll need from five to seven years of advance planning.
- Sell to your employees or partner (to sell to anyone else can only be done with great difficulty, absent a merger or a sale where you stay on).
- Stay on after the sale to train, counsel, supervise, and help everybody involved. Continuity for principals and customers is a must. The buyers need your expertise, and the buyers can get *current* tax deductions for their payments to you (Code Section 197). Remember, the more successful the buyer, the better off *you'll* be!

Chapter Thirty-Seven

Selling Your Rep Firm: Acquisitions and Mergers

While by far the most common change in ownership is to sell to your employees (including any partner), we have been increasingly involved in a considerable number of mergers of sales agencies, as well as some outright sales to other rep firms. (These activities seem to increase during recession times and decrease when business gets better.) In several cases, what was publicly announced as a merger was actually an acquisition (purchase) of one rep firm (usually larger) by another (usually smaller) agency.

ACQUISITIONS

The most usual problem in an acquisition is competing lines, and this issue is often solved in advance with a smaller line or two sometimes being dropped. Then, as long as the principals can be satisfied, the acquisition (although rarely called that) can go forward. To refresh your memory, there are two key points to selling any principal, whether it be a sale, merger, or acquisition. As long as you offer your principals both *continuity* and the prospect of *increased sales*, you can move forward. Remember, "the principle problem is the principal problem." Solve that and almost any two-line compatible rep firms can structure a successful acquisition (assuming, of course, the same or related industries).

The compensation package for the seller is usually composed of two parts:

1. Payment for the lines that are successfully brought into the combined firm, usually as a multiple of gross commission income and with 100 percent of one year's commissions being the most typical figure.

2. Additional compensation for services that will actually be rendered for the year or two the seller will really be working. If this "working" is only a fiction for public consumption and in fact the

seller will only "be around as needed," this payment can be eliminated.

Here is an example of a compensation package in an acquisition. The seller brings in $200,000 in annual commission income and agrees to actually work in the business for two more years to make sure all lines are held and the deal really works. There are two alternatives: the seller can be paid only for services during the first two years and then for the lines over the following five years, or the seller can be paid a combined amount for the lines and services together over the next five years.

Under the first option, she could be paid, say, $60,000 a year for services actually rendered (plus applicable expenses, or better yet use my combined compensation pool idea) in the first and second year and then $40,000 a year for the next five years (5 × $40,000 = $200,000). Under the second option, we could aggregate the $120,000 (2 × $60,000) for services actually rendered in the first and second year with the $200,000 for the lines for a total of $320,000 ($120,000 + $200,000). That total could be paid evenly over five years at the rate of $64,000 a year (5 × $64,000 = $320,000). Or the total could be paid unevenly over anywhere from six to 10 years, depending on the age of the seller, the motives of the seller, the negotiations, the financial strength of the buyer, and so forth.

CAVEAT

Don't forget Code Section 197! You must keep in mind that payments when *no* services are being rendered are only tax-deductible over 15 years, *regardless* of the length of the payments! (See Chapter 31.)

All the same ideas, structure, and safeguards discussed in all the other chapters on selling your agency can be applied to a purchase of one rep firm by another. Conceptually, an acquisition is very similar to the problems and goals of selling an agency to employees. Even the valuations and the principle consideration of solving any potential problems with the principals are similar.

For public consumption, all the trappings of a merger may be displayed (although this varies with the motives behind each sale):

- The name of the firm may be changed to include that of the seller.
- The seller may become an officer of the buyer corporation (typically vice president).
- The seller usually has a prominent office and high visibility to customers and principals.

- The announcements to the principals, customers, and the industry highlight the fact of the "merger" and all the implied advantages.

KEY POINT

The seller and the buyer should travel together in advance of the actual sale to visit all the major principals of the seller. This is to both get their blessing and to introduce the buyer. At such meetings, all the selling talents of both individuals should be turned on: sell your principals or the deal will fail!

Reread Chapter 32 as the seller should *keep* the old corporation. Then all the payments already discussed could be made to that corporation for reasons and advantages explained. This eliminates down payments, asset purchases, buying commissions receivable, and provides all the other benefits already discussed in that chapter. It's a big win-win and simplifies the entire acquisition to a tremendous degree!

As the seller, don't be insensitive to your employees! Of course there will be the usual problems of friction between the employees of the buyer and the employees acquired from the seller. Be prepared for friction, disagreements, ego conflicts, and even resignations; these problems will invariably occur. For example, each firm has a top salesperson, but now we have one combined firm. Further, employees of the buyer firm will always tend to act and think superior, since they "bought" the other firm. Sales ability, empathy, knowledge, experience, vigilance, watchfulness, and stroking are required.

As usual, money can frequently help. One of our larger rep-clients acquired a smaller but still substantial sales agency. The seller had a top salesperson, but the buyers not only had their own top salesperson, but that person was an owner-partner as well. The seller's top salesperson was thinking about leaving until the buyers raised his salary from $80,000 to $110,000 a year. He not only agreed to stay, but years later he is still there and has integrated perfectly into the buyer firm.

Even the seller should come in for special consideration. It's a real trauma to not be the boss and to suddenly be in a subordinate position. Reps are rugged individualists, and they start their own agencies so they can be boss. Abruptly, years later, again they are *not*. Some special solicitude and concern is called for.

Hopefully, synergism will take place at some point after an acquisition or merger. In other words, the combined firm will be more successful than each of the separate firms were before. As an illustration, if the buyer firm was doing $600,000 in commission income and the seller firm was doing $200,000, hopefully a combined firm with combined strengths and combined lines would shortly reach $900,000, rather than $800,00 in commission income.

MERGERS

Again, the *principal* problem is the one that must be solved first. Eliminating competing lines is a given, or the merger cannot go forward. My advice is for the two owners to personally visit each significant principal and *sell* them! Remember, *continuity* and the prospect of *increased sales* are the watchwords! It's a little easier to "sell" the principals in this case, because nobody really intends to leave the combined operation, even after a year or two.

The big difference between an acquisition and a merger, from a psychological standpoint, is that in a merger all the new owners of the merged firm must get along with one another indefinitely! Successful salespeople have big egos, by definition, which doesn't make the sudden sharing of power and authority an easy thing to accomplish. In effect, you have a "business marriage," and a new business "partnership" is created, no matter *what* the legal form may be. Additionally, you may have all the employee problems discussed under acquisitions. *Customer* problems as a result of a merger rarely occur, however, and generally they can be solved by reassigning salespeople.

So, to sum up, the nonmonetary merger issues are:

- Eliminating competing lines.
- Selling the principals.
- Sharing the merged ownership power and authority.
- Solving potential employee problems.

But before you jump into the merger, let me suggest a short delay before it's finalized. After all, don't you think it's always a good idea to get engaged first, before you go on your honeymoon? I know that may sound a little old-fashioned, but I'm not preaching morality in this case—just practicality. So first get an engagement ring and wear it a little while before you head for Niagara Falls.

THE ENGAGEMENT

I strongly believe in a trial period in the case of any merger, and I would suggest 3–6 months. During this period, either side can back out of the merger without giving any reason! This is an important point: You *don't* have to justify why you are calling off the merger. No arguments, no name-calling.

During the engagement period, each side to the merger carefully preserves their old corporations. Sometimes a "joint account" or a temporary partnership of the two corporations is used, or each corporation pays its pro rata share of expenses. The commissions may go into a new account and the joint expenses are paid first, after which the balance of the commissions are paid to each of the old corporations. Usually each side makes their own payroll payments, primarily to save payroll tax costs and convenience in payroll reporting, so any disproportionate payrolls are compensated in the commission split.

The average rep will shudder, "Complications that don't increase sales. Who needs 'em!" Consider the worst-case alternatives. You fold the two old corporations, form a new one, merge the entire operation from day one, and then find out that you cannot possibly live one day longer with your new "partner," his terrible employees, and his lousy lines! Just see what it will *then* cost you in legal fees, accounting fees, lost lines, lost face, lost selling time, litigation, embarrassment, stress, and so forth. All of which, thanks to our great legal system in this country, could then drag on for years!

THE PRENUPTIAL AGREEMENT

Assume that two agencies that are *approximately* equal in commission income are merging; you will never find two exactly the same, and even if you did there would still be differences in quality of the lines, longevity and security of the lines, principal contracts, granting of vested interests and other termination provisions by the principals, and so forth. There's a lot to negotiate, but let's first assume that we have a 50–50 merger.

The agreement would then provide for:

- An engagement period with the cancellation provisions and the temporary arrangements in accounting, money, banking, payments, and so forth, as discussed.
- The formation of a new corporation after the engagement term expires, with each of the owners in the new firm owning equal shares of the stock. Compensation, expenses, and perks are (usually) identical for each owner.
- The retention of their old corporations and collection of their previously earned commissions by each party.
- The fact that the lines go into the new corporation.
- The donation of the assets of the old corporations (office equipment, furniture, and autos) to the new corporation, or the acquisition of new assets. If the assets contributed are approximately equal, no equalization is required. If necessary, the donors can

be paid with extra compensation. If autos are leased, the new corporation takes over those payments (see Chapter 2).

- Legal safeguards, provisions, and protections. This final part of the agreement is by far the biggest portion. Of course, the key problem of the "3-Ds" must be covered: *d*eath, *d*isability, and *d*isagreement. Any of these can occur after the honeymoon period and must always be covered in the contract.

In a typical type of agreement, you might have "3-D" provisions something like this:

- **Death.** Each merger partner will carry sufficient life insurance (owned either individually or by their old corporation) on the other merger partner to buy out the surviving spouse of the deceased at a stated and fixed price. This price, hopefully, is about equal to the amount of life insurance proceeds.
- **Disability.** For three months of disability, the disabled owner receives full salary. For the second three months, the disabled owner receives one-half salary. A disability policy is purchased (either by a corporation or individually) with a six-month waiting period. After six months, the disability payments begin as the salary ends. If the owner is disabled for more than one year, the buyout provisions kick in, exactly as provided in the next section.
- **Disagreement.** This is the tough one! If the two partners split and each takes back exactly the lines brought to the merger, no problem and no payments. It's when some of the lines brought in by one stay with the *other* after a disagreement and demerger. Additionally, what about *new* lines brought in after the merger? It's usually done as a matter of arithmetic and negotiation. Say I keep one of your lines that pays $50,000 a year, and we demerge. Payment to you might be figured at $50,000, payable at $10,000 a year for five years—exactly as if you sold me the line. However, if we jointly bring in a $50,000 line *after* the merger and it stays with me, then I might pay you *one-half* (say $25,000 over five years), using the logic that our joint efforts got the line in the first place.

Of course the "3-D" suggestions and examples are just that, and there are no hard and fast rules. Use these to generate your own ideas, but, conceptually, these provisions run along the general lines I have outlined. Additionally, there will be a competent lawyer who will add whatever she feels is necessary (usually quite a bit), following the broad outlines of these merger concepts.

To further expand on the "Disagreement" problem, the contract should cover all such disagreement matters as:

- How the lines shall be divided in the event the merger fails.
- What compensation, if any, shall be paid between the parties, based on the line split. Compensation can include payment to one party *not* getting an original line back, because the principal now chooses to stay with the *other* party.
- How employees and assets of the corporation are divided.
- Who keeps, or what happens to, the new merger corporation.
- Who is responsible for leases, bank loans, future IRS audits (both any additional taxes and the costs of representation), payroll taxes, other liabilities, and final professional fees.
- Provisions for arbitration, rather than endless litigation.
- Who pays the extra legal and accounting fees incurred as a result of the split-up.
- Any covenants, warranties, guarantees between the parties, and possible noncompetition agreements.

Next, assume what I call a "permanent unequal merger." One rep is bringing $600,000 in annual commission income to the merger, and the other rep is contributing $300,000. In this example, the stock would usually be issued two-thirds to the first rep and one-third to the other (i.e., a ratio of 2:1, in proportion to their lines), but the tricky part is compensation. Just because one rep controls two-thirds of the business does not necessarily mean that compensation (and expenses, fringes, etc.) should be in a ratio of 2:1. This point is major and negotiable: If they function in the future as equal partners, with equal responsibilities, equal efforts, and equal success, they might very well draw identical salaries, expenses, and fringes. There is no fixed rule of thumb.

Then there is an "unequal merger that will be equalized." Assume the same $600,000 and $300,000 in commissions. The combined agency will be grossing $900,000. If each side brought in one-half the combined total, or $450,000, to the merged operation, the merger could be equal from day one. One, however, has a $150,000 shortfall. To equalize the stockholdings in the new corporation, the larger rep is thus "owed" $150,000, which is usually paid in the form of higher compensation to the larger rep contributor. The rep could be paid an extra $30,000 a year for five years, or the larger rep could be compensated for five years at a *ratio* of 2:1 over the smaller rep, whatever those amounts might actually be. After five years, both receive *equal* compensation. Frequently the larger rep retains voting control until the disproportion is paid, but sometimes not. Any combination of the two ideas could be put into effect, or whatever you feel is fair, and you can negotiate accordingly.

In both the "unequal" cases just discussed, all the other "equal" guidelines, ideas, and suggestions apply when drawing up the actual agreement. Just the "nonequalization" or "eventual equalization" requires special conditions, but the rest of the merger ideas are viable and should always be considered and factored into the merger agreement.

THE WEDDING

Ask anyone that has ever been married and they will assure you that their problems did not disappear on the day of the wedding. Notwithstanding an engagement period, despite a prenuptial agreement, regardless of the beautiful wedding, they now have to live together! Having a partner can be like having a second wife (only you see more of this one). And, too, expectations often exceed reality.

Now is the time for much give-and-take, particularly if you have never had a partner before. As mentioned, strong egos abound among owner-reps. A power struggle is not the way to begin a merger, and it could quickly end it! My advice is to be considerate of each other and work at the merger as hard as you ever worked at a successful marriage; this advice is perhaps as important as anything else in this chapter.

As an aside, I have rarely found that the merger of two unprosperous sales agencies to result in one strong rep firm. A merger doesn't seem to cure the problem, perhaps because there is no real management or administrative ability in either firm, or perhaps because the lines themselves are poor.

THE DIVORCE

The good news: If one of every two marriages in this country ends in divorce, I would estimate that only one out of ten rep mergers fail (and virtually no properly done acquisitions). That's still a scary 10 percent for all you merger candidates to worry about.

KEY POINT

My advice here relates to the merger agreement. The more careful and complete the contract is, the less likelihood of trouble to begin with. If a problem arises between the merger-owners and the solution is embodied in the contract, that fact, in and of itself, usually reduces the friction between the parties. Instead of arguing who is right or wrong, everybody calms down. And if one partner is contemplating a rash or unwise course of action that is covered and controlled by the merger accord, the problem may never begin. The *more* that is included and dealt with in the merger concord, the *less* likelihood that the provisions will ever have to be enforced.

If you do fall into that unlucky 10 percent, the more stipulations and provisos relating to disagreement the less painful the divorce will be! As mentioned earlier, that disagreement section of the agreement should cover such details as splitting lines (or not), compensation therefore, and so forth.

KEY POINT

In many cases, the old premerger corporations are kept, sometimes inactive or sometimes for new uses. They provide a wonderful fallback in the event the engagement is called off or later if there is a divorce. In California, it costs $800 a year (tax-deductible) to keep an inactive corporation alive, in good standing, and with the corporate name legally protected, which is frequently a worthwhile investment.

CONCLUSION

Well, we covered sales and acquisitions of rep firms, plus equal mergers, and two kinds of unequal mergers. We also ran the gamut of engagement, prenuptial agreement, wedding, and divorce. This is a chapter for the rep: seller, buyer, mergeror and mergeree. Take it all to heart, but do it very carefully.

Chapter Thirty-Eight

Selling Your Rep Firm: Protection

GUARANTEES AND COLLATERAL

Let's conclude this section of the book with assorted ideas designed to protect the seller from some of the damage that *failure* of the sale of the agency could cause. Most of these suggestions are legal in nature, and you should look to your lawyer for more thoughts than are included in this chapter.

The seller should look for personal guarantees or collateral to protect his position if there is default. If the entire sale fails, the seller will always suffer, but not as much if prior arrangements provide the impetus for the other party to see that the sale remains a success. It's the same thing the bankers do to make sure loans are repaid; the more the buyers may be hurt by their default, the less inclined they are to default.

Here are some ideas and suggestions to protect you. Keep in mind that the more you have in place, the better.

- Hold the stock of the newly formed buyer corporation as collateral for the sale.
- Structure an up-front, nonreturnable payment as initial extra payments under the consulting agreement. (In effect, this is a "nonrefundable deposit" or payment for an "option" to buy.)
- Obtain personal guarantees of the buyers and personal guarantees of family members of the buyers. Wealthy parents and parents-in-law are ideal, but wealthy brothers and sisters are equally good. Remember, the more, the better.
- Hold second mortgages on the buyers' homes. Request collateral, such as stocks, bonds, and so forth, pledged by the buyers, their relatives, their friends, or anybody you can grab.
- Structure a separate commission floor that triggers an entirely new board of directors appointed by the seller. Be on the board of directors of the new buyer corporation.

- Place restrictions on the buyers'salaries, expenses, autos, and so forth.

LIFE INSURANCE ON THE BUYERS

The sale of your rep firm presents a perfect opportunity for the business use of life insurance. It's virtually a given that the seller should require life insurance on the buyers. Life insurance usually represents the only chance for the seller to collect all the money in the event of death of a buyer. The seller usually collects the insurance proceeds and walks away, and all future payments due are canceled. Whatever happens to the agency after that is of no concern to the seller, who has been fully paid. If one of two or three buyers dies, the seller collects a proportionate percentage of the selling price, and the remaining buyers continue only *their* share of the payments.

The buyers are invariably younger and life insurance is generally cheap, so this is a perfect place to buy term insurance (and you only want insurance for a limited term equal to the payment period). The cost is usually insignificant. You can, if you want to, buy declining-value term that will match the decreasing amount the buyers owe, but the cost of insurance to cover the time span of the payment period is so nominal, I rarely recommend that you even bother with declining-value.

Corporate Alternative Minimum Tax

It is generally no longer as practical for either the old or new corporation to own and be beneficiary of life insurance. In very simple terms, the corporation may pay an Alternative Minimum Tax (AMT) of 20 percent on 75 percent of life insurance proceeds. Although there is no regular income tax due, if a corporation collects $500,000 in life insurance the AMT would be $75,000 ($500,000 × 75% × 20% = $75,000, ignoring the $40,000 AMT "exemption," which might be used up by other AMT items).

The alternatives are for the corporation to carry *more* life insurance than the face amount of the sale contract, so that the net *after* the AMT is equal to the amount owing, or for the seller to buy that life insurance on the buyers *personally*, especially since those costs are usually minimal. When the insurance is purchased individually, pursuant to a buy-sell agreement, all the individuals have an insurable interest in each other and any insurance proceeds collected individually (properly structured) will be tax-free.

LIFE INSURANCE ON THE SELLER

Life insurance on the seller's life may not always be necessary. The time to buy this type of insurance is in a situation where the death of the seller will seriously damage the rep firm and thus the buyers. This is usually true only if the transition to the new owners was not started some years before the actual sale. In such cases, the buyers may not be able to hold all the lines or may not yet have the ability to run the company without the aid of the founder-seller. Then they usually *do* need insurance on the seller. However, sellers are usually older and may be uninsurable. Any insurance is therefore much more expensive than insurance on the buyers.

Because of the much higher insurance cost, we always recommend that insurance on the seller be purchased individually by the buyers, which avoids the corporate AMT and thus eliminates any need for additional insurance coverage to pay that tax. Of course, it's tempting to be able to pay off the surviving spouse of the seller with the insurance and just be done. The buyers and seller will have to weigh the factors in each case and make individual decisions with the aid of their CPAs, lawyers, and other financial advisers.

Because of the usually high cost of insuring the seller, buying decreasing (i.e., declining) insurance coverage to match the payments should be considered. It's even possible, because of the limited term of coverage, that decreasing term insurance for that short time span may be cheaper than decreasing ordinary life insurance. Insuring the seller involves more time, effort, shopping, and consulting than insuring the buyer.

Finally, the surviving spouse of the seller will receive any insurance payments estate tax free because of the unlimited marital deduction (see Chapter 23), but such payments could be classified as "income in respect to a decedent" and subject to income tax. However, I feel that the situation could be avoided by naming the spouse the direct beneficiary of the policy purchased by the buyers. Life insurance proceeds start out, by definition, being income tax free; it's only in connection with a business that the proceeds might be considered income taxable. So, if the seller is to be insured, both sides should get careful advice on how to exactly structure the deal.

HINDSIGHT

We all have perfect 20/20 hindsight. These chapters on selling your rep firm are designed to give you the *foresight* not to regret the sale and to avoid as many mistakes as possible. Here is some of our hindsight based on our own involvement in many sales, a survey I did for the Electronics Representatives Association, and some informal surveys of our own. The biggest seller mistakes were:

• Too long a term for the buyout. Nobody was ever happy if the payments were longer than 10 years; That seems to be the absolute maximum amount of time. Two sellers who each used 20 years were quite bitter.

• Lack of floors and ceilings. Most, if not all, the sellers we interviewed regretted not having such provisions.

• Too low a selling price. Apparently some sellers sold on very extended terms and still used a multiple of one times a year's commission income, or even less.

• Difficult selling terms. You have to drag this one out of some sellers, since they don't want to admit it was their fault. Some structured their deals, so that the buyers could *not* deduct the payments (e.g., for company stock or other capital assets), in which case the buyers were trying to pay with after-tax dollars. Some sellers set the total valuation too high (e.g., three times a year's commission income). (I discussed the seller being in a control position and the mistake of taking advantage in Chapter 34.)

• Potential problems not covered in the contract or not covered in great enough detail. Said another way, many of the seller-reps, with the typical salesperson's impatience and disdain for detail, just brushed aside many of the safeguards and virtually went on a handshake, that is, a very short and simplified contract. After all, the buyers were the "trusted employees" of the seller. Hopefully, the preceding chapters have taught you that your entire financial future is at stake, and you simply cannot do that.

CONCLUSION

Use this hindsight as your own foresight. My last comments are indeed a fitting way to end these eight chapters on selling your rep firm. In Chapters 31–38, I've told you how to sell your agency; this last section is based on actual experiences of how *not* to do it. I expect all readers, sellers or buyers, to structure an absolutely perfect sale, with flawless and impeccable planning and unlimited success! *GO FOR IT!*

Chapter Thirty-Nine

A Look Back

THE CHAPTER FLOW

When I sat down to write this book, I began writing about the topics for sales reps that I knew were essential to their business. Two of the sources for topics were feedback from reps in our own CPA practice and speech requests by various rep trade associations. I had no grand or overall plan. Then, the book just grew over two years as I thought of another and still another topic to write about. Finally, the manuscript just flowed to the natural conclusion of eight chapters on valuation and sale of a rep firm. I feel there are no significant topics left, so I'm done!

But it is interesting to look back at the various chapter headings and see how they naturally fall into the various areas of business and tax information for sales reps. Not by design, but by normal and virtually automatic classifications, we first have a set of chapters preceded by the word "business":

Chapter 1. Business Entertainment.

Chapter 2. Business Auto Leasing.

Chapter 3. Business Travel.

Chapter 4. Business Use of Your Home.

Chapter 5. Business Auto Recordkeeping.

Then the shift is to employees and employee variations:

Chapter 6. Employee Expense Reimbursements.

Chapter 7. Statutory Sales Employees.

Chapter 8. Independent Contractor or Employee?

Chapter 9. Independent Contractor Audits and the IRS Tests.

Then come retirement plans:

Chapter 10. Retirement Plans and IRS Plan Audits.

Chapter 11. The New Threat to Retirement Plan Bank Accounts and Other News.

Followed by chapters on the various forms of business that a rep can consider:

Chapter 12. The Form of Your Business: The "Regular" C Corporation.

Chapter 13. The Form of Your Business: The S Corporation.

Chapter 14. The Form of Your Business: Partnerships.

Chapter 15. The Form of Your Business: Sole Proprietorships.

Next we had accounting-tax-bookkeeping subjects:

Chapter 16. Zeroing Out at Fiscal Year-End.

Chapter 17. A Bookkeeping System for the Manufacturers' Sales Agency.

Chapter 18. Equipment Leasing and Expensing.

Chapter 19. Record Retention Guidelines.

Then we talked about money going in and out of the sales agency:

Chapter 20: How to Steal Money from Almost any Rep Firm.

Chapter 21. Loans to and from Shareholders.

Chapter 22. Unreasonable Compensation.

Followed by some assorted "stand alone" topics, but each significant, as the titles indicate:

Chapter 23. Estate Planning.

Chapter 24. Business Insurance.

Chapter 25. How to Avoid an IRS Audit.

Chapter 26. Dealing with Your Banker.

Chapter 27. The Right Way (and the Wrong Way) to Take Money out of Your IRA.

Chapter 28. Assorted Taxtips.

Chapter 29. Your Family Working in Your Business.

Chapter 30. The Revenue Reconciliation Act of 1993 and Year-End Tax Planning.

And finally, the natural conclusion (and a virtual "mini-book"):

Chapter 31. Selling Your Rep Firm: IRS Background.

Chapter 32. Selling Your *Entire* Rep Firm.

Chapter 33. Selling Your Selling Only *Part* of Your Rep Firm.

Chapter 34. Selling Your Rep Firm: Valuation.

Chapter 35. Selling Your Rep Firm: The Payments.

CONCLUSION

I find it very interesting that the book virtually wrote itself, and the topics were easily selected and readily appeared. While it took two years of hard work, it was really a labor of love. You see, I selected the title of this chapter, "A Look Back" for two reasons. The obvious one is the one we just completed: reviewing the topics in this book and the natural pattern of the information.

But the information in this book also represents a look back at my entire professional career, throughout which I have spent my time working for, working with, speaking before, counseling, arguing, joking, advising, and teaching and loving each and every one of the hundreds of reps who have enriched my life! You have been the major reason my professional career is so productive, emotionally fruitful, financially rewarding, enjoyable, challenging, exciting, and wonderful!

So I give you this book with the hope that every reader gains many financial and tax benefits from all the guidance, ideas, cautions, tax-tips, and the various subjects discussed. Good Luck and God Bless!

ABOUT THE AUTHOR

Mel Daskal is a native Chicagoan, a CPA, and holds a Master of Business Administration (MBA) degree from the University of Chicago.

He has spent his entire professional career working for sales reps and also for a number of their trade associations. At various times, Daskal has been the accountant for the Electronics Representatives Association (ERA), ERA Insurance Trust, Chicagoland Chapter of ERA, Southern California Chapter of ERA, and Manufacturers' Agents National Association (MANA). He has been voted honorary life memberships in both the National ERA and the Southern California Chapter of ERA, as well as being awarded the prestigious "White Pin" by national ERA.

For over 20 years, he has written the monthly publication "Financial Fax," currently distributed nationally by the Manufacturers' Representatives Educational Research Foundation (MRERF), a group of 28 rep-broker trade associations. Additionally, he writes another monthly version of "Financial Fax" distributed nationally by various manufacturers' trade associations. He has authored literally hundreds of articles about money and taxes for reps and is in great demand as a speaker at management conferences for small businesses of all kinds, including, of course, sales reps.

He is still active, on a full-time basis, in the CPA firm of Daskal/Spector Accountancy Corporation (still standing, after the 1994 earthquake, in Sherman Oaks, California) and resides in west Los Angeles with his wife, Carol.

Index

S

U

V

W

Y

Z